Spinoza and the Politics of Freedom

Spinoza Studies
Series editor: Filippo Del Lucchese, Brunel University London

Seminal works devoted to Spinoza that challenge mainstream scholarship

This series aims to broaden the understanding of Spinoza in the Anglophone world by making some of the most important work by continental scholars available in English translation for the first time. Some of Spinoza's most important themes – that right is coextensive with power, that every political order is based on the power of the multitude, the critique of superstition and the rejection of the idea of providence – are explored by these philosophers in detail and in ways that will open up new possibilities for reading and interpreting Spinoza.

Editorial Advisory board
Saverio Ansaldi, Etienne Balibar, Chiara Bottici, Laurent Bove, Mariana de Gainza, Moira Gatens, Thomas Hippler, Susan James, Chantal Jaquet, Mogens Lærke, Beth Lord, Pierre Macherey, Nicola Marcucci, Alexandre Matheron, Dave Mesing, Warren Montag, Pierre-François Moreau, Vittorio Morfino, Antonio Negri, Susan Ruddick, Martin Saar, Pascal Sévérac, Hasana Sharp, Diego Tatián, Dimitris Vardoulakis, Lorenzo Vinciguerra, Stefano Visentin, Manfred Walther, Caroline Williams

Books available
Affects, Actions and Passions in Spinoza: The Unity of Body and Mind, Chantal Jaquet, translated by Tatiana Reznichenko
The Spinoza-Machiavelli Encounter: Time and Occasion, Vittorio Morfino, translated by Dave Mesing
Politics, Ontology and Knowledge in Spinoza, Alexandre Matheron, translated and edited by Filippo Del Lucchese, David Maruzzella and Gil Morejón
Spinoza, the Epicurean: Authority and Utility in Materialism, Dimitris Vardoulakis
Spinoza and the Politics of Freedom, Dan Taylor

Forthcoming
Affirmation and Resistance in Spinoza: Strategy of the Conatus, Laurent Bove, translated and edited by Émilie Filion-Donato and Hasana Sharp
Experience and Eternity in Spinoza, Pierre-François Moreau, translated by Robert Boncardo
Spinoza's Political Philosophy, Riccardo Caporali, translated by Fabio Gironi

Visit our website at www.edinburghuniversitypress.com/series/SPIN

Spinoza and the Politics of Freedom

Dan Taylor

EDINBURGH
University Press

Edinburgh University Press is one of the leading university presses in the UK. We publish academic books and journals in our selected subject areas across the humanities and social sciences, combining cutting-edge scholarship with high editorial and production values to produce academic works of lasting importance. For more information visit our website: edinburghuniversitypress.com

© Dan Taylor, 2021, 2022

Edinburgh University Press Ltd
The Tun – Holyrood Road, 12(2f) Jackson's Entry, Edinburgh EH8 8PJ

First published in hardback by Edinburgh University Press 2021

Typeset in 10/12 Goudy Old Style by
Servis Filmsetting Ltd, Stockport, Cheshire

A CIP record for this book is available from the British Library

ISBN 978 1 4744 7839 7 (hardback)
ISBN 978 1 4744 7840 3 (paperback)
ISBN 978 1 4744 7842 7 (webready PDF)
ISBN 978 1 4744 7841 0 (epub)

The right of Dan Taylor to be identified as the author of this work has been asserted in accordance with the Copyright, Designs and Patents Act 1988, and the Copyright and Related Rights Regulations 2003 (SI No. 2498).

Contents

Acknowledgements	vii
Abbreviations	x
Introduction: Masaniello's Moment	1

I The Politics of Servitude

1. Servitude	19
2. Nature	40

II Desiring Freedom

3. Power	67
4. Desire	93

III Commonality

5. Becoming Collective	125
6. We Imagine	160
7. The State	187
Cadenza: *Prudentissimo Viro*	214
8. Revolution	223
Conclusion: For One and All	247
Bibliography	257
Index	278

For k-punk

Acknowledgements

Given that my subject is collectivity in Spinoza, there's a vast number of people who should be thanked for helping the ideas come to life. It's been a collective effort, the sum of six years of conversations, attempts, crossings-out and fresh starts.

The work started as a PhD at the University of Roehampton, and I want to thank my two supervisors, Nina Power and Jenny Bunker, for their guidance and support. It was enriched by generous comments on earlier drafts from Eric Jacobson. Without a Vice Chancellor's Scholarship from the university, the work would've been impossible. Tina Beattie, Neil MacDonald and Ted Vallance helped in overcoming bureaucratic hurdles.

I am very grateful to Beth Lord and Étienne Balibar, who examined the PhD and, while passing it without corrections, offered meticulous and insightful feedback which has indelibly improved the work. Since then, my thanks to Carol Macdonald at Edinburgh University Press for her cheerful support and guidance, and to the two anonymous reviewers of an earlier draft of the manuscript, whose encouragement and criticisms sharpened the writing further. To Filippo Del Lucchese, for his suggestions and insights in crafting the later manuscript. My thanks also to Kirsty Woods and James Dale their help through production, to Caroline Richards for her keen eye in copy-editing and John Barker for indexing. Its remaining flaws are mine.

While studying any philosopher involves spending a lot of time alone, it needn't always be a solitary endeavour. I was able to think in public at many conferences over the last few years, and thank audiences at Royal Holloway, Turin, Goldsmiths, Kingston, Aberdeen, Groningen, UCL, Winchester, Chichester and elsewhere for helping me develop, refine or abandon loose ideas. I particularly want to thank Tiff Thomas, Corin Bruce, Torin Doppelt, Olivier Surel, Dimitris Vardoulakis and Filippo again. Many others were generous in their thoughts and conversation when I was still a rather green graduate student – I particularly thank Keith Green, Susan James, Matt Kisner and Mogens Lærke. And I also thank Laura Grace Ford, and the Mark Fisher reading group at Somerset House, which put collective joy and post-capitalist desire back on my mental map.

I want to thank the students I've taught and thought with while writing, too: my students at Roehampton and Goldsmiths, who have given me immense (and not unreasonable) hope about the future; and the children of several South London schools where I taught the first two parts of Spinoza's *Ethics*, who grasped it with remarkable *scientia intuitiva*. I also want to thank Austin Hill, Christian Kerslake and the wonderful group of philosophers I've taught for some years now at the Mary Ward Centre, where the more speculative edges of this book were first tried out. Equally, I want to thank my friend Ariel Hessayon who first taught me Spinoza and early modern philosophy at Goldsmiths many years ago.

Most books hide a secret history of their composition, and this one is no exception. Over the course of the work I cycled and camped across Britain, worked in inner London community advice centres and a homeless hostel, and had a spell as a disability support worker in East London. Conversations sometimes turned to the difficulty of democracy, the viability of collective power. My joys and perseverance in being were very much enhanced by these many different encounters, affecting and being affected as much as possible. They lifted my eyes to a more visionary, universal freedom, and the trickier, pragmatic questions about its realisation.

Then there are the people who were with me while I thought, and to whom I owe immense gratitude: to Sarah for her support and companionship in the early years, for helping me sound out early ideas and for her encouragement; to Grandma Ruth for mental and bodily nourishment, and the beauty of blossoming plants; to my Dad for his ever-constant love and belief; and to Christy, Lucy and Mum. For their friendship, George Hoare, Yari Lanci and Dave McEwan. To Vera, for all the laetitia and любовь, in which holds the greatest collective flourishing. And, in the final stages, to Sascha and Mila, спасибо, for helping look after little Yasha.

Lastly, this work has been dedicated to my late friend and former teacher, Mark Fisher, who passed away during the writing of this book. I had the great fortune of being taught philosophy by him at a further education college in South London, a place which drew in demotivated young people, ejected or exiled from mainstream education. His enthusiasm for difficult thinking in difficult times was infectious, and he had that rare Socratic gift among teachers of giving his students the confidence to think and express their own ideas as if they had arrived at them independently. He made our thoughts *ours*. He encouraged me and others to go to university when we were unsure if we were good enough, or if difficult thinking (or student debt) was worth the uncertainty. His prolific output on the *k-punk* blog brought many more of us into contact with new cultural and philosophical worlds, including that of Spinoza, while his *Capitalist Realism* (2009) gave a blueprint for radical change that galvanised many into the British student protest movements that raged in the years after.

Above all, Mark was a Spinozist *avant la lettre*. Not only his political thought, but his warm, self-effacing yet electrifying manner all bore the manner of a person for whom philosophy was a 'meditation on life', and on the very best of human life, of the vistas and vicissitudes of human freedom. But as he also put in an early, perceptive writing on the 'inhuman', anegoic aspects of Spinozan reason, 'being a Spinozist is both the easiest and hardest thing in the world'.[1] His final, incomplete thought was turning to a politics of 'post-capitalist desire' and 'collective joy', and while the remainder is *reliqua desiderantur*, this work is a very modest tribute to the collective joys and desires his conversation brought to life.

---

[1] Fisher 2004.

Abbreviations

Throughout I use Edwin Curley's translations in *The Collected Works of Spinoza*, published in two volumes by Princeton University Press (1985, 2016), with occasional reference to Silverthorne and Israel's translation of the *Theological-Political Treatise* (2007). All passages have been checked against the Latin original. Modifications in translation are clearly indicated, and usually occur in the discussion of a certain keyword, e.g. *vulgus*, with the Latin in square brackets.

Citations will follow the format of the Edinburgh University Press Spinoza Studies series, which has been designed for legibility and precision of reference. Each involves an abbreviated citation to the specific text at hand (*Ethics*, *TTP*, etc.), followed by a semicolon and an author–date citation to the page number of either Volume I or Volume II of Curley's *Collected Works of Spinoza* (*CWS* I and *CWS* II).

The following abbreviations are used for Spinoza's texts: CM = *Metaphysical Thoughts* (*Cogitata Metaphysica*, appendix to PP); *Ethics* = *Ethics*; Ep. = *Letters* (*Epistolae*); KV = *Short Treatise on God, Man and his Well-being* (*Korte Verhandeling van God, de Mensch en des zelfs Welstand*); PP = *Descartes's Principles of Philosophy Parts I and II* (*Renati Des Cartes Principiorum Philosophiae*); TdIE = *Treatise on the Emendation of the Intellect* (*Tractatus de Intellectus Emendatione*); TP = *Political Treatise* (*Tractatus Politicus*); TTP = *Theological-Political Treatise* (*Tractatus Theologico-Politicus*).

Citations to the *Ethics* give the part in Roman numerals, followed by the Proposition in Arabic numerals (without further abbreviation), then the page number in Curley's first volume. For example, Proposition 18 of Part 4 is abbreviated to *Ethics* IV, 18; *CWS* I, 555. Arabic numerals are used to indicate the item where there are multiple scholia, corollaries and lemmata. The following abbreviations are also used: App. = Appendix; Ax. = Axiom; Cor. = Corollary; DA = Definition of the Affects at the end of Part 3; Def.

= Definition; Dem. = Demonstration; Exp. = Explanation; GDA = General Definition of the Affects at the end of Part 3; Lem. = Lemma; Post. = Postulate; Praef. = Preface; Schol. = Scholium. For example: 'Desire is man's very essence, insofar as it is conceived to be determined, from any given affection of it, to do something', would be cited as *Ethics* III, DA 1; *CWS* I, 531.

Theological-Political Treatise (*TTP*): citations give chapter number in Roman numerals, followed by paragraph number added by Bruder as an Arabic numeral, and contained within *CWS* II (then followed by the page number in the *CWS*). For example, Chapter 20, paragraph 6 is *TTP* XX, 6; *CWS* II, 345.

Political Treatise (*TP*): chapter number in Roman numerals, followed by paragraph number in Arabic numerals, followed by the Curley translation. For example, Chapter 1, paragraph 5 becomes *TP* I, 5; *CWS* II, 505.

Letters (*Ep.*): letter number cited in Roman numerals, followed by addressee in square brackets, then a citation to the relevant Curley volume. For example, Letter 36 to Johannes Hudde is *Ep.* XXXVI [to Johannes Hudde]; *CWS* II, 24.

Treatise on the Emendation of the Intellect (*TdIE*): paragraph number in Arabic numerals as added by Bruder, followed by the Curley volume. For example, paragraph 14 of the *Treatise* becomes *TdIE* 14; *CWS* I, 14.

Short Treatise on God, Man and his Well-being (*KV*): citations give the part number in Roman numerals, followed by the chapter number in Arabic numerals, and then the section number added by Sigwart with Arabic numerals (included in *CWS* I). For example, section 2 of Part 1, Chapter 1 becomes *KV* I, 1, 2; *CWS* I, 61.

Descartes's Principles of Philosophy (*PP*) and *Metaphysical Thoughts* (*CM*): abbreviations for the *PP* follow the same as the *Ethics* above, followed by the Curley volume, while those for the *CM* give the part number then chapter number in Roman numerals, followed by Curley. For example, Part 1, Chapter 1 becomes *CM* I, I; *CWS* I, 300.

Hobbes's works are abbreviated as: *Leviathan* (*L*); *De Cive* (*DC*). For example, *Leviathan* Book II, Chapter 17, section 13 is *L* II.17.13, following the standard continental system, while *De Cive* gives the chapter number in Roman numerals, followed by section number in Arabic numerals, e.g. *DC* IV.2 is Chapter 4, section 2. References to most pre-1900 philosophical work will tend to give the book number where applicable, followed by chapter number and section (or other standard referencing).

Introduction: Masaniello's Moment

Among other pastimes like pipe-smoking and playing chess, the philosopher Benedict de Spinoza was fond of drawing. One of the figures seen in Spinoza's sketchbook was a fisherman named Masaniello, leader of a popular uprising against Spanish rule in Naples in 1647. The fisherman's face bore an uncanny resemblance to Spinoza's.

For a philosopher with a reputation for an austere, otherworldly ethical system, enveloped in what he himself conceded as a 'cumbersome' and obscure geometrical presentation,[1] it may be unusual to begin with artistic representation and the imagination. Spinoza often noted the difference between signifier and signified, or between 'something mute, like a picture on a tablet' and a true 'mode of thinking' in the understanding.[2] The former falls under the 'confused and mutilated' knowledge from human imagination, said to be of the first kind of knowledge, compared to the 'common notions' of the second.[3] His philosophy has very little to say about art (but this is also true of optics). But as Johannes Colerus, one of his earliest biographers, found upon visiting Spinoza's former landlord and the rooms of the late philosopher, there was 'a whole book of such draughts, amongst which there are some heads of several considerable persons, who were known to him, or who had occasion to visit him'.[4] While these eminent figures are not named, one character is explicit. Despite his modest background, over a seven-day period he became the unlikely leader of a violent uprising against

---

[1] *Ethics* IV, 18 Schol.; CWS I, 555.
[2] *Ethics* II, 43 Schol.; CWS I, 479.
[3] II, 40 Schol.; CWS I, 476–8. Consider Spinoza's later remarks on how disagreements in knowledge often stem from errors in applying the correct word to a particular thing in II, 47 Schol.; CWS I, 483.
[4] Colerus 1880: 418.

high taxation, Spanish rule, the excesses of the aristocracy, and its complicit clerical backers. While the face of the fisherman 'did perfectly resemble Spinoza', his dress was 'very much like that of Massanello [sic], the famous head of the rebels of Naples'.

For a few heady days in July 1647, Masaniello had been the iconic leader of a popular uprising that seized control of a city of 300,000, and a kingdom ten times that. A lower-class upstart, contemporary accounts ridiculed Masaniello's plebeian status and popularity with the lowest of the poor, the *lazzari*, yet nonetheless were puzzled by his apparent command of 'doctors, merchants, lawyers [. . .] and an infinite number of other men of talent, merit and experience, and all superior to him in status'.[5] After attacking the palace of the hated Viceroy, a puppet of Naples' Spanish overlords, Masaniello organised and summoned a new republican civil guard of the poor and middling classes, said to number the hundreds of thousands, among them many women. They seized the armouries, opened the prisons, increased bread supplies, and attacked the homes of the aristocracy, redistributing looted items to the poor. When monks and clergy came out in processions to placate the angered crowds, their crucifixes and holy relics were wrested from them.

Then in dubious circumstances, Masaniello was either (or both) poisoned or became mad, acting more like a tyrant than a tribune of the people, attacking his followers with a sword, spouting heresies in a crowded church, and dropping his trousers in public. He was assassinated soon after. Crowds first paraded his corpse around the streets, shouting 'death to the tyrant Masaniello!' but, after the Spanish imposed draconian bread rationing on the city, his body was then reclaimed, celebrated, and given a spectacular public funeral. To add to the peculiar nature of the story, a certain Tommaso Anniello (or 'Masaniello') of Sorrento had led a similar popular revolt in Naples against the Inquisition a century earlier. Echoing Marx, the tale of Masaniello began first as tragedy, then as farce.

Though probably intended to amuse friends and visitors familiar with his radical reputation, Masaniello is an apt motif to reflect on the rebel image of Spinoza. In becoming Masaniello, Spinoza allowed his visitors and himself to share in a joke at his own expense. Indeed, a sharp, incredulous humour occasionally pierces through Spinoza's writing, usually in the scholia or the letters. Consider his takedown of Hugo Boxel's belief in ghosts, prefaced by a dry joke ('Some, perhaps, would consider it an evil omen that the reason

---

[5] According to Giraffi, quoted, the chief contemporary historical source on the 'tumults' (Villari 1985: 120).

for your writing to me was spectres or spirits').⁶ Or his wry comparison of the multitude who obey religious instruction out of fear of the afterlife, or who, divested of such belief, instead choose to live hedonistically (this is 'no less absurd to me than if someone, because he does not believe he can nourish his body with good food to eternity, should prefer to fill himself with poisons and other deadly things, or because he sees that the mind is not eternal, or immortal, should prefer to be mindless, and to live without reason').⁷ But the image of Masaniello also points to the problems of rebellion, desire, and the power of the multitude that dominate his works.

Many readers of Spinoza will be familiar with the introduction to the early, unfinished *Treatise on the Emendation of the Intellect*. As he writes:

> After experience had taught me that all the things which regularly occur in ordinary life are empty and futile, and I saw that all the things which were the cause or object of my fear had nothing of good or bad in themselves, except insofar as [my] mind was moved by them, I resolved at last to try to find out whether there was anything which would be the true good, capable of communicating itself, and which alone would [. . .] continuously give me the greatest joy, to eternity.⁸

Soon into the account, Spinoza presents a conflict between the private self that seeks this true and lasting good, against the world of men preoccupied with a differently conceived highest good, of 'wealth, honour, and sensual pleasure'.⁹ Would it be possible to attain this good 'without changing the conduct of plan of life which I shared with other men'? Despite his attempts, the young Spinoza finds himself and others pulled back into what he would later call the 'servitude' of the passive affects, in particular the sadness that comes with their inevitable disappointment. The objects pursued by the common people only hinder what preserves our being. Instead, the pursuit of this true and certain good necessitates a change in the plan of his life. It will involve imagining and conceiving a human nature greater than his own. But its pursuit will also involve that we should strive for as many others to arrive at it as possible, 'so that their intellect and desire agree entirely with my intellect and desire'.¹⁰ In other words, Spinoza's well-known endorsement

---

[6] *Ep.* LII [to Hugo Boxel]; CWS II, 408.
[7] *Ethics* V, 41 Schol.; CWS I, 616.
[8] *TdIE* 1; CWS I, 7.
[9] *TdIE* 3; CWS I, 7.
[10] *TdIE* 14; CWS I, 11.

of the life of the mind is also one of a life in common. Taking pains so that 'many others' may understand this good 'as easily and surely as possible' is a feature of the philosophical life. It's one that leads Spinoza to endorse social institutions and processes that empower minds and bodies on a much wider scale, leaving behind the Scholastic corpus in favour of the pursuit of public education, medicine and mechanics.

But here, as is the case later, we also encounter the staging of a distance between the philosopher and the common people. Among other 'certain rules of living' he prescribes – a rhetorical device that returns in the *Ethics*[11] – he advises that we 'speak according to the power of understanding of ordinary people', and 'yield as much to their understanding as we can'. Not only does the philosopher counsel of the risks of imitating the lives of others, there should also be a gap between the circulation of ideas of the philosophers, and those of the common people who may not otherwise give 'a favourable hearing to the truth'. Philosophy appears as both liberatory and dangerous.

These qualities aren't to be overinflated – they appear fleetingly in a text otherwise concerned with the mutability of the human mind, and the right rule of the intellect over the imagination – but their early entrance is significant. These tropes will return in the *Ethics*, *TTP* and *TP*. They point to an underlying concern with the safety and flourishing of the individual in relation to the community surrounding them, and the lingering possibility of a more universal collectivity based on the common pursuit of true knowledge. This zone of tension between the individual, the communal and the universal is something this book will explore. In mapping their waxing and waning, my account will assess Spinoza's case for human freedom in its epistemological, psychological and political forms. Like others, I want to determine the role of the imagination and the affects for realising human power and freedom. But I'm going to explore that through some of the conceptual problems hinted here which deserve a fuller hearing – namely the influence of harmful ideas in derailing the pursuit of philosophical freedom, the dialogue or silence between philosophical speech and the common people, and the underlying gravitational pull of collectivity for flourishing and freedom.

For Spinoza's politics of human freedom is inherently cautious, identifying not merely that desire and the passions are fundamental to political authority, but that sad affects like fear, anger and hatred are most instrumental of all. Spinoza's aims across his works were professedly conservative and seemingly uncontroversial in nature – the blessedness (*beatitudo*) of human beings in the *Ethics*, or the political protection of the 'freedom to philosophise' in

---

[11] E.g. *Ethics* V, 10 Schol.; 20 Schol.; *CWS* I, 601–3; 605.

the *TTP*, or the conditions for the 'inviolability' of the State's laws in the *TP*. Yet his arguments were seen by contemporaries to threaten to turn the world upside down. His *TTP* was a 'godless' work that threatened religious order (Thomasius), a 'book forged in hell' (Blijenbergh), or 'sheer atheism with furtive and disguised arguments' (Velthuysen).[12] Denunciations of the *Ethics* and its substance monism were even more colourful, after it appeared in the *Opera Posthuma* in 1677: 'the fantastic ravings of the maddest heads that were ever locked up' said Bayle; a 'hideous hypothesis', warned the young Hume.[13] The image of Spinoza was one who might up-end moral and political authority in his rigorous pursuit of human freedom, like that of Masaniello and his moment.

Spinoza's drawing of Masaniello points not just to the image of the rebel, then, and the inherent topsy-turviness of rebellion, but also, lastingly, to the inherently affective nature of the political. While Spinoza was often critical of the 'passions' and 'foolishness' of the common people,[14] who he openly discouraged from reading the *TTP*,[15] he was also sensitive to the effectual and ineffectual ways in which lasting political change and revolution might occur. Accounts of Masaniello were popular in England, then amid revolution and its consequences, with frequent comparisons made between the fisherman and Oliver Cromwell in illicit, Amsterdam-printed works.[16] As Spinoza would later write of the Protectorate and subsequent Restoration, a 'people can often change the tyrant, but can never destroy him', unless they also 'change their form of state'.[17] The problem was that the English would inevitably allow tyranny to repeat itself unless they also addressed 'the causes of the prince's being a tyrant'.[18] Without removing the systematic causes for any kind of tyranny, a people were doomed to repeat history. Masaniello soon out-tyrannised the Viceroy.

Without addressing the fundamental causes of human servitude, any similar uprising would suffer the fate of tragedy, if not farce. Spinoza came even to see this in his own context, as the Dutch liberal republican leader, Johan de Witt, was set upon and killed by an enraged crowd in The Hague in 1672 during a crisis of authority in the midst of war, with implicit support from the Calvinist Dutch Reformed Church and William III of the House

---

[12] In Nadler 1999: 295, 246.
[13] In Lloyd 2002: 17; Hume 2007, 1.4.5.
[14] *Ethics* I, App.; *CWS* I, 441; *TTP* VI, 5; *CWS* I, 153.
[15] *TTP* Praef., 34; *CWS* II, 75.
[16] Villari 1985: 125–32; Boerio 2016.
[17] *TTP* XVIII, 32–3; *CWS* II, 329–30.
[18] *TP* V, 7; *CWS* II, 531.

of Orange-Nassau. The outcome was like the execution of an earlier liberal republican Dutch figurehead, Johan van Oldenbarnevelt, in 1619, orchestrated by similar foes. Spinoza's thought is concerned with the difficulties of thinking human freedom, then, in difficult times. What he will say on this topic, and its inherently political nature, is instructive.

*

In this book, I will argue that the philosophy of Spinoza is concerned with a freedom of an inextricably political kind, founded on a model of empowerment that is mutual, collective and socially liberatory. For one and all. The kind of freedom open to the reasonable individual of the *Ethics*, the 'free man',[19] involves life with others of a common nature, and the prudence to live with others of a different nature. But it also involves an underlying basis of material peace and security through which friendship and learning can flourish. The free man's desire for knowledge and friendship takes him into the world of others, into the political, and necessarily involves his interests and energy. For Spinoza, understanding the nature and laws of politics will become a preoccupation that first disrupts the *TTP*, with its unexpected political treatise contained in Chapter 16 that feeds into 17 and 20, but compels the return to politics later in the *TP* for important conceptual and contextual reasons.

Spinoza's vision of human freedom unites the self-concerned desires of the individual with the common good of the community in which they live. While there already exist a number of accounts of freedom in Spinoza, be it of the *beatitudo* of the individual in the *Ethics*, or the free deliberation of democracy outlined in the *TTP*, this study will identify a consistent preoccupation with the intrinsically social and political basis *of* (and not merely requirements *for*) human freedom in Spinoza's works, one I will explore around the concept of collectivity. I think this preoccupation is vital for understanding Spinoza's broader philosophy. And while some commentators have given wonderful treatments of Spinoza's politics, I want to explore how these epistemological and political problems inform each other and transform the broader edifice of his philosophy, while also observing the

---

[19] This will not sound right to modern ears, but Spinoza's language, like that of most early modern contemporaries, is inevitably gendered and speaks of the 'free man', just as it speaks elsewhere of the gendered term 'man' (*homo*) to describe humanity. Where possible I will refer to human beings, using 'man' where quoting Spinoza. But I agree with Hasana Sharp that we cannot responsibly conceal this lack of inclusive phrasing (see Sharp 2011: 1n1, 47).

particular claims and differences among his works as his thought develops through these questions.

I am going to present a new argument for freedom in Spinoza as something *viable* for all human beings, being a way of life wherein individuals become as knowledgeable as they can, usefully assist each other, enjoy each other's company and live well, collectively. Spinoza's work addresses the friendship and mutual advantage we can offer one another, but it's also alert to the hatred and fear that can simmer in our hearts and which lead to conflict and the breakdown of civil society. Spinoza's ambivalence about the difficulties facing such a joyous image of freedom need working out. In developing Spinoza's questions about servitude, harmful ideas, vacillation and desire, I will assess the challenges that threaten to destabilise a community's striving for its common good into debilitating superstition, tyranny and fear. It's necessary to begin thinking about what inhibits our power and makes us passive, prone to beliefs in fortune or free will that hide the causes of our affects and lead us into fogs of fury or paralysing fear.

I also want to intervene into a lively debate about the politically liberatory use of Spinoza's thought, making the argument that the individual's lasting freedom must be realised through empowering others to live as reasonably as they can, using a mixture of affective, imaginative and cognitive means to increase the power of one and all. Such a freedom is realised not merely at the level of personal relationships but also through the transformation of political and social institutions. At the heart of this thorny problem of human freedom is the concept of collective desire, which I want to present as a new tool, discerned in Spinoza's underdeveloped thoughts about collective power, to address problems in contemporary political thought around protest and political change, the State, populism and democracy, and in dialogue with more recent political theory.

I'm going to establish my argument through a detailed textual analysis of the *Theological-Political Treatise* (1670), the *Ethics* (1677) and the *Political Treatise* (1677), sensitive to Spinoza's Latin terminology and to developments and differences in his thought across those works. I'll present a conceptual framework for understanding human power in terms of collectivity, commonality, unanimity and interdependence – the affective, imaginative and societal structures in which individuals identify each other as of a common nature, and so join forces together and act, think and interact in ways that realise their mutual advantage.[20] The argument is grounded

---

[20] At this early stage, by *empowerment* I mean the power of an individual to self-determine their actions and ideas as much as they possibly can. By *individual* I refer, for now, to a

in the premise that the individual is already an 'ensemble of social relations' as Marx says,[21] and this study explores in particular the internal structures of individuation, by way of desire, imagination and emotions. At this early stage, I recognise I am bandying around rather complex terms, and the goal of each chapter is to elucidate these, both for the Spinoza novice and the more initiated.

My attention to collective individuation shares common ground with recent theoretical interest in the concept of 'transindividuality', that is, the processes by which an individual is constituted (and in turn constitutes) a collective, a process which is never-ending and always incomplete.[22] While I'm not the first to address Spinoza's interest in the social and relational nature of human freedom, my analysis of the relationship between desire and politics, and its importance for Spinoza, should contribute a new understanding of the inextricable connection between freedom of an individual *and* collective kind.

My initial interest in Spinoza's relevance to contemporary thought was piqued by what's sometimes called the 'Spinozan turn' in France, particularly the Spinozism of Gilles Deleuze. The term is a bit of a misnomer given the apparent unity it places over a politically and philosophically diverse tradition. But it's a useful one for grouping together a certain 'air' of May 1968 in these readings, as Negri puts it.[23] Gueroult, Matheron and Deleuze are usually considered of this tradition, all producing landmark studies in 1968–9. Althusser is sometimes omitted, though Knox Peden has restored his significance, alongside Cavailles, Desanti and Alquié.[24] Macherey, Balibar, Negri, Tosel and Albiac are sometimes considered 'descendants', but this simplifies what are diverse contextual, political and interpretive positions.[25] My analysis will diverge from this tradition in three ways: first, that Spinoza's thinking about human freedom and power develops over the course of his major works with significant shifts that require a more nuanced, textually determined and contextual account. Second, that while the *Ethics* has justifiably been given far more attention to derive a metaphysical account of freedom, the

---

human being (with the process of individuation outlined in Chapter 5). By *collective individuation* I refer to the process by which several individuals identify, think or act as one, as part of a single group or community.

[21] Marx and Engels 1998: 570.
[22] Simondon 1989; Balibar 1997b; Read 2016; Kelly and Vardoulakis 2018.
[23] Negri 2004: 113.
[24] Peden 2014.
[25] E.g. Montag and Stolze 1997. For a more critical view of these 'neo-Spinozisms', see Kordela (2007: 3–5).

TTP and often-overlooked *TP* provide a robust and compelling politics of freedom. In this I'm somewhat aligned with Matheron. Third, that Spinoza's thought cannot always be regarded as entirely liberatory, at least by the political references and ideals often used by late twentieth-century readers (and subsequently) – particularly regarding the role of obedience, imagination and the state. Instead, he makes several arguments about the necessarily limited powers of the people that cannot be so easily transposed onto subsequent political contexts, and which make up the subject of Part I.

That is not to discount these readings, far from it, and I don't want to be accused of what Sigmund Freud called the 'narcissism of small differences'. The underlying aim here is to draw together the best of these politically liberatory readings of Spinoza to derive a coherent and applicable political theory independent of them. For the proliferation of quasi-Spinozan concepts of 'desire', the 'affects' and the 'multitude' into critical theory via Deleuze and Negri has brought new, enthusiastic readers to Spinoza and opened up new ways of thinking about his politics. But in their haste to apply a model of desire as wholly liberatory, or revolutionary multitudes, or 'affects of capitalism' to the twenty-first century, there results in what Spinoza would call a 'confused and mutilated' account of his work.[26] Deleuze's *Spinoza: Practical Philosophy* (1970) and Negri's *Savage Anomaly* (1981) have been particularly influential in Anglophone critical theory since their translations (1988/1991 respectively), and both studies, and their readers, will be occasional sparring partners. Again, that is not to discourage polemic or heresy – the concern is rather that there is a great deal more that is useful in his thought that remains occluded by selective readings, unclear translations and an 'inadequate', that is, passive, reliance on other secondary interpretations. It will also necessitate exploring the political stakes behind different interpretations of Spinoza, from the Marxist to the liberal to the Straussian, and weighing up the opportunities and limitations presented by these different theoretical backgrounds.

While I intend to clarify some of the conceptual foundations of these debates, I'll avoid a lengthy detour in historically and politically accounting for them. Such a task has been accomplished by others, and the great virtue of the current vitality of Spinoza scholarship – currently in a golden age of new translations, critical editions, handbooks and monographs – means that such a commentary would soon be out of date. For me, Spinoza's work is broadly concerned with understanding how we can become freer, that is, in

---

[26] On the affects of capitalism, see Massumi (e.g. 1992: 122–8), Hardt and Negri 2000, Latour 2014, and indirectly, Lordon 2014.

increasing our capacity to think and act where we are as much a cause of our thoughts and actions as possible. Such a freedom is necessarily collective, as this ability develops through our dependence on and interaction with many others, and the gradual cultivation of a clear and distinct understanding of the causes of these encounters. My aim then is to offer a more secure foundation for conceiving the individual's freedom, the common good and collective's desire as all, broadly, apiece. Our fundamental concern is with collectivity, using Spinoza's own observations and underdeveloped ideas on this to outline a more robust foundation for thinking about collective political power in general.

This book appears at an interesting juncture in Spinoza scholarship, one in which excellent research in Spinoza's politics, ethics, epistemology and historical context have become increasingly oblivious of each other. There is a danger in imitating Odysseus in trying to return home to an 'uncontaminated' reading of Spinoza, plugging one's ears to the temptations of debating with the Sirens. They may be doing leftist politics in France or the United Kingdom, archival historicism in the Netherlands, or epistemological analysis in North America.[27] Since Bennett's cavalier dismissal of Wolfson's contextualist method ('the labour and learning are awesome, but the *philosophical* profit is almost nil'),[28] it has become common to consider Spinoza's epistemology detached from his politics or historical context. Charlie Huenemann warns of the limits of this 'collegial approach', where scholars subject the 'Great Ones' of philosophy to the same critique and reconstructive defence as one's own colleagues, placing questions or

---

[27] Based on a study of recent essay collections – Koistinen and Biro (2002), Koistinen (2009), Melamed and Rosenthal (2010) and Della Rocca (2017) – which include nothing on the rich contributions to Spinoza's political theory being made by more radical theorists; Kisner and Youpa (2014) do not include questions of context and influence in Spinoza's ethical theory; and Montag and Stolze (1997), Gatens (2009), Vardoulakis (2011), Lord (2012) and Kordela and Vardoulakis (2017) do not draw on the meticulous analytic work being undertaken in North America. A small number of collections buck the trend: Van Bunge et al.'s invaluable *Continuum Companion* (2011) is a welcome exception to this trend, as is Sharp and Melamed (2018) and Stetter and Ramond (2019). Monographs and articles worth highlighting include Balibar (2008), Steinberg (2009, 2018), Viljanen (2011), Sharp (2011) and James (2012). That Frank and Waller (2016) offer a guide to Spinoza's politics that includes no discussion of Deleuze, Negri, Balibar or Matheron (let alone Aristotle, the De la Courts or Jonathan Israel's 'Radical Enlightenment' argument) is an unfortunate oversight.

[28] Bennett 1984: §3.5.

thoughts into their minds that they could not have possibly entertained.[29] I don't seek to purge Spinoza of his contradictions or defend him against an array of excellent, meticulous, collegial criticism. But in bringing together diverse hermeneutic and political traditions and readings on the common ground of empowerment, I will also argue that there is a consistent if multi-faceted argument for human freedom of an ethical and political character, just as it is of an individual and collective nature.

At the same time, we should avoid what Yitzhak Melamed castigates as making Spinoza 'one of us', an untimely, anomalous modern who shares our ideas and values.[30] This is an understandable and old problem. 'I have a precursor, and what a precursor', writes Nietzsche ecstatically upon discovering Spinoza in 1881. Nietzsche's Spinoza denies 'freedom of the will, teleology, the moral world order, the unegoistic, and evil'.[31] For Hegel too, all philosophy, as in 'thinking, or the spirit', must place itself 'at the standpoint of Spinozism', that is, the all-encompassing oneness of substance.[32] And then there are the well-worn remarks of Novalis and other German Idealists. For many different eras and ways of thinking within them, the possibility and implications of viewing 'God or nature' from the standpoint of eternity have led to dizzying reflections on their own.[33] But in turning to Spinoza to find a precursor, there is a danger of letting him off the hook, in taking what is most modern in his thought at the expense of what is more difficult or contrary, or questions of his method in writing *for* human freedom amid very different intellectual and political references to ours. While deriving a liberatory politics from his works, we must avoid considering Spinoza apart from his context, thereby 'discovering' what can only be our own concepts (for instance, egoism, communism, feminism, radical democracy and so forth). That's not to say that Spinoza can't illuminate modern concepts, but it's unfair to claim that they are his.

We should also avoid reproducing vague, trite affirmations of joy and people power through this difficult and rigorous thinker. As Benjamin Noys argues, contemporary critical theory is hampered by a prevailing

---

[29] Huenemann 2014.
[30] Melamed 2013a.
[31] Nietzsche 1982: 92.
[32] Hegel 1990: 154.
[33] The most tremorous equivocation in the history of philosophy, *deus sive natura*, and one which scandalised contemporaries: it first appears in *Ethics* IV Praef., and IV, 4 Dem.; CWS I, 544; 548. Conceiving things 'under a species of eternity' (*sub specie aeternitatis*) first appears in *Ethics* IV, 62 Dem., then substantially in V, 22–3; 29–31; CWS I, 581; 607–10.

'affirmationism', that is, an incoherent affirmation of joy as a good in itself, derived in his view from the influence of Spinoza.[34] It is not an unfair criticism, and Chapter 4 turns an eye to the pitfalls of affirmation in Spinoza's politics. How then can we effectively politicise desire and the affects in Spinoza in a way consistent not only with his metaphysics of power, but also his critical appraisal about the sad and destructive passions of the multitude (indeed, of human nature)? And how does an account of desire and the affects also reckon with Spinoza's remarks on the troubled relation of reason and the imagination? This, fundamentally, is the task ahead.

The material of the book is organised around eight core concepts in Spinoza. While it will require some initial familiarity with Spinoza's ideas, each chapter aims to explain each concept within its appropriate contexts, and then elucidate its meaning for the viability of freedom more broadly.

Part I explores why we are not free, and what passivity means for us individually, and with others. Chapter 1 begins with servitude, under the premise that any philosophical commonplace, like the mind's freedom being through contemplating truths, is insubstantial, unless it can also account for why minds are not free, what their servitude consists of, and what prevents human beings from easily achieving such a freedom. It is principally concerned with the *TTP*, and broadly considers servitude as a state of being possessed by harmful ideas. It's both an internal state and a more extensive one than traditional readings admit, and the chapter assesses its links to fortune, superstition, and to political domination. Servitude is a state where disempowerment is made meaningful and rewarding, rather than intolerable, and this problem is used to connect ethical freedom to political rights, as well as to questions of fortune, prejudice and superstition which impede the circulation and understanding of true ideas.

Chapter 2 turns to the problem of 'nature' and natural right, exploring what human beings are according to nature, and how conflicting views of nature impede human power. It discusses the underappreciated significance of three laws of Nature in the *TTP*'s Chapter 16, before raising wider questions of the status of the free man and the slave, and Spinoza's various formulations of freedom and slavery. I relate these back to the contested areas of nature and naturalism, the historical context of slavery in the Dutch

---

[34] A withering takedown of continental philosophy's sacred cows, but Noys's (2010) politicisation of the negative does not explain why, in Spinoza, joyous affects are necessarily more empowering than sad affects. As *Ethics* III, 11–12 indicate, affects of joy correlate to a transition to a state of greater power, and when the mind imagines what causes it joy, it results in an increase in the body's power of acting (*CWS* I, 500–1).

colony of 'New Holland' in Brazil, and the broader avenues of conflict and cooperation between individuals.

Part II explores how we can become free, or rather freer, given that as modes of nature we are necessarily subject to causes and forces in a certain and determinate way. Chapter 3 investigates the account of power in the *Ethics*. It asks: why is the conatus so important? What's its relation to human power and finitude? What's the difference between a non-human and human conatus? Or the conatus of a body and of a mind guided by reason? The chapter distinguishes freedom from power, and within this, alights on the well-known *potentia/potestas* distinction, re-presenting these as two facets in the individual's becoming freer.

Chapter 4 then applies this theory of Spinozan power to human freedom. Its concern is a practical freedom, one that avoids tautological positions like 'power makes things more powerful' or which place freedom beyond the reach of most human beings. It argues for a more inclusive model of empowerment, one that values the imagination and the passive affects – things not in themselves empowering, but which can be used to greater power and self-knowledge. I want to distinguish desire from the conatus, and explore the features of this peculiar 'consciousness'. What matters most is not what a given desire is, but what it *does* for the agent. Neither desire nor the affect of joy intrinsically correlate with actual self-preservation, but are best realised through it, providing a new way to think freedom through desire and what I call an education of the imagination.

Part III then turns to aspects of collectivity over three different articulations in Spinoza: the *Ethics*, *TTP* and *TP*. What does it mean to be one with another person of a common nature, to become 'one body' and 'one mind', and why does Spinoza repeatedly emphasise this across his works? Chapter 5 identifies a tendency towards unanimity that develops across Spinoza's works unevenly. It is premised in his accounts of sociality and individuation in the *Ethics*, wherein individuals are conatively compelled to associate with one another, and find in reason the most effective common ground in doing so. The basic good of unanimity, or collective right, emerges in the *Ethics* and *TTP*, with fuller exposition in the *TP*. While some scholarship has focused on the political implications of group subjectivity (e.g. multitudes), I think there is a wider and more systematic thought of collective power that goes beyond momentary democratic eruptions (if this is even what Spinoza had in mind, which I am unsure of). This notion of collective right precedes the political as an intrinsic model of association, and is more flexible and universal than a specifically political manifestation. The chapter then explores interdependence through Spinoza, and in relation to later theorisations of interdependence and collectivity in Sartre and Camus.

Chapter 6 explores the role of the imagination as an individual and communal phenomenon. It enables individuals to recognise who is of a common nature, the basis by which they are useful to each other, a faculty I call commonality. The relation of imagination and intellect, crucial to Maimonides and preoccupying parts of the *TTP*'s discussion of philosophy and theology, will be first grounded in the epistemology of the *Ethics*. Then, focused on the *TTP*, I'll explore the socially beneficial effects that can follow from the use of the imagination in bringing communities together, through Spinoza's account of the prophet. What does it mean that, in Spinoza's irony-laden remark, 'today, so far as I know, we have no prophets'?[35] The figure of Jesus Christ, presented as both a prophet and a philosopher in the *TTP*, is one way of thinking through some of the possibilities and ambivalences of the philosopher's use of reason and imagination. Then, through a late assessment of the relation between the individual and the collective in Benjamin, Lukács and Spinoza, I will conclude on the pre-eminence of shared imaginings to communal identity, and the underlying difficulty for group identities in also producing capable, self-determining individuals. If 'Nature creates individuals, not nations',[36] then how might the individual distinguish and interrogate bonds of community (which bind us to a theoretically restricted group of those of a perceived common nature, like us) with awareness of our true universality as modes of God? This distinction of the communal against the universal needs to be prised out.

Chapter 7 turns to the State, and Spinoza's ideas in the *TP* about the role of the State in establishing the conditions for peace, piety and mutual assistance. Does Spinoza champion a proto-liberal sovereignty of reduced scale, founded in deliberation, toleration and free speech, or should the State actively intervene in the lives of its subjects? If he seems to emphasise both, why, and are the two compatible? What late and new role does the free multitude play in the establishment and maintenance of social cohesion? The *TP* itself has been underappreciated in providing a deeper exposition of the pre-eminence of the affects to political life. Here the multitude appear on stage, and their common feelings and desires take a primary role in the freedom and security of the State. I will identify Spinoza's aim here with this late, unfinished work as an attempt to describe a reasonable republic, that is, an optimum state whose foundation and laws are strictly, scientifically

[35] *TTP* I, 7; CWS II, 78.
[36] *TTP* XVII, 93; CWS II, 317.

reasonable. I'll also critically assesses Spinoza's attempt to load the burden of becoming freer onto the State itself, resulting in some potentially unresolvable paradoxes for individual freedom.

The chapter is then followed by a Cadenza (typically a more expressive, ornamental passage towards the end of a musical work, usually by a soloist), in which Spinoza and Gramsci's readings of Machiavelli's *Il Principe* are contrasted in terms of the symbolic and collective nature of power. In both one can discern a politics of *common sense* – a shared sense of being of a community or common – and of the importance of transforming shared ideas, beliefs and feelings to broader political freedom.

Can Spinoza's politics allow for a coherent theory of rebellion? The final chapter addresses this fundamental question for instigating political change, like the kind suggested in the *TP*. On the face of it, no, though some intractable difficulties in the text are contrasted against the historical context. I explore one opportunity raised by Matheron through 'indignation', then turn to the imitative affect of emulation as a powerful political affect for collective power and political transformation. The discussion of an ethics of solidarity then utilises the Cadenza's politics of commonality, exploring how movements can organise around a powerful signifier – for example, the People, at the centre of current debates around populism – while avoiding the foundation of a community being on a sad (and inherently disempowering) affect like fear or hatred for others. Through drawing on a range of contemporary political theorists, it concludes with an argument for making as many as they can to think for themselves, recognise their common good, and organise together in effective political movements that can realise this, politically. A freedom for one and all.

So often conceived as something *within* autonomous individuals, my lasting goal with this study of the politics of freedom seeks to restore significance to another feature, that of freedom *among* individuals, freedom as something conditional and realised through our relations with others. This is not the sole freedom Spinoza had in mind, but I think it is the most important. A freedom not merely of conviviality and friendship, *laetitia* and *hilaritas* multiplied, but of collectively becoming the best that we can be. A becoming that is dynamic and open-ended, but which supplies enough information to ascertain and realise the good life, collectively.

Part I

The Politics of Servitude

1

Servitude

Spinoza's works share a concern with human freedom, and he is not the first to identify this freedom in the mind's contemplation of universal truths, the blessedness (*beatitudo*) that results from what he calls the 'intellectual love of God'.[1] But in what precisely does this freedom consist? In the *Ethics* he describes as 'free' (*liber*) that 'which exists from the necessity of its nature alone, and is determined to act by itself alone', a definition broadly consistent across his work.[2] In contrast is 'necessity' or compulsion, in which a thing is determined 'by another to exist and to produce an effect in a certain and determinate manner'. As *natura naturata* (existing from the necessity of God's nature, i.e. modes) and not *natura naturans* (what is 'in itself and conceived through itself' alone, i.e. God), human beings are necessarily constrained and determined to act in a certain and determinate way by prior causes.[3] This determination to act in a particular way is expressed by our conatus or striving to persevere in being, which essentially individuates all things.[4] For human beings, this conatus is experienced through desires, a particular mental-and-bodily 'consciousness' of our appetites and ideas about them.[5]

Yet given the sheer range of ways in which we are only a partial and inadequate cause of such ideas, which are often of an imaginative or affective sort, what we may experience as our own free will is more often determined by ideas of which we're only a partial cause, and from an external source that

---

[1] *Ethics* V, 32 Cor.; CWS I, 611.
[2] *Ethics* I, Def. 7; CWS I, 409.
[3] I, 29 Schol.; CWS I, 434.
[4] III, 4–7; CWS I, 498–9.
[5] III, 9 Schol.; CWS I, 500. Spinoza's account of consciousness is notoriously vague, with no precise definition given. Simplifying, it describes the mind's ideas of the body's affections (analysed in Chapter 4).

renders us passive. Most of the time we're in a state of 'servitude' (*servitudo*), that is, overpowered by the strength (*vis*) of the affects, as Part IV of the *Ethics* is titled, and which the first line of its preface defines as 'Man's lack of power to moderate and restrain the affects' – a problem to which he devotes substantial attention.[6] Freedom, then, is inherently difficult for Spinoza, and his critique of Cartesian free will,[7] coupled with his causal determinism, leads to a more complex view of human agency. Compared to a long tradition in political philosophy that identifies freedom as naturally within or civically granted to us, Spinoza's thought remains somewhat estranged with the prominence it reserves to the ways in which we are not free, at least not as we might think.

Prejudices of Nature

This occurs in an intriguing way in the Appendix to *Ethics* Part I, one of the best places to become acquainted with Spinoza. In the preceding part, Spinoza has overturned the mind–body dualism of Descartes, as well as much of the prevailing Scholastic and neo-Aristotelian views about God. Over thirty-six short, sinewy propositions, Spinoza has reconceived God as a singular, eternal, immanent, necessary and all-encompassing substance, from whose infinite power all things are predetermined. But there remain 'prejudices' (*praejudicia*) in our understanding that could hinder the apprehending of his new philosophy and 'the connection of things as I have explained it'. This natural inability to grasp God's nature, as Spinoza conceives it, rests on one prejudice above all:

> All the prejudices I here undertake to expose depend on this one: that men commonly suppose that all natural things act, as men do, on account of an end; indeed, they maintain as certain that God himself directs all things to some certain end, for they say that God has made all things for man, and man that he may worship God.[8]

This simple prejudice is one of reasoning from final causes, of being predisposed to recognise purpose and design in nature where it happens to suit

---

[6] For Spinoza, affects are ideas of bodily affections that correspond to a change in the body's power of acting, joyous affects connoting an increase, sad affects a diminution (e.g. III, 11; *CWS* I, 500–1).
[7] II, 49 Schol.; *CWS* I, 484–90.
[8] I, App.; *CWS* I, 439–40.

what we perceive to be our advantage, while not thinking of the causes that dispose those desires in the first place. This leads many to conclude that nature has been designed with human advantage in mind – our 'eyes for seeing, teeth for chewing' – and to an anthropomorphic view of God who has 'made all things for man'.

Remarkably, Spinoza then explores this claim through a psychological account of fear and hope. All humans are born 'ignorant of the causes of things', and this ignorance often remains decisive as we pursue our desires for our own advantage, and experience this pursuit as an illusory state of freedom. Yet being largely ignorant of the causes of things, under the force of our appetites, and naturally predisposed to viewing anthropocentric purpose in nature, we confuse effects with final causes, what Matheron calls a 'finalism'.[9] As modes of nature, we are often subject to external causes more powerful than ourselves, leading to changes contrary to our wants and well-being. This leads many of us to 'vacillate wretchedly between hope and fear', as the *TTP* begins,[10] as the mind endeavours to think of ways to alleviate or forget its fears and embrace new sources of hope.[11]

While hope has an important role in much ethical theory – Kant famously asked 'what may I hope?' as among the three fundamental questions for philosophy[12] – it is as much in our susceptibility to epistemically weak bases of hope that superstition arises as in our natural predisposition to seek final causes. In this respect, Spinoza differs from a broader treatment of hope in early modern philosophy which tends to treat it as, if not rational, nonetheless of motivational service to becoming more virtuous (Descartes), moral (Kant), or courageous and loyal to the State (Hobbes). For Spinoza, hope and fear are affective counterparts, denoting an 'inconstant joy [or sadness], which has arisen from the image of a future or past thing whose outcome we doubt'.[13] In the Appendix, human beings are inherently hopeful when, as they observe a natural world seemingly ideal for human survival, they suppose that an anthropomorphic God directed 'all things for the use of men in order to bind men to them and be held by men in the highest honor'. Yet the consequences could not be more devastating for Spinoza. As men observe what they do not understand in nature, so they 'turn toward themselves' and meditate as per their 'temperament' (*ingenium*) or mentality, and

---

[9] Matheron 1988: 107.
[10] *TTP* Praef., 1; CWS II, 65.
[11] E.g. *Ethics* III, 25; IV, 50 Schol.; CWS I, 507; 574.
[12] Kant 1998: A805/B833.
[13] *Ethics* III, 18 Schol. 2; CWS I, 505.

so 'judge the temperament of other men', as well as that of God, 'from their own temperament'.[14]

For some, like Descartes, this might be called wonder, 'the first of all the passions', a 'sudden surprise of the soul' in the face of the new.[15] In the *Theaetetus*, Plato describes this 'wondering' as where 'philosophy begins and nowhere else';[16] for Aristotle, it is 'because of wonder that men both now and originally began to philosophize'.[17] But for Spinoza, this isolated reflection (which we might implicitly oppose to common deliberation) leads to conflicts of opinion and belief with others. Prejudice becomes 'superstition', as communities develop different ways of worshipping God to 'direct the whole of Nature according to the needs of their blind desire and insatiable greed'. The judgements of God are elevated to a pedestal beyond ordinary human comprehension, except to a minority of powerful clerics who in turn monopolise institutions of worship and knowledge. This not only effects a self-perpetuating, socially shared 'state of ignorance', it also leaves communities vulnerable to the ambitions of 'interpreters' and 'followers' who seek to mollify and exploit the prejudices, fears, hopes and uncertainty of the many to establish their own authority, and those of powerful political regimes who call upon their support.

Above all, the issue with these prejudices is that they arise from a failure to understand our natural environment and our relationship to it. In its place, we reach for ideas which not only make sense of our world, but as a more important psychological insight, make us feel strong enough to withstand or ignore what makes us feel uncertain or afraid. As Spinoza writes, the mind strives as far as it can 'to imagine those things that increase or aid the body's power of acting'.[18] There is a lot more to say about this individual, fragmentary but fundamental faculty of imagination, and it will return in the following chapters. For now, in this confluence of adversity and the pursuit of our desires, we cling to hopes and fears that become based on rituals, omens and superstitions. There is also more to say about the effects of hope and fear, and the relation of the affects to political domination, and we will return to this in the later sections of the chapter. First, I want us to explore where else Spinoza sets out the problem of being in thrall to erroneous

---

[14] *Ingenium* has been translated as 'mentality', 'socio-cultural character', or by Steinberg recently as our 'affective make-up' (2018: 19), and is discussed in Chapter 6. On its political importance, see Moreau (1994: 395–404), and Read (2016: 24–5).
[15] Descartes 1989: 52, 56.
[16] Plato 1997: 155d.
[17] Aristotle 1998: 982b.
[18] *Ethics* III, 12; CWS I, 502.

thinking, and how we might come to understand and reduce its effects. It is my contention that freedom cannot be understood in isolation from servitude, and that in Spinoza's mature thought we encounter one of the richest assessments of the limited scope of human freedom amid the servitude of the passive affects and powerful socio-political structures.

Defining Servitude

Both the *Ethics* and the *TTP* assign the emergence of servitude in the affects of hope and fear, to which superstition offers refuge, helping dispel the suffering caused by uncertainty. At the very beginning of the *TTP*, we can recognise a similar rhetorical move to the Appendix, as Spinoza contrasts an idyllic but absurd possibility while emphasising the value of understanding the affects for human psychology and politics:

> If men could manage all their affairs by a definite plan, or if fortune were always favourable to them, no one would be in the grip of superstition. But often they are in such a tight spot that they cannot decide on any plan. Then they usually vacillate wretchedly between hope and fear, desiring immoderately the uncertain goods of fortune, and ready to believe anything whatever.[19]

It's precisely because most of us cannot live unbendingly to such a plan, and that fortune does not always favour us, that we are troubled by uncertainty and its affects of hope and fear, and seek any means to alleviate it. This Preface has a lot to say about human credulity. 'If, while fear makes them turn this way and that, they see something happen which reminds them of some past good or evil,' Spinoza writes, 'they think it portends either a fortunate or an unfortunate outcome.'[20] In this way we come to associate certain signs with 'omens', and develop elaborate superstitions, sacrifices and prayers that separate us further from a true understanding of our situation, and 'invent countless things and interpret nature in amazing ways, as if the whole of nature were as crazy as [we] are'.[21] Instead, hope and fear consign us to passivity, vacillating between uncertain affects while remaining attached to ideas and desires beyond our control. These states of confusion arise from fundamentally natural circumstances: what compels us into the 'sanctuary of

---

[19] *TTP* Praef., 1; CWS II, 65.
[20] Praef., 3; CWS II, 66.
[21] Praef., 4; CWS II, 66.

ignorance' is the inevitability of fear, sadness and vacillation when, under the force of our appetites, we confuse effects with final causes, rendering us vulnerable to the grossest anthropomorphic delusions, as the Appendix memorably sets out. It is within this passivity in disempowerment that the conditions for servitude emerge.

But what exactly does Spinoza mean by servitude? Unlike Descartes, Spinoza says that error and falsity have no positive value in themselves, but merely emerge from the incorrect application of a word to an idea.[22] Can we speak then of servitude in any positive conceptual sense? Or is this servitude we are seeking merely an absence of internal capability or power? In a certain sense, yes – it is both, but as I want to set out here, servitude refers to a state of passivity in which we are under the influence of ideas that are harmful to us. While these ideas can result internally, out of prior associations, images and beliefs in our own minds about ourselves or others, for Spinoza they ultimately bear an external source which makes us passive in our reasoning, unable to recognise the cause of our idea. This will have important political consequences later. Let's now take a more systematic look at the appearance of forms of *servitudo* (servitude, slavery) across Spinoza's works, in order to recognise both its underappreciated importance as an ethical problem in his work, and the roads he identifies to restore human freedom.

Forms of *servit–* (incorporating various declensions of *servitudo*, as well as *servus*, slave) appear sparingly but decisively in Spinoza's works, with differing uses. Aside from making the title of Part IV, and appearing briefly in its preface to describe the power of harmful affects, we find it in explicitly in three other instances in the *Ethics*. Spinoza dismisses as false belief the apparent 'servitude' of obeying God's commands as a necessary burden for attaining the riches of the afterlife.[23] It later appears again as a false impression of harmony produced by flattery.[24] Lastly, at the end of the *Ethics*, it describes again the false hopes of those who follow moral codes so as 'to receive a reward for their servitude'.[25] Each articulation refers to a weakened and passive mind. However, in the *Ethics* Spinoza uses *impotentia* (impotence) more often to describe the mind's inability to restrain either the passions, particularly sad ones, or erroneous ideas of an anthropomorphic

---

[22] *Ethics* II, 33, 35; CWS I, 472–3.
[23] Translation modified: in this instance and the following two, Curley has 'bondage' instead. *Ethics* II, 49 Schol.; CWS I, 490. Cf. *Ep*. XLIII [to Jacob Ostens]; CWS II, 387.
[24] *Ethics* IV, App. 21; CWS I, 591.
[25] V, 41 Schol.; CWS I, 616.

God.²⁶ Yet the retention of this term and its variations is instructive, suggesting a consequential shared state that arises from such impotence, thereby necessitating the distinction. It presents a mistaken belief of believers who experience what ought to be empowering and joyous – the knowledge and love of Spinoza's God, resulting in a rigorous ethics – as a great burden.²⁷ Being attached to this false burden, a doctrine that makes their passivity meaningful rather than intolerable, seems to Spinoza as actual servitude.

In the same scholium, Spinoza adds that they would 'prefer to govern all their actions according to lust, and to obey fortune rather than themselves'.²⁸ In the first instance of servitude in the *Ethics* earlier, we also find in the following sentence the first use of fortune in the *Ethics* ('matters of fortune, or things which are not in our power').²⁹ They are linked in Spinoza's mind, if not explicitly: fortune refers to a false refuge for individuals, disempowered and vulnerable because of their lack of power to resist harmful ideas. Returning to the Preface of Part IV, we observe the same: in the following sentence after the definition of *servitutem*, fortune appears – 'the man who is subject to affects is under the control, not of himself, but of fortune'³⁰ – which is to say, of nothing. Or, more precisely, of an inadequate belief which makes this nothing into something, a domain of supernatural forces, one whose belief only further disposes the hapless individual to further actions or ideas that harm themselves or others. Later, the one who 'conquers' others using love over hate 'requires the least help from fortune', suggesting a polar relation between the two – fortune indicating a lack of power, whereas reason 'conquers fortune', indicating the route to empowerment.³¹

Spinoza's definition of fortune in the *TTP* is more wry: 'God's guidance, insofar as it directs human affairs through external and unforeseen causes', a commonplace belief but an absurd one by his causal reasoning.³² It again suggests that fortune's antithesis, reason, involves aspects of ability. 'If men could manage all their affairs by a definite plan' – as we will recall from the

---

²⁶ E.g. II, 3 Schol.; III, Praef., 55; IV, Praef., 17 Schol.; 18 Schol., 20, 45, 53–7; CWS, I 449; 491; 525; 543; 554–5; 557; 571; 575–7.
²⁷ Suggestive of the Marxist concept of 'false consciousness' much later, wherein dominant social relations of exploitation are concealed and misrepresented. For Althusser, the *TTP*'s account of the Hebrew Republic demonstrated the '*materiality*' of ideology (1997: 9–10).
²⁸ V, 41 Schol.; CWS I, 616.
²⁹ II, 49 Schol.; CWS I, 490. Compare V, 20 Schol.; CWS I, 606.
³⁰ IV, Praef.; CWS I, 543.
³¹ IV, 46 Schol.; 47 Schol.; CWS I, 573; ibid.
³² *TTP* III, 11; CWS II, 113.

Preface earlier – or if fortune favoured us, then there would be no superstition. Superstition, as we saw earlier, also arises out of the natural and inevitable uncertainty of human life in which we cannot be expected to always regulate our affairs with sure judgement, or be an adequate cause of our own ideas and actions. As Kant later writes, the concepts of fortune and fate 'circulate with almost universal indulgence' even though 'one can adduce no legal ground for their entitlement to their use either from experience or from reason'.[33] Pierre-François Moreau locates a 'critical theory of fortune' in Spinoza's remark, yet fortune – such a significant, autonomous 'goddess' for Machiavelli and much Renaissance humanism – seldom recurs in the *TTP*.[34] For neither fortune nor superstition cause servitude in themselves; rather, both are effects of it.

Servitude indicates, then, not a specific state of affairs or relationship, but a general condition of passivity and weakness. This is of the gravest ethical importance, because noble ideals and rules for living serve little use if the individual is unable to live up to them.[35] From our discussion already, it's clear that the passive affects, particularly hope and fear, hold decisive sway. What's interesting is how a similar form of servitude appears in the *TTP*, although explicitly concerned with socio-political conditions. Here, prejudices about religion are vestiges of our 'ancient servitude', and Spinoza warns against theologians who seek to manipulate the multitude against the supreme powers so that 'everything may collapse again into slavery'.[36] This would make sense of Dutch attitudes to living under hated Spanish Habsburg rule prior to their revolt over the late sixteenth century. A more common instance of servitude is that of the Hebrews under the Egyptians, as recorded in the Book of Exodus.[37] Both reflect the occupation or enslavement of the Dutch or the Hebrews, and elsewhere in the *TTP* Spinoza relies on an implicit relation between the two, presenting the early Hebrew Republic under Moses as a double-edged political exemplar for the United Provinces.

Yet Spinoza also describes as *servitute* passive obedience to biblical laws which Jesus Christ frees all from so that they can follow these with a free mind,[38] and later also describes the Hebrews' obedience to the laws as

---

[33] Kant 1998: A84–5/B117.
[34] Moreau 1994: 477.
[35] Like the problem of akrasia, explored in Chapter 4.
[36] Translation modified: 'servitude' for 'bondage', as before. *TTP*, Praef. 17; CWS II, 69–70.
[37] *TTP* II, 46; V, 30; VI, 42; and Annotation 16; CWS II, 107; 146; 161; 212 (and discussed in Chapter 6).
[38] III, 45; IV, 34; CWS II, 121; 134.

appearing more freedom than servitude.[39] We can already notice similarities to those of the *Ethics* earlier of being in thrall to false beliefs about God, but servitude here widens, concerning our *passively obeying* moral codes while ignorant of their true nature and advantage. There are also instances which reiterate the *Ethics*: that the 'true life, worship and love of God seemed more servitude than true freedom' under Moses' laws, referring to false belief.[40] Lastly, 'slavery to the flesh, or an inconstant and vacillating heart', shares something of the *TTP*'s Preface and *Ethics* Part IV, of a given mind's inability to control its affects.[41]

Spinoza's uses of servitude, then, are consistent, though neither uniform nor schematic, at times only reflecting different contexts of *servitudo*. This can be partly explained by the contexts of both. The *Ethics* is aimed at the learned, philosophical reader, demonstrated in 'cumbersome geometric order' as Spinoza himself admits (and ultimately published posthumously over concerns about personal safety), and emphasises a more internal affective servitude.[42] The *TTP* is aimed at a broader, educated liberal Dutch republican audience, and was published anonymously in 1670 but proliferated widely, and emphasises a more external, politically timely servitude. It deploys a naturalistic, historico-political critique of biblical scripture, divine revelation and ecclesiastical authority in secular matters to challenge the growing political power of anti-Cartesian Calvinists in the Dutch Reformed Church and Prince William of Orange in the affairs of the republic.[43] Yet there are some important commonalities. In each, minds are dominated by inadequate and harmful beliefs that they are not the cause of, and which determine them to think and act in ways harmful to their own being. They correlate to disempowerment but should not be reduced to it (which would otherwise be merely *impotentia*). For servitude provides a refuge in false belief, from the apparent good of unmoderated affects and the harmful desires or dependencies that arise, to being in thrall to false beliefs about God, or our own good. The servitude of the Dutch and Hebrews refers to a more basic lack of power to think and act reasonably under political domination – thus, in the latter case, the Hebrews were unable to form a democracy as they lacked sufficient reason.[44] While Moses ultimately prescribes reasonable laws

---

[39] XVII, 89; CWS II, 316.
[40] II, 47; CWS II, 107.
[41] IV, 21; CWS II, 130.
[42] *Ethics* IV, 18; CWS I, 555.
[43] Chapter 6 assesses the *TTP*'s historical context and influences.
[44] *TTP* V, 27; CWS II, 145.

and a social contract founded on their common good, the divided sovereignty of their state leaves it fatally compromised, and the Hebrews come to experience their laws as a burden, being passively compelled to obey them without realising their fundamental benefit, which ultimately weakens their state. Again, their servitude describes the rule of harmful ideas, and in most cases, servitude is attached to debilitating political consequences – but what counts is not the content of the ideas themselves, or the specific historical relation, but the underlying condition of passivity and weakness where individuals do not capably think for themselves.

The *Political Treatise*, written later and left incomplete, presents some further significant similarities. As well as 'not restraining our appetites', and being under their control rather than 'the dominion of reason', like the definitions of the *Ethics*, it otherwise consistently refers to an explicitly political servitude, like that of the *TTP*.[45] There is the 'slavery' and 'barbarism' of the Ottoman Turks – the image of tyranny invoked in the *TTP* and across early modern western Europe – transferring all power to one sultan.[46] Then there is the danger of servitude under popular military dictators, and the slavery that exists under an absolute ruler who conceals the workings of government from the people using the 'mantle of utility'.[47] Spinoza also remarks on the 'symbols of servitude' of statues and honorific titles.[48] Given that the *TP* is premised on a theory of popular sovereignty as the basis of political stability, the *servitudo* of the State is actually that of the subjects' minds, unable to think adequately or as guided by reason to their common good, and instead being in awe to compelling, harmful ideas that perpetuate instability and fear.

There's also an important shift from the earlier *TTP* that emphasises servitude as something associated with the mind. Early in the *TP*, Spinoza presents a revised account of human power associated with independence of thought. He gives four instances of where one person falls under the authority of another either in body or mind, including where one becomes subject to the right of another through deception.[49] By implication 'it follows that a mind is completely its own master just to the extent that it can use reason rightly'. Neither afraid nor deceived, it can think for itself, and since human power should be assessed 'not so much by the strength of the

---

[45] *TP* II, 20; *CWS* II, 515.
[46] VI, 4; cf. VII, 27; *CWS* II, 533; 559.
[47] VII, 17; 29; cf. VIII, 6; *CWS* II, 552; 560; 567.
[48] X, 8; *CWS* II, 600.
[49] II, 10–11; *CWS* II, 512.

body as by the strength of mind', it follows that 'people are most their own masters when they can exert the most power with their reason'. This kind of servitude, then, is where one is unable to reason or think for oneself. It thereby leaves one vulnerable to indoctrination by the more powerful, whose ideas and practices are passively received and adopted as one's own. While this use of terminology is subtle and not always prominent in the text, I would argue that it leads to an important early premise for the politics of freedom in Spinoza. Philosophy should aim for as many as possible thinking for themselves.

This notion of being so dominated that one cannot think for oneself is also what Spinoza refers to in his use of 'slave' (*servus*). In the *Ethics*, the slave is presented as the antithesis of the free man, led not by reason but solely by passion or opinion.[50] In the *TTP*, the slave is repeatedly said to be 'under the command' of another, particularly as the subject of a state that demands it transfer the entirety of their rights, including that of thinking for themselves.[51] Spinoza distinguishes between the obedience of the slave and the obedience of the child to a parent, or a subject to a reasonable sovereign: whereas the slave obeys orders only useful to the master, the child obeys orders that are useful to them even if unable to perceive their rational necessity; by implication, the subject will also obey the sovereign whose orders are useful to the republic, and therefore themselves.[52] In both cases, 'slave' describes being passively under the command of affects, opinions or instructions for which one is not an adequate cause, and which are effected by an external force.

While Spinoza captures all these terms under *servitudo* or *servus*, and we now recognise passivity and lack of power in each, we need to explain how a given state of weakness results in domination by others. When Spinoza writes that the 'prejudices' surrounding religion might be appropriated by ambitious clerics 'to turn the heart of the multitude, who are still at the mercy of pagan superstition',[53] the servitude he refers to is not of being only under monarchical or theocratic rule – rather, this servitude is a collective state of disempowerment, which is then used by religious or political authorities to establish obedience to a powerful regime. Hence the *vulgus* (common people, pejoratively) share in a kind of servitude without being what we would term 'slaves': they are a group of people who become a subject through

[50] *Ethics* IV, 66 Schol.; CWS I, 584; cf. *TTP* IV, 38; CWS II, 135.
[51] *TTP* XVI, 32–5; CWS II, 288–9.
[52] XVI, 35; CWS II, 289.
[53] Praef., 13; CWS II, 70.

their servitude to harmful ideas. In this sense *vulgus* is less a socio-political category, more an epistemological one, as Étienne Balibar notes – their status is defined by their epistemological passivity, or, more concisely, in that they are unable to think for themselves, rather than, say, in sharing a humble social origin.[54] The *vulgus* exist in a state of epistemic servitude, striving to interpret the world according to inadequate ideas about freedom, God or nature, and desire. Yet while this passive affective condition seems somewhat universal epistemologically, what matters is its specific socio-political manifestation, and the harm it perpetuates both for the common people and for the State.

Whereas fortune locates agency outside human control in the realm of beasts and gods, Spinoza is throughout the *TTP* and the *Ethics* more interested in what human beings can control. As the title of *Ethics* Part IV spells out ('Of human servitude, or the strength of the affects'), servitude connotes a lack of power to moderate strong affects. But this does not necessarily entail all strong joyous affects – unless it is titillation, which in pleasing one part of the body over others, destabilises its proportion of motion-and-rest, and so causes harm.[55] Spinoza also writes elsewhere that cheerfulness or desires arising from reason can never be excessive.[56] The affects whose strength needs restraining are those that determine us to think or act in ways harmful to ourselves or others like us. These are most likely to be sad passive affects – ideas of the body's affections as it undergoes a transition to a state of lesser power – and of these disempowering states Spinoza particularly has in mind, hatred and fear. But he writes of the affects in general and, were his intention simply to affirm the good of joy, the *Ethics* might conclude with its affirmation of friendship, theatre and green plants,[57] rather than the *beatitudo* of the mind in adequate ideas. Instead, its ethical prescriptions recognise a freedom of the mind achieved through moderating the affects, without being simply equivalent to that.

It's too early to determine what this might mean politically, but we can begin to identify what servitude is not. It's not simply part of the tragic condition of human life that we necessarily live in a kind of universal servitude to all affects whose control we cannot escape, nor is the implied solution one of overcoming the affects altogether for the *apatheia* of the mind. Rather, we're in servitude to the extent that our affects determine our behaviour and

---

[54] Balibar 1994: 11. These different terms are assessed in Chapter 5.
[55] *Ethics* IV, 43; CWS I, 570.
[56] IV, 42; 61; CWS I, 570; 581.
[57] IV, 45 Schol.; CWS I, 572.

mental states in such a way that we do not act reasonably, which is to say, in a manner that will demonstrably maintain or enhance our well-being. In that sense, servitude is in our hands but beyond our grip. To establish some freedom, we must come to understand the causes of these affects, no longer captive to the uncertainty of fluctuating 'wretchedly between hope and fear', as the *TTP* memorably begins, but without expecting to be free of them altogether.[58]

Political Slavery

Our servitude, then, arises naturally from a certain inevitable weakness in our reasoning, as we discussed through prejudice, and lends itself to fantastical hopes and fears. While there is something undoubtedly universal about all this, Spinoza is quick to explore both in the *Ethics* and the *TTP* the political consequences of such a vulnerability. While the Appendix tentatively broached the emergence of distinctive peoples with their own contrary forms of worshipping their gods, the *TTP* goes further in thinking through the social consequences of harmful ideas. Let's turn to how that plays out.

We left the Preface earlier midway through its critique of superstition, which continues in the following paragraphs. All human beings are 'by nature' subject to superstition, and given what in the *Ethics* will be called its fragmentary, inadequate basis, it is 'necessarily very fluctuating and inconstant'.[59] Superstition is associated with hope, hate, anger and deception (fear goes unmentioned – we might say it is its root). Yet the form superstition takes varies. At this point, Spinoza launches a denunciation of the common people, of a kind which marks the *TTP* more than the *TP*.[60] 'The common people always remain equally wretched', and are 'never satisfied for long'.[61] Their inconstancy and unpredictability have been 'the cause of many uprisings and bloody wars' and, writing later, they are not 'governed by reason, but carried away by an impulse to praise or blame'.[62] But Spinoza said at the start of the Preface that few if any of us are governed by reason, and it's initially unclear what this critique of the common people is supposed to amount to. What's interesting is where the critique leads:

---

[58] Kisner (2011: 23) presents a similar claim regarding the possibility of adequate knowledge. Chapter 4 assesses the affects and adequate ideas.
[59] *TTP* Praef., 7; CWS II, 68.
[60] Chapter 5 will explore why.
[61] Praef., 8; CWS II, 68.
[62] Praef., 33; CWS II, 75.

> To avoid this evil [of inconstancy], immense zeal is brought to bear to embellish religion – whether the religion is true or illusory – with ceremony and pomp, so that it will be thought to have greater weight than any other influence.
> [. . .] The greatest secret of monarchic rule, and its main interest, is to keep men deceived, and to cloak in the specious name of religion the fear by which they must be checked, so that they will fight for slavery as they would for their survival, and will think it not shameful, but a most honorable achievement, to give their life and blood that one man may have a ground for boasting.[63]

Spinoza seems to raise here the possibility that one may acquiesce or even will what causes one's weakness. For Deleuze and Guattari, this is 'the fundamental problem of political philosophy' and one that 'Spinoza saw so clearly',[64] namely, why subjugated members of a society not only assent to but even support rulers whose decisions damage or destroy their own lives or those they care about. It raises pressing questions about our agency and even willingness under powerful regimes that will inform the rest of the book.

Note the agency implied: they *will fight for slavery*. The Latin, *pro servitio*, recurs just once in the *Opera* regarding military service in the *TP*, and this activity in subjugation shouldn't be overstated.[65] Spinoza instead sets up a binary that appears elsewhere in his works: the free individual versus the slave. He gives the example of the Ottoman Turks, the prevailing model of political servitude also given in the *TP* in the last section, for whom Christian fears of invasion and occupation loomed large until their defeat in the Battle of Vienna the following decade. This rhetorical device to stir the audience is contrasted with the 'free republic' – explicitly described in the following paragraph as the one in which 'we live' – in which it is 'completely contrary to the general freedom to fill the free judgment of each man with prejudices, or to restrain it in any way'.[66]

This latter move is decisive, as weak ideas about omens and rituals become organised into formidable structures of belief that explain away uncertainty with narratives of damnation, salvation and a divinely ordained human command structure. It thus becomes not only thinkable, but honourable, to

---

[63] Praef., 9–10; CWS II, 68–9.
[64] Deleuze and Guattari 2013: 42.
[65] TP VIII, 9; CWS II, 569.
[66] TTP Praef., 10; CWS II, 69.

give up one's life for the perpetuity of a regime with which one identifies.[67] While a servitude to passive affects like fear is inevitable then, as are superstitious ideas becoming attached to our hopes and fears, Spinoza's warning is that unless a republic is sufficiently constituted to enable and defend the flourishing of reason (i.e. through protecting free speech, religious and cultural plurality, or democratic deliberative and executive processes), it will collapse into despotism, that 'ancient servitude' of earlier. This is exacerbated by ambitious figures, who emerge in any given society, who seek to summon and steer the hopes and fears of the common people for their own political ends.

While Balibar writes of the politically decisive 'fear of the masses',[68] it is as much the 'hope of the masses' in Spinoza that also perpetuates the rule of tyrants and oppressive regimes. For it is hope, among other affects, that was earlier instrumental in conditioning servitude; hope that leads men to attempt to read the judgements of the gods in the flight of birds or animal entrails, and which render 'nature and the gods [. . .] as mad as men' or 'as crazy as they are'.[69] In a recent analysis, Justin Steinberg argues that hope serves a greater political good than fear through producing more loyal and willing subjects, who bring stability, civic trust, peace, or '*securitas*'.[70] Drawing on a wealth of textual material, fear serves little political advantage – where men act from fear, 'they act very unwillingly', often motivated merely by the avoidance of death – and such societies like the Ottoman Empire are a 'wasteland' marked not by peace but the mere 'privation of war'.[71] While the debilitating nature of fear is undeniable, the danger of advocating a politics of hope is its necessarily uncertain and passive basis, vulnerable to the same adversities that lead prejudice to superstition. As Spinoza repeatedly counsels, the basis of hope and fear is the same – 'there is no hope without fear, and no fear without hope' – for each involves doubting a thing's outcome through imagining something else that excludes the presence of that thing.[72] Through this arises the belief in superstitions that Spinoza warns against in political terms in the *TTP*'s Preface. Furthermore, such hopes may be indistinct from fantasy, that is, forms of wishful thinking in which, to upturn a tenet

---

[67] In other words, the problem of what Étienne de la Boétie called 'voluntary servitude' a century earlier.
[68] Balibar 1994: 5, 27.
[69] *TTP* Praef., 4; *CWS* II, 66–7; *Ethics* I, App.; *CWS* I, 441; *TTP* Praef., 3; *CWS* II, 6.
[70] Steinberg 2018: 81.
[71] *TTP* V, 22; *TP* V, 4; VI, 4; *CWS* II, 114; 530; 533.
[72] *Ethics* III, 50 Schol.; III, DA 13; *CWS* I, 521; 534.

of Spinozan realism, we regard others not as they are, but as we would like them to be.[73]

The importance of the imagination for political obedience here – or as Spinoza conceives it, as the first kind of knowledge – cannot be overstated: the subject's willing or fearful obedience is an effect of how that subject has internalised and made sense of powerful social narratives about their conditions of existence. As Althusser writes, such 'ideology' exists both as a real (i.e. economic) relation and as an 'imaginary' or 'lived' relation; indeed, our participation in the former is dependent on our investments in the latter.[74] Worse, such hopes may themselves reflect what cultural theorist Mark Fisher called, after Deleuze, the 'frozen images' of reactive, repetitive and docile behaviours.[75] In his view, they're instilled by a late capitalist ideology that presents itself as natural, realistic, if not inevitable, veiling the conflict and contingency of its historical basis. In its place, Fisher calls on us to 'abandon hope',[76] just as Deleuze wrote of the emerging 'control societies' that '[t]here is no need to fear or hope, but only to look for new weapons'.[77]

But Spinoza already indicates what weapons are up to the task. 'The more we strive to live according to the guidance of reason,' he writes, 'the more we strive to depend less on hope, to free ourselves from fear, to conquer fortune as much as we can, and to direct our actions by the certain counsel of reason.'[78] Perhaps this circling of reason at the beginning and end of the sentence begs the question. But it indicates that the only meaningful way to overcome the rule of hope and fear is through empowering the hearts and minds of the many. In this the political realism of the *TTP* is instructive. If often damning of the capabilities of the common people (an anger that dissipates by the *TP*, and assessed in Chapter 7), the *TTP* nonetheless outlines how citizens can better participate in and become more empowered by the State they inhabit.

In a phrasing that has sometimes been paused over, Spinoza writes of the draconian and prescriptive laws of Moses' Hebrew Republic that '[t]o those who had become completely accustomed to it, this regime must have seemed no longer servitude, but freedom'.[79] Moses' gift as a prophet–statesman in Spinoza's view was to devise a legal and political system tailored to the

---

[73] After *TP* I, 1; *CWS* II, 503.
[74] Althusser 2005: 233–4.
[75] Fisher 2009: 73.
[76] Fisher 2015b.
[77] Deleuze 1995: 178.
[78] *Ethics* IV, 47 Schol.; *CWS* I, 573.
[79] *TTP* XVII, 89; *CWS* II, 316.

weakened capabilities of the not-long-liberated Hebrews that mobilised their hopes and willingness, giving the State further stability in turn and further improving the lives of its subjects. All the same, Moses' paternalistic state does little to lift the intellectual capacities of its subjects, who soon fall under the sway of the powerful Levites, with the State degenerating into a monarchy.[80] While hope and willingness are important affective resources for political movements (which should aim to not merely critique but develop viable alternatives), they shouldn't be advocated for their own sake. Causes of hope and willingness must be accompanied by processes that raise awareness of what causes disempowerment, and the difficulties surrounding change.

Caution around the affective power of hope leads us to appreciate a final dimension of Spinoza's political endorsement of free speech. Besides his arguments for its fundamental inalienability ('If it were as easy to command men's minds as it is their tongues'),[81] and its uses for disseminating reasonable ideas as widely as possible in democratic assemblies,[82] the value of free speech is its power to overcome what Hannah Arendt would later determine as foundational to totalitarianism: loneliness. Not merely fear, as early modern political realists might conjecture, or the epic unimaginative thoughtlessness that constituted the 'banality of evil' in Eichmann's case, but loneliness, a world 'deserted by all human companionship'.[83] That is, of advanced industrial societies rendering swathes of the population economically and socially 'superfluous', uprooting social ties and creating modern cities devoid of public spaces and civic life, where 'nobody is reliable and nothing can be relied upon'.[84] Without companionship or free speech, the circulation of ideas diminishes and the noise of those with divine or secular authority deafens dissent. While Spinoza would later write, after Seneca, that 'no one has sustained a violent rule for long',[85] Arendt's insight – that this loss of communication and sociality is conditional for the maintenance of powerful regimes – helps distinguish the connection between prejudice, superstition and a domination seemingly embraced by so many.

---

[80] XVII, 99–103; CWS II, 318–19. Chapter 6 assesses this.
[81] XX, 1; CWS II, 344.
[82] XVI, 30; CWS II, 288.
[83] Arendt 1979: 474.
[84] Ibid. 478.
[85] *TTP* V, 22; XVI, 29; CWS II, 144; 288.

Takeover

In this final part, we will develop something still implicit in Spinoza's account of servitude – how an individual's mind can be taken over by another, and how this debilitating reprogramming of one's desires might also indicate how one can become more robust and able to withstand such indoctrination. This problem preoccupies the *TTP*, whose Preface is consumed with the problem of affective and political forms of servitude, and whose defence of the freedom to philosophise largely takes the form of an investigation into how belief systems function at the level of custom, community, language, history and the imagination.

Now, why did some fight for their servitude as if it were their salvation? The foregoing discussion indicates that they act out of an internal weakness caused by being overpowered or possessed by ideas harmful to oneself and others. They are passive then in their fighting, but that doesn't explain how something seemingly internal and traditionally autonomous, the human mind, can be broken down, broken into and reprogrammed to act in such a self-negating manner. Nor does it explain how commonly shared sad affects can impede the possibility of collective action – what Frantz Fanon called a state of 'wretchedness' in the minds of the oppressed, 'this self-hatred, this abdication and denial' of agency.[86] It relates to how consoling beliefs, particularly faith-based ones that emphasise docility, passivity and obedience, can perpetuate a feeling of inferiority and self-contempt. As James Baldwin put it elegantly in *The Fire Next Time*: 'the passion with which we loved the Lord was a measure of how deeply we feared and distrusted and, in the end, hated almost all strangers, always, and avoided and despised ourselves'.[87] We find a similar observation in the *TTP*, when Spinoza describes 'the love of the Hebrews for their country' which results in a comparable xenophobia.[88] 'Their daily worship so encouraged and fed this piety, and this hatred of other nations', he writes, that these affects 'had to become a part of their nature'. While the complex racial politics of shame play no part in Spinoza's discussion, in both we recognise how certain affects become *part of our nature*, and how communities can share, reciprocate and intensify common passive affects of love, anger and hatred, which are further internalised and perpetuated within personal relationships, where much of the political takes place.

---

[86] Fanon 2004: 148.
[87] Baldwin 1968: 51.
[88] *TTP* XVII, 80; CWS II, 314.

But there's another facet of what Spinoza called *fighting for slavery* which we haven't yet untangled – how individuals not merely adopt a belief system passively imposed on them but come to experience it as involving their own agency. This is a peculiar development. Frédéric Lordon calls this process 'enlisting', wherein people not merely acquiesce in the 'master-desire' externally imposed on them, but come to recognise and pursue it *as* their own.[89] He observes a process of 'capture', wherein authorities enlist their subordinates to not merely assent to being dominated but actually to experience a sense of freedom, activity, even joy in their subjugation. The effect is a complete capture of the individual's 'interiority', a process of 'co-linearisation', in which the desire of the subject comes to totally coincide with that of the authority.[90] In this way, what are experienced as 'consent' and 'freedom' are instead dangerous prejudices and instances of what we define as servitude. 'To produce consent is to produce in individuals a love for the situation in which they have been put.'[91]

While love is not necessary to establish consent, the most powerful bonds of obedience involve forms of love and devotion. We'll recall the xenophobia that Spinoza called 'love' and 'piety' just earlier. It's a useful corrective to the tendency to ascribe liberatory powers to any form of passive joy. Pascal Sévérac and Jason Read both observe that the subject's passive joys are not themselves empowering, because they are not a cause of them.[92] It is 'precisely because we actively strive to interpret the world according to inadequate ideas of our freedom and autonomy', Read writes, 'that we are subject to it'. In this way, we experience our subjection as a kind of freedom – a freedom that belongs to someone else. Applying a finding about harmful ideas from the first section, a state of servitude is reinforced by believing one's consent, joys or free will is one's own. There is nothing normatively liberating about a given desire (a point developed later in Chapter 4). In Deleuze and Guattari's *Anti-Oedipus* we also find a similarly forthright account of the social investment of desire, explaining the individual's desire *for* and attachment *to* coercive forms, and their passive affective experiences of hope and joy within them. Desire precedes everything – '*There is only desire and the social, and nothing else*' – and so desire must be accounted for within every power formation.[93] That includes, in their view, an identification of one's

---

[89] Lordon 2014: 3–4.
[90] Ibid. 79–80.
[91] Ibid. 98.
[92] Sévérac 2005: 23; Read 2016: 258.
[93] Deleuze and Guattari 2013: 42.

desire with that of a powerful authority, even where that authority diminishes one's safety or living standards.

Whereas Lordon's account extends only so far as 'happy subjection', Deleuze and Guattari offer a more sophisticated model of desires, in which some are liberatory or 'molecular', and others contain an implicit desire for authoritarianism and are 'molar'.[94] They are particularly interested in the latter, often at the expense of the former's clarity. 'Repressing desire, not only for others but in oneself, being the cop for others and for oneself – that is what arouses',[95] they argue, considering sadistic desire as commensurate with support for political fascism. In attempting to explain Wilhelm Reich's question 'why did the masses desire fascism?' in 1930s Germany,[96] Deleuze and Guattari indicate the nature of libidinal investment in forms of authority within which one enlists one's desire and imagines participating within, if not *as*, an indispensable part of that authority. Hence the power of nationalism. Those who fight for their slavery under the monarch *do* desire such subjugation, according to this analysis.

Yet the more obvious implication, and one that Spinoza has in mind, is that they do not desire their own subjugation – rather, they imaginatively identify with the strengths of a larger and more powerful entity, and put themselves in its service, even if such willingness and devotion risks their own life. There will be some of the workings of the imagination here, clutching onto those things that increase or aid the body's power of acting, as we saw with III, 12 in discussing prejudices. In an argument that will be developed in Chapters 3 and 4, this difference in desire can be described as a *problem of consciousness*: no one will forego their right to think and act as they wish in society unless there is some perceived greater good. The problem then is the perception of this good: willing servitude raises difficult situations of when many might prefer not to, to echo Bartleby's phrase, but continue to acquiesce, believing it to be in their greater interest or for the common good to fight for a tyrant, or to not step in and fight against one.

We can also agree with Miguel Abensour that there is no 'collective political suicide' in such obedience, but even expedient, useful grounds for it, like the survival of oneself or one's family.[97] These problems cannot yet be resolved without an analysis of natural right and desire, undertaken over

---

[94] Ibid. 334.
[95] Ibid. 394. Deleuze and Guattari are clear about the fundamental influence of Spinoza in articulating their philosophy of desire (e.g. 41).
[96] Reich 1972: 216–20.
[97] Abensour 2015: §17.

the next three chapters. Yet there is already a weakness in merely affirming desire itself, or social withdrawal, or 'the inverse subordination and the overthrow of power'.[98] One cannot overthrow power except through a power of one's own, and attempting 'escape' may render one even more vulnerable to tyrants and ambitious clerics that Spinoza warns against.[99]

Instead, given the inherently social and relational character of freedom, such a freedom from servitude is only possible through the development and maintenance of empowering relations with others, ones which enable all sides to become more active in determining their own affects and ideas in place of the harmful ones explored in this chapter. As our argument can now show, freedom is necessarily achieved socially and inter-relationally in Spinoza. 'As many as possible, thinking as much as possible', writes Balibar, in a wonderful remark we will come back to.[100] For the free circulation of ideas to flourish, we must be attuned to the affective and imaginative determinants that lead us, by nature, into the misery and loneliness of servitude. It involves a reckoning with the political circumstances in which our minds can be taken over by powerful affects like hope and fear, often exacerbated if not caused by the bold claims of ambitious figureheads, which lead us to thoughts or actions we would not otherwise countenance. That in turn requires that we understand 'Nature', perhaps the most ubiquitous and difficult of all Spinoza's striking (re)formulations, and the ways in which 'by nature' we might become more capable of recognising harmful ideas for what they are.

---

[98] Deleuze and Guattari 2013: 416.
[99] Ibid. 317.
[100] Balibar 2008: 98.

2

Nature

In 1638, three years after the Dutch capture of Pernambuco, Northeast Brazil, from Portuguese hands, the governor of 'New Holland' wrote back to Amsterdam. Addressing the recently formed Dutch West India Company (WIC) who had organised and financed the occupation, Johan Maurits von Nassau-Siegen appealed for new colonists to the region, particularly those with capital:

> In order to make the factory they need, for it cannot be brought over from Holland as it is needed here, and to buy some Negroes, without whom nothing of value can be made in Brazil [. . .] [there] necessarily must be slaves in Brazil, and in no way they can be done without. If someone is offended by this, it will prove a useless scruple. [. . .] It is much needed that all the appropriate means are employed in the related trade of the African Coast.[1]

A similar call to overlook scruple appeared two years later from another experienced WIC agent in the region, Adriaen van der Dussen. His report includes one of the earliest 'racial', if not scientific justifications for the systematic enslavement of black Africans:

> Without Negroes nothing can be cultivated here, and no White – no matter how well disposed to work he may have been in the homeland – can dedicate himself in Brazil to such labors, nor can he bear them; it seems that the body, as a consequence of such an extreme climate change, loses much of its stamina; this takes place not only with the man, but also

---

[1] Alencastro 2018: 207.

with everything that comes from Europe to Brazil, including iron, steel, copper etc.[2]

From around 1630 (with the capture of Recife, renamed Mauritsstad) to 1654 (with their expulsion by the Portuguese), the Dutch maintained an uneasy foothold in Brazil. The lush, forested terrain and tropical climate was peopled by Portuguese settlers, African slaves and Amerindians, bound by uneasy alliances or more direct military control.[3] The expense and difficulty of controlling such a large and distant territory became clear during the First Anglo-Dutch War (1652–4), through which the Dutch were put on the defensive and unable to send relief to the colonies under Portuguese and local attack. At its peak, the Dutch West India Company also counted – across the Ethiopic Ocean – Elmina, Luanda and parts of the interior of Angola among its reach (1641–8). It was motivated principally by a desire to profit from the slave trade and the lucrative production of sugar, a crop introduced to Brazil from Southeast Asia via the Canary Islands and São Tomé. Among other things, the short life of Dutch Brazil resulted in a period of relative religious toleration, patronage of the arts, predatorial capitalism (what Marx would later call primitive accumulation), debt vassalage and slavery.

It's possible that both Van der Dussen and Nassau-Siegen were familiar with Hugo Grotius' 1625 *De Iure Belli ac Pacis* (*On the Rights of War and Peace*). This work, like *Mare Liberum* (*The Freedom of the Seas*, 1608) before it, set out an influential natural law framework for negotiating international conflict and trade in the new worlds of the East and West Indies.[4] For Grotius, there are two laws of nature. The first is self-preservation: 'nature drives each animal to seek its own interests',[5] and this is intrinsically true, even famously without God ('what I have just said would be relevant even if we were to suppose [what we cannot suppose without the greatest wickedness] that there is no God, or that human affairs are of no concern to him'). This is balanced by a second law, defined by a desire for society in

---

[2] Ibid.
[3] Like the Tupinamba peoples, many of whom, having been colonised by Portuguese missionaries, served as soldiers or farmers for the WIC. On Dutch Brazil, see Brienen 2006: 110–12 and *passim*, Alencastro 2018: ch. 6, Van Groesen 2014 and Feitler 2009. For an insightful view on Spinoza and slavery, see Tatián 2018.
[4] Grotius was also a Dutch East India Company (VOC) shareholder, with *Mare Liberum* occasioned by the Dutch seizure of a 1,500-ton Portuguese carrack in 1603 off Singapore, loaded with porcelain and lucrative wares.
[5] Grotius 2005: Prolegomena, 1747.

accordance with reason, which forms the basis of our respecting each other's rights. This is the 'source of *ius*, properly so called, to which belong abstaining from another's possessions, restoring anything which belongs to another (or the profit from it), being obliged to keep promises, giving compensation for culpable damage, and incurring human punishment'.[6] Among others, this extended the right of punishment to individuals and not just states, like the VOC, increasingly in conflict with local regional powers and European rivals.

It also granted, more subtly, the right to punish all those who 'offend against Nature' – including pirates, cannibals, anyone inhumane to their parents, but also indigenous peoples who had not sufficiently cultivated land given by Nature, or who prevented European access to 'settle in some uninhabited Land' where 'just occasion' required it.[7] For Grotius, there were also occasions in which slavery was justified where it led to preserving the slave's life. '[P]erfect and utter Slavery', he writes,

> is that which obliges a Man to serve his Master all his Life long, for Diet and other common Necessaries; which indeed, if it be thus understood, and confined within the Bounds of Nature, has nothing too hard and severe in it; for that perpetual Obligation to Service, is recompensed by the Certainty of being always provided for; which those who let themselves out to daily Labour, are often far from being assured of.[8]

We encountered many forms of slavery in the last chapter, though most concerned an epistemic sort of being passive to and under the driving influence of harmful ideas. In this chapter I want to explore whether we can follow Spinoza, Locke and other contemporaries in distinguishing (or rather, being blind to) political slavery, or epistemic slavery, as something distinct from the material and systematic enslavement of black Africans and Amerindians whose labour produced much of the wealth of the European 'Age of Discovery', as it's often troublingly described. As I see it, there can be no discussion or silence on slavery without a discussion of theories of nature upon which this trade in the living was predicated. The Dutch, like other European powers, believed they had a right to take and use what was theirs by right of nature. Without the free flow of African slaves, Nassau-Siegen wrote, New Holland would be 'useless and bear no fruits to the Compagnie'.

---

[6] Ibid.
[7] Grotius 2005: II.XIII.I.
[8] Ibid. II.V.XXVII.

When supply dwindled, the Dutch resorted, as the Portuguese and Spanish often had before, to captured Amerindians, who 'do not labor if not paid for in advance, and, on having the occasion, they flee and the master loses his payment', as Van der Dussen complained.

While reports appealed for white Dutch settlers, in practice, the colony was also reliant on Sephardic Jews, mostly from Amsterdam, many second or third generation Portuguese, with the advantage of fluency in a language that was the lingua franca of both the slave trade of the Central West African coast, and the Portuguese plantation and sugar mill owners that had fallen under Dutch control. The Amsterdam Jews also had the advantage of connections to credit and international trade needed by the beleaguered, broke colony. As well as making up a significant number of the WIC's occupying army and militia (of the latter, Wiznitzer estimates up to 50 per cent), the Jews also settled in New Holland in relatively large numbers, reaching a peak of 1,450 in 1645, or 11 per cent of the population.[9] The first synagogue in the Americas opened in Recife around 1636. This degree of toleration was undoubtedly unusual – Jews had relative freedom of worship, as did Portuguese Catholics, and some Marrano 'New Christians' converted back to Judaism over this period. As Jonathan Israel rightly observes, though, it reflected a pragmatic concession to 'sheer, straightforward necessity' rather than a shift of values.[10] Occupations varied, with a small number involved directly in the slave trade (6 per cent of all sugar mill owners were Jewish, calculates Wiznitzer)[11] but most indirectly (as were most others in the colony), either through retail, trade, or through supplying supplies and credit, loaning African slaves to heavily indebted mill owners, with rates of interest that would eventually stoke local Portuguese unrest.[12]

Spinoza was intimately connected with this world. His father Michael d'Espinosa was a Portuguese merchant of dried fruit, Algerian oil and pipes, and shared an Amsterdam warehouse with Philips Pelt that also contained sugar and brazilwood, used as a red dye in textiles production.[13] Upon his father's death in 1654, Baruch inherited the family business, which he oversaw with his younger brother Gabriel. It was here that Spinoza may have briefly encountered the temptation of 'riches' recalled in the *TdIE*,

---

[9] Wiznitzer 1956a: 43; Friedman 2017: ch. 6.
[10] Israel and Schwartz 2007: 24.
[11] Wiznitzer 1956b: 195.
[12] Against the incorrect claim that Jews were disproportionately involved in the Dutch slave trade (e.g. Feuer 1995: 257), see Friedman 2017: ch. 5.
[13] Nadler 1999: 36.

and his moral disquiet was a common refrain among Dutch Collegiant merchants like Pieter Balling and Jarig Jelles, who he met around this time. That same year, New Holland was finally retaken by a Portuguese naval blockade and insurgency, boosted by a local Maroon uprising led by the black military commander Henrique Dias. In one record we find Spinoza donating five guilders to 'the poor of Brazil',[14] being the Jews forced to return to Amsterdam after their expulsion, including their rabbi, Isaac Aboab, who would later sign the *cherem* against Spinoza. Saul Levi Morteira, who taught the young Spinoza at the Keter Torah Yeshiva, later becoming chief rabbi of Amsterdam, remarked on their miraculous escape not only from the Portuguese ('by natural inclination the greatest enemies of the Jewish people'), but also their 'army of soldiers, Negroes, mulattoes, escaped convicts, poor, starved, and barefooted individuals'.[15] Undoubtedly, such frightening anecdotes from the Pernambuco refugees would have circulated in Spinoza's childhood world.

In a 1664 letter to Balling that has long interested commentators, Spinoza recalls a terrifying dream of a 'black and scabby Brazilian' and 'Ethiopian' whose sight appals him until he focuses his thoughts on another object.[16] In an inventive and hopeful reading, Negri claims that this initiated a shift in the foundations of Spinoza's thinking, from inner mysticism to materialism and its political commitments.[17] Likewise, others have posed whether it indicates the 'haunting', or 'projective identification', of the perspectives of the outcasts, excluded and 'Maroons' of European society.[18] The more immediate historical context of the dream seems surer ground for interpretation. Spinoza's dream may reflect – aside from its obvious purpose to elucidate the workings of the imagination, and help a grieving father make sense of his thoughts – the memories of the Jewish settlers of their fears and losses in Pernambuco, of which there were occasional massacres of Jewish soldiers by the Brazilians and Portuguese.[19] Indeed, Lewis Feuer persuasively links it to Henrique Dias himself.[20] Death was also brought by disease, like the ominous scabs which Kevin von Duuglas-Ittu links to a certain Canary

---

[14] Yovel 1989: 77.
[15] In Wiznitzer 1954: 112.
[16] *Ep.* XVII [to Pieter Balling]; *CWS* I, 353.
[17] Negri 2003: 86–91.
[18] Goetschel 2016: 39n2 gives a good overview of these dream interpretations, which usually offer speculative, esoteric meanings. I then paraphrase the views of Rosenthal 2005: 218, Montag 1999: 88 and Ford 2018: 191.
[19] E.g. Wiznitzer 1956a: 46.
[20] Feuer 1995: 258.

Island physician convalescing from leprosy, whose home Spinoza is recorded visiting in 1659.[21]

In any case, Spinoza's dream can be understood in the context of the Jewish experience in Dutch Brazil, and of the broader vulnerability and opportunities that life there presented.[22] If, as per Grotius, the seas belonged to all and none in their natural state, then Jewish New Holland was a reminder of the feeble, if not impossible, premises of a benign Christian morality in nature that Grotius would later shoehorn into the second edition of *De Iure Belli ac Pacis*, and which characterise the later approaches of Pufendorf and Locke. While Pufendorf would envision as a fundamental principle of natural law that everyone must 'cultivate and maintain toward others a peaceable sociality that is consistent with the native character and end of humankind in general',[23] Locke would go further. 'The *State of Nature* has a Law of Nature to govern it, which obliges everyone', he writes in the *Second Treatise*, '[a]nd Reason, which is that law, teaches all Mankind [. . .] that all being equal and independent, no one ought to harm another in his Life, Health, Liberty or Possessions.'[24] Much rests on that dubious Christian *ought*.

All the same, Spinoza's fear shouldn't be overstated. The survival of the community rested on another foundation, one intimated in Morteira's repetition of 'our people', 'His people' and their escape by divine providence in his record: the advantages of mutual assistance and common purpose. While Spinoza would later write curtly of such beliefs ('the Jews never mention – nor do they heed – intermediate, or particular causes'),[25] his view of nature is indelibly marked by the benefits to one and all of communal life and cooperation. It also suggests a view of human power as marked by our capacity to react and withstand contrary forces as much as maximising our own advantage, something realised by working with others. Indeed, it is this ability to understand our existence in nature as it is, and not as our desires or anthropocentric beliefs would like it to be, that delineates whether we fall under the spell of the prejudices and superstitions discussed in the last chapter. It's this tension between nature conceived as a place of conflict and conquest, and cooperation and community, that I now want to explore.

---

[21] Von Duuglas-Ittu 2008.
[22] Gabriel would travel to Bermuda in 1656, becoming naturalised as an English citizen, later moving to Jamaica in 1671, where no more is known of him; Spinoza's sister Rebecca would later migrate to Curaçao, dying of yellow fever in 1695.
[23] Pufendorf 1994: II.3.15.
[24] Locke 2003: II.2.7.
[25] *TTP* I, 8; *CWS* II, 78.

Natural Right

In a gloss of his arguments of Chapter 16, Spinoza introduces a somewhat conventional concept of natural right (*jure naturali*) in the Preface, by the standards of Grotius and Hobbes.[26] It belongs to an individual and 'extends as far as each person's desire and power extend'.[27] Like Grotius, there is something dynamic about it – the individual can 'transfer' their right with others to a sovereign authority, who then takes on this right to protect them.[28] Unlike Hobbes, not all right can be transferred: an element always remains with the subject, that of their right to think and judge, and can never truly be bequeathed to the sovereign. But what precisely is this natural right? Is it merely equivalent or also reducible to one's desire or power? Does human natural right differ substantially from the natural right of birds or beasts? In what sense does a subject possess or transfer their power to another, and by what understanding of nature does such possession function?

In Chapter 16 Spinoza addresses these questions, in a broad-ranging treatise that covers natural right (paragraphs 1–14), the social contract (15–38), civil rights (39–51) and remaining questions of obedience to the sovereign (52–67). He begins with the analogy of how big fish eat smaller to indicate the state of nature. It's memorable if unusually blunt. Perhaps it reflects Grotius' and the Dutch interest in the sea (though *Mare Liberum* is more concerned with the rights of fishermen than fish), or offered a subtle comment on the particular natural source upon which Dutch wealth was based. It's soon followed by a definition of natural right which raises more questions than answers. It is said to be 'the rules of nature of each individual, according to which we conceive each thing to be naturally determined to existing and having effects in a certain way'.[29] Likewise, the example of hungry fish indicates that nature absolutely 'has the supreme right to do everything it can'.[30] But this does not actually define what these rules are, why they determine the nature of an individual thing thus, nor, should we pursue him further, what nature is, or existence, and so forth.

---

[26] On Spinoza and natural law, see Steinberg 2018: ch. 2 and Campos 2015 *passim*.
[27] TTP Praef., 29; CWS II, 74.
[28] Spinoza doesn't account for how subjects should react if the sovereign authority to which they have transferred their right does not protect them from harm, or even actively harms them (e.g. institutional or state violence or discrimination). The difficulties of a coherent theory of rebellion in Spinoza are mulled over in Chapter 8.
[29] TTP XVI, 2; CWS II, 282.
[30] XVI, 3; CWS II, 282.

We can be charitable: using the preface and the fish analogy, natural right seems to correspond to a thing's *doing* of what preserves its existence. Indeed, what Spinoza offers in this discussion is a précis of his *conatus* doctrine in *Ethics*, Part III. This is analysed in the following chapter through the *Ethics*, but for now, note that Spinoza defines each thing by its *conatus*, from the Latin *conor* (to strive) and meaning its 'striving to persevere in its own being'.[31] This conatus belongs to all things in nature,[32] and in human beings corresponds to our appetite, and when appetite is accompanied by consciousness, is desire.[33] Spinoza, lastly, is keen to impress that 'the right and established practice of nature [. . .] prohibits nothing except what no one desires and what no one can do'.[34] While this argument, like much of the chapter, bears Hobbes's influence, we can agree with Israel that Spinoza's attack on Christian natural law, like that of Aquinas, is much bolder,[35] and most importantly for our purposes, contains an implicit view of power. If natural right corresponds to what one can do, and reflects desire *or* power, then the very 'freedom' Spinoza seeks to define at the start of this chapter would be nothing other than the individual's activity or power within a given set of relations, the 'rules of nature of each individual' defined earlier.

It is still unclear, however, what this 'freedom' amounts to, and we should distinguish natural right – belonging to all beings in nature – from freedom, which so far reflects a given ability or liberty. The title page of the *TTP* writes of the 'freedom of philosophizing', the preface of the 'complete freedom of judgment' of life in the Dutch republic, Chapter 5 of the stateless Hebrews' 'being permitted, as they wished, to enact new laws', Chapter 14 of 'how far each person has the freedom to think what he wishes with respect to faith', and Chapter 16 of 'this freedom of thought, and of saying what you think', and later, in its description of democracy as approaching 'most nearly the freedom nature concedes to everyone'.[36] This use of *libertas* suggests the possibility of being able to do something. Yet Spinoza adds to his earlier preface definition that natural right is determined 'not by sound reason, but by desire and power'.[37] Its capacity *to do* does not necessarily include a normative predisposition to doing reasonable or morally salubrious things. This definition subverts any belief in a natural or universal human morality (contra

---

[31] *Ethics* III, 6; CWS I, 498.
[32] Cf. *TTP* XVI, 2; CWS II, 282.
[33] *Ethics* III, 9 Schol.; CWS I, 500.
[34] *TTP* XVI, 9; CWS II, 284. Cf. *Ethics* III, 9 Schol.; CWS I, 500.
[35] In Spinoza 2007: 197n2.
[36] *TTP* Praef., 12; V, 26; XIV, 2; XVI, 1; 36; CWS II, 69; 145; 264; 282; 289.
[37] XVI, 7; CWS II, 283.

Aristotle, Cicero and Christian natural law) while Spinoza's 'eccentric Hobbesian' flourish, to borrow Curley's phrase, is to even subvert Hobbes's objective foundation of a natural law of self-preservation.[38] For Spinoza, this natural right only extends so far as what a thing *judges* to be in its own interest,[39] which, lacking 'sound reason', may tend towards its own harm, as our earlier analysis of superstition makes clear. As he argues in the *Ethics*, there is no use in condemning human nature as 'a dominion within a dominion' or deriding or bewailing this natural state.[40] 'Nature is not constrained by the laws of human reason, which aim only at man's true advantage and preservation', he writes.[41] 'It is governed by infinite other laws, which look to the eternal order of the whole of nature, of which man is only a small part.' It is therefore a feature of the 'order and laws of nature', which prohibits nothing and strives to do everything it can.

Spinoza makes a similar declaration earlier in Chapter 5, which expands on this problem. 'Now if nature had so constituted men that they desired nothing except what true reason teaches them to desire, then of course a society could exist without laws.'[42] Later in the *Political Treatise* we encounter something similar. If 'the plebs could restrain themselves, and suspend judgment on matters they know little about, or judge things correctly from scanty information, they would be more worthy to rule than to be ruled'.[43] In both cases, Spinoza speculates on the possibility of popular government and a society without the external coercion of the law. While rejecting any kind of political *telos*, he argues that the reasonable individual will always grasp that it is in their own interest to assist their fellows and maintain the security of their state by obeying its laws. As Spinoza writes in a later annotation, distinguishing his view from Hobbes, 'the more a man is led by reason, i.e. the more he is free, the more will he steadfastly maintain the State's laws and carry out the commands of the supreme power to which he is subject'.[44]

---

[38] Curley 1996: 317; *DC* I.8–10.
[39] This use of *judge* is a placeholder for the analysis of desire, consciousness and evaluation in Chapter 4. At this stage it refers not to a rational evaluative judgement, but a combination of ideas (affects, beliefs of the first kind of knowledge of *Ethics* II, 40 Schol. 2, common notions of the second, and so on) which together constitute a decision.
[40] *Ethics* III, Praef.; *CWS* I, 491.
[41] *TTP* XVI, 10; *CWS* II, 284.
[42] *TTP* V, 20; *CWS* II, 144.
[43] *TP* VII, 27; *CWS* II, 559.
[44] *TTP* XVI, Annotation 33; *CWS* II, 289.

At the same time, the number of individuals who can acquire sufficient reason (and, by the definition given in the annotation, can be said to be free, reason and freedom being equivalent) are 'very few', and may only acquire this capacity after a good part of their life has elapsed.[45] '[E]veryone seeks his own advantage', he writes, 'but people want things and judge them useful, not by the dictate of sound reason, but for the most part only from immoderate desire [*libidine*]' and by affects which 'take no account of the future and of other things'.[46] Spinoza thereby returns to the problem of servitude, of being overwhelmed by harmful ideas and so subject to fortune, and to the more imminent political problem of the fear-led common people, whose fears and susceptibility to superstition are exploited by ambitious figures who seek power over them. By this stage, Spinoza has come to the worrying conclusion that natural right is the basis of political power, but such a right has no moral normative content and, being so often passive and in servitude to harmful ideas, often leads to mutual suspicion, conflict and greed. It may even seem that he has done little more than restate Hobbes's own account of natural right, whose implications would carry him towards monarchy.

To avoid such a position, Spinoza must do more than merely reassert the coextensiveness of right and power[47] – he must instead prove that human beings are naturally disposed to allying with each other for a greater good, and that their resulting relations are empowering and liberating from servitude. Such a universal predisposition of human nature would enable his account to explain how individuals become more active and self-determining, capable of conquering their dependence on fortune, superstition or other harmful ideas which lead to their domination. This will then provide a basis for his account of democracy as both the most natural political form and more powerful than monarchy. Let's assess his attempt.

Laws of Nature

'True law is right reason, consonant with nature, spread through all people', writes Cicero in *De Re Publica*.[48] Though Hobbes and Spinoza were fond of displaying their contempt for 'the Schoolmen',[49] both borrow heavily

---

[45] VIII, 3; XV, 45; XVI, 7; *CWS* II, 192; 282; 283.
[46] V, 21; *CWS* II, 144.
[47] E.g. *Ep.* L [to Jarig Jelles]; *CWS* II, 406.
[48] Cicero 1999: 71.
[49] E.g. *L* I.8.27; *TP* II, 15; *CWS* II, 514.

from classical sources, and Spinoza particularly reaches a peculiar hybrid of natural law, combining mutual conflict and self-preservation with a classic republican ideal of the pre-eminence and rule of reason, under laws like Cicero's, 'constant and eternal'. Interestingly, this involves the observation of three laws of nature which also bear on our ongoing questions of servitude, power and politics. Together, they present a cogent if underdeveloped theory of empowerment which is given depth in *Ethics*.[50] It's my view that these laws contain the key to how Spinoza's thought overcomes an initial ambivalence around the dangers of politics, towards a naturalistic account that accommodates both desire and self-interest and the inherent advantages of community and friendship. As we will see, they also implicitly involve a much greater role for the affects and imagination for securing peace than considered by previous natural law thinkers.

Following Hobbes's *De Cive*, Spinoza presents a concept of 'divine law' (*lex*), which 'aims only at the supreme good [*summum bonum*]' and is 'the true knowledge and love of God', discerned through natural reason.[51] This is distinguished from 'human law' (*jus*), whose 'only purpose is to protect life and preserve the country', and which culturally varies, resulting in differences around ceremonies, customs, language, historical narrative and so on.[52] In turning to politics in Chapter 16, it is surprising that *lex* rather than *jus* should appear in a handful of instances.[53] It attests to a similar method as that applied to biblical scripture, deploying a critical method to elicit what is reasonable from within the medium, identifying three universal principles in nature that are then applied to human societies.

---

[50] Commentaries on freedom and power in Spinoza have largely tended to focus on the later *Ethics*, where Spinoza offers a more coherent, comprehensive account. Santos Campos (2012: 118–19) is an exception, but also tends to use the *Ethics* to explain lacunae in the *TTP*'s account of natural law, whereas my argument is that the *TTP*'s account of natural right and power in Chapter 16 should be assessed on its own merits in order for it to be then considered a response to the problems of servitude and domination identified in its Preface, and as assessed in the last chapter.

[51] *TTP* IV, 9; *CWS* II, 127; *DC*, IV.

[52] Compare Hobbes (*DC* II.1–3, III.31–3 and VI.16). Others present *lex* with different findings: Balibar (1997a: 192) argues there is an equivalence of *jus/lex* in the chapter, which I cannot see the text bearing out. Rutherford (2010: 144) provides a compelling if convoluted schema that separates descriptive laws (like these) from prescriptive ones (such as civil laws, *jus*). Our focus is on these elementary or 'descriptive' laws – Chapters 6 and 7 assess their political ramifications.

[53] Their significance is also obscured by inconsistent translations, which tend to use 'right' or 'decree' (*jus*) and 'law' (*lex*) interchangeably, rendering vague what are in Latin clear laws. Curley's 2016 translation is an exception.

The first concerns the concept of natural right just discussed, which, under the 'rule of nature', is the primary expression of sovereignty: 'the supreme law of nature is that each thing strives to persevere in its state, as far as it can by its own power'.[54] This will be expanded in the *Ethics* as the conatus, with a metaphysical basis. Spinoza adds that this law does this 'not on account of anything else, but only of itself', by which it is aligned with the thing's own being or interest, but then adds, less convincingly, that 'it follows that each individual has the supreme right to do this'. If we incorporate our discussion of right as *doing* earlier, then this becomes less complicated, leaving the conatus as demonstrated from nature, rather than by the more complex metaphysics of power in the *Ethics*.

This principle of self-preservation and pursuing what one judges to be a good leads Spinoza to account for the natural formation of society. This was a common trope of early modern political thought. Aristotle had famously established sociability and speech as signs of humanity's political nature, one in which basic associations of hierarchical difference in the household (husband–wife, master–slave, parent–child,) merge into larger associations – the village, and ultimately the city-state. And yet for Aristotle a mass of people in one location does not a city make. 'The state is an association intended to enable its members, in their households and the kinships, to live *well*', and whose purpose is perhaps most important of all, being 'a perfect and self-sufficient life'.[55] Early in this chapter, Grotius offered two laws of nature, the latter tending to human advantage and mutual protection. Elsewhere in *De Iure Belli* he stresses that the right of all societies, public and private, is in the majority ('who naturally have the Right and Authority of the whole').[56] Within this tradition, one of Hobbes's specific contributions was the emphasis of fear and the desire for survival for the emergence of civil society. In agreeing to defend themselves from foreign invaders or one another, the people of the commonwealth would 'confer all their power and strength upon one man [or assembly] [. . .] that might reduce all their wills, by plurality of voices, into one will'.[57] This 'covenant of every man with every man' was embodied into the collective individual of the commonwealth, or Leviathan, which would rule through love, devotion and terror like a '*Mortal God*'.

Spinoza sits somewhere between these traditions in the *TTP*. Civil society emerges out of a group of individuals in nature recognising the benefits

---

[54] *TTP* XVI, 4; *CWS* II, 283.
[55] Aristotle 1981: 1280b.
[56] Grotius 2005: II.V.XVII.
[57] *L* II.17.13.

of 'mutual aid' and 'the cultivation of reason', as well as the common protection of property, through which they form a basic political agreement that inaugurates the State.[58] It is significant that this happens so quickly: Spinoza uses the law of natural right to explain why individuals, necessarily weak, vulnerable and in servitude to harmful affects in the state of nature, are predisposed to allying together. While this becomes the basis for Spinoza's account of the social contract, it first appears as a combination of multiple individuals who together become one united entity – or what will hereafter be called a *collective* – whose right is far greater than any individual's alone. Thus Spinoza writes that 'without mutual help and the cultivation of reason', human beings necessarily live in great misery, and thus 'for security, it was best to live as one' (translation modified).[59] There is little of Hobbes's emphasis on fear or the advantages of rule under monarchy here. This minimal social association, founded on security amid hostility and unreason, then becomes the foundation for their empowerment, and Spinoza maps out this process from the initial social agreement. This would ensure that 'they would have collectively [*collective*] the natural right each one had to all things', thus ensuring the agreement was useful to each, and that their collective right would 'no longer be determined according to the force and appetite of each one, but according to the power and will of everyone together'.[60]

This results in the 'agreement' (*pactum*) to transfer their individual rights into the collective of 'all of them together', rather than merely vertically up to the sovereign monarch, as Hobbes has it. This aspect of combination and unity remains underdeveloped in the text, but one can recognise a new theoretical outgrowth from Hobbes. Societies are instead established according to this 'sole dictate of reason', the mutual empowerment and collective right of all, which, in order to remain secure, requires an obedience to this agreement. There are similarities here to the *recta ratio vivendi* (or 'right ways of living') of *Ethics* Part V, including restraining one's appetites, moderating one's conduct to treat others as one would wish to be treated, and protecting the rights of one's fellow subjects – which all empower oneself and others and lessen the servitude of harmful ideas.[61]

---

[58] *TTP* XVI, 13; *CWS* II, 284.
[59] XVI, 13; *CWS* II, 284. This *oneness* is more significant than translators suggest. Curley has: 'to live, not only securely, but very well, men had to agree in having one purpose' (2016: 284). Israel/Silverthorne: 'it was necessary for people to combine together in order to live in security and prosperity' (2007: 197). But *in unum conspirare* is more forceful than 'agree' or 'combine'.
[60] Ibid.
[61] *Ethics* V, 10 Schol.; *CWS* I, 601–3. The *recta ratio vivendi* follow from what Spinoza

This becomes the basis of a second 'universal law of human nature', that 'no one neglects to pursue what he judges to be good, unless he hopes for a greater good, or fears a greater harm'.[62] This appears in the context of the social contract (and note the intrusion of 'human' into this nature) but, *contra* Aristotle or Grotius, empties out any teleological associations around virtue, *koinonia* or sociality. Instead, of 'two goods, each person chooses the one he judges to be greater; between two evils, the one which seems to him lesser'.[63] So long as *we judge* our place in a community to be more beneficial or useful than being outside it, we will remain within it. This second law also destabilises Hobbes's reliance on the social contract as a single intractable moment for politics, placing priority not with the sanctity of the oath itself, but with the utility in obeying it. If our social bonds are based on the choice of the greater of two goods – which also coincides with self-interest, a view propagated by the influential Dutch republicanism of the De la Courts – then the well-governed republic will realise the common interests of its people.

We therefore live in societies where it is 'in our interest', otherwise the utility of remaining in such an agreement is lost and the contract 'remains null and void'.[64] This reflects a judgement of our relationships with others, which, like any idea, can be active or passive and based on inadequate ideas, like those of the last chapter. Yet it also indicates the basic good of civic participation which Spinoza develops later in his politics, because it establishes desire, in the form of seeking a greater good or avoiding a greater evil, as the basic principle for political stability. It also explains why rebellion emerges, when civic participation is no longer for the good or safety of the subjects. This principle plays a decisive role in the foundation of the State, in that there must be a motive for not violating the agreement, like one that results 'brings more harm than utility to the one who breaks it'.[65] If the republic cannot provide enough to motivate the individual's loyalty, then it must condition enough fear to stifle disobedience. But this isn't where Spinoza is heading. Instead, an understanding of natural right and the greater good should lead us to identify what causes human servitude.

---

presents as the 'dictates of reason', and broadly correlate to what will result in self-preservation (cf. IV, 18 Schol., the prescriptions of the 'free man' in IV, 67–73; V, 10 Schol. earlier; and their role in the *beatitudo* of V, 20; CWS I, 555; 584–8; 601; 605–6). On these rules, see Rutherford 2008 and Steinberg 2014.

[62] TTP XVI, 15; CWS II, 285. Cf. *Ethics* IV, 65; CWS I, 583.
[63] TTP XVI, 15; CWS II, 285.
[64] XVI, 20; CWS II, 286. Spinoza uses Hobbes's example of lying to a highway robber (e.g. *L* I.14.27) to substantiate this claim. See Garrett 2010 for an incisive comparison.
[65] Ibid. For Hobbes's original point, see *DC* II.16.

Spinoza's third law illuminates this, and appears in his argument for democracy, the model most naturally expressive of collective right and participation in a state, ensuring its security and continued peace. In a definition that is much more expansive than his later account in the *TP*'s final, unfinished chapter, he describes democracy as 'a general assembly of men which collegially [*collegialiter*] has the greatest right to all that is in its power' (translation modified).[66] *Collegialiter*, like the Latin *collective* before it, is an unusual and uncommon phrase in his work. It appears twice in Chapter 5, describing what is paraphrased as democracy – 'the whole of society, if it is able, should hold command collegially' (translation modified) – founded in collective right and ability.[67] This distinction in terms is significant, mapping out the agency of subjects within the agreement. *Collegialiter* reflects a capacity for deliberation, as distinguished from the more general, passive right of the many subjects transferred to the State's sovereign. This underlies democracy's pre-eminence as a political form in the *TTP*, as well as its relation to free speech.[68] Its superiority over monarchy and aristocracy lies in the greater circulation of reasonable ideas in its deliberative assemblies. Mimicking Hobbes, though for very different ends, it is also the most 'natural' form of government.[69] For societies *can* be formed 'consistently with natural right' and every contract 'preserved with the utmost good faith' only if 'each person transfers all the power he has to the social order'.[70] Such a 'supreme natural right over all things' like that possessed by this society, which can count on the obedience of all its subjects, is not a coercive monarchy like that of the Ottoman Empire,[71] but a 'democracy', for only here can all subjects participate in civil life.

In turn, each of its citizens must obey the directives of the sovereign power, however absurd – again, a Hobbesian argument – though with another twist: these decisions express the collective desire of the people, being the imma-

---

[66] *TTP* XVI, 25; *CWS* II, 287. See also XVI, 30; XX, 38; *CWS* II, 288; 351. Diverging from Curley (2016: 144) and Israel/Silverthorne (2007: 200): Spinoza uses *collegialiter* here and XX, 2 to describe democracy, rather than *collective* as earlier in XVI, 5 (*CWS* II, 283), used just once in the text.
[67] *TTP* V, 23; V, 27; *CWS* II, 144–5; cf. Giancotti Boscherini 1970a: 187. Again, diverting from the translators. The root word later makes it into the *TP*, where Spinoza gives a veiled endorsement of the democratic power of guilds (or corporations, *collegia*), VIII, 5; *CWS* II, 567.
[68] E.g. XX, 6; *CWS* II, 344.
[69] *DC* VII.5.
[70] *TTP* XVI, 25; *CWS* II, 287.
[71] Praef., 9; *CWS* II, 68.

nent power of the State. Thus Spinoza imagines that this obedience will not involve coercion, but consent and free participation, and that such a collective right, collegially expressed in large deliberative assemblies, will result in the natural triumph of reason over unreason.[72] Hence, 'very rarely can it happen that the supreme powers command great absurdities', he writes in one of his more hopeful passages.[73] To protect their 'own interests' and retain power, it is 'incumbent on them most of all to consult the common good, and to direct everything according to the dictate of reason'. The obedience of the subject to the sovereign is premised on the third instance of *lex* in this chapter: 'in a republic, and a state where the supreme law is the well-being of the people [*salus populi*], not that of the ruler, someone who obeys the supreme power in everything should not be called a slave, useless to himself, but a subject'.[74] The *salus populi* is a common trope of Roman republicanism, particularly Cicero, and even Hobbes presents it as 'the end' of the sovereign ('to which he is obliged by the law of nature').[75] Spinoza's use of the classic motif appears, however, in an account of sovereign power rooted in democracy. The most orderly state is the one that most powerfully realises the common interests and desires of its constituent parts, 'everyone together', whose rights have been freely transferred into the collective.[76] Their collective right, or desire, is the basis of the reasonable and free political state.

He remarks on this again in Chapter 19 even more forthrightly, reasserting this *lex* as prior to all others: 'the well-being of the people is the supreme law. All laws, both human and divine, must be accommodated to this'.[77] Of course, Spinoza knows by his own reasoning that all laws of nature belong to one order, human and divine, without humanity being 'a dominion within a dominion', so the emphasis on the people's welfare here is unusually strong, and not something taken from Hobbes or elsewhere. In turn, only effective institutions and laws, like those which best represent the common good, justice and piety, will ensure that the greater of two goods is desired and the State remains in existence. In this way Spinoza argues that the free State is

[72] See Chapter 6 for a critical account of this argument.
[73] XVI, 29; CWS II, 288.
[74] XVI, 34; CWS II, 288–9.
[75] L 2.XXX.1. Spinoza is not the first to link this to democracy: the De la Courts argue similarly in *Politike Weeg-schaal* (1662), a popular Dutch republican work which Spinoza had likely read by this point (Weststeijn 2012: 270). Contextualising the influence of *salus populi*, see James 2012: 237.
[76] TTP XVI, 10; CWS II, 285.
[77] XIX, 24; CWS II, 337.

the most reasonable one.[78] Human freedom is only possible in a stable State, and the goal of the State is, in the final case, 'to free everyone from fear so that they may live in security', enabling them to develop their abilities and live well in peace. To this extent, 'the end of the republic is really freedom'.[79]

What does that then mean for servitude and freedom? Servitude was defined in the last chapter as an individual's internal state in being dominated by ideas that dispose it to think or act in ways harmful to oneself, under the influence of ideas that we are unable to restrain. This internal state involves a set of ideas about one's disempowerment which render it meaningful if not acceptable, rather than intolerable. All the same, such a condition is a passive and not a voluntary one. The closing discussion of takeover considered some ways in which individuals can be so effectively dominated that they experience another's right and desire as their own. Indeed, the account of natural right earlier in this chapter found it coextensive with desire and power. It comes with no moral or reasonable inclinations, and Spinoza goes further than Hobbes in emphasising the role of judgement in determining what we desire or do, and upon our participation (or not) in society. Our active desires, that from which the dominated are seemingly alienated, therefore have some instrumental role in freedom.

To this, we now have three laws of human nature as they apply to politics, explaining why natural right is the basis and stability of the State, and why desire, in seeking the greater of two goods, is instrumental in maintaining societal obedience to the utility of the common good. As with natural right, however, this still doesn't help us overcome harmful ideas. If desire is a means by which individuals can come to seek ends that realise the good of all collegially, how then are harmful desires replaced by beneficent ones? To put it more concisely: how does one go from having a mind owned to a mind of one's own? The case of the three laws has established, for now at least, the conditions of reason in politics inherent to the *TTP*, a reason that correlates to the empowerment and freedom of *one and all*. But what do these laws of nature indicate about our place in nature, and *as* nature?

One with Nature

There are few words in Spinoza more common than *Natura*. 'For nothing, considered in its own nature, will be called perfect or imperfect', he

---

[78] XVI, Annotation 33; CWS II, 289.
[79] XX, 12; CWS II, 346. This important passage is analysed later in Chapter 7, while the foregoing discussion of justice and piety is discussed in Chapter 6.

writes in the early *TdIE*, 'especially after we have recognized that everything that happens happens according to the eternal order, and according to certain laws of Nature.'[80] While never given a systematic definition, it generally has two meanings: first, the traditional (and Scholastic sense) of a thing's essence as distinct from its properties, for example, the nature of God, a triangle, or a human being – though here we may note that the use of *natura* rather than *essentia* implies a more scientific form of observation than Scholastic contemplation; second, as a way of describing the entirety of all things in existence – the *rerum natura* often referred to in *Ethics* I – bound by universal laws, a whole greater than the sum of its parts.[81] As a shorthand, we might distinguish these as 'nature' (essences) versus 'Nature' (all existing things). Yet these uses shouldn't obscure that we are dealing with one order of Nature, one constituted by the power and being of the modes, which is why I'll refer to both as 'nature' to avoid confusion. Given that everything necessarily follows from God's given nature, there is no way that 'the order of Nature' could be different.[82] In *Ethics* I Appendix, the devastating prejudices that arise in us concern a confused view of Nature – 'that all natural things act, as men do, on account of an end', and, after being considered solely in terms of human advantage, the inference that 'there was a ruler, or a number of rulers of nature, endowed with human freedom'.[83] We saw in the last chapter that this makes 'nature and the Gods [. . .] as mad as men'. But it's worth noting that this madness arises from an inevitable (indeed, naturally) flawed process of reasoning which has led our belief systems time and again to consider themselves as apart from the rest of Nature, a dominion within a dominion.

Spinoza repeatedly criticises those who fall foul of such thinking. In the *TTP*, there are the 'common people' (*vulgus*) who think that 'God's power and providence are established most clearly when they see something unusual happen in nature', like miracles, which leads them to imagine two distinct powers, that of God and of natural things.[84] They imagine God's power as 'the rule of a certain Royal majesty', a commonly held image of God as an authoritarian lawgiver that Spinoza also chides at the end of the *Ethics*.[85] In

---

[80] *TdIE* 12; CWS I, 10.
[81] As Moreau explains in the indispensable *Continuum Companion to Spinoza*, this explains the *natura naturans/naturata* distinction: *naturans* is God, the sole free cause, as substance and attribute, and *naturata* are the things (Van Bunge et al. 2011: 271).
[82] *Ethics* I, 33 Dem.; CWS I, 436.
[83] I, App.; CWS I, 441.
[84] *TTP* VI, 1; CWS II, 152.
[85] VI, 3; CWS II, 153; *Ethics* V, 41 Schol.; CWS II, 616.

both instances, Spinoza makes a rhetorical switch in perspective between a misguided contempt and a love of Nature – blessedness is 'not the reward of virtue, but virtue itself'.[86] For if miraculous events were supposed to 'destroy, or interrupt, the order of nature [...] to that extent [they] could give no knowledge of God', and would even 'take away the knowledge we naturally have and make us doubt God and everything else'.[87]

In claiming to have a unique knowledge of God's commands beyond the ordinary workings of nature, the prophet (if they are a 'true' one, and not merely ambitious) perceives but does not understand basic truths about societal harmony which are only grasped indirectly. Likewise the theologians who 'curse human affairs' and the 'melancholics' who despise human society and prefer a life 'uncultivated and wild', accompanied only by animals, is for Spinoza no less absurd.[88] The great clarion call of Spinozism – 'not to laugh at human actions, or mourn them, or curse them, but only to understand them' – is premised on understanding such actions as within the singular order of nature, whereby the affects 'love, hate, anger, envy, love of esteem, compassion, and other emotions' should be considered as much properties of nature as 'heat, cold, storms, thunder, etc., pertain to the atmosphere'.[89]

The goal is understanding our oneness with nature and as nature. As Hasana Sharp has rightly argued, one of Spinoza's great contributions is the upending of the Cartesian elevation of man (either in his dualism, or anthropocentrism), a perspective open to what she calls 'renaturalization', one that recognises 'the nonhuman forces operating within everything we think is ours, or our own doing'.[90] This involves reckoning that nature is in no way defective or to be despised. Those who claim to see imperfections or failure in nature are bound up in 'fictions', accustomed more 'from prejudice' than from 'true knowledge of those things'.[91] We are 'a part of nature' and cannot be understood without it.[92] Therefore our natural right in no way offends nature, nor do the laws of political reason of what Augustine would call 'the Earthly City' offend those of 'the City of God' – they are one and the same, 'God, *or* Nature' (*Deus, sive Natura*), Spinoza's famous equivocation in *Ethics* Part IV. It also indicates another important difference from Hobbes, earlier – life under the 'mortal God' might bring some short-lived

[86] *Ethics* V, 42; CWS I, 616.
[87] *TTP* VI, 26; CWS II, 158.
[88] *Ethics* IV, 35 Schol.; CWS I, 564.
[89] *TP* I, 4; CWS II, 505.
[90] Sharp 2011: 9.
[91] *Ethics* IV, Praef.; CWS I, 544–5.
[92] IV, 2; CM II, 9; CWS I, 548; 333.

security, but the individual cannot surrender what is inalienable by natural right – the capacity to think, judge and disagree. Reason instead compels us not just to an agreement with but an understanding, if not intellectual love, of Nature. That requires that we understand the affects which drive our behaviour, and our broader relations with others and the social and political structures in which they function. It requires knowing 'what the body can do',[93] and connects back to the advantages of medicine and mechanics that the young Spinoza envisioned in the *TdIE*.

In a final way, it also connects backs to the intrinsic good of community and collective power that we have been thinking about. 'By singular things I understand things that are finite and have a determinate existence', he writes.[94] 'And if a number of individuals so concur in one action that together they are all the cause of one effect, I consider them all, to that extent, as one singular thing.' For Spinoza, the autonomy of the isolated individual is not the highest good of his politics, and Spinoza's thought clashes with a trend in English political thought (particularly Hobbes, Harrington and Locke) that C.B. Macpherson called 'possessive individualism', in which '[t]he individual is essentially the proprietor of his own person and capacities, for which he owes nothing to society'.[95] Just as we are a part of nature, so we are a part of a society in which we were cared for and raised long before questions of political consent and contract enter the scene.[96] The solipsistic concern with the atom-like individual in this tradition is illusory – everywhere relations with others constitute, condition and transform us. Collectively we are brought to life and collectively we draw from and contribute to the many benefits of society, and we become more powerful in affecting and being affected as much as possible. It may be this feature, what I call the collectivist Spinoza, that has made him attractive in different ways to left-Spinozists like Althusser, Deleuze and Matheron. To render it in the terms set out in the Introduction, Spinoza's collectivist thinking has a true knowledge of nature tending individuals towards what is universal, becoming common, then becoming collective. To regard existence 'under a species of eternity' necessitates nothing less.

But wonder shouldn't get the better of us here. Even amid his endorsements of the good life together, Spinoza often reminds us of the more often

---

[93] *Ethics* III, 2; CWS I, 495.
[94] II, Def. 7; CWS I, 447.
[95] Macpherson 1962: 263.
[96] This hasn't been lost on some feminist philosophers. Aurelia Armstrong has written on Spinoza and relational ethics of collaboration and cooperation (2009: 59), while Sharp has persuasively placed this relationality within a broader Spinozist 'feminist ethics of care' (2011: 108), one also alert to the 'aleas of fortune' (2019: 279).

contrary and conflicted nature of our relations with others. '[I]t rarely happens that men live according to the guidance of his reason', he remarks, just before endorsing the advantages of society, and 'their lives are so constituted that they are usually envious and burdensome to one another'.[97] It's for this reason that friendship is so important to the free man later, 'to lead himself and the others by the free judgment of reason'.[98] 'Only free men are very useful to one another', he writes, and only they can be 'very thankful to one another'.[99] The ignorant person, by contrast, is isolated. They judge situations by their own temperament (*ingenium*)[100] which, as we know from the last chapter, is one often riven by strong present passive affects whose force conceals their causes. In an earlier section, Spinoza puts this across even more clearly. While the free man is 'led by reason' and 'does only those things he knows to be most important in life, and therefore desires very greatly', the slave (*servus*) is 'led only by an affect, or by opinion', and 'does those things he is ignorant of'.[101] The slave does not recognise the proper order of nature, and is therefore most susceptible to the prejudices, superstitions and other harmful ideas that characterise Spinoza's general view of slavery as an epistemic condition. So, how does that shape our discussion of slavery in Brazil?

The Black Jew

There is a remarkable moment halfway through his *Autobiography* where Malcolm X, somewhat cavalierly, dismisses the entire history of Western philosophy, which he has been studying while in jail. 'I don't respect them because it seems to me that most of their time was spent arguing about things that are not really important.'[102] Michel de Montaigne would have agreed ('within those piles of knowledge and the profusion of so many diverse things, they have found nothing solid [. . .] only vanity').[103] One thinker, however, escapes his censure. 'Spinoza impressed me for a while when I found out that he was black. A black Spanish Jew.' Aside from his persecution by the Jewish community, though, he doesn't explain what impressed him.

It's often said that Spinoza has meant many things to many different intellectual and political traditions. In his drawing of Masaniello, he had a

[97] *Ethics* IV, 35 Schol.; CWS I, 564.
[98] IV, 71 Dem., following IV, 35; CWS I, 586; 563.
[99] IV, 71 Dem.; CWS I, 585.
[100] IV, 70 Dem.; CWS I, 585.
[101] IV, 66; CWS I, 584.
[102] Malcolm X and Haley 1973: 275.
[103] Montaigne 2003: 557–8.

passing interest in fashioning himself. Over this chapter, we've been drawing out an emerging line of thinking about society and collective power that's also attuned to the conflicts and sad affects that also inevitably rise in our experiences with others. It's tempting to think of Spinoza and his philosophy of human freedom within the wider arc of revolutionary and rebellious struggle. In one sense, there are few activities more Spinozan than what second-wave feminists would call consciousness-raising: an affirmation of 'the affective, of the validity of personal experience', wrote Karlyn Kohrs Campbell, 'of the necessity for self-exposure and self-criticism, of the value of dialogue, and of the goal of autonomous, individual decision making'.[104] But consciousness-raising usually occurred in small groups, like the models of friendship of free men Spinoza had in mind. Establishing how a small, free community extends outwards and incorporates the sad, frightened or ignorant through friendship and a love of what is lasting, universal and open to all, God or Nature, is a question Spinoza paused over. It yields different approaches and outcomes in his two political works, which we'll consider in Part III.

But liberatory thinkers of various civil rights traditions have also spoken highly of hope. In Baldwin's *The Fire Next Time*, glimpsed in the last chapter, he pleads for hope, even for what is impossible or unrealistic. 'But in our time, as in every time, the impossible is the least that one can demand', for history 'testifies to nothing less than the perpetual achievement of the impossible'.[105] Similar sentiments often appear in Dr Martin Luther King ('[w]ith this faith we will be able to hew out of the mountain of despair a stone of hope').[106] More recently in the Trump era, Martha Nussbaum articulates 'practical hope', being 'a vision of the good world that might ensue, and, often at least, actions related to getting there'.[107] We could dismiss these as the words of very different contexts and times, where motivating the brutalised and dispossessed has been of more profound importance. But they usefully place in relief the urgency of Spinoza's caution about passive affects, like hope, which can obscure understanding the causal basis of our situation in nature with wishful thinking. Such fantasies make freedom-lovers less useful to each another.

[104] Campbell 1973: 79.
[105] Baldwin 1968: 111.
[106] King 1992: 105. The first synagogue in Recife was called the Kahal Kadosh Tsur Israel (Holy Congregation of the Rock of Israel). There's a curious resonance in the two stones or rocks.
[107] Nussbaum 2018: 205.

A century after Henrique Dias, Toussaint Louverture led a successful rebellion of black slaves in Saint Domingue (now Haiti) against French plantation owners, then defended the newly free republic from French and British invasions. Writing to the Directory of the new French Republic which he served, Louverture rejected racist criticisms that the people of the island were ignorant and uncouth, unfit to rule themselves. 'No doubt they are, for without education there is only ignorance and crudity', he writes. 'But should they be criminalized for this lack of education, or should we accuse those who used terrible punishments to prevent them obtaining it? Is it only civilized people who can distinguish right and wrong, and know charity and justice?'[108] On the slavery of Dutch Brazil, or the wider slave trade more broadly, there is a silence in Spinoza, as among most Dutch contemporaries.[109] Perhaps he took this trade for granted, another natural instance where right coextends to power. We find in Spinoza – like we do in Locke, or the American Constitution, or the Declaration of the Rights of Man to which Louverture presented such a challenge – a blindness to transatlantic slavery, and a concern with *servitudo* of an epistemic and less often political sort, of a European context. This kind of slave appears briefly at the end of the *TP* as one of those excluded from Spinoza's democracy, by which time Spinoza has long held his thoughts away from the scabby Brazilian.[110]

The great hope of the multitude-theorists of Spinoza is to assume that he (or we) can become part of this multitude, that we will be accepted and not endangered. In the Brazilian context, the Maroon threatened Jewish settlers, just as in Amsterdam, Spinoza was expelled by the Jewish community under Rabbi Morteira's instruction and, according to Colerus's biography, was lucky to survive a knife attack in the street.[111] And yet, if 'nature

---

[108] Geggus 2014: 144.

[109] An exception is Franciscus van den Enden, Spinoza's Latin teacher, who in 1662 drafted a political constitution for a utopian Mennonite colony in 'New Netherland' (now Delaware), which opposed slavery as 'in contradiction with all human fairness and compassion' (in Mertens 2007).

[110] *TP* XI, 3; *CWS* II, 603.

[111] The *cherem* was also signed by Rabbi Aboab, who had just returned from Brazil. Maxime Rovere argues, however, that the whole event has been overstated ('a ceremony made entirely by the ignorance of historians'): the *cherem* was a hastily copied document from an earlier excommunication, it contains no detail nor does an investigation file survive, no one attended the banishment. Its crux was not so much apostasy as a conflict between Dutch and Jewish law over Spinoza's legal declaration of being a minor in order to avoid repaying the debts on his late father's estate. The apocryphal stabbing may also relate, in his conjecture, to a disputed debt with the

creates individuals, not nations',[112] then Spinoza's thought contains within it the possibility of a cosmopolitan universalism, one guided by a common interest in understanding the order of Nature and, through it, flourishing. But it would take Kant a century later to think through, politically at least, a cosmopolitan law of 'universal hospitality' that would try to upend Grotian diplomacy with an indictment of European colonial projects and their 'inhospitable conduct'.[113] For Spinoza, cosmopolitan universalism would also require overcoming sad passions and hateful ideas about others on a mass scale, to enable particular groups and nations to common together as one. Perhaps it would be like hoping that a cat could live by a lion's nature – Spinoza does not seem so optimistic in parts of the *TTP*.[114] But his observations about the laws of politics, or the advantages of democracy and free speech, indicate that an awareness of the affective nature of social life, and an implementation of appropriate social and political processes and structures, might alleviate the confusions and fears that naturally arise in our own lives, and guide us towards becoming more powerful together; that the processes of politics – the organisation and empowerment of minds and bodies on a large scale – offer great, untapped resources for making societies more powerful, harmonious and enjoyable places to live. But what does it mean, then, to consider human freedom and power as one with nature? And in what does our power consist?

Alvares brothers (Rovere 2017: 172; 186–90). For the traditional account which links it to his excommunication, see Colerus 1880: 416; Nadler 1999: 110.

[112] *TTP* XVII, 93; *CWS* II, 317.
[113] Kant 1991: 106.
[114] *TTP* XVI, 7; *CWS* II, 283.

Part II
Desiring Freedom

3

Power

In a letter from a friend, Spinoza is pressed to explain how his view of freedom differs from that of Descartes. 'I also think, with Descartes,' the ever-attentive Tschirnhaus writes, 'that in certain things [. . .] we are not in any way compelled, and so have free will.'[1] The view he offers is one of what we might now call compatibilism – 'I acknowledge, indeed, with you, that there are causes which determine me to write now', he says, apologising for his delay in replying, 'but such things do not on that account compel me', and 'I really could, withstanding these reasons, refrain from doing this'.

Spinoza's reply is very interesting. He would have faced confusion around his account of freedom before. What does it mean to speak of freedom without free will? He begins by restating his definition of freedom as acting without constraint – 'I say that a thing is free if it exists and acts solely from the necessity of its own nature'[2] – a state that can only belong to God as 'natura naturans'.[3] By contrast, modes of nature are finite, 'natura naturata', necessarily determined by a causal chain 'to exist and produce effects in a fixed and determinate way'.[4] To illustrate this, he then gives the peculiar example of a stone struck into motion by an external cause. Now, what if this stone were to begin thinking?

> conceive now, if you will, that while the stone continues to move, it thinks, and knows that as far as it can, it strives to continue moving. Of course, since the stone is conscious only of its striving [conatus], and not

---

[1] *Ep.* LVII [to Ehrenfried Tschirnhaus]; CWS II, 425.
[2] *Ep.* LVIII [to G. H. Schuller]; CWS II, 427.
[3] Cf. *Ethics* I, Def. 7; I, 17; 29; KV I, 8; CWS I, 409; 425; 433; 91.
[4] *Ethics* I, 31 Dem.; CWS I, 434. Cf. *Ep.* LVIII [to G. H. Schuller]; CWS II, 427; CM II, 9; KV I, 8; CWS I, 91; 333.

at all indifferent, it will believe that it is very free, and that it perseveres in motion for no other cause than because it wills to.

Experiencing only the motion of its given state, unaware of the external causes that have determined it in a particular way, the stone would necessarily believe itself to be its own free cause and agent. Spinoza then invites his friend to compare this wry thought experiment with that 'famous human freedom everyone brags of having', which amounts to little more than that 'men are conscious of their appetite', which, Spinoza defines elsewhere as 'desire',[5] being 'ignorant of the causes by which they are determined'. Spinoza gives further examples in the letter that are then repeated verbatim in the *Ethics*:

> So the infant believes that he freely wants the milk; the angry boy that he wants vengeance; and the timid, flight. Again, the drunk believes it is from a free decision of the mind that he says those things which afterward, when sober, he wishes he had not said. Similarly, the madman, the chatterbox, and a great many people of this kind believe that they act from a free decision of the mind, and not that they are set in motion by an impulse.[6]

Each fails to recognise the causes of their actions, which are effectively involuntary, compelled by forces under which they have no control. Spinoza called such a condition 'servitude' in Chapter 1. In each, Spinoza is arguing that a belief in free will (as in Descartes) is precisely that, a belief, one that he describes here as 'innate' to our natural condition. In the *Ethics*, the term 'innate' is dropped,[7] and he instead subtly emphasises the inevitability of such ideas from our natural interactions, like his account of prejudice in Part I Appendix. Our delusions of choice reflect rather the conflict of an appetite against custom or moral instruction weakly understood. The servitude that men fight for is inside their own heads, being the power of harmful ideas that offer miraculous, hopeful, stupefying consolations for their weakened state, and which reward, not just secure, obedience and defeat.

Returning to the *TTP*, Spinoza notes that in nature, the wise man has as much 'supreme right to do everything which reason dictates' as the 'ignorant and weak-minded have the supreme right to do everything that appetite

---

[5] *Ethics* III, 9 Schol.; CWS I, 500.
[6] III, 2; CWS I, 496.
[7] Ibid.

urges'.[8] This is not to demote the life of reason, but to compare two different experiences of desire, one committed to the rational actualisation of its powers wherein freedom lies, the other bound by appetite and fortune and described as servitude. We thought about this epistemic slavery in the last chapter, when contrasting the friendship of the free man against the isolation of the slave. Like the stone, both authentically experience their activity as *theirs*, and each will pursue their appetites with passion, though the intemperate person won't recognise the causes of their desires, or might feel unable to do anything about them, and their harmful ideas will weaken their power of acting and those around them. Spinoza makes the comparison again in the *Ethics*, where he notes that 'there is also no small difference between the joy which guides the drunkard and the joy possessed by the philosopher'.[9] The joy of the former is necessarily short-lived, accompanied later by sad affects that correlate to a diminishment of power; the latter by the joyful passive affects of love, and active affects of fortitude, generosity and courage, which by nature are more intensive and enduring.[10] Though one who is reasonable pursues the same conative drive as someone driven by fear and ignorance, the former will experience greater joy as their activities widen and power increases.

But as Spinoza often reminds us, much of human life is spent clouded by the imagination and sad passive affects, making us vulnerable to fears, superstitions and an ignorance of the order of nature, like that discussed in the last two chapters. As Heidi Ravven notes, no one is a *tabula rasa*, free to choose as they wish, but we each come programmed by a vast number of imaginative, affective, cultural and historical determinants, predisposing us to act and react within a limited number of ways.[11] At the same time, Spinoza makes some of the most strident claims for the possibility of human freedom in the history of philosophy. While what we judge to be our own 'will' and 'desire' is often illusory and premised on an ignorance of its causes, as we concluded in Part I, Spinoza will insist that an understanding of desire and the affects is necessary to ethical and political flourishing. Yet paradoxically, much of our freedom also consists in recognising what is beyond our control. How then can the source of our servitude become a means for liberation? Or as Tschirnhaus said, how can we talk about a freedom that accounts for the causes that determine me now as well as my ability to resist and refrain from them?

[8] *TTP* XVI, 6; *CWS* II, 283.
[9] *Ethics* III, 57 Schol.; *CWS* I, 528.
[10] III, 59 Schol.; *CWS* I, 529.
[11] Ravven 2002: 197.

Within this riddle is the difficulty of desire. All the problems of political domination – an illusory feeling of choice to live under tyranny, or of being subject to and taken over by a more powerful authority's systems of belief – involve desire. As I'll show in this chapter and the following, desire is a particularly human consciousness of what we judge to bring us pleasure or reduce our pain. Desire is what animates the child, the drunk, the madman, the chatterbox and the rest of Spinoza's dramatis personae. In each, a person might experience a sense of what we might now call 'self' – freely chosen habits, fantasies, hopes or decisions – whose actual causes are obscured from their understanding. To reach desire, we must first determine what it is a consciousness of – a basic form of individual power, or striving, realised in all things, which Spinoza calls the conatus.

Focusing on the *Ethics*, we'll first tackle what Spinoza means by power, and then explore what freedom means within the context of his determinism, the 'hideous hypothesis' that had appalled Hume. We'll then pinpoint what this means for human freedom by outlining the conatus argument, and explaining its centrality to his psychology and ethics. Lastly, I want to delve into its collectivist implications, with some interpretive digging into what's sometimes called the 'physical digression' (II, Proposition 13). This prepares the ground for an ethics of power concerned with making all human beings as free as possible – a *becoming freer*. First, what does Spinoza mean by power?

Potentia/Potestas

English translators of Spinoza often remark on the difficulty of prising apart two different forms of power in Latin, *potentia* and *potestas*, incorporated into the one English word. A similar problem is presented by *puissance* and *pouvoir* in French. But like servitude and nature, Spinoza's uses of power tend to be idiosyncratic and not ostensibly defined, with *potentia* sometimes used interchangeably with *potestas*,[12] *vis* (force),[13] *virtus* (virtue),[14] *conatus* (striving),[15] *imperium* (political power)[16] and *essentia* (essence).[17]

Spinoza uses *potentia* most often, which broadly refers to a thing's power of acting. God's *potentia* is 'his essence itself' and that by which he and all

---

[12] E.g. CM II, 12; *Ethics* IV, Def. 8; CWS I, 341–2; 547.
[13] Ibid. II, 45 Schol.; CWS I, 482.
[14] III, Praef.; IV, Def. 8; CWS I, 492; 547.
[15] III, 7 Dem.; CWS I, 499.
[16] II, 49 Schol.; V, Praef.; CWS I, 595; 601.
[17] V, 9 Dem.; CWS I, 601.

things are and act.[18] God's *potentia* is his freedom to act from the necessity of his own nature alone, while his 'power of thinking is equal to his power of acting'.[19] *Potentia* here describes what is able to or necessarily exists.[20] Unlike the early *Short Treatise*, though, where God's power (*magt*) is of a different order to the weak, divided modes,[21] one of the most exciting developments of the *Ethics* is how the modes are a part of, and constitute, God's infinite power. The logical necessity of recognising humanity as part of and one with nature demands no other outcome. That's why Deleuze wrote that what interested him in Spinoza most was the finite modes, in particular 'the hope of making substance turn on finite modes' and being understood through them.[22]

Human beings realise the same *potential*, then, when they act according to the dictates of reason. 'By virtue or power I understand the same thing', in that we become more powerful the more we live under the guidance of reason. This describes an internal capacity rather than the effect of a given interaction, though our points about collectivity so far indicate that, where individuals can join and produce a common effect, so they become more powerful. Elsewhere, *potentia* describes an individual's 'power of imagining' and 'power of thinking', and their power to control their actions and affects.[23] The title of Part V refers to the mind's *potentia* to control the affects. Part III, 11 is most concise, describing the body's power of acting (*agendi potentia*) and the mind's corresponding power of thinking (*cogitandi potentia*).[24] Each corresponds to the other, for we are describing one kind of power belonging to an individual, understood through the two different attributes of extension and thought. Each indicates an internal capacity to act, and this sense is used across the remainder of the *Ethics*.[25] It's this power or capacity to act I want us to keep in mind, one founded in our activity.[26]

---

[18] I, 34; CWS I, 439.
[19] I, 36; II, 7 Cor.; CWS I, 439; 451.
[20] E.g. I, 11; 34; 36; III, 8 Dem.; CWS I, 417; 439; 439; 499.
[21] KV II, 5; CWS I, 105.
[22] Deleuze 1990: 11.
[23] *Ethics* II, 17 Schol.; 21 Schol.; III, Praef.; CWS I, 465; 467; 491.
[24] Ibid. III, 11; CWS I, 500.
[25] E.g. III, Praef.; Def. 3; Post. 1; 12–13; 15; 19–20; 27; 53–9; GDA; IV, Praef.; 3–5; 8 Dem.; 20 Dem.; 30–1; 35 Cor.; 37 Schol.–Schol.2; V, 25 Dem. There is no real distinction between *potentia* and *potentia agendi* or *cogitandi*, given that power is necessarily expressed in actual effects (cf. Kisner 2011: 20; Deleuze 1990: 93).
[26] It is tempting to use the English word 'capability' here, but this implies a potentiality separate from actuality belonging to the Aristotelian notion of *dynamis*, whereas Spinoza's concept of power is wholly identified with activity. For an overview of

Though Spinoza didn't explain it well in his reply to Tschirnhaus, this is also the keystone of his argument against free will. A mind is only as powerful as a body, and can only do what its body can. We cannot hope then that the mind's will can act as a separate and free cause that might interfere in the chain of determined causes that has led to our current physical and mental state and associated affects. Hence the bulk of the *Ethics*, Parts III and IV, concerns not platitudes or devices for mental self-restraint but a science of the affects, which are ideas of the body's affections, through which we can understand and disarm their disempowering effects. It also means that an individual's strength is in affecting and being affected, as much as possible. 'For the more the body is capable of affecting, and being affected by, external bodies in a great many ways, the more the mind is capable of thinking.'[27] Later, he will say that it is 'no more in our power to have a healthy body than it is to have a sound mind'.[28] In each case, the individual is constituted by a unity of two separate and equal attributes, a body and a mind.

Yet there is also the power connoted by *potestas*, referring most often to a thing's power or command over itself. The human mind is said to have a weak but viable *potestas* to control the affects and bring about effects which follow from its own nature, hence Spinoza's interest in 'the mind's dominion over the affects', and 'what kind of dominion it has for restraining and moderating them'.[29] Likewise, God has a power (*potestas*) to produce effects that follow from his nature.[30] A state also has power over its subjects to compel them to obey laws that realise their common good.[31] Again, this refers to an ability to command (or at least steer) some of the effects that arise from oneself as a cause. Developing one's *potentia* requires some *potestas* over ourselves, to respond as actively as we can to external forces and the affects they produce in us – a practical programme for freedom addressed in the next chapter.

Where does that take us? For now, power involves similar instances involving a capacity or authority to act or effect. Spinoza dissolves the Aristotelian distinction between potentiality/actuality and understands power as the essence of God, constituted by the continuous activity of its modes. This power is immanent and not transcendent. Our freedom then is very much

---

the debate, see Saar 2013: ch. IV (who also opts for something like 'capacity to act' [*Handlungsfähigkeit*] at 184).

[27] *Ethics* IV, App. 27; *CWS* I, 592.
[28] *Ep.* LXXVIII [to Henry Oldenburg]; *CWS* II, 480.
[29] *Ethics* III, 2; V, Praef.; *CWS*, I, 495; 595. Cf. *Ethics* II, 49 Schol.; IV, Def. 8; V, 4; 10; 42 Dem; *CWS* I, 489; 547; 598; 601; 616. See also *TP* II, 7; *CWS* II, 510.
[30] *Ethics* I, 17 Schol.; 33 Schol.; 35; II, 3; *CWS* I, 425; 436; 439; 449.
[31] IV, 37 Schol. 2; *CWS* I, 566–8; *TTP* XVI *passim*.

associated with our power, but this power incorporates elements of *potentia* and *potestas* for its realisation. The *potentia* versus *potestas* debate of recent years then is a bit of a red herring. Against Negri, I'd say that an individual's *potentia* is enabled by its *potestas*, and it would be some overreach to say that Spinoza presents a liberatory form of power (*potentia*) against a repressive state force (*potestas*).[32] Instead, we should recognise the value of political organisations capable of steering, determining and maximising the power of their parts against countervailing forces that would compel them into dissolution and passivity. But before we get to that, let's now explore how the early metaphysics of power shapes Spinoza's account of human freedom.

Freedom

Spinoza gives a definition of freedom early in the *Ethics* which he uses throughout his work. We'll remember from Chapter 1 that he calls free that which 'exists from the necessity of its nature alone, and is determined to act by itself alone'.[33] In Letter 58, shortly before the thinking stone and the hungover chatterbox appear, Spinoza gives the same definition near verbatim. In contrast is compulsion or necessity, in which a thing is determined 'by another to exist and to produce an effect in a certain and determinate manner'. We discussed this in Chapter 1 in relation to *natura naturans/naturata*. For finite modes like us determined to act in a certain way, our existence is not free but necessary, and so freedom at least of this unfettered kind doesn't seem possible.

Proposition 17 of Part I – Spinoza's case for immanence, concluded in Proposition 18 – and its second corollary argue that only God is a 'free cause', acting from the necessity of his own nature alone, from which infinitely everything follows and within which everything is contained.[34]

---

[32] Negri 2003: 72. Others have noted the *potentia/potestas* distinction, but without the same degree of criticism or attention to its occurrences in the text, for instance Balibar 2008, 88; Barbone 2002: 102–3; Saar 2014: 19; Van Bunge et al. 2011: 293–6; Viljanen 2011: 64; and Curley in Spinoza 2016: 649–50. Negri's distinction stems from its courageous if untenable refusal to endorse any form of higher-order organisation that might become hierarchical, and its source material in the text is too small and selective. That said, as a work of *living Spinozism*, rather than Spinoza scholarship, there are few works of greater *animositas* and *fortitudo* than the prison-produced *L'anomalia selvaggia*. I'll make the case for higher-order political organisations that avoid some anti-hierarchical pitfalls in Chapter 5.

[33] *Ethics* I, Def. 7; CWS I, 409.

[34] *Ethics* I, 17–18; CWS I, 425–8. Propositions 1–15 are primarily concerned with substance, understood as 'what is in itself and is conceived through itself' (I, Def. 3; CWS

From this, he presents the *natura naturans/naturata* distinction (what is 'in itself and conceived through itself' alone, i.e. God, against everything which exists from the necessity of God's nature, i.e. modes).[35] This also means that '[i]n nature there is nothing contingent', because just as God exists necessarily, by Spinoza's peculiarly monist ontological argument, so 'the modes of the divine nature' also follow from it necessarily.[36] Spinoza then claims that God has no free will, in the sense that any effect must be produced by a certain cause and cannot arise 'voluntarily' without one.[37] This proposition uses the earlier definition of I, Definition 7 (as does I, 17 Corollary 2).[38] Will itself is only an erroneous 'mode of thinking', given that every effect follows necessarily from its cause, linking back to God. He'll return to this argument at the end of Part II.[39] Instead, God acts from the necessity of his essence as an infinite, free and perfect being. These qualities are defined across Part I,[40] and this essence is his power (*potentia*), from which follows the necessarily existing activity of causes and effects.[41]

What does this tell us so far about freedom? It's being self-determined to exist by one's nature alone. We'll recall from the last chapter that in Part IV Spinoza describes a 'free man' who acts from his own nature alone (IV, 67–73), and Part V also presents the 'freedom of the human mind', and its eternity through the intuitive third kind of knowledge.[42] Should we speak then of different orders of freedom?

Jonathan Bennett thinks so. He observes three different occurrences of freedom in Spinoza that correspond to these parts: God's freedom, and that of the free man, both being self-caused and the latter a 'theoretically convenient limiting case', alongside a third freedom from the passions that Part V attempts with its 'psychotherapy' of the passions in Proposition 10.[43] But I disagree. The challenge of the *Ethics* is to recognise humanity as part

---

I, 408). Proposition 14 identifies substance with the essence of God, and thereafter God is used predominantly in its place, with substance not reappearing at all in Part V. As per convention, what is God's is 'his', but Spinoza has no anthropomorphic notion of God, and 'its' would be technically correct.

[35] I, 29 Schol.; CWS I, 434.
[36] I, 11; 29 Dem.; CWS I, 417–18; 433–4.
[37] I, 32; CWS I, 435.
[38] CWS I, 409; 425.
[39] II, 49 Schol.; CWS I, 486.
[40] E.g. I, 33; 8; 11; CWS I, 436; 412–15; 417.
[41] I, 34; 35–6; CWS I, 439.
[42] V, 32; CWS I, 611.
[43] Bennett 1984: §72.3.

of the order of nature, and our freedom as intelligible in the same terms as God's freedom. For Spinoza, we can experience this freedom in our minds, through the contemplation of the essences of things, which is 'intuitive science' or the third kind of knowledge.[44]

Instead, one should conceive these as one order of freedom, and one that is possible for finite modes. As finite modes we are realisations of God's freedom to the extent that we are active and not passive, that is to say, limited or overwhelmed by external forces. Our freedom is therefore in becoming as powerful and as active as we can, and thus at our most active and adequately self-directed, we *are* realisations of God's freedom or nature's power:

> Therefore, when we say that the human mind perceives this or that, we are saying nothing but that God, not insofar as he is infinite, but insofar as he is explained through the nature of the human mind, or insofar as he constitutes the essence of the human mind, has this or that idea.[45]

This prompts one of the few moments in the *Ethics* where Spinoza steps from behind the cumbersome geometrical order and appeals to his readers (now at 'a halt') to 'continue with me slowly, step by step, and to make no judgment on these matters until they have read through them all'.

This comes through understanding and accepting the necessity of what follows from God's nature.[46] By contrast, the human illusion of freedom as free will arises out of an ignorance of what causes our actions – voluntarism's weak basis, concisely put – thereby construing them to be self-caused and freely chosen, like the thinking stone earlier. Our power is equivalent to our virtue, we'll recall, but elsewhere our virtue is 'nothing but acting from the laws of one's nature'.[47] Chapter 2 spelled out the importance of living and agreeing with nature. Our freedom is also equivalent to our rationality. Spinoza presses this twice in short succession: a free man 'lives according to the dictate of reason alone'; 'I call him free who is led by reason alone. Therefore, he who is born free, and remains free, only has adequate ideas.'[48] Our freedom as finite modes, then, is in living virtuously, which is 'nothing

---

[44] *Ethics* II, 40 Schol. 2; V, 25; *CWS* I, 478; 608.
[45] II, 11 Cor.; *CWS* I, 456.
[46] V, 10 Schol.; *CWS* I, 601–3. Cf. II, 49 Schol; *CWS* I, 490.
[47] III, 18 Schol.; *CWS* I, 555.
[48] IV, 67 Dem.; 68 Dem.; *CWS* I, 584; ibid. But who only has adequate ideas? That's surely not possible for finite modes like us. We'll come back to this problem in the next chapter.

else but acting, living and preserving our being [...] by the guidance of reason', which produces corresponding affects of joy.[49]

There is a particular freedom Spinoza describes as *beatitudo*, experienced by the mind alone, outlined in Part V.[50] Whereas Bennett is caustic ('the second half of Part 5 is negligible' and 'pretty certainly worthless'), and Margaret Wilson wonders whether it was 'misspoken', included by editorial error, *beatitudo* can be considered as the mind's attainment of a greater proportion of adequate ideas which are universal and eternal truths.[51] Thus, there is nothing of *my* mind that endures, only the adequate ideas it was a transient realisation of in its contemplation.[52] The 'perfection' and 'intellectual love of God' that arise from the third kind of knowledge are the mind's experience of a self-determined, adequate activity that correlates to God's actual power.[53] Although the latter features of this freedom are described in human terms, and I'll come back to this in the next chapter, they are based on an ontology of power that describes things in general.

Let's round this up with a theoretical distinction. While the *absolute* freedom of being totally self-caused and unaffected by external forces *is* impossible for organisations of finite modes, they can experience a *relative* freedom when their activity correlates to it, in activity that is reasonable and conducive to the perseverance of their being. But how does that translate into human terms?

Conatus

The conatus, simply put, is the essential striving of each thing to persevere in its own being, and the foundation of all life. We explored this in the last chapter with the *TTP*'s account of natural right, but Spinoza's argument was enveloped in Hobbesian claims about nature and society. In contrast, the *Ethics* is more incisive, giving the conatus a metaphysical basis in power and freedom. What I'd like to do here is first explore how the conatus argument is formulated, then consider some problems raised by commentators, and lastly identify how appetites and desires can be considered the same for philosophers and drunkards, the free and the enslaved.

---

[49] IV, 24; CWS I, 558.
[50] E.g. V, Praef.; CWS I, 594; cf. II, 49 Schol.; CWS I, 490.
[51] Bennett 1984: §85.1; Wilson 1996: 129.
[52] For more sympathetic attention to *beatitudo*, see Nadler 2001: ch. 5, Garrett 2009, Viljanen 2014, and Schmaltz 2015.
[53] *Ethics* V, 33; 36; 32; CWS I, 611; 612–13; 611.

Now, a comprehensive survey of theories of self-preservation in early modern philosophy is beyond our scope, and has been accomplished well elsewhere.[54] Instead, we'll begin by identifying the precise role of the conatus as a foundation for ethical and political life. Through this, we can then turn to our core problems of freedom, agency, individuation and power which make up the rest of this chapter. With a little reconstructive work, what emerges is a conceptual structure for collective desire through and beyond Spinoza: that while desire's emergence in passive affects and the imagination renders it vulnerable to the forms of servitude identified earlier, the underlying criterion of power manifested by our conatus gives us sufficient information to understand our desires and increase our capacity to act. This awareness develops through the strength and diversity of our relations with others.

Spinoza's conatus argument is presented in four propositions at the beginning of Part III, and is derived from only four previous propositions, two somewhat indirectly. Let's consider what they are.

In III, Proposition 6 he says:

Each thing, insofar as it is in itself, strives to persist in its own being.[55]

This principally draws on two preceding propositions:

No thing can be destroyed except through an external cause. (Proposition 4)
Things are of a contrary nature, i.e., cannot be in the same subject, insofar as they can destroy the other. (Proposition 5)[56]

Two further propositions develop its logical consequences:

The striving by which each thing perseveres in its being is nothing but the actual essence of the thing. (Proposition 7)

---

[54] Being the foundation of Spinoza's ethics, the conatus has been given many good readings. I'll do my best in the space here to capture the state of the art, but for a wonderful, thorough if now slightly out-of-date introduction I recommend Garrett 2002, then Viljanen 2011. For an inventive argument for the conatus's centrality to Spinoza's thought through the lens of danger, habit, the pleasure principle and 'conatus-memory', see Bove 1996: ch. 1.
[55] Curley confusingly adds 'power' to this simple proposition where it doesn't appear, making it: 'Each thing, as far as it can by its own power, strives to persevere in its being' (CWS I, 498).
[56] CWS I, 498.

> The striving by which each thing strives to persevere in its being involves no finite time, but an indefinite time. (Proposition 8)[57]

The final associated Proposition 9 is most interesting. The proposition itself doesn't add much, but the scholium will be important for our discussion later:

> Both insofar as the mind has clear and distinct ideas, and insofar as it has confused ideas, it strives, for an indefinite duration, to persevere in its being and it is conscious of this striving it has. (Proposition 9)
> When this striving is related only to the mind, it is called will; but when it is related to the mind and body together, it is called appetite. This appetite, therefore, is nothing but the very essence of man, from whose nature there necessarily follow those things that promote his preservation. (Proposition 9, Scholium)[58]

First context, then meaning. The conatus has a foundational role in Part III, which addresses the origin and role of the affects, defined as the mind's ideas of the modifications or affections of the body, which involve an increase or decrease in its power of acting.[59] These are states that correlate to the individual's experience of their own power. In Part I, Spinoza presents a monist, necessitarian and determinist account of substance. Part II presents its implications as they relate to the human individual, understood as a collection of finite modes manifesting through the parallel attributes of thought and extension as a mind and a body,[60] whose capacity for understanding is then determined. Spinoza's necessitarianism states that whatever is, was necessary (or rather, there is no other way what is possible could be otherwise, following I, 33).[61] His determinism proceeds similarly: all effects necessarily follow from their causes (thus barring any free will, divine or otherwise).[62] It follows then that any faculty of free will is impossible.

In the scholia and appendices he wages a digressive war against the belief in an absolute faculty of free will and divine teleology, and the anthropocentric ignorance arising therefrom.[63] Given that he does not impute any

---

[57] Ibid. 499.
[58] Ibid. 500.
[59] III, Def. 3; III, 11; CWS I, 493; 500.
[60] II, 7; CWS I, 451.
[61] CWS I, 436.
[62] Following I, 28; CWS I, 432–3.
[63] E.g. I, 33 Schol. 2; I, App.; II, 3 Schol.; 35 Schol.; 48–9; CWS I, 437; 441; 449; 473; 483–8.

meaningful motivational power to the will, how can human beings – merely finite modes, determined by forces beyond their control – have any kind of agency whatsoever?[64] Unless Spinoza can describe an internal motivational force and a capability to cultivate an awareness of it, he will be left with a cold, atomistic account of life as merely colliding forces, where power is indiscriminately but causally distributed.[65]

This primary principle of self-preservation in nature was familiar to his readers, being a 'commonplace of popular wisdom', as Wolfson puts it.[66] The Latin term *conatus* originated with the Stoics, chiefly Cicero, who observed an instinctive principle of self-preservation in animals across nature. From birth 'a living creature feels an attachment for itself, and an impulse to preserve itself and to feel affection for its own constitution', a view indebted to the earlier prevailing Aristotelian–Peripatetic account of *hormê* (impulse).[67] There are similar statements of a law of self-preservation in medieval Christian philosophy (e.g. Augustine, Aquinas, Duns Scotus) and Jewish philosophy (Gersonides, Morteira).[68] These all refer to animal life, however, nor do they see any agency to this animal law, as they share a conception of human free will like that of Descartes, which Spinoza was determined to disprove.

Spinoza's conatus argument was equally informed by the New Science of Galileo and Descartes, which replaced Aristotle's teleological account of striving to actualise an end – that is, reasoning from final causes, criticised in Chapter 1 – with a physical law of inertia. Descartes' first law of nature in the *Principles of Philosophy* is that 'what is once in motion always continues to move', unless prevented by some other cause.[69] 'When a body is once in

---

[64] Where possible we should use 'human beings' instead of 'humanity'. It's an awkward phrasing but reflects Spinoza's own nominalist criticism of reliance on 'universals', frequent in Aristotle and Scholastic discourses, which he calls 'beings of reason' (II, 48–9; CWS I, 483, 490; cf. Ep. II [to Henry Oldenburg]; KV II, 4, 7; CM I, 1; CWS I, 167; 103; 299). The conatus refers to 'Each thing . . .' rather than 'Everything. . .'. Spinoza also claims that there is no abstract faculty of will or desire, only particular willings and desirings (e.g. I, 31 Schol.; II, 48 Schol.; CWS I, 435; 483; cf. Sévérac 1998: 42–3).

[65] This dynamic view of reality as bodies interacting and opposing forces colliding is called the 'contest' view of force by Gabbey and was influential in contemporary physics (1980: 243–4; cf. Carriero 2005: 133; Viljanen 2011: 90).

[66] Wolfson 1962: II, 196.

[67] Cicero 1931: III.5; cf. IV.7, V.9.

[68] See Wolfson 1962: II, 195–204. On the influence of Gersonides, see Harvey 2012; for a more up-to-date study of medieval sources, Viljanen 2011: chs 3–4.

[69] Descartes 1985: II.37.

motion', we also find in Hobbes, 'it moveth (unless something else hinder it) eternally.'[70] Yet these accounts tended to describe this inherent force or power of self-preservation in terms of motion, and were thus unable to explain how a thing can retain a given state and 'resist changing', as Leibniz would criticise Descartes, and which Tschirnhaus may have had in mind in his letter to Spinoza earlier.[71] This physical element is important for Spinoza: sidestepping Part II's account of human minds and bodies,[72] Part III begins on the properties of *things* (rather than, say, human souls, or animals), from which the conatus is derived. However, this mechanistic notion of striving as a form of continued perseverance in a given state is crucial for human desire, as will become clear.

The conatus, introduced and defined in Proposition 6, combines both classic and modern senses outlined. 'Each thing, insofar as it is in itself, strives [*conatur*] to persist in its own being.'[73] Applied to living creatures, there is nothing in the proposition's second half that Cicero would disagree with. Nor should adding 'each thing' bother Descartes and Hobbes. But the 'insofar as it is in itself' (*quantum in se est*) may cause problems. Della Rocca questions whether it is even necessary or merely an 'equivalence' of different claims, and Viljanen wonders how any mode can be said to exist in itself, given that it necessarily exists through others.[74] But drawing on Cohen, Viljanen observes that this Latin phrase originates in Lucretius and was used by Descartes and Newton to describe something 'by nature' or 'without external force'.[75] For a thing to strive *insofar as it is in itself* is to strive as a feature of its nature, without being affected by external causes. It corresponds to its essence. In the *Ethics*, Spinoza sometimes encourages us to think of a thing's existence as separate from duration, as he does in III, 8 and 9.[76] Its ability to strive is determined by its power to inhere or remain in itself, its '*being in*' itself or inherence, as Garrett notes, through which it is and is conceived through.[77] A thing's elemental striving indicates and occurs through its power. This suggests the possibility of understanding agency even in modes passively determined in a certain and determinate way.

---

[70] *DC* I.2.2.
[71] Leibniz 1989: 172.
[72] The one relevant proposition (II, 13) is curiously unlinked – see Garrett 1994 for conjecture why.
[73] *Ethics* III, 6; CWS I, 498.
[74] Della Rocca 1996: 194–206; Viljanen 2011: 72.
[75] Cohen 1964: 147.
[76] CWS I, 499.
[77] Garrett 2002: 135.

This striving is also an efficient and not a final cause – it strives *as* its nature, rather than *for* its self-preservation. Proposition 7 restates this definition of the conatus, adding that this elemental striving is the 'actual essence' of the thing itself, and Proposition 8 adds that this essence does not involve 'finite time', given that duration would necessarily internally limit its striving.[78] A thing's essential striving is equivalent to its power by which it is defined and individuated.[79] A thing by essence strives, and this peculiar confluence of modern physical forces and medieval metaphysical essences is best appreciated when we turn to the derivation of Proposition 6, and how it leads to Proposition 7 and beyond.

We'll recall that Proposition 6 was premised on two preceding propositions, and its derivation has also disquieted some. Through examining the cause of this confusion, and two attempts by Garrett and Viljanen to solve it, the relationship between power and freedom that underpins the conatus becomes clearer. Proposition 4 states that nothing can destroy itself except through an external cause, and Proposition 5 adds that things are 'of a contrary nature' insofar as one can destroy the other. Bennett is most critical of the construction of the conatus argument: the first proposition is 'otiose', the second 'drastically ambiguous', and the whole derivation 'glaringly fallacious'.[80] For him, it stands on four weak equivocations of terms that are not defined, and only subsequently defined by later propositions, heaping confusion on confusion, and implying a subtle, undeniable teleological reasoning where we try to do what will increase our power.[81] These claims are important. If Spinoza has no coherent explanation for the conatus, the source of all activity, organic or otherwise, then he cannot explain the possibility of agency and freedom in a deterministic universe.

Bennett finds Spinoza's conative explanation of suicide particularly weak.[82] No one 'kills himself from the necessity of his own nature', says Spinoza, except only when 'compelled by external causes'.[83] Spinoza gives the example of Seneca, who took his own life at the order of Emperor Nero, and another where someone's imagination and body are so disordered that there is no corresponding idea in the mind.[84] While certain factors might explain suicide in these cases – a death sentence that cannot be refused, or

---

[78] *Ethics* III, 7–8; *CWS* I, 499.
[79] III, 7 Dem.; *CWS* I, 499.
[80] Bennett 1984: §57; cf. Della Rocca 1996: 206; Garber 1994: 60.
[81] Bennett 1984: §57; cf. Garrett 2002: 128–9; Della Rocca 2008: 137–41.
[82] Bennett 1984: §56.
[83] *Ethics* IV, 20 Schol.; cf. III, 10; *CWS* I, 557; 500.
[84] III, 10 Schol.; *CWS* I, 500.

very severe depression – it presumes that suicide can never be a rational, voluntary act, because all human beings must always want to remain alive. But this isn't to seriously think about many other instances, like terminal disease or devastating life traumas, or other instances where life is no longer bearable. Although more charitable, Curley and Della Rocca have found more examples of ticking time-bombs and lit candles that indicate how things can be destroyed by internal causes.[85] Spinoza would say external forces are still involved here – the passage of time, as well as circumstance and life events in my examples – but the account of suicide here and elsewhere is unsatisfactorily simplistic.[86]

Bennett and Della Rocca's criticisms stem from their meticulous focus on Propositions 4–6, at the expense of another two propositions used by Proposition 6 from Part I. These are:

> Particular things are nothing but affections of God's attributes, or modes by which God's attributes are expressed in a certain and determinate way. (I, 25 Corollary)[87]
>
> God's power is his essence itself. (I, 34)[88]

Defending the conatus, Garrett, Lin and Allison have used the latter two to reinforce its derivation.[89] These two are vital for the account, as they explain why the being of modes is, in essence, power, and how such power is limited in scale. Finite things, be they as simple as stones or as complex as human beings, express God's power, modifying it in a specific and limited way. God is by essence power, so finite modes exist as they actualise God's power under a certain attribute, as we considered earlier. Hence, the conatus argument indicates that, in terms of their essential definition, things cannot act in ways that are self-destructive, and will resist contrary forces to remain in being.[90] They express this essential power in a way that strives towards persevering in being, insofar as it is not determined by external causes.[91] Thus power and its particular realisation in finite modes is the basis of the conatus. This is an important development, as it indicates that becoming powerful and becoming freer are equivalent. It also signals that our power or virtue lies

---

[85] Curley 1988: 102–10; Della Rocca 1996: 199–200.
[86] E.g. *Ep.* XXIII [to Willem van Blijenbergh]; *CWS* I, 390.
[87] *CWS* I, 431.
[88] *CWS* I, 439.
[89] Garrett 2002: 128–35; Lin 2004: 25–9; Allison 1987: 131–3.
[90] Following III, 4 and 5, respectively; *CWS* I, 498.
[91] III, 6; *CWS* I, 498–9; cf. Viljanen 2011: 103.

in our understanding of and agreement with the order of nature, something we were thinking about in the last chapter with the free man and the slave.

Bennett raises another problem: it is still unclear how one moves from a negative inability to destroy oneself to a positive striving to persevere in existence.[92] In other words, can we get from self-preservation to purposefully acting towards what advantages us? Commonsensically, yes, but it's unclear whether the text can or should bear it out. Matheron claims it is in the necessity of acting – '*If* its nature is to produce certain effects, it is certain that these effects will agree with its nature and therefore tend to preserve it.'[93] In itself, Bennett is right to dismiss this 'activity' as insufficiently demonstrated and somewhat meaningless.[94] However, when connected to the two propositions from Part I earlier, we can extrapolate another characteristic of power that enables a recognition of its freedom. Singular things are modifications of God's power, under the form of any given attribute, existing in a certain and determined way. As modes of God's power, there are ways in which a clear and distinct understanding of our affections and their causes can lead to an ability to alter their effects. This subtle shift is decisive in the case for human freedom. But formulating this at length (beyond Spinoza's concision) is difficult, and the viability of human freedom in gaining power over the affects is only significantly addressed at the close of Part III and across Part IV. Let's see how four leading commentators have illuminated it – Deleuze, Lin, Garrett and Viljanen.

The importance of *expression* has been highlighted by Deleuze, who identifies a marginal concept in the *Ethics* to explain how substance's 'expression' of essences through attributes, and attributes' expression through finite modes, offers a way of reconceiving Spinoza's ontology as founded on the unfolding power of finite modes.[95] These modes do not merely manifest substance, but also constitute it – they are 'expressive precisely insofar as they imply the same qualitative forms that constitute the essence of substance'.[96] Thus, God's power is continuously expressed and unfolded by the modes, and cannot be understood without it. The argument is methodologically precarious, weighted on a conceptual borrowing from Leibniz.[97] But

---

[92] Bennett 1984: §57.4.
[93] Matheron 1988: 11.
[94] Bennett 1984: §57.4.
[95] Expression appears in *Ethics* I, Def. 6 but goes undefined. Deleuze 1990: 13–14.
[96] Ibid. 186.
[97] Deleuze could well make the same point against my case for collectivity, so I'll be mindful of the English phrase about throwing stones and glass houses. The metaphysical basis of collectivity will be outlined, though, in Chapter 5.

it illustrates our point that reality is an intrinsic and total sum of power, of causes producing effects, expressed or realised by the activity of modes, under an infinity of attributes including thought and extension. Like Deleuze, Martin Lin also observes a Neoplatonic influence on the conatus, as modes manifest the nature of their causes, emanating God's power through their conative strivings.[98] Taken together, we can even think of a kind of divine conatus that correlates to the striving of the modes, one which 'eventuates divine action', explains God's existence and 'produces everything of which it is capable'.[99]

Garrett, by contrast, described earlier how modes inhere or *be in* substance, and this inherence is akin to their power. A mode's *being in* substance isn't about spatial containment or parts to wholes, he says, but that it is conceived through it, and that its striving power is understood '*in itself*', separate from external causes.[100] This approach remains usefully close to the text. Similarly, Viljanen identifies a geometrically causal model of power or 'dynamic essentialism', whereby things are by essence powerful causers, and through their essences dynamically 'produce effects and determine each other's power of acting'.[101] Relying heavily on *Ethics* I, 34, he observes that for Spinoza, God's power is his essence itself, and through this essence or power, is the cause of himself and all things. Power is the 'intrinsic causal activity of all things', and this power is the means by which God's essence is realised.[102] Thus – to resolve Bennett and Matheron's disagreement on activity – God is intrinsically active, and this power is actual, being the ability to cause effects.

Whether one says they express, manifest, inhere in or dynamically realise God's power (Spinoza's thought allows for equivocation), power is the essence of God or nature, and nothing but the totality of substance, and it is intrinsically causally active. To the extent that the power of each thing is limited and determined to differing extents, it exists by degrees, and thus there are degrees of power by which we can measure a thing's capacity to

---

[98] Lin 2004: 31–40. Curley highlights Suarez (in Spinoza 1985: 223), whereas Carriero 1991 argues for Avicenna's influence. There is a good if overstated case for the influence of emanation on Spinoza's account of God's productive causality in Wolfson 1962: I, 372–5; and an insightful discussion of Neoplatonist and Scholastic influences in Deleuze 1988: chs 3 and 11, and Viljanen 2011: chs 2–3.
[99] Lin 2004: 43.
[100] Garrett 2002: 148.
[101] Viljanen 2011: 53.
[102] Ibid. 62.

think or act independently.¹⁰³ Our power is not one of Aristotelian potential nor metaphysical contemplation of truths, but in thinking and acting, and one whose processes are intelligible to us, like all other things in nature. As singular things, we realise being through our striving to persist in our being.

By that token, it is in our interest to become as powerful as we can. The key question of whether this is through an 'egoistic' manner at the expense of others, or through a collective endeavour of mutual empowerment, is the problem ahead, and to which we return in the next two chapters. For now, there are a couple more foundational premises to cover. Given that the essential striving of each thing is determined in a particular way, the power that properly belongs to us is that which arises from our own nature, without regard to (or in spite of) external forces around us. In this way Matheron describes 'autonomy' in Spinoza as a power of acting, or 'the individual's aptitude to do what follows from the laws of its nature alone'.¹⁰⁴ It is the intrinsic power of a thing to determine its own direction to the greatest degree it can. It is realised through being a cause of one's own states, in an adequate way.

That may be too much for us, given that we're also necessarily limited by external forces that inevitably overpower us. 'There is no singular thing in nature than which there is not another more powerful and stronger', Part IV begins ominously.¹⁰⁵ What might it mean, then, to be an adequate cause? Spinoza's definition of adequate is technical and purposeful, and refers to an intrinsic, objective understanding. Applied to an idea, it has all the intrinsic characteristics of a true idea, without reference to an external object.¹⁰⁶ Applied to a cause, its effect can be clearly and distinctly perceived through it alone, that is, intrinsically and truthfully understood without reference to an external object.¹⁰⁷ Human beings cannot be adequate causes given our natural vulnerability to external forces that produce changes in us, and so we cannot ever escape the passions that these external effects produce. So, a traditional view of autonomy as something entirely self-caused wouldn't be possible for us finite beings. While the conatus describes the essence of each singular thing, we must determine why some things are said to be more powerful or free than others, from which to grasp how human beings can do *what*

---

[103] On power existing 'by degrees', I'm indebted to Kisner 2011: 32–4; there's a similar view in Bennett 1984: §72.3; Della Rocca 2008: 187; Garrett 2002: 142; Lin 2004: 46, and 2006: 405; Steinberg 2009: 41; and Viljanen 2011: 66.
[104] Matheron 1988: 50.
[105] *Ethics* IV, Ax.; *CWS* I, 547.
[106] E.g. II, Def. 4; *CWS* I, 447.
[107] III, Def. 1; *CWS* I, 492.

they can to become as powerful as possible. Interestingly, this takes us back to the advantages of mutual assistance and common venture we thought about in the *TTP* in the last chapter.

Many Into One

Let's bring back that thinking stone from earlier. By the foregoing reasoning, the stone is composed of finite modes in the same way as the person who threw it. Both belong to one order of nature, so what – if anything – separates their individuality or striving power? What makes us an individual, and what does Spinoza mean when he describes various kinds of individuals as being composed of parts that cohere and persist in a certain proportionate way? What makes the whole greater than the sum of its parts? Getting some clarity on these questions should help us distinguish the power or freedom of individuals from the more general field of forces from which they arise. For while Spinoza does distinguish the particular individuality of the haemoglobin cell or 'worm in the blood' from the higher-order individuality of the bloodstream, or the mammal in which it flows beyond that, we first of all need a general foundation for determining individuality.[108]

Let's turn to Part II, 13, the 'physical digression'. It has an unusual place in the *Ethics*, being the only place where he deals with bodies and physics at any length, and has the air of an introduction to a very different, unfinished work. Definition 7 defines 'singular things' as finite and with a determinate existence, and adds that numerous individuals can compose 'one singular thing' so long as they are the combined cause of a single effect.[109] This was quoted at length in the last chapter in conjunction with Macpherson's 'possessive individualism' thesis. It leads to the striking implication that a singular thing (that which, following III, 6, conatively strives) can include *collectives* of human individuals acting in concert to produce a singular effect. But on a physical level, how does a singular thing or individual persevere in its being? Part II, 13 first proposes that the body is 'the object of the idea constituting the human mind', and 'nothing else'.[110] A human being is a union of a mind and a body, then, being modified under two parallel attributes by which it is expressed, following II, 7.[111] To understand this union, Spinoza sets out to explain the nature of bodies, but his account presents a theory of

---

[108] *Ep.* XXXII [to Henry Oldenburg]; CWS II, 19.
[109] CWS I, 447.
[110] *Ethics* II, 13; CWS I, 457.
[111] CWS I, 451.

complexity that explains why some things are more powerful than others.¹¹² This will become important for understanding freedom as a social, if not collective venture.

The physical digression begins by noting that the human body is intelligible according to the same laws determining other bodies in nature, which 'do not pertain more to man than to other individuals, all of which, though in different degrees, are nevertheless animate'. But Spinoza adds a criterion that both ideas and objects can differ from others to the extent that they contain more 'reality' and are thus more 'excellent'. This reality corresponds to their power (II, Definition 6 earlier equivocates 'reality' and 'perfection'),¹¹³ hence the more 'reality' a thing is said to have, the more active and less passive it is.¹¹⁴ To avoid a tautology like 'power makes things more powerful',¹¹⁵ this reality/power applies to human minds and bodies to the extent that they are (a) capable of affecting and being affected, as much from their own nature as possible (i.e. independently), which (b) indicates their complexity, composed of many parts that combine into one individual that collectively produces a single effect. That argument is rather compressed, so let's unpack it:

> *(a) capable of affecting and being affected, as much as possible* . . . This refers to a 'proportion' between bodies and minds, that 'as a body is more capable than others of doing many things at once, or being acted on in many ways at once, so its mind is more capable than others of perceiving many things at once'.¹¹⁶ The mind's capacity to perceive, through which it develops knowledge, extends only as far as the body's range of interactions with other bodies. These interactions can either be *active* or *passive*, that is to say, either involving ourselves as an adequate cause, *or* as a partial cause or not a cause at all. Both affecting or being affected by other bodies is advantageous, as IV, 38–9 later confirms, but Spinoza qualifies that as a body's actions 'depend *more* on itself alone' (my emphasis), so

---

¹¹² Hence I agree with Henri Atlan's recent argument that the 'physical digression' (*petite physique* in French) is 'misnamed' – it instead describes the 'psychophysical' and 'compound' union of mind and body (2018: 70). For me, the power of this union is suggestive less of metabolic organisms and more of relational and collective forms of power.
¹¹³ *CWS* I, 447.
¹¹⁴ *Ethics* V, 40; *CWS* I, 614–15.
¹¹⁵ This tautology comes to mind when reading works advocating the intrinsically liberatory power of multitudes – that as there are many, so they are powerful (and predisposed to egalitarian democracy and autonomy). My challenge instead is to determine how a group of agents become more singularly and harmoniously self-determining.
¹¹⁶ *Ethics* II, 13 Schol.; *CWS* I, 458.

its mind is capable of understanding distinctly.[117] This *more* confirms that Spinoza envisions power as something measurable in degrees of activity, or what Deleuze calls 'intensity' of power.[118]

(b) . . . indicates their complexity, combining into a single effect. This refers to the nature of bodies themselves, and the extent to which they can be capable of many interactions. II, 13 Lemma 1 defines simple bodies in terms of 'motion and rest', determined to exist in these varying states by other bodies, in a causal chain that continues to infinity.[119] But these bodies move up in complexity when a given number of them combine into one unified body or individual, defined by its maintenance of a 'certain fixed manner' or 'ratio of motion and rest', communicated internally among its constitutive parts.[120] Thus a composite body or individual can contain multiple parts of a different nature – for example, the organs, blood and cells of a human body – which change over time. This offers a more robust solution to the ship of Theseus paradox or continuity of personal identity than Locke's reliance on memory and consciousness.[121] These parts can also differ internally – what matters is the harmony or proportion between them that's maintained.

Therefore, an individual like a human being is a composite of bodies, which are in turn composites of other bodies, that maintain and share in producing a common activity. An individual's power is determined by the extent of its interactions, and an individual is more powerful to the extent that these interactions result from its own self-determined activity. Yet there seems to be no limit to what counts as an individual for Spinoza. So long as each retains its ratio of motion and rest (its physical identity), the thinking stone and the philosopher each count as individuals of varying degrees of complexity and power. Individuation increases in complexity as composite bodies form higher-order composite bodies up to infinity, so that 'we shall easily conceive that the whole of nature is one individual, whose parts, i.e., all bodies, vary in infinite ways, without any change to the whole individual'.[122] The individual *is* to the extent that it operates *as*.

---

[117] CWS I, 568; II, 13 Schol.; CWS I, 458.
[118] Deleuze 1990: 417–18.
[119] Lem. 1; Lem. 3; CWS I, 458–9.
[120] Ax. 2", Def.; Ibid. Lem. 5; CWS I, 460–1.
[121] Locke 1997: II.XXVII.
[122] Lem. 7, Schol.; CWS I, 462.

What determines an individual is its complexity and ability to realise the conative power of which it is already a manifestation. To the extent that they are as active as possible, and as much a cause of their own mental and physical states as possible in their interactions with others, then individuals are said to be powerful. By contrast, to the extent that they passively accede to or are overwhelmed by external forces and the mental and physical states they produce, they are not a cause of either their own activity or of others with which they interact, and are therefore passive, weak and in a state of servitude, like that in Chapter 1. This gives a metaphysical grounding to the passivity there discussed – in having opinions about the world that are neither ours nor particularly accurate, or feeling sad passions which grip and debilitate our thinking and depress our power of acting – our activity is diminished, and other forces act upon us.

There is much more to say about this metaphysics of power through individuation, and we return to this hotly contested passage and its consequences for collective subjectivity in Chapter 5. But there remains an ambiguity in our account, illustrated by Marx and Engels' formulation of the *real* movement of communism in *The German Ideology*. 'Only within the community has each individual the means of cultivating his gifts in all directions', they write, and therefore 'personal freedom becomes possible only within the community'.[123] Whereas individuals have hitherto formed an 'illusory community' in the State and relations of private property, Marx and Engels envision a 'community of revolutionary proletarians' in which individuals participate 'as individuals' rather than mere 'members of a class'.[124] There is wondrous promise in the abolition and overturning of 'all earlier relations of production and intercourse' they herald, and Spinoza shares in this rationale of beginning politics again in the service of democratic, egalitarian human freedom.[125] But we are still faced with the problem of domination and stasis: how does one overpower the imaginings and affects of a powerful existing belief system, with a new social vision and political philosophy that might appear to one's fellows as an unrealistic (if not impossible) utopia?

---

[123] Marx and Engels 1998: 86.
[124] Ibid. 89.
[125] Ibid.; cf. 51–4. See also the *Communist Manifesto*: 'In place of the old bourgeois society, with its classes and class antagonisms, we shall have an association, in which the free development of each is the condition for the free development of all' (2008: 66). Marx is known to have copied out extensive passages of the *TTP* – in *Cahiers Spinoza* I these are reproduced with an excellent commentary by Matheron (1977) on the young Marx's interest in its apparent dichotomy between democracy and theocracy (cf. Kouvelakis 2003: 415).

Infinite Space

Let's summarise. Through Spinoza's somewhat abstruse reasoning we can now recognise the significance of his definition of power: it *is* reality, through which all things are expressed, as causers of effects that persevere their own being. Things become more or less powerful to the extent that they are *as* active causes of their own states or of others as they can be. While the argument has drawn on a range of critical material, it has brought together the reliance of the conatus on substantial, immanent power with the physics and composition of forces, from which to now assess the ethical implications of striving humans as we passively or actively persevere in existence in relation to other external forces, and from that how to maximise joyous encounters and develop common notions through which we become freer.

It is an ambitious argument I'm making, but these last few sections provide an ontological foundation with which to now discuss human desire, affects and imagination. Establishing this ontology of power prior to discussing human desire and the affects is crucial, because Spinoza considers us a subset of nature, without any privileges, no dominion within a dominion. What is it, then, to consider human actions and appetites as if they were 'lines, planes or bodies', with certain and determinate laws?[126] Lastly, while we can agree in part with Peden that 'ontologies cannot entail the content of political positions', we don't need to accept his conclusion that Spinoza's ontology offers only ethical, not political, positions.[127] Power pertains to the very basis of the *polis*, and what empowers individuals is a fundamentally political concern, as Spinoza was all too aware.

But let's not get too ahead of ourselves. If there are political consequences to the metaphysics of power, it should be considered an ontology in itself and prior. For George Santayana, the highest part of Spinoza's philosophy was 'in his physics', which alone 'revealed what was fundamental, eternal, and in his sense, divine'.[128] The *Ethics* is unique in communicating what we might now call a scientific perspective that God or nature is intelligible to human understanding, and that we can proceed from a knowledge of the part (from our own particular perspective, of the second kind of knowledge of common notions) to the whole (intuitive science, the essences of things). It pursues Galileo's enthusiasm that the 'language' of the universe is 'written in mathematical language, and its characters

---

[126] *Ethics* III, Praef.; CWS I, 492.
[127] Peden 2015: 99–100.
[128] Santayana 1913: xx.

are triangles, circles, and other geometrical figures'.[129] Spinoza repeatedly praises mathematics for providing 'another standard of truth' by which we could truly understand nature, no longer fogged by the anthropocentric finalism of Part I Appendix. A view freed from the passions. Plato with his divided line might agree.

But then Spinoza also claims that we can understand the affects as of the same order as geometric figures or 'heat, cold, storms, thunder'.[130] In this, it is these motions of power that are most interesting. Spinoza's vision of God or nature is that contains and realises an infinite becoming, of all possible ideas, actions, affects and worlds, some recognisable, some not yet thought or imagined before. Perhaps Rainer Maria Rilke had something like this in mind in his *Letters to a Young Poet* when he wrote that 'The future stands firm [...] but we move in infinite space'.[131] Or in William Blake's hesitation in the 'Auguries of Innocence':

To see a World in a Grain of Sand
And a Heaven in a Wild Flower
Hold Infinity in the palm of your hand
And Eternity in an hour.[132]

In Spinoza's metaphysics of the modes, in his intellectual love of God or nature, we can still find resources for a profound appreciation and wonder at the infinite majesty of the universe, constituted by a power contained within the sum of its parts.

Our account can now explain why human beings strive, and how this striving individuates us, but we have yet to determine how we become more powerful, what the extent of our powers is, or even how we experience our conatus. This problem can be illustrated with one of Spinoza's favourite analogies, a ship assailed by the stormy seas.[133] Facing the right direction of the wind, its sails compel it towards port. Yet without a knowledge of the winds, the boat's structure or how to steer the vessel, it remains largely passive and of limited capability. At this stage, the conatus remains at the

---

[129] Galileo 2008: 183.
[130] *Ethics* III, Praef.; *CWS* I, 492; *TP* I, 4; *CWS* II, 505.
[131] Rilke 2004: 50.
[132] Blake 2008: 490.
[133] Although a commonplace, its inspiration may be Ariosto's *Orlando Furioso*, 'as a ship on the high seas will sometimes be driven and buffeted by two contrary winds' and emotions overwhelm our capacity for reason (2008: Canto XXI, stanzas 53–4) – we'll return to this text in the next chapter.

mercy of external forces, its own internal weaknesses, and a reliance on random, passive, fortuitous encounters. To address this, let's now turn to how the conatus is affectively experienced as desire, and from that, understand how desire can bring power.

4

Desire

Spinoza isn't often read for his counsel on love. We do not know the extent to which he knew love, and his words on physical love tend to be distrusting and unsentimental. In a scholium on jealousy, he gives the example of 'love toward a woman' – one of the few instances where women appear in his work:

> For he who imagines that a woman he loves prostitutes herself to another not only will be saddened, because his own appetite is restrained, but also will be repelled by her, because he is forced to join the image of the thing he loves to the shameful parts and excretions of the other.[1]

Spinoza was also wary about sensual pleasures in the *TdIE*, and his concern seems to be with the desire to exclusively possess someone else, and resting our happiness therein.[2] In the *TTP*, Spinoza draws upon a text well known throughout sixteenth- and seventeenth-century Europe for its ironic treatment of love, Ariosto's *Orlando Furioso* (1532). In this epic and complex poem, we follow the journey of the knight Orlando, who falls in love with the pagan queen Angelica. Orlando's love is spurned when Angelica falls in love with another knight, and as a result he goes mad, rampaging across Europe and Africa until his friend Astolfo travels to the moon to literally recover his senses. In the *TTP*, Spinoza gives the text as an example of

---

[1] *Ethics* III, 35 Schol.; CWS I, 514.
[2] Buried later in the definitions of the affects, he does mull the possibility of marriage agreeing with reason, so long as physical union is 'not generated only by external appearance', but also a 'love of begetting children and educating them wisely', and by a love caused by 'freedom of the mind' (III, DA 20; CWS I, 591). Readers may otherwise have in mind the exclusion of women from democracy on grounds of natural weakness at the end of the *TP*.

where, to understand strange or incomprehensible things, it is important to know the motives and context of the author:

> I know I once read in a book that a man named Orlando the furious used to ride a winged monster in the air, that he flew over whatever regions he wanted to, and that by himself he slaughtered an immense number of men and giants. The book contained other fantasies of this kind, which are completely incomprehensible from the standpoint of the intellect.[3]

In a provocation that seems to have gone unnoticed, Spinoza then equivocates this with Perseus in Ovid, whose winged sandals helped him slay Medusa, Samson's slaughter of a thousand Philistines with the jawbone of a donkey (Judges 15:15), and Elijah's burning chariot that flew to heaven (2 Kings 2:11). 'These stories, I say, are completely similar.' Only their context and purpose separate them.

While the remarks are laced with his usual caustic wit, they also indicate the value of fiction in Spinoza's thinking. An inventory of his book collection at his death contains a surprising amount of literature for a philosopher with a reputation for austere metaphysics. Much of it is in Spanish, the language of learning in the Sephardic community he grew up in, while his works are dotted with references to Latin poets and playwrights like Ovid and Terence.[4] Terence's *Eunuchus* in particular deals in the troubles of the heart. Spinoza knew this play well. It's thought he acted in a public production as a young man, staged by his teacher Van den Enden, but in what role we do not know.[5] He alludes to it later in *Ethics* Part V when the theme of the unfaithful lover returns:

> So also, one who has been badly received by a lover thinks of nothing but the inconstancy and deceptiveness of women, and their other, often sung vices. All of these he immediately forgets as soon as his lover receives him again.[6]

This seems to be riffing on the first scene of the play, in which the lovestruck protagonist, Phaedria, despairs after being ejected from the house of Thais,

---

[3] *TTP* VII, 61; *CWS* II, 183–4.
[4] E.g. Cervantes, Quevedo, Gongora, Perez de Montalvan, Pinto Delgado and Baltasar Gracian; in Latin: Ovid, Lucian, Martial, Petronius, Virgil and Horace. Van Sluis and Musschenga (2009) provide a full inventory.
[5] Nadler 1999: 109.
[6] *Ethics* V, 10 Schol.; *CWS* I, 602–3.

who he hopes to seduce. Parmeno, his plain-speaking slave (a model for Sancho Panza in Cervantes' *Don Quixote*, perhaps), warns his master about the consequences of losing his wits. He then offers his own advice on the drama and dangers of love:

> In love there are all these evils; wrongs, suspicions, enmities, reconcilements, war, then peace; if you expect to render these things, naturally uncertain, by dint of reason, you wouldn't effect it a bit the more than if you were to use your endeavors to be mad with reason.[7]

Spinoza has a lot to say about the challenge of trying to make what is uncertain certain. It crops up in the *TdIE* when he asks whether he might be 'willing to lose something certain', the life of the mind, for the 'uncertain' existence of sensual pleasure, riches and honour.[8] It's foundational to the work of *Ethics* Part IV, which outlines a science of the affects that's also a physics of the affects, dealing with their respective power, force and causality. The lovesick man might be added to our dramatis personae from the last chapter, for whom it's no more in his power to have a healthy body than it is a sound mind. Parmeno warns Phaedria of his 'captivated' state and, like someone sold into slavery, pleads with him to 'redeem yourself [. . .] at the smallest price you can', to pay the ransom, avoid falling any further in love.

Remarks about the madness of love, the absurdity of chivalry and the like were common over the sixteenth century. Cervantes' Don Quixote is the knight who tilts at windmills in his fight for Dulcinea del Toboso, a non-existent princess. Shakespeare's works bristle with the folly of love, a 'madness most discreet'. The star-cross'd lover of *Romeo and Juliet* is another who labours under the spell of powerful delusions in a kind of servitude. It's a pressing issue of desiring what, in being impossible, harms us with delusions of attractiveness or grandeur that easily become passions of jealousy, hatred and plots for revenge. In its own way love, defined simply by Spinoza as 'joy with the accompanying idea of an external cause', has been wrongly overlooked by his readers.[9] As I want to show here, love and desire are at the heart of human power, if understood rightly.

But we are here to explore freedom. Now, given that we are no dominion within a dominion, and our appetites and actions are just another subset of nature, intelligible to reason, what does human freedom consist in? Yes, we

---

[7] Terence 1874: I.i.14–18.
[8] *TdIE* 2; CWS I, 7.
[9] *Ethics* III, 13 Schol.; CWS I, 502.

can extend the frequency of our interactions and try to be as much a cause of our own activity as possible. But as collections of striving matter and ideas, what might this amount to in our everyday lives, beyond aggressive self-interest and the avoidance of death (of a crudely Hobbesian kind)? How reliable is such a freedom when what we perceive of these interactions is necessarily formed by passive affects and the imagination? Having spent some time on power, freedom and the conatus, I want us to now understand how this hinges onto human beings, through desire, the conscious experience of the conatus that each of us has.

But what does this consciousness – a term loaded with so many modern connotations – amount to? How do we get from explaining the nature of the affects and desires themselves, and on to the cognitive and affective processes by which we can steer and direct our striving? And how does our inevitable immersion in forms of inadequate, imagination-based knowledge lead to confusion about what our desires are? This is another avenue to some of our earlier problems, like belief in free will or a human-like deity, but it also takes us to akrasia – the inability to follow through on good intentions. At its centre is desire, that all-too-human consciousness of our drives and power that compels us to pursue what we judge will bring us some good or reduce some harm. Such a consciousness, formed by affects, memories, images and common notions is the source through which we fall for falsehoods and superstitions, and yet, for Spinoza, the one means for becoming freer, happier and more powerful. A great deal rests on desire. So, I want us to understand precisely what Spinoza means by desire (and whether his account can offer some precision), before establishing how desires and the affects are to be used for our well-being and flourishing. As with the previous chapters, this line of thinking will take us back to the basic goods of friendship and collective power in his thought. By the end of this chapter, we should be able to begin recognising how friendships and communities are established and maintained through our desires.

Consciousness

Spinoza's account of desire (*cupiditas*) follows from the conatus argument of the last chapter, and is relatively simple, being established in two propositions (III, 9 and 11), and given a summary definition later.[10] These are:

---

[10] Cf. III, 56–9; IV, 15–18; 37; 60–1 App. 1–4; V, 4 Schol.; 26; and 28, where Spinoza develops this definition of desire to construct an ethics of freedom.

> Between appetite and desire there is no difference, except that desire is generally related to men insofar as they are conscious of their appetites. So desire can be defined as appetite together with consciousness of the appetite. (Proposition 9)[11]

The meaning of this is clearer when we recall the account of the conatus earlier. Spinoza is defining appetite as human conatus, but the additional feature of consciousness needs work. Then:

> The idea of any thing that increases or diminishes, aids or restrains, our body's power of acting, increases or diminishes, aids or restrains, our mind's power of thinking. (Proposition 11)[12]

This becomes the basis of introducing the three kind of affects, joy, sadness and desire, which we'll explore in a moment. Lastly:

> Desire is man's very essence, insofar as it is conceived to be determined, from any given affection of it, to do something.[13]

This doesn't add much directly to the preceding propositions, but Spinoza brings a new emphasis to desire which confirms its place at the heart of his ethics and psychology.

Let's break these down. They begin in the same proposition where we left our conatus argument in the last chapter. The Demonstration to Proposition 9 establishes that the mind strives to persevere in its being, and has a conatus constituted of both adequate and inadequate ideas.[14] This follows plausibly from what's sometimes called Spinoza's parallelism: that is, that the human being is a single mode, perceived from the perspective of two different, parallel attributes, thought and extension. 'The order and connection of ideas is the same as the order and connection of things', he says, which leads to the curious formulation that 'the object of the idea constituting a human mind is a body'.[15] Thus, the mind is necessarily conscious (*conscientia*) of its striving through the body's affections, given that the mind and body are manifestations of one individual in two unified attributes, of which the

---

[11] CWS I, 499.
[12] CWS I, 500.
[13] III, DA 1; CWS I, 531.
[14] CWS I, 499.
[15] II, 7; 12; CWS I, 451; 456–7. Cf. II, 23; III, 3 Dem.; CWS I, 468; 498.

mind is the idea of the body.[16] These affections can produce ideas which are called affects, which are experienced when the body undergoes a transition to a greater or lesser degree of power.[17]

The purpose of Proposition 9 Scholium is explain how the conatus manifests in human beings. When related to minds, it is 'will' (*voluntas*), and when it relates to mind and body together, it is 'appetite' (*appetitus*).[18] Appetite is 'the very essence of man, from whose nature there necessarily follow those things that promote his preservation'. Appetite would therefore seem to be the conatus as manifested in a human being, but Spinoza then adds a definition of desire that incorporates human consciousness, and so is 'appetite together with consciousness [*conscientia*] of the appetite'. In other respects, there is no difference between appetites and desire. This stress on appetites as an efficient cause of our desires in Proposition 9 is important, as it explains human behaviour and motivation without relying on either the invalidated faculty of free will or reasoning from final causes, through a peculiar formulation of consciousness.

But consciousness of what? While forms of the verb *conscire* and adjective *conscius* appear fifteen times in his Latin works, Spinoza gives no precise formulation of the term, irritating some commentators.[19] Two broad patterns of use emerge, though. The first refers to the mind's ideas of the body's affections, and its ideas of these ideas.[20] These are more conducive to one's perseverance in being to the extent that the mind is a cause of these ideas, and not subject to external causes which make it a partial cause of them (i.e. inadequate) – but this initial use of consciousness is dealing only with a mental awareness of bodily affections. The second refers to the mind's reason and understanding of itself, in contrast to an ignorance of external causes that leads to error[21] – in other words, a distinction between

---

[16] Following II, 7 and 15 Dem.; CWS I, 451; 463.
[17] Not all affections result in affects in the mind, for instance trembling, paleness and sobbing (III, 59 Schol.; CWS I, 530). The affects are also relative – one who is already an adequate cause of their own activity or in a powerful state may not experience any joy whatsoever (cf. III, GDA; CWS I, 542–3).
[18] III, 9 Schol.; CWS I, 500.
[19] The prospects of a coherent theory of consciousness are 'dim' by Miller's reckoning (2007: 203), echoing earlier criticisms by Bennett (1984: §44) and Wilson (1996: 133). Garrett (2008: 23–4) and Nadler (2008: 585) also find it unclear, but reconstruct it using bodily power and functional complexity respectively. For a good survey of the debate, see Nadler 2008; for a tripartite view of consciousness in Spinoza, LeBuffe 2010b.
[20] E.g. *Ethics* III, 9 Schol.; 30; IV, 8; CWS I, 500; 510; 550.
[21] I App.; II, 35 Schol.; III, 2; and a lesser extent, V, 39 Schol.; CWS I, 440; 473; 495; 614; *Ep.* LVIII [to G. H. Schuller]; CWS II, 427.

being conscious and understanding oneself as a conscious being. While each person is individuated by a striving to persevere in being that is the initial cause of their behaviour, this striving is modified by myriad factors unique to that individual: their bodily power or functional complexity,[22] the ideas they have about themselves, their environment or their affects, as well as the weight of external forces through which they become passive, their ideas being inadequate and not a realistic reflection of their situation. So, we can speak of desire as consciousness, but one liable to poor judgements and weak motivation.

This is what Steinberg calls a 'biconditional formula', one he sees operating in II, 23, a proposition we skirted by when introducing parallelism.[23] 'The mind does not know itself', he writes, 'except insofar as it perceives the ideas of the affections of the body.'[24] As Steinberg usefully points out, the mind is only conscious of itself insofar as the body is affected, *and* the mind necessarily perceives these ideas. So again, our consciousness is produced by the body's affections, and the mind's ideas of these, called affects.[25] But there is nothing in this consciousness that is predisposed to an objective universal standard of the good, as moralists of nature like Pufendorf and Locke supposed in Chapter 2. Rather:

> From all this, then, it is clear that we neither strive for, nor will, neither want, nor desire anything because we judge it to be good; on the contrary, we judge something to be good because we strive for it, will it, want it, and desire it.[26]

Thus desire also involves a consciousness produced by the ideas of our bodily affections, which determines what we value and judge as a good. But we'll recall from the discussion in Chapter 1 of Part I Appendix that such judgements often stem from our inevitably self-centred and weak reasoning.

Desire then reappears in 11 Scholium in the context of the affects. The proposition itself is rather straightforward and follows consequentially from the earlier parallelism arguments. The idea of what increases our body's power of acting will similarly effect our power of thinking. But

---

[22] As Garrett 2008: 23–4 and Nadler 2008: 585 respectively stress.
[23] Steinberg 2016: 72.
[24] *Ethics* II, 23; CWS I, 468.
[25] III, Def. 3; III, GDA; CWS I, 493; 542–3.
[26] III, 9 Schol.; CWS I, 500.

the consequences of that are more interesting, in confirming the power of the mind as established through the power of the body. But what kind of power are we talking about? In this context, desire is one of three primary affects, alongside joy (*laetitia*) and sadness (*tristitia*), out of which all other affects arise.[27] Whereas joy and sadness are passionate states that correspond to the mind's transition to greater or lesser perfection, that is to say, reality or power (following II, Definition 6), the role of desire is initially unclear.[28] It does not directly correspond to a transition in power, yet has a number of affective functions with their own capacity to determine behaviour.

The first of these introduced is emulation, 'the desire for a thing which is generated in us from the fact that we imagine others like us to have the same desire'.[29] This will have interesting social and political consequences in Chapter 8. Spinoza also names quite a few other passive affects of desire: benevolence, timidity, consternation, cowardice, longing, gratitude, anger, vengeance, cruelty, daring, courtesy, ambition, gluttony, drunkenness, greed and lust.[30] Of the active affects – that is, those which arise in the mind insofar as it acts in accordance with reason, and which involve joy and desire – it includes courage ('the desire by which each one strives, solely from the dictate of reason, to preserve his being') and generosity ('the desire by which each one strives, solely from the dictate of reason, to aid other men and join them in his friendship').[31]

But it's often hard to distinguish these from sad or joyous affects. Take for instance anger, one of the key affects of servitude, and 'a desire by which we are spurred, from hate, to do evil to him we hate'.[32] The desire seems to arise from the initial sad passion (likewise with vengeance).[33] Or lust, like that of Phaedria's, which is rendered in characteristically detached fashion as 'a desire for and love of joining one body to another'.[34] Ambition is more interesting. Like lust and greed, it is also a 'species of madness', in

---

[27] III, 11 Schol.; CWS I, 500–1.
[28] CWS I, 447.
[29] III, 27 Schol. [1]; CWS I, 509. Repeated in III, DA 33 but with 'like us' removed (CWS I, 539).
[30] Listed in III, DA 35–48.
[31] III, 59 Schol.; CWS I, 529. Curley translates *animositas* and *generositas* as tenacity and nobility, which feel a little too archaic and indirect for what Spinoza (or at least I) have in mind.
[32] III, DA 36; CWS I, 539.
[33] III, DA 37; CWS I, 539.
[34] III, DA 48; CWS I, 541.

that it involves a highly distorted view of oneself.[35] Spinoza describes it as a 'striving to do something [. . .] solely to please men', which is then expanded to include 'striving to bring it about that everyone should approve his love and hate'.[36] But it's hard to see how these desire affects, in themselves, could constitute an affective experience that was not also coloured by joy or sadness.

Spinoza admits as much elsewhere. 'The desire that arises from sadness or joy, and from hatred or love, is greater, the greater the affect is.'[37] A given affect may diminish or increase our power of acting, and in response we strive to either preserve what brings us joy or remove the sadness. This might include through the mind, in blotting out one image and replacing it with another more to our liking, as was the case with hope in Chapter 1. We should instead think of the desire affects as distinguishing different kinds of motivating forces on our behaviour. This helps us then elucidate what is otherwise a challenging proposition earlier, III, 12, where Spinoza describes how a mind imagines things that will increase the body's power of acting (and thus its own power). Just like the body, the mind is predisposed towards that which increases its power of acting, which here takes the form of the ideas it imagines. But unlike the body, the mind can summon up images of what is neither present nor doesn't exist to bolster its ability to withstand the vicissitudes of human life. I'm sure we can all think of instances of this. But it also means that the despairing lover might also imagine that the object of their desire holds them in greater (or in Phaedria's case, lesser) regard than they actually do, or in grief, might stamp out the pain of rejection through rage and rampaging, like Orlando. Thus, desire is the mind's consciousness of its own appetites, and reflects an internal striving that can make itself more active through the imagination. Once more, it also has no morally normative character: the mind's ability to imagine *what it can* to increase the body's power of acting is only limited by the range of that body's interactions, from which its ideas are produced (following the physical digression in the last chapter).

As he concludes in the closing definition of the affects, desire is our 'very essence, insofar as it is conceived to be determined, from any given affection of it, to do something'.[38] Consciousness is again decisive, one understood as our mind's ideas of the body's affections which, in being often externally

---

[35] IV, 44; CWS I, 571.
[36] III, 29 Schol.; 31 Schol.; CWS I, 510; 512.
[37] III, 37; CWS I, 515.
[38] III, DA 1; CWS I, 531.

determined by 'fortuitous encounters with things', produces a fragmentary and confused knowledge of an affective or imaginative sort.[39] Yet desires can also involve adequate ideas, acquired through common notions or other existing adequate ideas, and which involve a clear and distinct understanding of their cause and effects, and in which we are the cause of our own ideas or actions.[40] But Spinoza has in mind most the desire (*cupiditas*) of figures like Phaedria and Orlando, which overwhelms their judgement and paralyses their reason.

> [T]herefore, by the word desire I understand any of a man's strivings, impulses, appetites, and volitions, which vary as the man's constitution varies, and which are not infrequently so opposed to one another that the man is pulled in different directions and knows not where to turn.[41]

This distinction will become important later as we explore the akratic problem of desiring the better end, yet pursuing the worse, or not knowing where to turn. Appetite exists regardless of our consciousness of it, whereas desire incorporates all forms of 'strivings, impulses, appetites, and volitions' as they generate affections, by which an essence is conceived to be determined to do something. To sum up then, desires are a set of ideas that constitute a singular consciousness, involving ideas of the body's affections, as well as ideas of these ideas, be they representational (i.e. involving the imagination, or first kind of knowledge) or cognitive (i.e. common notions or intuitive knowledge, involving the second and third kinds). This consciousness provides the mind with information regarding its own striving power, and by which it can imagine things that further increase the body's power of acting.[42]

This enables us to further distinguish conatus, desire and will. Appetites are of the body's conative striving to persist in being, and they are the initial cause of our bodily behaviour, but desire essentially individuates us, as it involves our consciousness of these affections and associated ideas. Against Descartes, will is essentially indistinct from the understanding, and the origin of error is not in an overreach of will over intellect, but in inad-

---

[39] II, 29 Cor.; CWS I, 471.
[40] Following II, 40 Schol. 2; CWS I, 478.
[41] III, DA 1, Exp.; CWS I, 531.
[42] A later definition reiterates this: 'desire is the very essence, or nature, of each individual insofar as it is conceived to be determined, by whatever constitution it has, to do something' – desire is defined as a constitution of affects and ideas that produces a specific dispositional awareness (III, 59 Dem.; CWS I, 527).

equate causal knowledge.⁴³ Once we form a clear idea of a given passive affect, we are no longer entirely determined by it. Good is what is conducive to understanding, bad what hinders it.⁴⁴ At the same time, will cannot be a sufficient cause for modifying desires, because desires involve ideas of bodily affections, whose causal order necessarily involves the body.

Yet just as there is nothing morally normative about our desire, so there is nothing intrinsically liberating about it either: the affections that determine our striving in a given way might themselves be sourced in inadequate ideas or sad passive affects, leading some to pursue disastrous courses of action out of ambition, hatred or fear. 'What a man sees, love can make invisible', as Ariosto describes Orlando's blinding passion. 'A poor wretch will readily believe whatever suits him.'⁴⁵ For the reason-loving individual to follow the path of the *Ethics* and experience *beatitudo*, they will need to align their desire with forms of thinking and acting that they can reasonably infer will coincide with their self-preservation. Yet desire itself stands as a weak, reactive guide, unless our minds can become more powerful causes of what we desire. This is no small proposition. The examples of servitude in Chapter 1 include instances of where, through life's inevitable adversities, we fall under the spell of hopes and fears that render us credulous to fortune, omens and superstition. Likewise, the slave in Chapter 2 is one who not only judges (wrongly) from their own temperament but is led by an affect to do things they are ignorant of. The slave doesn't recognise the true order of nature and is paralysed by fear into avoiding associating with others. By contrast, reason dictates the pursuit of nurturing relations with others of a common nature, sharing and acquiring an understanding of ourselves and the universe in a setting of peace, cooperation, cheerfulness (*hilaritas*) and friendship. But before we even get to such relations, there is one obstacle facing all desires, a problem for lovers, ethics and politics.

Akrasia

Spinoza was fond of a saying by Medea in Ovid's *Metamorphoses*, that 'I see the better, yet I do the worse'.⁴⁶ It appears several times in the *Ethics* and in his correspondence, and suggested some riddle that ethical philosophy

---

⁴³ II, 49 Schol.; CWS I, 489.
⁴⁴ IV, 26; CWS I, 559.
⁴⁵ Ariosto 2008: Canto I, stanza 56.
⁴⁶ Ovid 2004: 7.20–1 – echoing Phaedra in Euripides' *Hippolytus*. In both, there is a conflict between sexual desire and moral judgement.

needed to account for.[47] The phrase encapsulates the problem of akrasia, whereby one acts in a way contrary to one's better judgement, understood as a moral or intellectual evaluation of a given situation, which one then disregards for a course of action more likely to result in less beneficial outcomes. In Spinoza's time, it was reflected in the analogy of the charioteer in Plato's *Phaedrus*, of wayward bodily passions needing mastery by the soul's reason and will.[48] Given that he disregards free will as an operative faculty, the challenge facing Spinoza is to present an account of agentic change that incorporates his determinism and model of desire so far reconstructed. If the individual mind's moral or intellectual evaluations can remain intact but are unable to influence actual behaviour, then what is their worth? Fortitude, generosity and courage are all well and good, but Spinoza needs to demonstrate how, like Macbeth, we might screw our courage to the sticking-place.

Spinoza gives one option in the Preface to Part IV: though commonly conceived as a weakness of will, akrasia reflects the power of external causes in determining our ideas over those of our mind's own making, resulting in vacillation; he also remarks later of the relative power of things present to those future or past.[49] Akrasia is that 'human servitude' of being under the power of the affects, the title of Part IV, and where we are only a partial cause of our own ideas (reminiscent of desire's definition as not normatively empowering, earlier). Awareness of this servitude should be enough to overcome it. But this solution is too neat for the inherent difficulty of changing desires amid powerful external causes, and Spinoza spends much of Part IV investigating this problem.

What I want to explore, then, is how an understanding of our desires can lead to a transformation of the effects that follow from them. This will be key to explaining how we become active, and not passive, an issue of Chapter 1 and of the discussion of power in the last chapter. We will proceed with two problems: first, whether we can separate the freedom of the philosopher from the illusory free will of the thinking stone, the drunken chatterbox, the jealous lover and the other dramatis personae. And second, in what way precisely an understanding of desire can overcome the vacillation and poor judgement associated with akrasia.

---

[47] *Ethics* III, 2; IV, Praef.; IV, 17 Schol.; *CWS* I, 495; 542; 554; *Ep.* LVIII [to G. H. Schuller]; *CWS* II, 427.
[48] Spinoza implicitly undermines this in his critique of Stoic and Cartesian free will in *Ethics* V, Praef.; *CWS* I, 596–7.
[49] IV, Praef.; IV, 16; *CWS* I, 543; 554.

Now, the conflict of a present good versus a future one preoccupies *Ethics* Part IV, where several passages deal with how reason often fails to overcome the passions. The passive affects are more intense where they concern something imagined as present or necessary than contingent (IV, 10–13). But this is complemented by a more disquieting problem for ethical philosophy:

> No affect can be restrained by the true knowledge of good and evil insofar as it is true, but only insofar as it is considered as an affect. (IV, 14)[50]
> A desire which arises from a true knowledge of good and evil can be extinguished or restrained by many other desires which arise from affects by which we are tormented. (IV, 15)

Even a true knowledge of good and evil – one guided by reason and conducive to our power – cannot by itself overcome strong passions, particularly those which seem immediate, visceral, present-focused, if not necessary. Thus, Phaedria vacillates at Parmeno's counsel until Thais comes out in the next scene and puts his mind at rest about her affections.

It might seem that Spinoza is tending to an ironic, if not tragic, view of humanity's follies and foibles, like that of Montaigne or Pascal. But we know that's far from the case. For what these issues raise is the supposition that the mind's volitions can exit the order of causality of the body's affections – in other words, that the mind's knowledge will be enough to withstand whatever tempting images or appetites the body assails it with. But that is the Cartesian view of free will and the view of the *Phaedrus*. Instead, the instances of akrasia indicate where the mind is assailed by competing strong affects *and* does not possess enough knowledge of these affects to determine their causes and overcome their strength. The task instead, then, is to recognise that true knowledge of good and evil is nothing if not accompanied by affects of joy.

> A desire that arises from joy is stronger, other things equal, than one that arises from sadness. (IV, 18)[51]

The path that the *Ethics* takes from this proposition, whose scholium forcefully introduces the value of friendship and collectivity, is also towards the development of what was intimated in IV Definition 8, considered in the last chapter: that, as our virtue is in our power or perfection, so where

---

[50] CWS I, 553.
[51] CWS I, 555.

the individual strives to persevere in being 'by the guidance of reason', they will gain in understanding and experience greater and more lasting joys.[52] Of course, there's a bit of a leap there, and it's only later in Part V that Spinoza offers some guidance for how else we might reduce the influence of the passive affects: 'So long as we are not torn by affects contrary to our nature, we have the power of ordering and connecting the affections of the body according to the order of the intellect.'[53] In other words, by applying the science of the affects given in Parts III and IV, we can form a clear and distinct idea of the affections of the body and thereby restrain the sad passions with a 'greater force', be it avoiding a worse sad passion that we believe might result in pursuing it, or experiencing some kind of joy where we summon up the kind of being we might aspire to be who wouldn't fall prey to such feelings.

What's interesting is how Spinoza uses joyous (and to a lesser extent sad) passions in overcoming akrasia.[54] To borrow Eugene Garver's phrase from a recent survey of the imagination in Spinoza, he's 'bootstrapping' the passions in the service of reason.[55] Or, to get it even nearer the mark, he demonstrates how the good life guided by reason is one that is necessarily rich in joys and desires of the most lasting and rewarding sort. We can illustrate this with an example of akrasia some may know. Spinoza himself was fond of smoking a pipe, as was Hobbes. Now, aside from nicotine addiction, the joy and desire for smoking cigarettes are very present-oriented and powerful. Going without seems impossible – few habitual users view cigarettes as contingent, and smoking can be associated with joyous or empowering feelings like the act itself, fitting in, feeling grown-up, or taking time out for oneself; all of which makes quitting even more difficult. Smoking kills: yes, few smokers dispute this rational principle. But success in stopping often involves a package of affective measures, from fear of disease, wanting to save money, premature ageing or an early death, shame when smoking in public or around non-smokers, to substitutes like vaping that offer a similar pleasurable experience with less nicotine. In other words, what we are dealing with is a *reprogramming* of the affects, and how they determine desires.

This is a compelling case, but does it not sin against the spirit of what Spinoza sets out to accomplish in Parts IV and V of *Ethics*, that is, to explain how the mind's acquisition of adequate knowledge enables it to become as

---

[52] IV, 24; *CWS* I, 558.
[53] V, 10; *CWS* I, 601.
[54] The problem of akrasia is also broached by Lin 2006, Marshall 2008 and LeBuffe 2010a: 113–16.
[55] Garver 2018: 102.

much a cause of its own affects and activity as possible? If our better desires are overwhelmed by strong passive affects, then Spinoza's ethics can only assist us to the extent that we retune our individual affective mechanisms. This approach is sometimes called the 'psychotherapy' reading, one which highlights V, 10 Scholium as providing a psychological toolkit for the individual to deal with their own sad passions.[56] But this seems to disregard some of the other key concepts that appear later in Parts IV and V regarding the free man, adequate ideas, common notions, and the mind's eternity through the intellectual love of God ('rubbish which causes others to write rubbish' as Bennett has it) – which leaves little intact of Spinoza's broader view of human freedom.[57] For while Spinoza does set out some 'right ways of living' (*recta ratio vivendi*) in the aforementioned scholium to help reduce the power of sad affects, it by no means follows that he seeks to remove the affects from the good life altogether, or that the end of his philosophy is merely a restatement of Stoic *apatheia* and individual tranquillity before death. Joy, desire, friendship and freedoms of a collective, political kind play a far more decisive role.

Indeed, the free man's life is characterised by joys and desires of an active sort. He 'desires very greatly', particularly that which is 'most important in life'.[58] His wisdom is a 'meditation on life, not on death', and he strives to join others to him in friendship, as we discussed in Chapter 2, and these friends 'strive to benefit one another with equal eagerness for love', which makes them most thankful to each other.[59] His courage and generosity empower him and those around him, and he chooses to live in a state and among others (unlike the 'melancholics'), and maintain the principle of 'common life and common advantage'.[60] This affect-driven approach is mirrored in Deleuze, who argues that pursuing joyous passive affects will lead to our empowerment. Whereas sad passions indicate 'when we are most alienated' and weak, the *Ethics* is 'necessarily an ethics of joy: only joy is worthwhile, joy remains, bringing us near to action'.[61] But there is a tendency in Deleuze's work to endorse all joys, whereas the findings of Chapter

---

[56] It appears in Bennett 1984 (e.g. ch. 14), and later proponents of a psychotherapy-type reading include DeBrabander 2007: ch. 2, LeBuffe 2010a: 190, Pereboom 1994 and Smith 1997: 135. Broadly, each argues for overcoming our passions and the errors these produce to achieve a state of individual psychological tranquillity.
[57] Bennett 1984 §85.3.
[58] *Ethics* IV, 66 Schol.; CWS I, 584.
[59] IV, 67 Dem.; IV, 70 Dem.; CWS I, 584; 585.
[60] IV, 73 Dem.; CWS I, 587.
[61] Deleuze 1988: 28.

1 should make us caution whether our desires and passive joys always lead to our self-preservation. For what Spinoza has in mind is a different order of joy and desire to what we might associate with hedonism, or the lover's lust. Spinoza is clear about the dangers of *titillation*, an excessive joy that threatens to disorder our internal stability, as well as joyous affects and desires that necessarily limit our ability to think or cooperate with others, like ambition, self-love or greed. Some sad passions can also help us understand our situation, or recognise the limits of our abilities, for instance pain (*dolor*), which helps us restrict a pleasure from becoming excessive.[62] It's through this that we can then become more powerful, or seek others of a common nature who may be also experiencing the same affects and join forces with them. Later, existentialist thinkers like Kierkegaard would even identify this *angst* as the condition and vertigo of freedom.

This explains how we can desire something harmful and why we should do something about it. It harms us because it's externally caused and we're passive. We should do something about it so that we can be happier and pursue things we can be surer are good for us. Akrasia, then, refers to the weakness of our better judgements to counter the affects that also determine our behaviour, the 'human servitude' of Part IV, implicitly supposing an opposition between them. But akrasia can be experienced by the philosopher as much as the chatterbox, the lover and the child. There is one order of human freedom. What separates the philosopher is that she can use her understanding of the affects to recognise how they are caused and reduce their harmful effects, and pursue activities and friendships she knows are most conducive to her flourishing. With that in place, how precisely do the affects, images and cognitions (i.e. common notions) that constitute desire's consciousness interact? From Part IV, there are two final points to make: (a) affects are necessary elements of human life, with a dynamic internal relation to each other that in turn disposes our desires, but (b) the mind's adequate ideas themselves produce joyous affects which can overcome even strong sad affects. Let's unpack that:

> *(a) affects are necessary elements of human life* . . . As beings in nature we are necessarily limited by external forces (IV, Ax.; IV, 2–4)[63] – this is part of belonging to the order of nature, as discussed in Chapter 2. These forces act on us, and we act on them, and we are thereby determined to interactions that will modify our bodies and produce ideas of these as affects.

---

[62] *Ethics* IV, 43 Dem.; CWS I, 571.
[63] CWS I, 547–9.

Affects are relative in power to each other, with present-orientated affects more powerful than future-orientated ones, given that the causes for determining these future effects are less clear to us, and so are perceived inadequately.[64] One affect can only be diminished or replaced by another stronger affect.[65] Even desires arising from a true knowledge of good and evil can be overwhelmed by stronger affects that compel us to error, as discussed earlier.[66] Yet a desire that arises from joy is stronger than one arising from sadness, given that it includes an image of something that increases the mind's power, even if it is based on inadequate ideas.[67] By that token, the solution to akrasia seems to lie with an individualist affective psychotherapy.

(b) the mind's adequate ideas themselves produce joyous affects . . . In IV, 8, Spinoza says that the 'knowledge of good and evil is nothing but an affect of joy, or sadness, insofar as we are conscious of it'.[68] Ideas of what concerns our good then, defined in IV Definition 1 as what is useful to us, involve an affect of joy.[69] Proposition 14 claims that no affect can be diminished by the cognition of a truth of our own good in itself, but only diminished by the extent to which that cognition has a corresponding affect.[70] We discussed this earlier: true knowledge can't overcome a strong affect except by summoning an even stronger counter-affect, or reducing the power of that affect, for example, by understanding its causes. In the Demonstration to IV, 20, Spinoza states that '[v]irtue is human power itself, which is defined by man's essence alone'.[71] Proposition 23 develops that line of thinking: one does not 'act from virtue insofar as one is determined to do something by inadequate ideas, but only insofar as one is determined by one's understanding' – that is, doing something from one's essence alone (we should also add the caveat *as much as possible . . .* before 'from', so that this remains possible for human beings).[72] And then Proposition 24: 'Acting absolutely from virtue is nothing else in us but acting, living and preserving our being (these three signify the

---

[64] IV, 9–12, 16–17; CWS I, 551–4.
[65] IV, 7; CWS I, 550.
[66] IV, 15; CWS I, 553.
[67] IV, 18; III, 21 Dem.; CWS I, 556; 506.
[68] CWS I, 550.
[69] Ibid. 546.
[70] Ibid. 553.
[71] Ibid. 557.
[72] Ibid. 558.

same thing) by the guidance of reason, from the foundation of seeking one's own advantage.'[73] From this, Spinoza deduces that reason guides our striving to further understanding, by which the mind increases its store of adequate ideas, which in turn determine desires that directly correlate to its actual self-preservation. This knowledge is of a universal kind, found in common notions, being 'the knowledge of God', which is also a knowledge of nature.[74] Hence, with enough understanding, we can be determined to act by reason alone rather than by our passions,[75] given that these involve acting from our own nature alone and will thus involve our greatest empowerment.

In other words, Spinoza explores how the mind's conatus comes to gain more power and reality through what it understands. This makes us more active and less passive, and because we become more powerful, we experience greater joy in the world we shape and share with others. But Spinoza's reasoning becomes opaquer here, and there are some general structural issues in the latter half of Part IV which might explain Proposition 59's late and unexpected enthusiasm for reason's power to override the passions, something seemingly discounted by Proposition 15 in (a). Spinoza needs an argument for the greater power of adequate ideas in determining behaviour over passive affects, otherwise his case in Part V for the freedom and *beatitudo* of the mind through the third kind of knowledge will collapse. How can we reconcile that with Spinoza's claim that the free man only acts from adequate ideas? Is he implicitly supposing two orders of freedom – of Gods and free men, who are truly free, against everybody else?

We thought about this in the last chapter with Bennett. But we should also keep Spinoza's rhetorical purposes. The free man is presented because, as he says earlier in Part IV, 'we desire to form an idea of man, as a model of human nature which we may look to'.[76] He doesn't explain why we should desire this, but it arrives in the context of a discussion of the merits of conceiving certain models (e.g. of houses or towers) by which we plan and judge a thing's perfection. In the *Short Treatise*, often considered as a very early draft of the *Ethics*, he writes of the value of conceiving 'an idea of a perfect man in our intellect', a 'being of reason' by which we might imagine and dis-

---

[73] Ibid.
[74] IV, 28; CWS I, 559.
[75] IV, 59; CWS I, 579.
[76] IV, Praef.; CWS I, 545.

cover the qualities that lead to 'true freedom' and a unity with God.[77] Both, then, reflect a pedagogical interest in exemplars or models which enable us to imagine and emulate the processes and activities that will make us freer. While absolute freedom is out of our grasp, we can acquire a relative freedom to our earlier abilities, something I wanted to distinguish in the last chapter. Nor should the conclusion follow that a free life is one without the passions. As Spinoza says in a wonderful, well-known passage later in Part IV:

> It is the part of a wise man, I say, to refresh and restore himself in moderation with pleasant food and drink, with scents, with the beauty of green plants, with decoration, music, sports, the theater, and other things of this kind [. . .] For the human body is composed of a great many parts of different nature, which consequently require new and varied nourishment.[78]

We can resolve the apparent difference between Spinoza's overall objective of liberating human individuals, and its stringent cognitive programme later in Part V, by identifying that these are the conditions for the mind to become an adequate cause of its own activity, that is to say, acting from its own nature alone. It is not that Spinoza prizes one kind of absolute freedom over all others; rather, his ethical and political works share the same objective of enabling people to become freer, in different ways, and with different degrees of power. As such, the good life that Spinoza's wise man pursues will involve affects of joy as well as sadness, nor will it be freed from akrasia. The wise person will, however, be better able to determine the causes of the affects impinging on their desires and fall less under the spell of external causes.

From what has now been established, the means for increasing our power of acting and becoming relatively freer is through our desires, understanding what images, affects and cognitive ideas form a consciousness from which they arise. Expanding this further, we can observe a limited form of agency, through the understanding of these inadequate ideas and their causes, by which to redirect and overcome their influence with other stronger affects.

---

[77] KV II, 4, 5; CWS I, 103.
[78] IV, 45 Schol.; CWS I, 572. The benefits of being among blossoming plants has long been recognised in Japan, where the practice of *shinrin–yoku* or 'forest bathing' has been prescribed for its medicinal benefits. Or we might think of their place in the poetry of Coleridge or Wordsworth, who in different ways treasured Spinoza – Coleridge who 'kissed Spinoza's face at the title-page' when borrowing the *Opera Omnia* from Henry Crabb Robinson (in Halmi 2012: 191), and Wordsworth in the *Prelude*, for whom 'Our destiny, our nature, and our home / Is with infinitude, and only there' (2000: 464).

Further, while there is no faculty of Desire – Spinoza writes that there are only specific desires[79] – each desire is composed of ideas, including those of the imagination (e.g. memory, purposiveness, images that might evoke kinds of joy or sadness), because as individuals in nature we cannot but interact with external forces. But they might also include ideas of which our minds are an adequate cause, which can guide our desires in a more effective way to persevering in being. We can infer then, following Garrett, that Spinoza's account of desires presupposes a multi-aspect view of our ideas, involving representational, affective and cognitive aspects.[80] Crucially for Spinoza, and against an overly Stoic reading of his work, ideas for which our minds are a cause (i.e. adequate, involving understanding) are necessarily joyous, given that they involve an increase in our power of acting.[81] In this way, Spinoza's desire can explain and overcome the problem of akrasia thus: we are more able to see the better and actively pursuing it where we can understand the causes of our desires in their multiple aspects. In this way, we become more able to recognise the external causes that determine these ideas. The intensity of our desires or motivations may or may not lessen despite this causal knowledge, and we will experience moments of vacillation like a ship in a storm buffeted by two contrary winds, to use Ariosto and Spinoza's image. But an understanding of the causes of conflicting ideas will enable us to act in ways that more effectively realise our perseverance in being.

This gives another answer to the problem of servitude: our captive subjects need a clear and distinct understanding of what causes their hatred, fear, hope or love. The value of reason to our lives is not merely epistemic: if we truly hold reasonable ideas then they will guide our affects and desires, and we will experience them with joyous affects. Reason's good is in the service of human empowerment. To increase our capacity to think and act, then, we must acquire more rational ideas (or *potestas*) with which to guide our desires, as otherwise nature disposes us to servitude to harmful ideas, from which erroneous beliefs like free will and divine purpose arise, and by which other powerful social forces will mercilessly exploit us. We explored this problem in Chapter 1 but weren't yet able to consider remedies. This journey to acquiring more understanding is long and difficult, and its first steps begin in the imagination and passive affects which inform our everyday beliefs. This is significant. It lifts Spinoza from the cold, ethereal plains of

---

[79] *Ethics* I, 31 Schol.; II, 48; *CWS* I, 435; 483–4.
[80] Garrett 1996: 296.
[81] Kisner writes helpfully of 'virtuous passions' which serve the good life by indicating what activities are good and bad for us (2008: 761).

a rigorously rationalist reputation that obscures the centrality of imagination and experience in his epistemology. Further, it gives the imagination considerable individual and social value in establishing conditions of peace and mutual assistance. What matters then is our perspective, something more plastic and contingent than we might suppose. 'To the eyes of a miser a guinea is more beautiful than the sun', writes William Blake, in words I think Spinoza might approve.[82] He continues:

> the tree which moves some to tears of joy is in the eyes of others only a green thing that stands in the way. Some see nature all ridicule & deformity, [. . .] & some scarce see nature at all. But to the eyes of the man of imagination nature is imagination itself.

While in terms of their epistemology, Spinoza and Blake's religion of the imagination is poles apart, they share a similar wonder at and love of the order of nature of which humanity is a part. This is a view of human life that emphasises not ego-death and finitude in the greater arc of time, but an affirmation of life's fullness and diversity. Nor despair, as Camus proposed, between humanity's insatiable need for meaning 'and the unreasonable silence of the world', which leads some to suicide, others God, others the serial conquests of a Don Juan-like figure.[83] Philosophers need not revel in the absurd, or worse still the heartbroken pessimism of what E. M. Cioran called 'the disease of being born'.[84] Spinoza's response is, again, more interesting – that here in the silence is the eternal and immutable order of nature, one that's intelligible to human understanding, and able to produce in us great states of joy and love – not a disappointed love for meanings lost, but what Hannah Arendt would call, after Augustine, *amor mundi* (love of the world).

Returning to the example of smoking, there must be an internally directed motivation for quitting, and the way this emerges is through desire and the affects. It doesn't matter what precisely they are, so long as we can sustain our desire to stop smoking with what will actually increase our power of acting.[85] Joy is instrumental, being more powerful than sadness given that it involves an image of ourselves becoming more powerful, but Spinoza will

---

[82] Blake 2008: 702 (excessive capitalisation removed for legibility).
[83] Camus 2005: 26.
[84] Cioran 1970: 69.
[85] Akin to Plato's distinction between factual knowledge and true belief in the road to Larissa analogy in *Meno*.

reserve just as much influence for fear of greater evils, particularly in his political works. What matters is not the experience of passive joy itself, but a transformation in what we desire and enjoy in order to meaningfully become freer. In other words, a re-education.

Educating Joy

We naturally pursue what we judge will bring us pleasures or reduce our pain (except in rarer cases of self-denial for a greater future good, or in periods of depression), but we've also been thinking about where immediate, present-focused joys might not correlate with our perseverance in being, like for the fixated lover or the drunk. Joy should not be confused for what correlates with self-preservation. What would it mean, then, to educate our joys?

We desire what we associate with our states of pleasure and are determined to pursue it. Any attempt at becoming freer must begin with what is already enjoyed, drawing strength from this powerful affective source, to then begin reprogramming the kinds of desires one associates with it. As Steinberg says, 'we can only change our minds if we find ways to change our hearts'.[86] Realising what we are capable of, our activity, requires at least some internal direction towards becoming more active and self-determining in the first place, but this needs an affective energy able to redirect our current dispositions. In this way, we can get the measure of Pascal's cryptic remark that the 'heart has its reasons, which reason does not know'.[87] The heart, desire, is pulled by passive affects of external origin, at times beyond its control. Few great novels go without such dramatic plot lines. What makes such literature so edifying is the insights it can give into the impact of the emotions or past experiences in shaping our own desires; that the affects are acting on us, and through us, all the time.

The *Ethics* counsels a life not free of the passions, but one as joyous as possible. Pleasure is of great importance for the philosophical life, be it through green plants, theatre, friends, music, anything that increases the power of our mind and fosters a cheerful disposition and self-contentment (*acquiescentia in se ipso*), which is the highest pleasure available to us.[88] What matters is not the object/image associated with joy, but one's relation to it. Unlike different ancient traditions of mental freedom – like, say, Epicurean *ataraxia* – which involve the mind's separation from emotion and desire,

---

[86] Steinberg 2016: 85.
[87] Pascal 1966: §277.
[88] IV, 45 Schol; cf. IV, 42; 52 Schol.; CWS I, 572; 570; 575.

through Spinoza we can conceive of reprogramming desires and joys so that neither are 'overcome' (something only possible through actual death), but are instead maximised and intensified. For there are no affects of the mind, insofar as it acts, that are not related to desire or joy,[89] and it will always experience its own activity with a kind of joy, even in spite of negative interactions (this may instead contribute to the agent's resilience and fortitude). Of all desires, those that arise from reason 'cannot be excessive', as they are always concerned with our own well-being.[90] But there's something in Spinoza's model that suggests that the acquisition of knowledge and enjoyment of life only engender an even greater desire for these things. As he writes, the 'more capable the mind is of understanding things by the third kind of knowledge, the more it desires to understand things by this same kind of knowledge'.[91] We should not seek to overcome or master our desires, but to understand them as much as possible, and from that, to seek the most lasting forms of joy.

What about where we don't get what we want? That, after all, is the premise of *Eunuchus* and *Orlando Furioso*. It might be something we've reasonably determined to be conducive to our perseverance in being – a promotion, a friend's recovery, a relationship to weather the storms. Spinoza insightfully shows that the first time we understand ourselves is in the frustration of our desires, the adversity that leads to a belief in fortune and anthropomorphic gods 'as mad as men', like in Chapter 1. In quite a different setting, frustrated desires are central to our subjectivity in psychoanalysis. For Jacques Lacan, a keen reader of Spinoza in his youth, desire seeks some object which can only give partial gratification, for the fundamental desire is rooted in our earliest sexual development and can never be fulfilled.[92] In an insightful seminar (VII), Lacan challenges a traditional ethics of desire that assigns guilty meanings to desire and finds ways to postpone acting upon it – 'Carry on working, work must go on'.[93] It may well be that desires offer no meaning, except in their articulation; nonetheless, these desires act upon us like the 'laws of heaven'. For Lacan, an understanding of desire calls for a new edict: 'Have you acted in conformity with the desire that is in you?' But this giving ground to the ineffable and unutterable of desire is a backstep from

---

[89] III, 59 Schol.; *CWS* I, 529.
[90] IV, 61; *CWS* I, 581.
[91] V, 26; *CWS* I, 608.
[92] The *objet petit a*. Lacan became devoted to Spinoza while at school, an influence that remained over his works. We could say that he took Hume's 'hideous hypothesis' seriously, at least in terms of the philosophy of desire.
[93] Lacan 1997: 314–18.

what makes Spinoza's contribution so interesting. That desire, like any other thing of nature, can become intelligible to us when perceived clearly and distinctly, and is as worthy of scientific investigation as another aspect of nature (if not higher).

Yet much of Spinoza's counsel is about accepting our own limits. He tells us at the end of Part II to accept fate and 'bear calmly both good fortune and bad'.[94] Within this Stoic commonplace is an argument that identifies some agency amid necessity, not merely a fatalistic resignation. For here Spinoza first mentions 'matters of fortune', defined as 'things which are not in our power', and, as our discussion in Chapter 1 concluded, belief in fortune acts as a consoling refuge for our disempowerment, involving attachments to images or desires of transient or unattainable goods, resulting in sad affects that expose us to superstition. Spinoza instead directs us to identify the causes of what has become so necessarily. This not only enables us to accept the inconstancy of life, but to alter where we can our actions and circumstances to avoid miserable repetitions.

By recognising the actual causes of a given situation and establishing rules or patterns of behaviour to avoid the causal recurrence of a disempowering effect, we can thereby reduce, maintain or possibly even increase our power of acting as a response to a given situation where one is initially disempowered. Wherever we freely obey what is causally necessary, that is, responding in a way determined by ideas arising from our own nature as much as possible, we are more active than one who resigns themselves to a love of fate; and even if there was no way we might have anticipated a given event, we are consequently more capable of avoiding it in future through adapting our behaviour, and otherwise, to be content 'to act well, as they say, and rejoice'.[95]

Let's try to put this reprogramming into a rough model, based around a series of questions we might ask of a given desire. *Can I recognise the cause of the desire? Am I at least a partial cause? Is it likely to increase my capacity to act? Is it compelling me towards something that would aid the well-being of another person like me?* If the answer to the preceding questions becomes uncertain, then more information about the cause and nature of the desire is needed. If the answer is negative, then the desire may be harmful and unlikely to result in a lasting joy. To challenge the force of the desire we might wish to overcome, we need to draw on a stronger emotional response, for instance the likely negative consequences of following it, or the more lasting happiness

---

[94] *Ethics* II, 49 Schol.; CWS I, 490.
[95] IV, 50 Schol.; CWS I, 574.

that might result from an alternative course of action. If the answer to each stage is affirmative, then we can pursue it freely, provided we regularly check that the changes it is producing in us have not now rendered the desire harmful to us, for instance by excess.

What's good about this joyous desire test is that it applies what has now been understood about the composition of affects and cognitions in human desires over this chapter and the last. It recognises that there is nothing morally or rationally normative about desires, but identifies a means for redirecting these by which ethical agency is restored. It is also somewhat consistent with Spinoza's own ethics, though goes beyond it. It combines elements of IV Preface's account of perfection as envisioning a model of human nature by which to compare our own actions, while also drawing on V, 10 Scholium's instruction to reorder and reconnect a given affect and its cause, thereby acquiring greater self-control. It concedes nothing to teleology, being confined to only what is probable or known to have occurred on other occasions, which is itself strengthened by the understanding.

The test has its limits. It requires being able to recognise the causes of our desires and to understand their composition in inadequate ideas. Among these causes, one must also be able to recognise where one is only a partial cause of (or even passive to) one's desires. It demands a reasonable knowledge of what counts as human power and what generally aids our self-preservation. Above all, it requires society, that is, the ability to interact with others, and to recognise things of a common nature with ourselves. It requires then a good deal of prior strengths, through knowledge, friendship, life experience and reflection. For Spinoza makes a challenging case for reason's guidance in maximising our powers by uniting with others of a common nature, forming communities that live peacefully and cooperatively. Maximising our joyous desires is, like everything else in Spinoza's philosophy of human freedom, a collective endeavour.

This could be a stumbling block. Much of what will nourish an adequate idea of the nature of our desires, or particular desires and affects themselves, is free and constructive dialogue with others. Yet it's an easy implication of Chapter 1, and Spinoza's reticence in publishing his work and the lengths taken to disguise his authorship, that others are dangerous. Our discussion of desire hinges, then, on the quality of relations we have with others, and the state of the society in which these take place. Spinoza is clear and repeats his dismissals of the misanthropes who despise human society. It's an uncontroversial claim therefore that for Spinoza individual freedom is only possible in society, and reflects a political, collective good. Yet few societies can foster the kind of freedom necessary for the philosopher, nor few attain the maturity and motivation Spinoza believes is necessary for the pursuit of a true knowledge of God. We saw as much with the *TTP* in Chapter 2. All individuals are necessarily limited by others, and to varying extents causally dependent on them. Long before we might seek to develop our understanding we are socialised into a particular community, under a particular language, social position, identity, belief system and so forth.[96] There is a political issue that follows from this: which kinds of societies are most conducive to human freedom? What role does the imagination and affects take in identifying – or being led to identify – who we can live with and trust? While nothing is more useful to man than man, Spinoza was well aware of historical and contemporary examples of how societies had collapsed into civil war and sectarian violence. What leads us to view each other as of a common nature? What maintains or dissolves those bonds of commonality? These are some of the problems to which we will now turn.

Walking the Path

So, where does the discussion of freedom, conatus and desire get us? If there is a lasting ethical dictum from the analysis so far, it is *to be as active as one can*. It also offers a useful corrective to a tendency to melancholy and misanthropy in some regarding the miseries of living with others. To Schopenhauer's maxim that 'almost all our sufferings spring from society', or as Sartre more concisely puts it, 'hell is other people', such sufferings can now be explained as desires arising from inadequate ideas.[97] By understanding the affective and cognitive causes of our desires, and how we might begin reprogramming these to maximise our joys and improve our well-being, we can reconnect *almost* all our joys as having to do with others. But Sartre's remark reminds us that such inadequate ideas are often socially conditioned and reinforced, and warn against the hopeful delusion of finding refuge in individual self-development alone, where communities and public institutions decline. Instead, our becoming freer is contingent on the world we make and remake around us. Chapter 1's less cheerful findings also cautiously remind us that many people live under sad affects and, to the extent they are passively determined by them, could harm us.

It is not that the loss of concepts like free will or rational motivations

---

[96] This importance of developing a prior capability in people to think, feel, value and act in ways that result in more lasting well-being is indebted to the capability approach of Amartya Sen and Martha Nussbaum.
[97] Schopenhauer 1974: 424; Sartre 1989: 45.

sinks any ethical system: rather, it demands more work of it. When Hume tells us that 'reason is [. . .] the slave of the passions', we can reply with Spinoza that the freedom of the passions comes through reason.[98] Desire is an 'emergent property' (a term used in neuroscience to describe mental states),[99] a consciousness that arises from the complexity of its constituent parts and which it can partly be explained by, but not necessarily reduced to. Like any given thing, its power is measurable by the degree of harmonious common functioning of its internal parts, its passive and active ideas, its ratio of motion and rest, as discussed in Chapter 2. In this way, the most lasting joys and rewarding desires will flow from our nature. As John Martin Fischer puts it, our freedom is in 'how we walk down that path', not the path itself.[100]

In this way, I want to challenge the claim that Spinoza's ethics is 'egoistic' or 'radically individualistic', as Lee Rice says.[101] This view emerged in the late twentieth century from several American scholars who observe similar premises to mine about the conatus, desire and power, but then infer that Spinoza's entire project is about individual self-empowerment. Steven Barbone says that it would be 'very difficult to deny cogently that Spinoza's philosophy is individualistic and egoistic'.[102] This relies on an earlier claim that two individuals cannot share one nature as otherwise they would become one individual.[103] But this seems to misunderstand what *common* means, which is something that one shares in and is part of, and not necessarily identical with. Likewise, Rice claims that Spinoza is 'a precursor of contemporary libertarianism', in that his politics is concerned with the rights of individuals that are negotiated in a small state.[104] In the American context, libertarianism would include the anti-socialist Friedrich Hayek or virtuous selfishness of Ayn Rand. Rice's position draws on the earlier work of Douglas Den Uyl, which also reads Spinoza as a theorist of 'psychological egoism', but also takes his politics as concerned with Randian heroic

---

[98] Hume 2007: 2.3.3.
[99] E.g. Gazzaniga 2012: 107. This unexpected entrance of neuroscience isn't of one-way benefit. In a recent insightful work, biophysicist and philosopher Henri Atlan warns against a prevailing 'vulgar biologist' reading that reduces mind to mere brain. The task for emergent theories is 'to still face the question of the causal relationship between body and mind' (Atlan 2018: 47; Introduction; ch. 7 *passim*).
[100] Fischer 2007: 82.
[101] Rice 1990: 274.
[102] Barbone 2002: 107.
[103] Ibid. 110.
[104] Rice 1990: 274.

individuals motivated by self-interest.[105] This is a thousand miles from the philosophy of democracy, mutual assistance and the free man one associates with Spinoza.

Of course, such readings are no less ideological than Deleuze and Guattari or Negri's materialist reading of Spinoza through the concepts of immanence or the multitude, or Althusser's detour through to Marx in order to grasp the formation of ideology. Nor are they any less ideological than the laissez-faire 'psychotherapy' readings concerned with individual self-healing discussed in this chapter that reflect the individualised mentality of our own neoliberal era. But any claim that Spinoza's concern with the individual simply ends there, and views society and the collective as a mere means to an egoistic end, cannot seriously be describing the same philosopher as Part IV of the *Ethics* and the *Political Treatise*. From what has been considered so far, anything that aids the self-preservation of an individual is virtuous and reasonable, but such things cannot be found within the individual alone. Knowledge of the second and third kind is of a universal sort, but there is no possibility of its acquisition whatsoever unless the individual is raised, educated and made able to participate in a well-organised, peaceful community, surrounded by friends and nurturing relationships, opportunities for learning and leisure, and among citizens who share peaceful, cooperative beliefs.

Understanding the causes that determine them to act, the reasonable person will discern that their individual freedom is reliant and limited by the freedom or power of their community (or communities), and the people that make up them. Personal freedom therefore becomes possible only in the community, as Marx and Engels remarked earlier. Recognising this involves a deprogramming from a tradition of what C. B. Macpherson called 'possessive individualism', which Jeremy Gilbert has recently reprised.[106] For Gilbert, like Macpherson, this emerged in the contractualism of Hobbes and proceeds through Locke's re-foundation of the political order on private property. While unfairly lumping the two and short-selling both, Gilbert's modern socialist challenge points back to the political stakes of reading early modern thought through a contemporary lens. To what end do we read or read into Spinoza – as liberal and individualistic, reflecting late twentieth-century neoliberal capitalism and Randian aristocratic values? Or as a detour to Marxist and anti-capitalist struggles, a prophet-pioneer of the revolutionary multitudes whose nicely indeterminate status avoids trickier questions about working-class composition and political affiliation?

[105] Den Uyl 1983: 67–8.
[106] Gilbert 2014: 36–44.

Either are confused and fragmentary to a full view of Spinoza, but both are insightful. The track I take, the collectivist Spinoza, is one I want to begin rooting in Spinoza's own metaphysics, taking the remarks about power, and collectivity, and exploring them by way of mutual association and desire. This cannot bring us into the presence of a pure, unadulterated, authentic Spinoza – no honest work of interpretation could. But it's my proposal that Spinoza's politics of collective freedom and desire contain a potent remedy to several problems in past and present political philosophy, one rooted in an implicit politics of collective power, mutual assistance, friendship and love. We'll begin exploring how in the next chapter.

A difficult task lies ahead, then, drawing on everything now discovered about human power, individuation, freedom, desire and joy, and applying that to the scale of groups, collectives and peoples. What kind of freedom, if any, can be said to be collectively realised and desired? Can commonly shared feelings, images and ideas be reprogrammed with adequate ideas, so that communities can live more peacefully, equitably and cooperatively with each other, or are we, too, falling guilty of utopian desires, dreaming of what Spinoza would call a poet's golden age?

Part III
Commonality

5

Becoming Collective

Before her career as a novelist, George Eliot was a translator of Spinoza. She spent over a decade translating Spinoza's *Ethics* in what would have been its first English-language edition (1856), had it not been for a dispute with a publisher, which confined it to a cupboard for another hundred years. While some scholars have detected Spinozan affinities in Eliot's more philosophical novels like her debut *Adam Bede* and her masterpiece *Middlemarch*, there is a curious resonance in *Felix Holt, the Radical*, which bears on the problems of servitude, the affects and desire we've been discussing.[1] The novel concerns the conflict between two moral and political outlooks – the poverty-stricken but principled intellectualism of Felix Holt against the complacent, materialistic opportunism of Harold Transome. Harold is seeking election to parliament in a tightly fought local race, and both seek the hand of Esther Lyon, whose choice between them and subsequent shift in consciousness make her the novel's intellectual protagonist. Eliot's remarks on the necessity and difficulty of working together are illuminating. She writes:

> Fancy what a game at chess would be if all the chessmen had passions and intellects, more or less small and cunning: if you were not only uncertain about your adversary's men, but a little uncertain about your own; if your knight could shuffle himself on to a new square by the sly; if your bishop, in disgust at your castling, could wheedle your pawns out of their places; and if your pawns, hating you because they are pawns, could make away from their appointed posts that you might get checkmate on a sudden. You might be the longest-headed of deductive reasoners, and yet you

---

[1] On Eliot and Spinoza, there's the classic Atkins 1978, then some wonderful recent work, e.g. Gatens 2012, Arnett 2016, Fay 2017. See also Clare Carlisle's introduction to the recently republished translation (Eliot 2020).

might be beaten by your own pawns. You would be especially likely to be beat, if you depended arrogantly on your mathematical imagination, and regarded your passionate pieces with contempt.[2]

The chessboard is an interesting place to think with Spinoza. Like pipe-smoking and drawing, it's one of the few pastimes we can tentatively associate with Spinoza (a chessboard was included in a posthumous inventory of his belongings).[3] Success in chess involves a proficiency in causal reasoning – grandmasters think many moves ahead. Each piece has a different position and purpose, but all belong to one side or the other. Victory is through strategy, in organising pieces to work together to capture the king. In Eliot's thought experiment, though, this working-together is disrupted by the passions. The lie of chess is that the pieces might be like us – or, in her critique of the ambitious and egotistical Mr Jermyn in the novel, that other people are to be viewed as mere pawns:

> Yet this imaginary chess is easy compared with the game a man has to play against his fellow-men with other fellow-men for his instruments. He thinks himself sagacious, perhaps, because he trusts no bond except that of self-interest: but the only self-interest he can safely rely on is what seems to be such to the mind he would use or govern. Can he ever be sure of knowing this?

We know that Spinoza's difficult style has made it easy for some to misinterpret him, willingly or not. Neither Hume nor Hegel claimed to be able to recognise the prospect of human freedom in the *Ethics*. While loving Spinoza and his rationalistic precepts, Coleridge, like other contemporaries in England and Germany, found the philosopher incompatible with the more mystical aspects of Christianity he wanted to protect. 'Did philosophy commence in an IT IS instead of an I AM, Spinoza would be altogether true', he said. 'I, however, believe in all the doctrines of Christianity.'[4] One could wonder if Eliot is challenging Spinoza with this rebuke of the 'mathematical imagination' and deductive reasoning, but I think it reflects an appreciation of what differentiates Spinoza from other contemporaries: his appreciation of the passions and disdain for this crude kind of self-interest. Hobbes lists chess as merely one among many 'contentious games', like 'tables', 'dice,

---

[2] Eliot 1997: 237.
[3] Nadler 1999: 289.
[4] In Halmi 2012: 191.

tennis [. . .] and hunting'.⁵ Locke uses the game to demonstrate the relativity of place: in play, each 'chess-man' has a defined place on the board, but afterwards, all are stored in one bag, where a king is no different to a pawn.⁶ We refer then to their place as a physical location, like a bag in a box on a bookshelf, rather than one designated part of the board. While chess makes no entrance onto Spinoza's thought, it bears affinities with Spinoza's rigorous causal metaphysics of power, one which considers human affects and actions as belonging to the same order of nature as geometric figures and types of weather.

In his early *Elements of Law*, Hobbes conceived of the human passions as instead like a race:

To endeavour, is *appetite*
To be remiss, is *sensuality* [. . .]
To lose ground with looking back, *vain glory* [. . .]
To endeavour to overtake the next, *emulation*.⁷

And so on. It's interesting how the definition of emulation differs from Spinoza's of the last chapter in subtly emphasising competition over imitation and admiration. Indeed, the net effect is to view all passions, like all people, as in one condition of striving to survive a state of competition, if not outright war. Hobbes's 'mortal God' would share a similar approach as Mr Jermyn to his pieces under his sovereign authority, and as critics of absolute monarchy like Spinoza have long been aware, subject to the same defects.

Spinoza also differs from Hobbes in his emphasis on not only the viability of understanding nature and one's place in it, but also that as many as possible can also enjoy this perfect good and blessedness. 'The greatest good of those who seek virtue is common to all', he writes in the *Ethics*, 'and can be enjoyed by all equally.'⁸ This mellifluous note characterises a particular kind of Spinozan love of life, which is also a love of others loving what we love, which can be heard in the free man passages, the beginning of the early *TdIE*, and in important social propositions like *Ethics* IV, 18 Scholium, and IV, 37 and later in Chapter 5 of the *Political Treatise* and its treatment of the highest good. But it is not a consistent note, and there are many other

---

⁵ Hobbes 1840: 441.
⁶ Locke 1997: II.XIII.8.
⁷ Hobbes 1999: 59.
⁸ *Ethics* IV, 36; CWS I, 564.

passages where Spinoza seems to share a kind of Hobbesian suspicion of others' capacities and motives.

The Broken Middle

We'll recall from the Introduction Spinoza's youthful remarks in the *TdIE* on the difficulty and rapture of philosophy. Spinoza described there an urgency with which we should go about that others seek after this same perfect good envisioned. Spinoza also suggests an accompanying social programme, one strikingly different to the typical Scholastic or Renaissance humanist package then taught in the universities, prioritising the education of children, medicine, mechanics and other areas that boost human life alongside philosophy.[9] But Spinoza was also cautious about the freedom of the philosopher in the society around them. Among his rules of living there are '[t]o speak according to the power of understanding of ordinary people [*vulgus*]' and to 'yield as much to their understanding as we can'.[10] This appears in the context of 'attaining our purpose and advantage', and relies on an earlier distinction between the certain good pursued by the philosopher, and the good ordinarily strived for by the *vulgus* which harms, if not destroys, their being.[11]

Spinoza's caution about social persecution appears more openly in the *TTP*. In a letter to Henry Oldenburg five years before its eventual publication, Spinoza sets out three challenges:

(1) the prejudices of the theologians; for I know that they are the greatest obstacle to men's being able to apply their minds to philosophy [. . .]
(2) the opinion the common people [*vulgus*] have of me; they never stop accusing me of atheism, and I am forced to rebut this accusation as well as I can; and
(3) the freedom of philosophizing and saying what we think, which I want to defend in every way[12]

While his words on the theologians and defending the freedom to philosophise are usually grabbed onto, I want to pause here on this aspect of the common people who threaten the philosopher's life. There is a strain of

---

[9] *TdIE* 15; CWS I, 11.
[10] *TdIE* 17; CWS I, 12. These inclusions of the Latin are deliberate – we'll distinguish *vulgus* from *populus* or *multitudo* later in this chapter.
[11] *TdIE* 7; CWS I, 9.
[12] *Ep.* XXX [to Henry Oldenburg]; CWS II, 14–15.

caution if not outward hostility to the *vulgus* throughout the *TTP*. 'The common people always remain equally wretched', he writes in the Preface, so they are never satisfied for long',[13] and who remain 'addicted to superstition [*superstitioni addictum*] and loving the remnants of time more than eternity itself'.[14] Spinoza warns them against even reading the work, and puts this into practice later when instructing friends to prevent a Dutch translation from appearing in print around 1671.[15] There is also the anecdote about the knife attack on Spinoza recorded both by Bayle (outside a theatre) and Colerus (outside a synagogue), the latter of whom heard it more reliably related by Spinoza's landlord.[16] Even if spurious – no contemporary source corroborates it – its circulation as myth reflects the fact of Spinoza's scandalous reputation. 'The mob [*vulgus*] is terrifying, if unafraid', he writes in the *Ethics*, which in its finale impugns the common people (*vulgus*) said to pursue virtue out of hope for eternal reward or fear of damnation, not for virtue itself.[17] Then there is its 'cumbersome' and difficult geometric method which, as Stuart Hampshire describes, uses 'an absurdly crabbed and inelegant Latin, as much to conceal his meanings as to impart them'.[18] Even if we reject the claim that it intentionally sought to conceal – I think we should – undoubtedly the style and language reduce its readership, compared to, say, Descartes' *Meditations*.

[13] *TTP* Praef., 8; CWS II, 68.
[14] Praef., 25; CWS II, 73.
[15] *Ep.* XLIV [to Jarig Jelles]; CWS II, 390. This was probably prompted more by personal safety than anything else – Spinoza's friend Adriaan Koerbagh had died in prison in 1669 after publishing a work that set out in Dutch to demystify theological, legal and political concepts.
[16] Colerus 1880: 416; cf. Rovere 2017: 172.
[17] *Ethics* IV, 54 Schol.; V, 41 Schol.; CWS I, 576; 616. The first remark is itself a quotation of Tacitus; intriguingly, Spinoza will later quote the same material in order to refute its attribution of general human vices to the common people in particular in the later *TP*. Confusingly, Curley translates the line completely differently. See *TP* VII, 27; CWS II, 558. On the development of Spinoza's thought between the *Ethics* and *TP*, see Chapter 7, and Taylor 2019b.
[18] Hampshire 2005: vii. I don't accept this view whatsoever: Spinoza's Latin is modelled on the concision and economy of Seneca, not the rhetorical flourishes of Cicero, and any flaws (and there are not so many) reflect that Spinoza, unlike most early modern authors, learnt his Latin in his twenties and not from early childhood. The argument is reminiscent of Leo Strauss's interpretation of the *TTP* and its fear of persecution, discussed in Chapter 6. On Spinoza's Latin and its relation to meaning, see Lærke (2014) and Van Rompaey (2015). Rovere notes, however, that, in the *Opera Posthuma*, Spinoza's Latin may have been refined by Pieter van Gent and Lodewijk Meyer's elegant editing (2017: 529).

But the *Ethics* offers a more substantive account of how a passive affect can be felt, communicated and shared by different people. He scrutinises how, from the earliest of ages, we tend to imitate the feelings of others, be it pity ('sadness that has arisen from injury to another'), esteem ('when we rejoice because we have affected another, like us, with joy, then we regard ourselves with joy') or emulation, like in the last chapter.[19] We tend to love what others love and hate what they hate. This judgement, then, of what is common to others, or who we recognise as in common with us, is what I'm calling commonality and is something I want to develop in this chapter and the next.

What I'm also circling around is a tension I see present in Spinoza between the individual and the communal, which results in two different attempts to politically resolve it in the two political works. I want to call this tension a *fracture*, by way of the concept of the 'broken middle' in Gillian Rose. For Rose, a Hegelian philosopher writing in a very different context, there's an inevitable tension that ethics and philosophy try to resolve 'between freedom and unfreedom, the struggle between universality, particularity, and singularity'.[20] Enlightenment ideals (she has in mind Kant) make utopian promises that seek to mend the 'middle' between universal categories and concrete particulars, between an emphasis on subjective inner experience and on communal forms of morality and law that seek to restrict or shape that subjective experience. For Rose, the task of philosophy is to face up to that difficulty. 'With what does the ethical begin?' she asks. 'With the difficulty that cannot rest with either perfection or repugnance.'[21] This is to risk 'comprehension' and coming to know, a risk that inevitably involves uncertainty and not knowing, and of accepting the impossibility of ever bridging this middle.

How does that bear on Spinoza? After all, an irresolvable dialectical tension is straight from Hegel's conceptual playbook. Rose's broken middle involves being alert to the difficulty of resolving the contradiction between theory and practice, or of the contradiction of nature conceived 'under a certain species of eternity'[22] and of the historical and political processes that condition and create not just nations, but individuals. Between 'power and exclusion from power', writes Rose later in *Mourning Becomes the Law* – between state institutions, constitutionalism and statecraft, and the disruption of protest and individual difference.[23]

---

[19] *Ethics* III, 22 Schol.; III, 34 Dem.; CWS I, 507; 513.
[20] Rose 1992: xii.
[21] Ibid. 60.
[22] CWS I, 481.
[23] Rose 1996: 30.

It is a fracture between two concepts of social life: on the one hand, the conception in the *Ethics* of the individual as a modal unit of God's power, who has the facility to understand nature and join with others of a common nature into a collective individual, producing a singular effect; on the other, that of life in a community, appearing in the *TTP*, *TP*, and to a lesser extent *Ethics* Part III and Part IV's first half, which deal in a science of the affects and the imagination. It views society as inherently contingent, unstable and constituted (for better or worse) by the immanent power of the common people, whose unstable, passive and reactive states must be understood and steered by wise statesmen (or in the past, a prophet–statesman like Moses – we'll explore this in the next chapter). In the first concept of social life, Spinoza's concern is with the individual's knowledge and participation in a more universal collectivity that can incorporate the entirety of Nature; in the second, one that understands community as contingent and imagined, formed by historical and political circumstances, customs, narratives and cultural markers, and which cannot result in universal agreement or knowledge – a fracture that exists for the individual between the universally collective and the contingently communal.[24]

The community is necessarily limited to those whose social or inherited characteristics mark them 'as us', whereas the collective is necessarily unlimited and might welcome all human beings, if not living beings, into its totality of nature. Both, undoubtedly, are what Spinoza calls *ens rationis*, beings of reason and not mind-independent.[25] Spinoza describes these demonstrations later as 'the eyes of the mind', enabling us to recognise clearly what's perceived confusedly through the imagination.[26] Nonetheless, thinking of a fracture or tension in Spinoza's thinking between the freedom of the individual and the collective, and the relative power and well-being of the community and the people, is a fruitful one. I also suggest that analyses emphasising the inherent good of singular plural subjects (e.g. the multitude) don't face up to the difficulty of forming, organising and living in

---

[24] The reader might be thinking of Matheron here, who argues in *Individu et communauté* (1969) that 'singular things cannot exist but *in community*' (1988: 19). I'm differentiating myself from Matheron's view of collectivity which tends to inflate the ease and advantages of communal association, hence I propose a spectrum later and add the concept of community as a kind of imaginative/affective middle ground which captures the more everyday and less perfect examples of common life. We'll engage with Matheron more readily in the last two chapters, where his 'communism of minds' imagines something equating to an ideal of collectivity as I conceive it.

[25] E.g. *Ethics* II, 49 Schol.; *CWS* I, 490.

[26] V, 23 Schol.; *CWS* I, 608.

such communities, or being excluded by them, particularly when they come under strain or are dominated by the sad passions of Chapter 1.

Let's approach this difficulty in one more direction before we get into Spinoza's text. It's reminiscent of another series of problems Hannah Arendt observed of modern industrialised societies. In *The Human Condition*, she describes how sweeping economic, political and technological changes were making increasing numbers of people superfluous. Industrial developments had deskilled human work, submerging many in 'sheer automatic functioning' and the 'most sterile passivity', while automation and advanced capitalism had made many others unemployed.[27] Bureaucratic processes were permeating everyday life, reducing government to a distant rule by experts and reducing the spaces in which citizens could democratically participate. In *The Origins of Totalitarianism*, this has more disturbing historical resonances, in creating the conditions of mass loneliness, the final condition necessary for the rule by terror and total domination of totalitarianism. We thought about this form of loneliness, deserted by all human companionship, in Chapter 1, and there we paused over its dangerous effects for the circulation of ideas. But it has a second bearing on this problem of the fracture. For Arendt describes this modern state of loneliness as 'not belonging to the world at all'.[28] We could describe it as the opposite end of the spectrum to collectivity, a condition that might be suggested by the word 'atomised', though even that involves a part in the whole. Arendt's condition is more terrifying – it's of becoming nothing whatsoever, of being nullified.

Their contexts are different, but what Rose and Arendt approach is a similar problem to Spinoza.[29] The freedom-loving individual needs friendship in order to flourish, but they also need a secure community and social or economic position. For Rose, this prompts the search for inner salvation and the self's commitment to living; for Arendt, this was an inherently political problem, and one that demands we address not merely human rights but political rights, and the establishment of democratic political spaces by which individuals might encounter each other. Though she did not draw on Spinoza, Arendt's emphasis on political rights resonates with the argument

---

[27] Arendt 1998: 322.
[28] Arendt 1979: 474.
[29] All three are also Jewish thinkers, informed by that tradition and upbringing but also bearing a troubled relation with it. Perhaps each could be identified with what Arendt called the 'pariah', one who is marginal and on the outside, a specifically Jewish status in her view. All took the view that thinking was necessarily difficult but among the most vital activities of human life.

we're identifying in Spinoza, that the freedom that the philosopher seeks can only be accomplished through living with and learning from others of a common nature, and in a peaceful civil society in which intellectual power and free speech is protected and cultivated.

What, then, is Spinoza's solution to this fracture between the freedom-loving individual and the kinds of communities in which they take part? Is it possible to easily distinguish between a community (based on a given affect or identification of a contingent nature, like personal characteristics, custom, history) *and* a collective (based on an equally shared love of God or nature and guided by reason)? What are my grounds for calling Spinoza a collectivist? I will first introduce collectivity in Spinoza, then consider three approaches (literalist, metaphorical, and my own). We'll discuss why some of the scholarly debate around Spinoza hasn't been able to recognise or fairly engage with the importance he gives to collectivity. I'll then propose a unanimity outline in his work, before thinking through some of his different terms for group subjects and why I think they change. Towards the end we'll come back to this problem of the broken middle for the individual themselves by way of the concept of interdependence. Reflecting Spinoza's own sensitivity to the distinction between 'theory' and 'practice',[30] the following chapter will then explore how the *TTP* uses prophecy in the Hebrew Republic to develop a politics of commonality, rooted in the affects and the imagination.

Collectivity

So, what do we mean by collectivity in Spinoza? After all, there are not many textual instances and Spinoza doesn't set it out in any definition. We'll recall from Chapter 2 the use of *collective* and *collegialiter* to describe how reasonable ideas flourish in democratic assemblies in the *TTP*. But I want to argue that there is an important outline of collectivity in the *Ethics* which deserves our attention. In it, I'm going to consider two claims: that the freedom of the reasonable individual is only possible in a community; and that any given community to which an individual might belong has an internal and relative degree of power that, in its most organised and coherent form, resembles that of an individual. The latter is already controversial and will need some elaboration.

In the *Ethics*, Spinoza makes a somewhat defensive apology for his 'cumbersome geometric method' and offers to concisely outline the 'dictates of

---

[30] *TTP* XVII, 1; *CWS* II, 296.

reason' before continuing any further.[31] It's an unusually candid aside and interrupts the flow of Part IV, which has otherwise proceeded rather drily through the relative past/present intensity of the affects. Now Spinoza wants to give a digest of his ideas. He earlier provided these in his Definition and General Definition of the Affects at the end of Part III, perhaps in response to confusion from the circle of friends then reading the manuscript and corresponding by letter. Among these, he argues, joyous passive affects are necessarily more powerful than sad ones, but Spinoza also introduces a new line of argument and the first in the *Ethics* with obvious political implications: 'nothing is more useful to man than man' (translation modified),[32] which becomes the basis of IV, 37 Scholium 2, the work's most explicit political statement on civil society and the State. But in this instance it results in what can be distinguished as a weak (*self-interest*) and a strong (*collectivist*) argument for communal participation.

The *self-interest argument* is of a naturalistic sort, that the security and material advantages of living with others makes it far preferable to solitude. This kind of self-interested reasoning is predominant in IV, 35 Scholium and 37 Scholium 2, where Spinoza equates seeking our own advantage with being useful to one another.[33] For example:

> the more each one seeks his own advantage, and strives to preserve himself, the more he is endowed with virtue (by IV, 20), or what is the same (by IV, Def. 8), the greater is his power of acting according to the laws of his own nature [. . .] Therefore (by IV, 35 Cor. 1), men will be most useful to one another, when each one most seeks his own advantage.[34]

I've strategically removed some important references in between to the 'guidance of reason' which I'll come back to – my sense is that some of the commentators I'll discuss shortly also tend to skim over these. In Chapter 16 of the *TTP*, Spinoza also makes a similar claim in his view of the fish and the emergence of civil society out of our natural state, one marked by 'force' and 'deception' and governed by desire and power.[35] We explored this natural right argument in Chapter 2. Undoubtedly, there's the influence of Hobbes, and some commentators have tended to view Spinoza's

---

[31] *Ethics* IV, 18 Schol.; CWS I, 555.
[32] IV, 18 Schol.; CWS I, 556.
[33] CWS I, 563–4, 566–8.
[34] IV, 35 Cor. 2; CWS I, 563.
[35] *TTP* XVI, 7–8; CWS II, 283–4.

arguments as an 'eccentric' take on Hobbesian precepts, as Curley put it earlier, differing largely in the arguments for democracy or free judgement. Noel Malcolm (a Hobbes scholar) is more withering: 'little more than a developer of theories within the Hobbes-influenced Dutch republican tradition', biblical criticism and socio-political analysis of religion excepted.[36] The self-interest argument has generally received more attention from commentators, who tend to present it as the only argument Spinoza gives for communal participation.

Yet it's derivative of a claim that is more consistent with the earlier metaphysics of power. This collectivist argument appears in various guises across *Ethics* IV, between propositions 18–40. Broadly, it states that there is a superior good for the individual who joins with others of a common nature. Not only will they increase their power exponentially with each person incorporated into their collective ('an individual twice as powerful as each one'), but this union is necessarily an empowering one ('Insofar as a thing agrees with our nature, it is necessarily good').[37] Part IV expands on this. Proposition 20 states that this greater power through combination is one that any reasonable person will desire, and Propositions 22–27 expand on this, stating that our striving to preserve ourselves is 'the first and only foundation of virtue', one that arises insofar as we are determined by the understanding, or guidance of reason.[38] Crucially, it's by extending the range and frequency of our bodily interactions, affecting and being affected by others as much as possible, that our minds become capable of a great many more ideas. Thus, in a definition considered when discussing power in Chapter 3 – 'the more the body is capable of affecting, and being affected by, external bodies in a great many ways, the more the mind is capable of thinking'[39] – we can now appreciate the underlying social element that is vital to this, thereby increasing our power collectively. 'He who has a body capable of a great many things has a mind whose greatest part is eternal.'[40] In other words, the rare and difficult path to blessedness necessitates living, sharing and learning with others like us.

---

[36] Malcolm 2002: 485. But Dutch influences should be considered too, like Marcus Zuerius Boxhorn, professor at Leiden where Spinoza may have studied, whose *Institutiones Politicae* (1657) considers the origin and goal of society in naturalistic, self-interested terms, or the De la Courts, with a similar view (see Weststeijn 2012: 30–8, 145–50).

[37] *Ethics* IV, 18 Schol.; 31; CWS I, 556; 560.

[38] IV, 22 Schol.; 23 Dem.; 24 Dem; CWS I, 558.

[39] IV, App. 27; CWS I, 592.

[40] V, 39; CWS I, 614.

So, individual freedom is also a collective good. We can break this argument down into two further claims. Without the help of others, our lives will be cut short and marked by suffering (*self-interest*); not only do communities enable many of us to live in peace and contentment, they also provide the conditions for how we might increase our understanding and enjoy our lives (*collectivist*). While the influence of passive affects makes individuals variable and inconstant,[41] jeopardising these reciprocal bonds of commonality, living with others provides plenty of opportunities to develop a clear and distinct idea of the passive affects and the causes of our desires. Therefore, this greatest good is common to all and can be enjoyed by all equally without conflict, as we heard earlier. Belonging to a community is conditional to becoming freer, then, in his model, and communities are more powerful to the extent that they contain influential and proactive individuals who live according to reason and encourage and assist others likewise.

The necessity of collective belonging is made even more apparent in Spinoza's model of the free man at the close of Part IV. This was discussed in Chapter 2, but let's explore why some disagree about its purpose. Kisner takes this doctrine to be a 'thought experiment' and Bennett merely forgotten material from an earlier draft, while for Matheron it's an ideal of human equality.[42] But this material serves an important practical function. The 'free man' serves the purpose set out in IV Preface, to present an exemplar (or ideal model) of human perfection, by which to better conceive and compare how one becomes more reasonable and free. It has a 'strategic' imaginative function, says Sharp, providing a model for critically understanding ourselves by a 'Trojan horse', says Steinberg, by which reason's dictates suffuse memorably into the imagination.[43]

But it's much more than that, because it indicates the fundamental role of friendship and collective life in Spinoza's thought. Of the doctrine's many striking features, one that tends to be overlooked is its collectivist nature. The free man by nature is perfect, a perfection unattainable for actual human beings, as we've explored already with adequate ideas. He possesses absolute self-determination (66), resourcefully avoids danger (69) yet never tells lies (72).[44] One would expect some kind of ascetic solitude to follow,

---

[41] Following IV, 32–4; CWS I, 561–2.

[42] Kisner 2011: 175; Bennett 1984: §68.4; Matheron 1988: 155. This is hard to square with its rhetorical purpose as an exemplar, and the distinction it makes between the ignorant/slave and the free man (IV, 66; 70–1; CWS I, 583–6).

[43] Sharp 2011: 107; Steinberg 2014: 196.

[44] CWS I, 583–6. Garrett 1990 attempts to resolve the liar paradox by doing away with the necessity of emulating the free man, an analysis which would be clearer if he

but Spinoza insists that the free man actively seeks the friendship of others like him (71), and prefers to live in a state and obey its laws (73).[45] Why?

Adherents to the self-interest argument can only suggest material gain, a kind of conative pragmatism, perhaps, but this doesn't account for why he desires to aid others, as guided by reason. The free man avoids the favours of the ignorant because he 'strives to join other men to him in friendship' and to 'lead himself and others by the free judgement of reason'.[46] This necessitates avoiding anything that might affect in others sad passions (such as by appearing ungrateful, or overly grateful and partial to one person, rather than all), by which they might come to wish harm on the free man. Spinoza refers to IV, 35 Corollary 1 here ('There is no singular thing in nature that is more useful to man than a man who lives according to the guidance of reason'), which alongside IV, 37 argues for the mutual good that follows when all pursue their own interest, understood of course by Spinoza as the intellectual love of God.[47] There is some traction for the self-interest argument, in that there is personal gain in making others around us reasonable, as they become easier and more useful to live with. Therefore 'men will be most useful to one another, when each one most seeks his own advantage'.[48] In other words, the desire to bring it about that others also enjoy the good we strive after (i.e. empowerment, by reason) is increased the more knowledge we have.

But it increases exponentially, not out of any motivation for personal utility. One motivated by self-interest (or 'Pride', as Spinoza might term it), like Mr Jermyn in Eliot's tale, would contain such formidable internal obstacles to knowledge that they could not act by the dictates of reason, and thereby become freer. Instead, it's a consequence of our own power – the more reasonable we are, the more we cannot help but aid others to become more capable and share with us the happiness this results in. 'The good which everyone who seeks virtue wants for himself, he also desires for other men', Spinoza writes, 'and this desire is greater as his knowledge of God is

---

also conceded that it functions as an imaginative standard, an exemplar for conduct. Rosenthal (2002: 228–30) offers an excellent, nuanced critique of its exemplar function, 'beings of the imagination', which helps us imagine a more general standard for making value judgements. Kisner is most critical of the free man's utility (2011: 162–7).

[45] CWS I, 586–7.
[46] IV, 70 Dem.; CWS I, 585.
[47] CWS I, 563; 564–5.
[48] IV, 35 Cor. 2; CWS I, 563.

greater.'⁴⁹ Its significance for politics shouldn't be underestimated. Here, as much as issues of local political crisis and context, have we an internal necessity for the two political works that arises out of Spinoza's metaphysics. For the philosopher committed to transforming and improving the society in which they live, politics must become be understood not as an art but a science, drawing on a rational knowledge of the affects, constitutional forms and processes, political institutions and their relation to religion, and the lessons of history.

By his nature, then, the free man strives to help others – it is a feature of his own freedom. Yet, if he is already 'perfect', functioning as an exemplar for the absolutely reasonable, self-determining model of human nature Spinoza would like us to imagine emulating, why should he want to actively seek the company of other free human beings (as 71 states)? Their friendship is one of 'the greatest necessity',⁵⁰ as through it the individual is guided to greater understanding of the world by their peers, has their enthusiasm for this knowledge intensified or reinforced by sharing it with others, and through it can love, that extraordinary capacity on which Spinoza rests the highest importance, and which is impossible alone. For while Spinoza is unreservedly supportive of cheerfulness, fortitude, generosity and courage, the highest joy that his ethics recognises is love – the intellectual love of God, preceded only by a more general love of God. Perhaps he was cautious about endorsing love wholeheartedly, given how its affective attachments are the source of some of the saddest passions presented in the *Ethics*, like those of the last chapter. A foundational premise of Spinozan love might be that love is a quality of a relation, not of a loved object.

Spinoza's free man is also freer in a state,⁵¹ and so freely obeys its laws, however unreasonable they are – anything that affords the cognitive, affective and material advantages of living with others is necessarily a good. To claim that it serves as merely a tool for a 'self-reflective therapy' is to miss what is truly liberating about the model.⁵² It's to only see the gains of Spinoza's ethics in terms of the individual, something that may tell us more about our own era than his. For everywhere, the study and love of nature tends to an understanding of what is not just for one, but universal.

Once again, political life is central to Spinoza's understanding of human freedom, but curiously he gives no account here of what forms of politi-

---

⁴⁹ IV, 37; CWS I, 564–5.
⁵⁰ IV, 71 Dem.; CWS I, 586.
⁵¹ *Ethics* IV, 73; CWS I, 587.
⁵² LeBuffe 2010a: 190.

cally organised communities are more successful in realising the common advantage of all. In the *Ethics* at least, Spinoza does not explicitly endorse democracy or any other political model. Whatever form it might take, its overall good is measurable in the internal harmony of its constitutive parts. To his claim for mutual utility, Spinoza adds that one can 'wish for no more than all should so agree in all things that the minds and bodies of all would compose, as it were, one mind and one body'.[53] By the terms of the collectivist argument, human beings unite with others judged of a common nature, and the communities they form are stronger to the extent that they are unanimous, upon which reason is the most reliable basis. Yet the singularity of mind and body Spinoza envisions is not merely one of shared opinions but reflects an underlying (and underdeveloped) *unanimity outline*, one which can help us think about collectivity and interdependence in a non-metaphorical way.

The Unanimity Outline

Let's return to the physical digression, whose account of individuation was introduced in Chapter 3. We'll recall that all bodies are defined in terms of 'motion and rest'.[54] Simple bodies combine into more complex ones that, to the extent they maintain this proportion in a certain and determinate way, can be called individuals. Spinoza's quite clear about that. So long as they 'communicate their motions to each other in a certain fixed manner',[55] that is, maintain an internal organisation of their constitutive parts that collectively continues their persistence in being, then they can be described as individuals. They are individuated by a proportionate internal stability of relations.

Spinoza adds that individuals are 'not distinguished in respect to substance', or the nature of their constitutive parts, but in the 'union of bodies' that results.[56] These can be 'affected in many ways' and preserve its nature, so long as these affections are 'retained' by that individual (that is, they have some control over them), and the resulting motions are communicated to each other.[57] This order of individuation ascends upwards, from the thinking stone to the jealous lover right up to 'the whole of nature', conceived as a

---

[53] IV, 18 Schol.; CWS I, 556.
[54] *Ethics* II, 13, Lem. 1; CWS I, 458.
[55] Ibid. Ax. 2", Def.; CWS I, 460.
[56] Ibid. Lem. 4, Dem.; Ibid. Ax. 2", Def.; CWS I, 461; 460.
[57] Ibid. Lem. 7, Schol.; CWS I, 461.

singularity.⁵⁸ Spinoza puts it rather colourfully as up to 'the face of the whole universe'.⁵⁹ 'And if we proceed in this way', he writes in the physical digression, 'we shall easily conceive that the whole of nature is one individual, whose parts, i.e., all bodies, vary in infinite ways, without any change of the whole individual.'⁶⁰ The whole of nature can be thereby conceived as one individual composed of diverse parts that vary, change and renew over time, while remaining unified.

This puzzling formulation hasn't gone unnoticed. Readers like Bennett, Rice and Barbone have claimed that this peculiar passage can only be understood in terms of animal organisms.⁶¹ But Spinoza gives no sign that this model is said to apply to any particular kind of thing, be it a human, animal, stone or a constitutive part of each, while his remark about the 'entirety of nature' permits us to consider a higher order of individuals than mere human beings. Instead, Spinoza seems to be encouraging us to consider collectives as kinds of individuals, of varying strengths, and this consideration appears, fleetingly, in the *Ethics* and the *TTP*, and becomes extensive in the *TP*, with its repeated consideration of the citizens or multitude as guided as if by one mind.⁶² This explains why it's necessarily good for human beings to associate with and assist each other, and why even Spinoza's free man model of human perfection naturally strives to combine with others of a like nature. Both *Ethics* IV, 37 and *TTP* XVI argue that humans naturally associate not out of fear of a greater evil, but for the greater good of security, prosperity and happiness, something only possible by combining 'as one [*in unum*]' (translation modified).⁶³ Even in the most depleted and weakened of such societies, marked by fear and violence, all communities indicate the workings of a natural propensity in human beings to associate, and increase their powers, collectively.

I want to outline what I regard as six implicit premises to the thought of collectivity in Spinoza. I accept that these do not appear as an explicit outline in the text, and so the usual interpretative caveats apply. However, by observing these premises together, we can appreciate why individuals are said to strive towards agreement with others:

---

⁵⁸ Ibid.; CWS I, 462.
⁵⁹ *Ep.* LXIV [to G. H. Schuller]; CWS II, 439.
⁶⁰ *Ethics* II, 13, Lem. 7, Schol.; CWS I, 462.
⁶¹ Bennett 1984: §26.2; Rice 1990: 272; Barbone 2002: 91.
⁶² Textual instances of people forming collectives or becoming of one mind/one body include E IV, 18 Schol.; IV, App. 12; *TTP* III, 13; XVI, 13; *TP* II, 13; 15–16; 21; III, 2; 5; 7; VI, 1; and VIII, 6.
⁶³ *TTP* XVI, 13; CWS II, 284.

1. *Things combine into groups that produce a common effect* (by II, 13).[64]
2. *These collectives are more powerful than if their constitutive parts acted alone* (by II, 13; III, 6; IV, 18; and V, 8).[65] We'll recall the conatus argument in Chapter 3. The important elements are now IV, 18 Scholium: of the useful things necessary to survival, 'we can think of none more excellent than those that agree entirely with our nature'.[66] V, 8 is more oblique but worth keeping in mind: 'The more an affect arises from a number of causes concurring together, the greater it is.'[67] That reinforces again the physical view of power Spinoza often has in mind.
3. *Conative perseverance in being includes desiring what one judges to increase one's power of acting* (III, 6–7, 9 and 12).[68] This follows the basis of the conatus and desire explored in Chapters 3 and 4. But it brings in III, 12, that fascinating little passage which invites a whole problem of judgement into Spinoza's ethics, as the mind endeavours to imagine what it judges will increase its power of acting, whether grounded in reason or the most deluded hopes.
4. *Human beings experience this as a desire to join with others of a common nature* (IV, 18 Scholium).[69] Nothing is more useful, as per earlier.
5. *Reason is the most secure and unanimous basis of this commonly observed good* (IV, 35 and 37).[70] We thought about the key passages here when discussing the shift from self-interest to collectivist arguments for communal life earlier.
6. *Communities that are led by reason increase their power by cohering particular desires into a collective desire, that is, one that's universal, non-exclusionary and based on a clear and distinct understanding of that desire, in a way that correlates to their common good.*

The last premise is my inference from the previous five. By Spinoza's reasoning, unanimity is realised when a group of groups of bodies unites into producing a singular effect. In working together as one, they share a fixed ratio or proportion among their parts which integrates them together, as in the physical digression in Chapter 3, while also potentially remaining partially

[64] CWS I, 460–2.
[65] Ibid. 498; 556; 600.
[66] Ibid. 556.
[67] Ibid. 600.
[68] Ibid. 498–502.
[69] Ibid. 556.
[70] Ibid. 563–8.

independent and not in other respects necessarily agreeing in nature. We thought about this in Chapter 3 on the physical level of bodies using II, 13, but what's suggested here is that there's also a unity of minds that occurs through the common love of virtue and guidance of reason, among parties of varying affects and interests.

Indeed, for Spinoza we are conatively predisposed to allying with others and combining our efforts for the security, peace and access to material goods this provides, but our ability to establish good relations with others depends in part on our own power of acting. Commonality is subjective – there are no hard facts about what we can or cannot judge as being of a common nature with us, and the imagination often plays the decisive part in determining how we judge the stranger a friend or enemy.[71] But by Spinoza's reasoning, the looseness of this category suggests that the more reasonable we become, the more we extend our commonality to all human beings, and beyond. In this way, the imagination becomes more capable by its greater constitution of desires and affects that arise more adequately, and one's sense of commonality is extended by the acquisition of common notions.

That opens all kinds of questions: given the dangerous role ambitious clerics and public opinion manipulators can play in stoking fear, as per Chapter 1, what role can socially progressive individuals and groups play in extending outwards how people imagine commonality? And what's the role of the State in all this? In the *Ethics* and *TTP*, Spinoza seems to encourage us to accommodate ourselves to the existing law of the State and avoid sedition. But in the *TP*, he proposes new models of states with the common premise of establishing peace and security through popular government. I'll explain how in the penultimate chapter.

My account is not the first to draw political implications from II, 13, with the reconstruction of a unanimity outline. Two groups of readers have clustered around this passage with conflicting claims regarding its implications for political states, a debate which Lee Rice calls the 'literalist' versus 'metaphorical' reading.[72] At its root is a conflict over the political stakes of Spinoza interpretation, with one side involving American scholars who elsewhere claim Spinoza as a kind of ontological individualist or even 'egoistic'

---

[71] Perhaps in this respect there's an affinity with Carl Schmitt's friend/enemy distinction as the foundation of politics, and as a public matter. But unlike Schmitt (or Hobbes), Spinoza has a more ambitious vision of politics as achieving peace and harmony through uniting individuals otherwise set apart by their sad affects and superstitious customs.

[72] Rice 1990: 271.

(as at the end of the last chapter), and continental Marxists who follow a trajectory like Althusser's in Chapter 1 in detouring through Spinoza to reach a de-Hegelianised Marx.

The debate was first initiated by the notion of a social or collective conatus in Sylvain Zac's 1963 *L'idée de vie dans la philosophie de Spinoza*. 'Society is an association of conatus', writes Zac, a kind of abstract living force by which 'despite the diversity of individual natures is the life of God which always remains the same'.[73] But the proposition that the political state might attain a more literal (or 'formal') individuality appears in Matheron's 1969 *Individu et communauté chez Spinoza*, which uses *Ethics* II, 13 to distinguish a 'formal' individuality (conferring unity and conative definition) as opposed to a 'material' one (composed of actual physical elements).[74] For Matheron, this state–individual is a 'system of movements that, operating in a closed cycle, produces and reproduces itself constantly', constituted by social groups and institutions.[75] Like Zac, Laurent Bove has also written of the State as a higher-order individual with its own conatus, expressing 'the "absolutely absolute" self-organisation of the collective body'.[76] Rice also adds fellow American William Sacksteder to the literalist camp, with his claim that the State is 'a single power which constitutes the corporate body of any political order'.[77] My argument so far differs from this reading in two ways: I'm not loading the State with the explanatorily difficult burden of supra-individuality, but consider it a looser community of individuals, a move whose advantages will become clear. I also conceive individuation as on a more nuanced scale based on an internal capacity to act – therefore a literalist-type claim that 'all states are individuals' can be replaced with 'communities can be individuals to greater or lesser extents'. At the same time, we should be wary of attempts to amplify to absurd lengths positions not held by Matheron and others.

But Rice would say that our effort is 'wholly erroneous'. In his critique of Matheron, he warns against any unwarranted extension of Spinoza's physics to political theory.[78] We'll recall Knox Peden giving a similar warning against extending ontologies to politics in Chapter 3. There are good grounds for agreeing. His case for dismissal relies on Spinoza's own vagueness

---

[73] Zac 1963: 225.
[74] Matheron 1988: 51–4.
[75] Ibid. 346.
[76] Bove 1996: 173.
[77] Sacksteder 1984: 208.
[78] Rice 1990: 271.

about applying these models any further than II, 13, and on the claim that Spinoza's politics does not explicitly treat the State as an individual. But I'm not sure that's right. The physical digression does inform the rest of the *Ethics* and its treatment of collective power,[79] while the *TTP*'s vision of a social contract established through popular support and participation (more on this later) and the *TP*'s presentation of civil harmony 'as if one mind' (*una veluti mente*) do give grounds to consider a unanimity to political bodies.[80]

But perhaps all Spinoza intends is a 'metaphorical' understanding of the State–individual, wherein such an individuality is a very loose metaphor to describe the sum of relations within it. This is a tougher problem. McShea calls Spinoza a nominalist in this respect. Any term for a collective individual like 'society' refers only to collective nouns that describe various concrete individual relations.[81] Gueroult also warns against reading the State as anything more than a '*dictamen Rationis*', or thing of reason, and not a reality. But Gueroult steps too far in the other direction – even if a saying or thing of reason doesn't have mind-independent existence, it doesn't follow that it cannot serve to advance our thinking further, as the remark on the 'eyes of the mind' indicated earlier. Instead, the metaphorical position of Rice (and Barbone subsequently) is that Spinoza is interested only in the 'organization of individual powers' (Den Uyl), and so treats the State as an 'aggregate whose members may, on occasion and depending on environing conditions, operate in a more or less unified manner'.[82]

Given Spinoza's professed distrust of the polysemic nature of words and symbols, it is unlikely he would have rested such significance on what was intended merely as a metaphor.[83] Even by the terms of Rice and Den Uyl, an

---

[79] With the benefit of the online tool *Ethics 2.0*, we can trace II, 13 and the axioms, lemmata and postulates over the rest of the *Ethics*. They bolster many further propositions in Part II, and appear across the remainder: III, Post. 1–2; 3 Dem.; 10 Dem.; 17 Schol.; 51 Dem.; 57 Dem.; GDA; IV, 18 Schol.; 39 Dem.; V, 4 Dem.; 23 Dem.; and 29 Dem. See www.ethics.spinozism.org.

[80] Both propose that the power of a state is founded on a direct investment of support and cooperation among subjects, in different ways – Chapter 6 introduces the social contract, and Chapter 7 evaluates the development of Spinoza's political thinking by the *TP*.

[81] McShea 1969: 133–43.

[82] Gueroult (1974: 170 n78); Den Uyl 1983: 71, one of this position's main resources; Rice 1990: 274–5.

[83] Spinoza makes several critiques of symbols, words and their polysemy in Part II which deserve further critical investigation – e.g. II, 18 Schol.; 40 Schol.; 43 Schol.; 47 Schol.; and 49 Schol. (*CWS* I, 466; 476; 480; 483; 485).

aggregate of individuals acting in a unified manner *is* an individual (albeit of a very weak, loose sort), as the definitions of II, 13 above make clear.[84] Hence there is no problem with describing a composite of individual relations as individuated, to the extent that they act in concert – it *is* in operating *as*, through singularly producing an effect. Rice and Barbone rely too heavily on the assumption that II, 13 applies only to animal organisms, and construct a metaphor that effectively makes humanity a 'kingdom within a kingdom', apart from the natural order. Instead the naturally intelligible and universal process of individuation applies to all forms.

At the same time, Barbone's wry analogy of a pile of stones said to have collective individuality is a reminder not to extend an anthropocentric idea of individuation too far.[85] Clearly, bonds of cooperation and common purpose among, say, a football team, rock band or school of mackerel are of a different order from the organs of a human body that are fundamentally interdependent. At the same time, Spinoza's account of individuation is unusually broad enough to explain individuation as resulting from many kinds of coordinated, common activities. One can also avoid the excesses of Matheron's position by cautioning that unanimity could apply to smaller communities first, and that individuation reflects internal degrees of organisational power, in the form of a coherency and harmony of internal, interdependent relations.

A large state marked by violence, fear or profound cultural differences may not amount to an 'individual' at all, then, but several, within a political administrative form. By taking into account *Ethics* IV, 18 Scholium and 37, and adding V, 8 ('[t]he more an affect arises from a number of causes concurring together, the greater it is'), one can derive a model of collective individuation *and* a basic means of distinguishing the relative power of some collective individuals over others.[86] It also allows us to appreciate, in

---

[84] In their 2000 preface to Shirley's translation of the *Political Treatise*, Rice (and Barbone) make no mention of the 'counterfactual' nature of *una veluti mente*, and instead describe the State as a 'quasi individual' made up of 'natural individuals', perhaps reflecting a shift from Rice's earlier views (Spinoza 2000: 26–7).

[85] Barbone 2002: 100.

[86] *CWS* I, 556; 564–8; 600. Not all readers fall into either camp. Lloyd has written perceptively on interconnection using II, 13 (1994: 10–11); see also Gatens and Lloyd 1999: 120–2. Moreau (1994: 427–65) has also provided a good critical compromise, prioritising not individuation itself, but what kind of individual the State might be (I would again caution *could be*), through a scale of complexity. See also Balibar (2005: 88–90) for an excellent summary and resolution to some of these interpretative challenges. My reading differs in its identification and prioritisation of an emerging

abstract form, the force of universal claims for the disempowered: by joining together into communities that are well organised and able to identify and effectively pursue a common project and goal that will benefit them all, they become more powerful and can achieve lasting change, of which the history of political struggles gives innumerable examples.

One in particular stands out. Rosa Parks's well-known refusal to obey the bus driver's command to give up her seat in December 1955 led to indignant black Americans in Alabama organising into a community that then successfully boycotted Montgomery's segregated bus system. This became an iconic event in the civil rights movement and in raising awareness nationally of the systematic injustice of racial segregation. Parks had apparently not planned to protest that day but said afterwards 'she had been pushed as far as she could'. In an insightful discussion of this, Sara Ahmed observes this as 'the willingness of a community that allows an act to acquire the status of willful *for* others'.[87] While the protest required the wilfulness of one individual to push back and represent an oppressed community (Claudette Colvin had, less conspicuously, refused before), it nonetheless acquired meaning through years of prior community organisation and activism. There's something interesting there, then, about what we mean by 'wilful desire', as Ahmed calls it – of instances where the freedom-loving individual takes a stand and opposes the community, and risks their own safety in order to defend what they consider true and under attack. Others may stand with them, after all, and so powerful protest movements begin. But just as often they do not. Spinoza may have been compelled by this desire at various points. Leibniz relates the story that his landlord, the same who spoke to Colerus, had to forcibly restrain Spinoza from leaving their home in The Hague just after the murder of Johan De Witt in order to post up a placard declaring '*Ultimi Barbarorum*' ('You are the greatest of barbarians').[88] In an early twenty-first-century context this risk might seem noble; in Spinoza's time, it could be fatal.

Chapter 1 also found little normatively liberating about collectively individuated powers, and Spinoza's model of collective individuation can equally apply to more societally harmful and superstitious elements that organise themselves into cults, think tanks and thought collectives, propagating their doctrines through influential channels. In other words, there is nothing nec-

---

hypothesis of unanimity as a good, rooted in Spinoza's accounts of sociality and individuation.
[87] Ahmed 2014: 142–3.
[88] Nadler 1999: 356.

essarily liberating about a shared set of ideas or beliefs. While the 'collective struggle presupposes a collective responsibility from the rank and file and collegial responsibility at the top', writes Fanon, years of oppression can also have the effect of creating what James Baldwin called 'self-hatred' earlier, a servitude arising from a prior state of epistemological–political weakness, 'dirtying our hands in the quagmire of our soil and the terrifying void of our minds'.[89]

In this way, we should distinguish the communal from the collective, and begin thinking about a spectrum of collectivity. Collectivity is the processes by which individuals combine with others they judge of a common nature, and act together. Individuals join together with others based on a common feeling or interest, or because they live in a society which defines and recognises them as of a certain grouping, based on cultural, physical or historical markers, like religion in the way Spinoza analyses it in the *TTP*. Smaller communities can combine into larger, though this tends to jeopardise their stability or coherence, unless subject to stringent organisation or powerful common ideas and desires. In all cases these groups vary in power to the extent of their internal coherency and harmony, and the powers of the parts composing them. So long as this internal proportion of self-organisation is retained, the community remains in a kind of existence, and, by deduction, it therefore falls under the conatus argument, and so possesses a conatus to persevere in its existence.

At the same time, communities can also be reactive and exclusionary, and belonging to them harmful. Some of the earliest moments that might constitute our subjectivity are grounded in moments of exclusion – of feeling that one does not or cannot belong to the others, of lacking what Arendt called a 'world' with them. If we use the Montgomery bus example, that might be the community of the white bus driver who had Parks arrested, or the white Americans either complicit or supportive of segregation laws. Perhaps what Arendt doesn't welcome enough (and this is a rather Hegelian point) is that such moments of loneliness can lead to profound self-discovery. Descartes, writing in 1630 of his adopted city Amsterdam, said, 'I could live here all my life without ever being seen by anyone.'[90] For him, this anonymity was a wonderful opportunity. For others, such self-discovery can give us the ability to best recognise others of a more welcoming and empowering common nature to us.

[89] Fanon 2004: 140.
[90] Watson 2007: 28.

The collectives themselves we're describing are at the furthest end of the spectrum, being communities that have achieved a unique singularity of effect, internal harmony and common purpose. Bodies and minds are integrated by a direct recognition of how their joint striving is maximised together. The collective's individuality is an 'emergent property', to take up a term from the last chapter – a property belonging to complex systems but not reducible to its constitutive parts.[91] I hope the reader can think of some examples. I have in mind loving romantic or familial relationships, musical bands that have achieved proficiency after rehearsing together, groups of friends working on a common project like writing a book together, or on a community garden or protest campaign. Collectives tend to be much smaller, and their collectivity is often not a permanent feature but a temporary achievement of close integration. These moments are some of the most life-affirming we will encounter.

From *Vulgus* to *Populus*

There's another way in which we can observe Spinoza's ideas about groups, collective individuation and its political importance changes over his works, and that's in the terms he uses to describe social actors. Spinoza's Latin is terse, concise, crisp, modelled on the clarity of Terence and concision of Seneca. He also tends to be very careful about words and for the most part consistent throughout (power in Chapter 3 and consciousness in Chapter 4 excepted). In which case, why do his terms for different groups shift so markedly over his three major mature works?

Some commentators have remarked upon the shift in terminology between the *TTP* and *TP*, yet there has been no precise linguistic record of how Spinoza refers to social groups across his works. Therefore, I've compiled a table using a keyword search of Spinoza's *Opera*:[92]

---

[91] While this is the first time a claim about collective individuality as an emergent property has been made, there are discussions of emergent properties in Spinoza with reference to panpsychism and the mind in Bennett 1984: §33.3; self and consciousness in Damasio 2003: 325n21; and Atlan 2018 *passim*.

[92] *Popul–* obviously excludes *populare* (popular), while *civ–* excludes *civitas* (commonwealth), *civilis* (civil), etc. Anonymous scholars have uploaded a digitised edition of Gebhardt's *Opera* (Spinoza 2009, http://spinoza.tk), with searchable text. I have cross-referenced this with the *CWS* for accuracy and Giancotti Boscherini's invaluable *Lexicon Spinozanum* (1970a: 153–6; 1970b: 728–9, 840–1, 846–7, 1121–4).

Term	English	Latin (nominative), singular/ plural where applicable	*Ethics*	*TTP*	*TP*
pleb–	plebs	plebs/plebes	0	23	25
vulg–	rabble	vulgus	17	74	3
popul–	people	populus/populi	0	147	4
multitud–	mass	multitudo/ multitudines	1	6	69
civ–	citizen	civis/cives	6	37	85

On first inspection, the *TTP* uses *vulgus* and *populus* a lot, the *TP* uses *multitudo* and *cives* instead, and the *Ethics* tends to use *vulgus* and on occasion *cives*. The *plebs* appear evenly in the *TTP* and *TP*, and seemingly something separate from the *vulgus* (or the latter conceived in a different way). The *TTP* and *TP* are separated by seven years, with the *Ethics* written and revised over that period, and there are some important shifts between their politics which we'll think about in Chapter 7. But the terms don't just reflect different rhetorical styles, they also indicate how Spinoza's ideas about collective power were changing over the period.

Let's explore these different concepts, and then comment on their changes. While Spinoza doesn't present an explicit theoretical outline of these terms, unlike Hobbes, there's a clear pattern of use. First, *vulgus* (common people), which is most common and appeared earlier in the chapter. Broadly, the *vulgus* have been determined by a sad affect (usually fear) or superstitious belief to act in ways that destabilise the State. Elsewhere in the *TTP*, Spinoza undermines Maimonides' view for scripture's metaphorical meaning by noting that then 'it would be written not for ordinary people [*plebs*] – and the uneducated common people – [*vulgus*, and note the distinction] – but only for the wisest, and especially for philosophers', and elsewhere in the passage speaks of 'the weakness of the common people [*vulgi imbecillitatum*]'.[93] There's a similar use in the *Ethics*: '[b]y God's power ordinary people understand God's free will', that is, erroneously.[94] Ambition is described as the desire to please the common people, while the love of money is wont to obsess the minds of the common people.[95] The *vulgus* exist

---

[93] *TTP* XIII, 27–8; *CWS* II, 262–3.
[94] *Ethics* II, 3 Schol.; *CWS* I, 449.
[95] III, 29 Schol.; IV, App., Def. 28; *CWS* I, 510; 593. In each instance, Curley's translation is unusually inconsistent, referring variously to ordinary people, men or the multitude when the use is always the same, so it's modified here.

under the kinds of epistemic servitude mapped out in Chapter 1, as they are always passively determined to act or think in harmful ways. In the *TTP*, they are an obstacle to the freedom of the philosopher.

Why doesn't Spinoza like the *vulgus*? It would seem to contradict his support for democracy elsewhere in the *TTP* and sins against the spirit of *Ethics* IV, 36 and its vision of a virtue open to all. Balibar has very insightfully written of a double-edged 'fear of the masses' in the *TTP*: a fear of the masses as a danger to the philosopher's safety, and a sympathy to the fear that the masses feel.[96] But the meaning of *vulgus* comes into relief when compared to the *populus* (the people) in the discussion of the social contract in the *TTP*. Those who freely transfer their natural right to the State's supreme power are the *populus*, and they actively participate in the State. The Hebrews under Moses are often described as 'the people' or 'one people'.[97] We'll recall, too, Spinoza's third political law, *salus populi suprema lex*. The *populus*, then, are a politically organised entity that are also powerful enough to determine their affairs. By contrast are the *plebs*, who are subjects of the State but otherwise passive and unable to participate in its affairs.[98] Spinoza doesn't appeal to the *vulgus* because he doesn't want it to exist. Instead, the view of collective power that he terms 'democracy' in Chapter 16 is one in which the *plebs* can become politically enfranchised and, through their participation in public life, become part of the *populus*.

This becomes clearer where Spinoza uses multiple terms in the same discussion. Take, for instance, Chapter 8 of the *TTP*, where the Hebrew people form a covenant with God via Moses's Ten Commandments: 'When he had finished reading these and the plebs [*plebs*] had understood them, the people [*populus*] bound themselves to them with full consent' (translation modified).[99] When speaking of a politically organised collective group that possesses sovereignty (as the Hebrews are said to, with their theocracy

---

[96] Balibar 1994: 5.
[97] *TTP* I, 20; IV, 17; CWS II, 83; 129.
[98] This category is largely replaced by *multitudo* in the *TP*, with *plebs* being used to describe the historical lower classes of a given society. For Balibar, the *plebs* are a 'socio-political' category, defining the mass of people opposed to those who govern, the '"inferiors"' (Balibar 1994: 11).
[99] *TTP* VIII, 23; CWS II, 198. This deviates from Curley, whose translation strangely blurs into one what are obviously different uses: 'Once these conditions had been read out, and without doubt grasped by all the ordinary people [*plebs*], they [*populus*] bound themselves with full consent' (Spinoza 2016: 198).

under God), then they are a *populus* (following Hobbes).[100] Likewise in the Preface, Spinoza criticises how ambitious priests have turned churches into theatres,

> each possessed by a longing, not to teach the people [*populus*], but to carry them away with admiration for himself, to censure publicly those who disagree, and to teach only those new and unfamiliar doctrines which the common people [*vulgus*] most wonder at.[101]

There is no *populus* without the agreement (*pactum*) that brings the State into existence, and which maintains it, but not all subjects of any given state are of the *populus*. The path to collective freedom travels, then, from *vulgus* to *populus*, along a spectrum of closer integration of a more harmonious and stable character. In his use of terms, Spinoza tangentially indicates a route towards popular freedom, in overcoming the servitude of the passive *vulgus* to socially harmful ideas, by developing more cooperative relations, more peaceful societies and more representative social institutions.

This does change in the *TP*, which removes all mention of a pact (*pactum*), has little to say on the social contract, and tends to refer to citizens (*cives*), subjects (*subditos*) and *multitudo*, and speaks of *civitas* much more than *republica*. We can already see difficulties with inferring, as Negri has and others subsequently, that the multitude is at the heart of Spinoza's work. If anything, it's a rather late entry, though nonetheless an important one within the *TP*. Montag concedes some of these interpretative problems yet, with Matheron, argues that the conditions for their possibility are established in the third and fourth parts of the *Ethics* where they are an '*immanent* cause' of politics, as Matheron writes of democracy elsewhere.[102] But this stretches the text too thin, and I don't think that the category of the multitude – what Balibar calls a 'right of number' and 'interaction of forces' – is altogether necessary to understanding Spinoza's coextension of natural right and power, say, in contrast to the more general dynamism of collective power like the unanimity outline we're discussing.[103] There is one important exception: the 'free multitude' that fleetingly appears in *TP* Chapter V, said

---

[100] *DC* XII.8.
[101] *TTP* Praef., 15; CWS II, 70.
[102] Montag 2005: 671n2; Matheron 1988: 378; 1997: 217.
[103] Balibar 1994: 15. A similar view appears in Rosenthal's concept of direct 'participation in public life' (2017: 410); for an earlier physical account of power, see Matheron (1988: 37–8).

to be 'guided by hope more than by fear' and who seek to 'cultivate life' rather than merely 'avoid death', in contrast to the 'slave multitude'.[104] But for the most part, Spinoza's problem with the *vulgus* and *multitudo* (in the TTP) is that they are not responsible for their own thoughts and feelings and have been taken over by powerful, ambitious interests. His interest in collective empowerment is through forms of political organisation on grounds of mutual assistance and common purpose, which produces the *populus* or *cives* – who are said to act as 'one body',[105] or think 'as if led by one mind'.[106] That body is an *ens rationis* to describe the power of the State as constituted by its active parts; that mind is not a singular person's or shadowy group's interests that brainwash everyone else, but a clear and distinct understanding of the common order of nature, open to all.

This takes us back to that old problem of the affects and their inherently conflictual nature, which we've been mulling over since Chapter 1. The challenge for Spinoza is that there is nothing intrinsically reasonable about the affects and desires of human beings, which tend to conflict over cooperation. Yet sociality, friendship and cooperation are at the heart of Spinoza's metaphysics of power, as this chapter has also demonstrated. How can this contradiction be resolved?

One solution is presented by Balibar, who traces a politics of 'communication' founded in human sociality and the free transmission of opinions as the basis of a state's good.[107] By this broad term he captures not just conversational interactions, but the content of all inter-relational exchanges, be they imaginative, affective, economic or intellectual – a *'relational* ontology' he calls it elsewhere.[108] This relies on an affirmative, liberatory potential in free tongues, our freedom of speech correlating to a 'multiplication of everyone's power'.[109] This sounds promising. But Spinoza's argument for free speech is rooted in a more cautious response to Hobbes's emphasis on outward

---

[104] A striking distinction, and discussed extensively later in Chapter 7, section 2. TP V, 6; CWS II, 530.
[105] TTP III, 13; CWS II, 114.
[106] TP II, 13; 15–16; CWS II, 513–14.
[107] Balibar 2008: 98–9.
[108] Ibid. 124; 1997b: 7. Later here, Balibar develops Simondon's concept of 'transindividuality', a collective being constituted out of immanent relations of activity and passivity (1997b: 15–32; cf. 1994: 27), relations constituted by this wide form of communication. *Transindividuality* is a helpful term for conceiving collectivity in Spinoza, but this chapter's definition of collective individuals captures the same phenomena within a more expansive theory of individuation (the *trans*– also seems superfluous).
[109] Balibar 2008: 118. See Sharp 2011: 44 on the tongue as an instrument of 'collective sovereignty'.

conformity of the tongue and verbally binding oaths ('[p]rofession with the tongue is but an external thing'): 'Were it as easy to control people's minds as to restrain their tongues.'[110] This inalienable faculty can only be censored to the detriment of the sovereign power, but which contains little reasonable in itself.

The challenge is implicit in Paolo Virno's more recent call for 'a grammar of the multitude' – to get beyond what Heidegger called 'idle talk', which he associates, in a rather curmudgeonly fashion, with infantile modes of communication under contemporary capitalism.[111] By the last premise of the unanimity outline, in order to become harmoniously individuated a *vulgus* or *multitudo* require a sense of commonality together, through which they can begin to associate and communicate. But this sense of being common rests principally in the imagination, that inherently partial, passive and 'mutilated' knowledge, yet also the most elementary and universal, thereby upending the values of Spinoza's epistemic hierarchy in II, 40 Scholium.[112] Imagination unites and divides us, enchants and stupefies. The *vulgus* bound by a common fear or anger are a community, after all – later in the *TP*, Spinoza will claim that political change is often established by a 'common affect' of hope, fear or desire to avenge a common loss.[113] Communities are established with the aid of the imagination, given its role in recognising commonality with another. As Arendt took from Kant, the goal of an ethics is to cultivate an 'enlarged mentality', that is, 'one trains one's imagination to go visiting'.[114] To grasp Spinoza's politics of collective power, then, we need to understand how the imagination operates in shaping our perceptions of commonality, and how it might bridge the fracture – from a community of an exclusionary, personal characteristic-based sort to an inclusive, cosmo-politan collectivity that embraces the face of the whole universe.

Yet at this still-theoretical stage, Spinoza's three laws of Nature from Chapter 2 indicate a standard by which some imaginings are superior to others: those that enable a collective to associate their desires with what most aids their well-being. Even if it takes some time before many in a *populus* (for this is not a *vulgus*) acquire the common notions to recognise why these principles are worth living by (or how they can be changed if not), they can help establish and maintain a community that lives according to

---

[110] L III.42.11; *TTP* XX, 1; *CWS* II, 344.
[111] Virno 2004: 90.
[112] *CWS* I, 477.
[113] *TP* III, 9; *CWS* II, 521.
[114] Arendt 1992: 43.

reason. While the politics of the imagination will be addressed in the next chapter, a final remark is due on another element of collectivity given more scholarly attention outside Spinoza.

Interdependence (or, on Sartre Misreading Spinoza)

In his posthumously published *Notebooks for an Ethics*, Jean-Paul Sartre set out to develop an ethical philosophy out of his *Being and Nothingness* that could connect existentialist individualism to historical consciousness and relationality. It's a not dissimilar problem to that of self-interest and desire over this chapter and the last. Sartre observes that the individual becomes '*conscious* of society' only to the extent that it 'falls outside him'.[115] But this 'Society' isn't an abstract formulation: 'the concrete form in which he represents the totality of other people is precisely that collective unity we call Society'. The individual becomes aware of these unities through '*the gaze of the other*', that is (and simply put), through the way we conceive ourselves within a broader web of social relations. The individual can either conceive themselves in terms of social relations (as a 'proletariat', or as a 'Jew') or refuse them outright.

Sartre attempts to explain what is a vague formulation in the notebooks by comparison to Spinoza. He writes: 'I am like a thought that is isolated from a consciousness while remaining in consciousness or, more precisely, I am like Spinoza's mode that never re-joins the substance from which it emanates [*émane*].'[116] It is unclear in the text whether this somewhat Neoplatonic reading of Spinoza is intentional – the reference is made in passing, and the very few other instances of Spinoza in the text betray an idiosyncratic and fragmentary understanding ('The temptation of objectivity: Spinoza and the Stalinists: objectify everything in order to suppress the consciousness of the other and finally one's own').[117] In any case, modes in Spinoza do not emanate from substance nor are they alienated from it: they are immanent realisations of its power. They therefore cannot exist in a transcendent relation to it, being unable to rejoin it, for they already always participate in it and constitute it, even if finitely. Spinoza dissolves the subjective/objective distinction upon which Sartre's ethics of the I/Other is premised. As we've explored over this chapter and the last, one's affects and desires are already constituted by one's upbringing, socialisation and

[115] Sartre 1992: 110.
[116] Ibid. 112.
[117] Ibid. 13.

education, one's cultural markers and the contingent social identifications these carry, one's daily relations with others, and one's passivity or activity in relation to external forces.

Yet Sartre's view of collectivity is illuminating in other ways. He says that a 'collective idea is one of the unifying structures of a given collectivity'.[118] It implies dependence on others, and cannot be rationally intuited by an individual, isolated member alone. It becomes 'social when others are its guarantee'. Giving the example of a political journalist who sets out to articulate 'public opinion', there exists a sense of 'internal objectivity' of collective thought which the journalist expresses as an idea. Dare it be said, perhaps Sartre had a pre-cognition of Twitter, wherein popular users publish views that both speak in their style and generate voluminous approval. The idea 'will be *true* if it really brings about the unitary fusion of consciousness', being 'the potential unity of the group, having become what it was'.[119] Such a unity is constituted through an interdependent, mutually constituting relation of gazes: the individual feels the 'collective value of the idea' when they are 'looked at by *another* who has this idea [. . .] and who looks at me as the expression of the whole' or collective. In this way, 'the collective idea is never thought by anyone' but exists through its recognition as a relation between others of a like-minded and common nature.[120] In this way, 'I realize the collective desire, I give body to it'. One actualises the collective desire in being an objective part of it.[121]

Sartre's subjectivist foundation for this marks the limitations of imagining oneself as somehow apart from the collective, upon which all manner of meta-individual values is imposed. One of the risks of the individual of Rose's broken middle, unable to enjoy community, or Arendt's lonely, superfluous subject, is the deeper burrowing into one's own thoughts and identity as a defence against a seemingly hostile world. Spinoza warns against overemphasising what the *I* perceives. In a subtle move, he overturns Descartes' 'I think therefore I am' (*cogito ergo sum*) into 'Man thinks' (*homo cogitat*).[122] It's a challenge to philosophies subsequently that begin with individual subjective or phenomenological experience.

For Mark Fisher, this is also to become trapped within 'the face' – of becoming attached and captive to a bored, miserable and narrow sense of

---

[118] Ibid. 113.
[119] Ibid. 114.
[120] Ibid. 115.
[121] Ibid. 116.
[122] *Ethics* II, Ax. 2; CWS I, 448.

subjectivity that's characterised by unsatisfying consumerism, anxiety and narcissism of life under contemporary capitalism.[123] To escape the face is part of a wider process of becoming aware of 'the outside', of a new way of living, seeing and thinking that's wholly different to this current malaise. This 'new humanity' impinges upon our depressed era and is contained within past historical struggles (for instance, late 1980s rave, the late 1960s counterculture or early 1970s worker militancy in Italy and the United States, as his unfinished *Acid Communism* project was exploring). Awareness of the common order of nature and its infinite, eternal nature takes us out of the self and into a more expansive awareness of one's being.

So, collectivity in Sartre is one's awareness of one's common nature with others, relations that are interdependent, then. This is to identify collectivity in the strength of our relations with others. Our sense of collectivity is not a natural fact but becomes realised through our cooperative activity towards a shared goal. This point links to more recent philosophical work on collective intentionality. Margaret Gilbert describes how a walking-group becomes a plural subject in being 'jointly committed to doing something as a body', a commitment that involves a degree of normative obligation to fulfil one's duties as a member of the group.[124] Such a joint commitment requires a prior willingness, mutual understanding and capability. Philip Pettit proceeds from different epistemic bases but arrives at a similar position. For Pettit, group agency requires a 'minimum of rationality'.[125] A group becomes a singular collective agent through identifying common goals, developing a 'body of judgements for rationally guiding action' in support of these goals, and then identifying who on occasion should pursue these goals.[126] In a similar vein, Holly Lawford-Smith derives a politics of coordinating individual obligations and 'mutual responsiveness', and Schmid argues that 'plural identity' is realised by habitual communal dispositions within members, enabling them to act together in joint evaluations – a 'plural pre-reflective self-awareness', or sense of 'us'.[127] In each instance, then, collective intentionality is predicated on a kind of group awareness or sense.

Yet this seems to rest on a voluntaristic view of agency and choice, where individuals choose (or not) to join with others. Spinoza's insights on the affective and physical nature of collective power outlined earlier in this

---

[123] Fisher 2018: 766.
[124] Gilbert 2006: 145.
[125] Pettit 2001: 241.
[126] Pettit and Schweikard 2006: 33.
[127] Lawford-Smith 2015: 227–32; Schmid 2014: 9–12.

chapter indicate that collectivity is inherently political, because the social is always political. It concerns what Del Lucchese analyses as 'constituent power', premised on interdependent and egalitarian relations of a free multitude within a common political project.[128] In this way we can appreciate Camus's remark that 'In order to exist, man must rebel, but rebellion must respect the limit it discovers in itself – a limit where minds meet and, in meeting, begin to exist.'[129] Rebellion is not premised on totality or universal truths; it cannot know whether it will succeed (but necessarily hopes that it does). The rebel 'prefers the "We are" to the "We shall be"', writes Camus, because the latter devalues the present in its appeal to a universal truth or unrealised epoch.[130] This reflects Spinoza's arguments for the inherent power of present affects to future ones discussed earlier.[131] By contrast, the *we shall be* tyrannises in the name of the cause, and ends up forfeiting its ethical legitimacy and popular support.[132] It refuses transcendence in favour of immanence, where the means *are* the ends. Suffering is discovered to be a 'collective experience' which, in luring us from our solitude, enables our self-awareness. 'I rebel – therefore we exist'.[133]

There is an echo of Camus in the work of cellular biologist Kriti Sharma, who closes her discussion of interdependence in nature with 'I am because we are'.[134] In an analysis of signal cell transduction, Sharma argues that identity is '*mutually constituted*'. In a point that mirrors Spinoza's critique of ascetic misanthropes in the *Ethics*, self-sufficiency is a delusion, for individuals cannot exist in isolation.[135] Instead one emerges in an already existing world whose relations and structures enable one to survive. From a cellular level, complex organisms like flowers or human beings are comprised of a vast number of diverse parts, cooperating on the basic level of signal and response, which often come in and out of existence or contact with our body.[136] It's reminiscent of Heraclitus' well-known analogy of the moving river. Our cognitive processes or 'folk essentialism' present objects as coherent, independent unities, but these, like even one's sense of selfhood, *cogito*

---

[128] Del Lucchese 2016.
[129] Camus 1991: 22.
[130] Ibid. 281–2.
[131] E.g. *Ethics* IV, 10, 15–16; CWS I, 551, 553–4.
[132] Camus 1991: 281–2.
[133] Ibid. 22.
[134] Sharma 2015: 130.
[135] *Ethics* IV, 35 Schol.; CWS I, 564.
[136] Sharma 2015: 6–10, 22–5.

ergo sum, are themselves perceptions.[137] Mentalities can be enlarged – the question remains how. All the same, when brought to Spinoza it offers a rebuttal to the frequent over-prioritising in philosophy of one's experience of being *in* an individual mind and body, at the expense of being *among* many others that determine its existence.[138]

Attempting to locate the original, pure source of an individual idea, affect or 'self' leads to an infinite regress, for in Spinoza, as in Sharma, everything is interdependent and inter-relational. Might this collapse with it the whole edifice of truth? In *Of Grammatology*, Jacques Derrida writes of the impossibility of finding 'a metaphysics of presence', an authentic outside or point of universal truth beyond the text.[139] But Spinoza might reply that this reflects a failure to think seriously, one that avoids the risk of facing what unites us with the entirety of nature by a retreat into solipsistic difference. Individuation continues up to the 'whole of nature',[140] and, as mere *natura naturata*, human minds and bodies are defined by the relations with other minds, bodies, ideas and things. This should lead us to view reality as comprised of contingent, interdependent relations and processes that constitute its perception. It's therefore our participation in the world which makes it, and which empowers ourselves and others to live as well as we are capable of, *becoming freer as one and all*. In restoring importance to these relations, this model of interdependence takes us back to our earlier accounts of joyous desires in the last chapter, and love in this one, wherein the possibility of empowerment and freedom comes not in some given feature of the object, idea or action, but our relation to it, one that is dynamic and continually evolving.

At the same time, this isn't a linear journey to personal enlightenment. It involves continuous work and negotiation. Friends fall out, communities disintegrate, drift apart or fade into inactivity. Sometimes our bonds of col-

---

[137] Ibid. 12.
[138] Sharma does not discuss Spinoza, unlike biophysicist Henri Atlan, who in discussing changing understandings of DNA (from determining one's essential make-up to a recent appreciation of epigenetics and how the organism itself dynamically shapes and is shaped to use the passive genetic code), reflects on *Ethics* II, 13. He writes: 'we cannot fail to see in this conservation of the individual, despite the possible renewal of all their parts from external bodies, an anticipation, from a dynamic point of view, of what we now call the metabolic activity of an organism open to its environment, long before its current biochemical and energy supports have been discovered' (2018: 81).
[139] Derrida 2016: 24.
[140] *Ethics* II, 13, Lem. 7, Schol.; CWS I, 462.

lectivity are overcome by factors beyond our control, like death, overwhelming opposition or the waning of love. Sometimes the views of people around us can be shocking or threatening. Still, we must act well and be glad, and leave something open in ourselves to the other.

So, then, in this chapter we have mapped out collectivity using *Ethics* IV, 18 Scholium and the self-interest and collectivist arguments for communal participation. We've thought about the free man as a collectivist in desiring to combine with others and share the joyous life that is guided by reason. We've also considered unanimity as an underlying conceptual process in Spinoza's metaphysics that informs his politics. The emerging view of freedom, then, is one that is not only relational, but realised through and maximised by our association with others.[141] It's where individuals come together and are able to achieve far more together than alone, through working together in an organised fashion to accomplish goals they share. These individuals might differ in their abilities, outlooks or personalities among themselves – what matters is what they accomplish together.

Therefore, we can explain the different images of collectivity that might come to mind – a human body, a sports team, a musical band, a walking group, and so on. Collective individuality debates have more trouble moving this onto the terrain of wider society, though, and the State. How in Spinoza can we speak of the imagination and affects as collectively shared? How is collectivity effectively realised in actual human societies, without being uselessly abstract? What political forms are more conducive to unanimity than others? What prevents unanimity from becoming coercive conformity and the kind of servitude assessed in Chapter 1? To address the limitations of this still-theoretical account of collectivity, I want to turn to the *TTP* and its politics of the imagination and commonality, a viable route to collective flourishing.

---

[141] This reading correlates with Armstrong (2009: 59), Kisner (2011: 231–2) and Sangiacomo (2015: 19), who read Spinoza in terms of 'relational autonomy', that is, of freedom not understood through individualistic self-mastery of a kind associated with, say, Descartes, Locke or Kant, but through personal relationships, care, cooperation and our socio-political environment. See also the Introduction to Armstrong et al. 2019.

6
We Imagine

Over the last few chapters we've been thinking about the implications of a worldview thrown up in Chapter 2. Given that the natural right of each of us is determined by 'desire and power', and 'prohibits nothing except what no one desires and what no one can do',[1] then what is the scope of an ethics in which traditional morally normative precepts do not seemingly apply? How does the freedom-loving philosopher and their collective, if they are fortunate to have established one, live through the fracture of acting, living and thinking among others who may be governed by the sad passions?

We saw in Chapter 1 how such states can turn a fearful and disempowered people into a 'savage multitude', willing in desperation to rally and fight for figureheads who indirectly oppress them.[2] Elsewhere, Spinoza repeatedly counsels against inflating the capacities of all to freely live according to reason:

> Before men can know the true principle of loving and acquire a virtuous disposition, much of their life has passed, even if they have been well brought up. Meanwhile, they are bound to live, and to preserve themselves, as far as they can by their own power, i.e., by the prompting of appetite alone. Nature has given them nothing else. It has denied them the actual power to live according to sound reason. So they're no more bound to live according to the laws of a sound mind than a cat is bound to live according to the laws of a lion's nature.[3]

---

[1] *TTP* XVI, 7, 9; CWS II, 283–4.
[2] *TTP* XVIII, 24; CWS II, 328.
[3] *TTP* XVI, 7; CWS II, 283.

We'll recall from Chapter 3 Spinoza's remark that it's no more in our power to have a sound mind than it is a healthy body in the *TP*. The thinking stone, the chatterbox, the jealous lover – while each live according to the same first law of the conatus, in the *Ethics* Spinoza says that the joys of the drunkard and a philosopher are 'of no small difference', something we could extend to all the dramatis personae under different spells of affective servitude.[4] Yet the *Ethics* ends with an endorsement of the rare and difficult path to freedom through adequate knowledge, whereas the *TTP* frequently admonishes the 'fickle' and 'capricious' *vulgus* for their incapacity to restrain their sad passions. This apparent distinction results in some interesting differences in interpretation, like the view of Leo Strauss that the *TTP* conceals an inherent elitism as Spinoza sought to avoid persecution by concealing his true doctrines behind bland, exoteric ones.[5] Or, on the other end of the political spectrum, Negri's esoteric politics of multitudinal 'counter-Power' against all forms of authority.[6]

The problem for Spinoza, as we've explored since Chapter 1, is how to not only recognise the rule of harmful ideas in our own lives – like the 'monarchy of fear', as Martha Nussbaum has called it – but go about reducing their effects in others.[7] On one level, it's a matter of self-interest if not survival, as we explored in the last chapter with the two arguments for collectivity. But the greatest advantages also follow from society and life with others for the philosopher. We thought about this in the last chapter with the implications of IV, 36 ('The greatest good of those who seek virtue is common to all, and can be enjoyed by all equally'). This mellifluent chorus of collectivity resonates in the civil society passages of the *Ethics*: nothing is more useful to man than man, and that 'the good which everyone who seeks virtue wants for himself, he also desires for other men'.[8]

Why is that? Spinoza gives several reasons – on an imitative level, we love with more conviction what we see others loving.[9] But Spinoza has in mind a form of 'friendship' in which those who live by the guidance of reason (i.e. to pursue their own actual self-advantage, which is to understand) strive to bring together others like them to pursue and share in this life in common. Bodies and minds affect and are affected more constantly with joys, as these

---

[4] *Ethics* III, 57 Schol.; CWS I, 528.
[5] Strauss 1988: 183.
[6] Negri 2003: 112.
[7] Nussbaum 2018.
[8] IV, 18 Schol.; 37 Dem.; CWS I, 556; 565.
[9] IV, 37 Alt. Dem.; CWS I, 565.

collectives better bring about what they agree in desiring. Therefore, the free man strives for friendship and strives to live in civil society, not as a misanthropic recluse out in the wilds. Garver puts this across nicely: 'to be a knower, one must be a citizen'.[10] But this work can and must be undertaken at a more ambitiously wide level if it's to be effective – not just among our own small collectives or wider communities, but at the level of the State more broadly.

We also explored in the last chapter the importance of collectivity, and the metaphysical basis by which groups of individuals come together and form one individual bound by an organised ratio of parts and effects. Yet we also stumbled on the issue of commonality: how we judge someone as being of a common nature to us. Judgement, an ill-defined category for Spinoza, plays a crucial role in our desires for what we consider a good or lesser evil. Their basis is largely in the imagination. So, if we're going to figure out how commonality can be extended outwards, embracing the entirety of nature, we need to understand the role of the imagination in forming and maintaining bonds of community and enmity. In a problem that takes us back to the education of joy in Chapter 4, we also need to explain how Spinoza's politics might result in the becoming freer of as many as possible, using means that are reasonable but do not demand an advanced individual capacity for reason.

What then is the relation of the imagination to reason for political thought? How can the former – necessarily inadequate, passive, fragmentary and confused in Spinoza's view – be of service to realising the ends of the latter? Does each present two different access points to a common kind of freedom, tailored to the varying powers of thinking and acting in a given society? Or does it reflect a more sinister side of the fracture – a subtle elitism within Spinoza's withering remarks on the *vulgus*, the validity of prophecy and the tenets of the universal religion (which contradict core Spinozan teachings on God)? We also need to satisfy Spinoza's own concerns about his safety from the *vulgus*. How do we reduce our reasons for fearing others – or the fears or hatred felt by others who may deny their commonality with us? In other words, we're approaching two sets of questions. On a political level, what has been the role of past leaders and political processes in establishing peace and piety? On an epistemological level, what role can the understanding play in improving or edifying the imagination that individuates a community and which mostly defines the mental lives of its members?

In this chapter, we're going to explore some of Spinoza's attempts at these problems. We'll consider his distinction of reason and imagination first in

[10] Garver 2018: 157.

the *Ethics*, then in its more extensive survey in the *TTP*. The concerns with biblical scripture can also be considered as a comprehensive analysis of how language, customs, histories and texts shape and maintain a common imagination of nationhood. Spinoza also explores the role of prophets who use their imaginations in ways that preserve their communities and lead members with enfeebled abilities to ways that preserve 'justice and loving-kindness'.[11] The figure of Christ is one who, in this analysis, offers the key break between a passive relation to truth (as in customs, worship, prayer and the universal faith) and an active, direct relation to a true understanding of God or nature that's universal and open to all. We'll consider Christ's important, unexpected role in the *TTP* in terms of two access points to reason. But we'll also weigh up some of the limits of the *TTP*. Its forms of commonality are still largely based on exclusionary nation-states, while the reclamation of Christ as a philosopher-prophet sent 'to teach the whole human race [. . .] common and true notions' comes against a larger assault on theologians who use the 'Word' of Christ against philosophers.[12] The *TTP*'s remedies in democracy and free speech, and the abandonment of prophecy, while sound in themselves, don't leave enough to theoretically address the collapse of the liberal Dutch government later in 1672 after a series of popular riots and insurrections. It's this which, among other things, necessitates the expanded role of the State and diminishment of religion in the later *Political Treatise* (1677), explored in the next chapter. But first, let's examine how Spinoza establishes a basic difference between imagination and intellect, and how that shapes the distinction between philosophy and theology.

Philosophy and Theology

In Chapter 14 of the *TTP*, Spinoza writes:

> What remains now is for me to show, finally, that there are no dealings, or no relationship, between faith, or theology, and philosophy. No one can fail to see now, who knows that these two faculties aim at, and are based on, completely different things. For the goal of philosophy is nothing but truth. But the goal of faith [. . .] is nothing but obedience and piety. Furthermore, the foundations of philosophy are common notions, and must be sought only from nature. But the foundations of

---

[11] *Justitia* and *charitas* are frequently paired in the *TTP*, e.g. Praef., 26; 28; XIII, 20, 22, 29; XIV, 3, 17, 19, 24, 27, 33, 39; XV, 25, 34; XVIII, 26; and XIX, 6–9.
[12] *TTP* IV, 31; CWS II, 133.

faith are histories and language, and must be sought only from scripture and revelation.[13]

We'll recall from early in the last chapter that this separation was one of the challenges Spinoza foresaw for the *TTP* when writing to Oldenburg. It's reflected in the book's title page, showing 'that the republic can grant freedom of philosophising without harming its peace and piety, and cannot deny it without destroying its peace and piety'. Like much else in Spinoza, these two commonplace words have been subject to redefinitions: philosophy refers not to the disputes of ancient Athens mocked by Montaigne or the Scholastic diet which passed for it in the universities. In the early *Metaphysical Thoughts* that append his study of Descartes, Spinoza mocks 'philosophers' who 'fall into these verbal or grammatical errors' where 'they judge the things from the words, not the words from the things'.[14] Philosophy in the *TTP* instead refers to the objective pursuit of universal knowledge of nature, without reference to free will, anthropomorphic gods or supernatural forces.[15] Likewise, theology doesn't refer to the study of the nature of God or systematic ideas around it, but to a series of beliefs whose use is solely for social obedience, and which contain ideas that do not stand up to critical scrutiny, like prophetic knowledge from revelation. Thus, Spinoza seeks to re-establish the proper bounds of theology within a narrow and humbler footing. It is concerned with 'obedience and piety', through the means of histories and language, while philosophy is concerned with the human understanding and the 'sciences' or, plainer still, 'truth'.[16] The question remains of the precise purview of each, and how we might, at the level of political thought, identify and contextualise processes of community formation and maintenance founded in historical narratives, customs and beliefs devoid of a true understanding of nature.

Central to understanding the proper role of theology is the role of the prophet, in particular Moses, who had the ability to persuade the many minds of the recently liberated Hebrews to live according to justice and loving-kindness, and in a community bound together by laws and practices that protected and maximised their individual interests. It is through under-

---

[13] *TTP* XIV, 37–8; *CWS* II, 271.
[14] *CM* I, 1; *CWS* I, 301.
[15] Curiously, in the *Ethics* philosophy is never mentioned, and the meaning held by the *TTP* seems instead to be connoted by the 'order of nature'. Elsewhere, Spinoza refers to philosophy's touchstone of truth as 'the natural intellect', in contrast to theology (*Ep.* XXIII [to Willem van Blijenbergh]; *CWS* I, 387).
[16] *TTP* XIV, 38; XIII, 29; XIV, 37; *CWS* II, 271; 263; 271.

standing and mobilising the minds of the many by the imagination that communities first gather strength and identity, and flourish. This poverty of reason (if we may call it that) is compensated for by the wisdom of the prophet–statesman, who designs laws for stable states in tune with existing beliefs and emotions of their people.

Steinberg has recently characterised Spinoza's project as governed by a political psychology wherein state leaders are attuned and seek to channel the '*ingenia*' (or 'affective make-up') of the many towards more peaceful, hopeful ends.[17] For him, the *TTP* demonstrates how people are better led not through fear (as in Hobbes or Machiavelli) but willing 'devotion', whose route is through the imagination and affects – as recognised and determined wise statesmen.[18] While this admirably ties together into a common project the politics of the *TTP* with the *Ethics* and later *Political Treatise*, it relies on consoling shared imaginings whose utility is in securing obedience to any kind of ruler. One could hopefully, if not devotedly, follow a tyrant after all, as we posed in Chapter 1.

More importantly, the view chafes against Spinoza's intellectualism elsewhere in his works, which strives to make everyone as knowledgeable as possible, and for which adequate ideas are pursued for their own sake, from which follows the 'greatest human perfection'.[19] The issue isn't Steinberg's reading but an underlying ambivalence in the text that any excellent interpretation will struggle to solidify. Why does Spinoza set aside one form of difficult, rare truth for philosophy concerned with the knowledge and love of God, and another form of accessible, imaginative beliefs concerned with obedience to universal precepts of justice and loving-kindness? If we are to consider them as two paths to a common kind of salvation, then for what use is the latter given its foundation in what Spinoza describes in the *Ethics* as the first kind of knowledge, being 'passive', 'confused', 'fragmented' and necessarily 'false'?[20] We'll get to those definitions in a moment.

This difficulty interests Michael LeBuffe, whose recent work also appraises the socially salutary effects of the former of the 'two kingdoms', theology. While both are concerned with restricting 'harmful passion', in his view, the power of theology is to provide people with a 'fixed plan' with which to live by, buffeted otherwise by the uncertain winds of fortune.[21] It draws on

---

[17] Steinberg 2018: 115–22.
[18] Ibid. 90.
[19] *TdIE* 14; *Ethics* V, 26; 27 Dem.; CWS I, 11; 608–9.
[20] II, 40 Schol. 2; 41; 477–8.
[21] LeBuffe 2018: 139–56.

singular objects and events like miracles to focus our imaginative and affective grasp on willingly obeying rules that aid our lives, ensuring peace and stability through which opportunities arise to cultivate reason. While the citizen may first be motivated by religious ideas, in 'the exercise of freedom, however, ideas of reason become more and more powerful'.[22] This mirrors somewhat the processes around the education of joy and collectivity in the previous chapters, though my emphasis has been on sociality and friendship for acquiring these ideas of reason. Indeed, the common notions arise out of peaceful encounters with others and the world around us, through affecting and being affected,[23] and a stable state offers a sound foundation from which journeys begin to discover knowledge in the fabric of the universe.

LeBuffe and Steinberg's accounts also benefit from their consistency with the *TP* with its psychological interest in politics, beginning with the word *Affectus* and concerned with treating people 'as they are' and not as we 'want them to be', whose passions can be understood in the same deductive spirit as meteorological phenomena.[24] But the *TTP* does not offer the same kind of political psychology, nor should we uncritically share this view of the political as inherently answerable to psychology, which seems a more modern preoccupation for political thought. Instead, I propose that we do not neglect the *TTP*'s political epistemology, concerned with ensuring the salvation of as many as possible, thereby tailoring the message of justice and loving-kindness in a medium the many can understand, through which the peaceful republic prospers.

*

It's useful to contextualise that political epistemology within the wider epistemology of the early *Ethics*, whose theory of the imagination in Part II remains largely consistent over this works and does not undergo substantial redevelopment from the earlier *Short Treatise*. In the *Ethics*, the nouns *imaginatio* (imagination) and *imago* (image) and verb *imaginari* (to imagine) refer to the mind's ability to perceive external bodies as present to us, even where such objects are not.[25] 'The human mind does not know the human body itself, nor does it know that it exists', he writes, 'except through ideas of affections by which the body is affected.'[26] These affections are often known

---

[22] Ibid. 172.
[23] *Ethics* IV, 38; CWS I, 568.
[24] *TP* I, 1; 4; CWS II, 503–5.
[25] E.g. *Ethics* II, 17 Schol.; 18; CWS I, 465; 466.
[26] II, 19; CWS I, 466.

to us as images. When we imagine, what our body perceives is not the external thing itself, but the way in which its body is affected by it. 'Although the external bodies by which the human body has once been affected neither exist nor are present, the mind will still be able to regard them as if they were present.'[27]

Thus memory, fantasy, hallucination and dreams all fall under the imagination,[28] bringing to us as present that which does not exist, like the image of the 'scabby Brazilian' in Chapter 2. These 'affections of the human body whose ideas present external bodies as present to us' he calls 'images of things'.[29] Spinoza adds that they are indicative of the body's own constitution rather than the direct nature of the object represented. In that same letter, Spinoza outlines to Balling his theory of the imagination. Images sensed by the body impress themselves upon us, leaving behind ideas or vivid 'traces', until another image is brought to disrupt that trace – for example, Spinoza's turn away from 'the same black man' to a book.[30] Spinoza will summon up a similarly physical image of the ideas in his mature account of the affects in terms of present-focused forces.

Spinoza also presents the imagination as being part of the first kind of knowledge which, alongside that 'opinion', is said to be 'mutilated' and 'confused'.[31] It arises out of the 'random experience' of encounters with other bodies, or from signs and symbols through which objects and ideas are recollected and perceived.[32] The imagination is described as a 'cause of falsity',[33] in contrast to the second (reason, *ratio*) and third kind (intuitive science, *scientia intuitiva*). These involve adequate knowledge and are 'necessarily true': the former of the properties of things, the latter of their essences.[34] The mind generates knowledge of the second kind through recognising common notions, identifying within a particular thing properties and general principles that it shares with others. We explored this in terms of its collectivity in Chapter 4, but we should appreciate that here it refers to what's internal to an individual mind.

The effect of such knowledge is to conceive a given object not merely through one's own subjective relation to it (as in the first kind), but to

[27] II, 17 Cor.; CWS I, 464.
[28] II, 18 Schol.; CWS I, 465–6.
[29] II, 17 Schol.; CWS I, 465.
[30] *Ep.* XVII [to Pieter Balling]; CWS I, 353.
[31] *Ethics* II, 40 Schol. 2; CWS I, 477.
[32] II, 29 Schol.; CWS I, 471.
[33] II, 41; CWS I, 478.
[34] Following II, 40 Schol. 2; CWS I, 478.

understand it in its own right, as something necessarily arising from God or nature. Thus 'all ideas, insofar as they are related to God, are true'.[35] By contrast, the first kind of knowledge is necessarily inadequate and passive, given that we cannot be a cause of the representations with which we are presented, and in which their cause is often not apparent to the senses. Given that most people, in Spinoza's view, 'do not know themselves',[36] or have adequate knowledge of the causes of their ideas, we are wont to imagine our own purposes and advantages in nature, leading to an anthropomorphic view of nature as created for us by a human-like God.[37] This has debilitating consequences for philosophy, as communities compete to seek favour from human-like deities which serves to make nature 'as mad as men', and from which beliefs in superstitious omens and clairvoyance arise, as explored in Chapter 1. Hence the *TTP* chides those who rely on 'the delusions of the imagination',[38] particularly the prophets, whose 'random and inconstant' nature renders prophecy 'inferior to natural knowledge'.[39]

Yet the value of the imagination mustn't be understated. On an elementary level, without it we would lack knowledge of our body or the external world, and most of our everyday mental representations fall under its category. Spinoza observes degrees of power in our ability to imagine, reflecting our own functional complexity,[40] indicating that some imaginings (and imaginations) can enrich the good life. Moreover, the affects, which operate through the imagination, occupy a decisive role in the mature Spinoza's ethics: sad passions can only be overcome by stronger passions, and Spinoza writes that the mind strives to imagine what will increase its power of acting.[41] Thus, while the imagination itself is necessarily partial and inadequate, its nature must be understood, utilised and maximised by the philosopher who seeks the good life, and who seeks to persuade those around them to live according to 'justice and loving-kindness'. Garver describes this as the 'cunning' of the imagination – that while we are naturally drawn to each other to increase the power of our bodies, so the imaginings and joyous affects that follow can lead by the 'backdoor' to empowerment and adequate ideas.[42]

---

[35] II, 32; CWS I, 472.
[36] *TTP* Praef., 2; CWS II, 66.
[37] Ibid.; *Ethics* I, App.; CWS I, 439–46.
[38] *TTP* Praef., 4; CWS II, 66.
[39] *TTP* Praef., 4; I, 47; II, 6; CWS II, 66; 93; 95.
[40] *Ethics* II, 13; CWS I, 460–1.
[41] III, 12 Schol.; CWS I, 502.
[42] Garver 2018: 100, 219.

The question remains whether knowledge of the imagination alone is enough. The Appendix makes clear that the danger arises when men 'mistake their imagination for intellect', while we should recall that the ideas of the imagination are also said to be confused or incomplete because they belong to a single body, and cannot represent the true causal order of nature, only its subordinate and passive parts. Nor, at this stage, should we give the imagination too much liberatory scope. Even empowering imaginings – that is, those the mind uses to boost its powers after *Ethics* III, 12 – will not get us closer to a true knowledge of nature if we remain just in a world of images. In other words, while they might enable us to experience more joy and peace, they can – as Garver says of the universal faith – so satisfy our minds that we do not strive to replace them with adequate ideas.[43]

At this stage, the question remains why Spinoza did not endorse the authority of philosophy itself, as his friend Lodewijk Meyer had, following Maimonides, in making reason the right interpreter of scripture.[44] In his insistence on the equal but different domains of philosophy and theology, or intellect and imagination, and on the socially salutary effects of doctrines of obedience, Spinoza's account focused not on statesmen per se, but prophets. For all the problems with prophecy that he raises, and his wry scepticism about the decline of prophecy in his own times, prophecy seems to have had some success where philosophy cannot, in instilling ideas of justice and loving-kindness that are *in line with* our common tendency to anthropomorphise and observe final causes in nature. These are the natural 'prejudices' we inevitably fall into as the Appendix to *Ethics* Part I presents. Precepts capable of cats, not just lions.

While the *Ethics* proceeds in geometrical order to demonstrate a philosophical path to the intellectual love of God, the *TTP* contrasts methods of 'mathematical' certainty, 'which follows from the necessity of the perception of the thing perceived or seen', with that of prophecy, whose certainty is 'moral', and whose end is that 'men become blessed by obedience and faith'.[45] The *TTP*'s political epistemology can be considered as a logical step from the problems of the Appendix, presenting a form of salvation for those otherwise unable to think by the exacting standards of the *Ethics*. 'Everyone, without exception, can obey', he writes, but 'only a very few [. . .] acquire a

---

[43] Ibid. 103.
[44] Meyer's *Philosophy the Interpreter of Holy Scripture* was published in 1666, and subsequently banned with the *TTP* by the States of Holland in 1674 along with the *TTP* and Hobbes's *Leviathan*.
[45] *TTP* II, 12; XV, 34; CWS II, 97; 280.

habit of virtue from the guidance of reason alone. So, if we didn't have this testimony of Scripture, we would doubt nearly everyone's salvation.'[46] But Spinoza's remark doesn't dispel all our earlier concerns. What about those who do not believe in Judeo-Christian scripture, but 'whose powers are not strong' to grasp philosophical knowledge of God?[47] Or what about those who utilise imagistic and affective means to mobilise the many to compel willing obedience to regimes that are despotic and unstable? What assurances can Spinoza's account of the two domains offer given its reliance on imagination, necessarily errant and inadequate? To determine these questions and assess the precise role of theology in Spinoza's political epistemology, I want to now explore the peculiar uses of prophecy, before contrasting it with the universal truth said to come from Jesus Christ, who occupies a median place between prophet and philosopher.

True Prophets

One of the expressed aims of the *TTP* is to separate philosophy from theology, demarcating the proper bounds of each. The freedom to philosophise involves such boundary-setting. Spinoza's letter to Oldenburg sets out to defend this freedom and remove the 'prejudices of the theologians' which prevent men from 'being able to apply their minds to philosophy'.[48] But we'll recall our discussion early in the last chapter about Spinoza's concern about dispelling his reputation among the common people for 'atheism' – an important consideration both for personal safety and for the successful publication of the *Ethics*, upon which work had begun at least three years earlier.[49] Likewise, while the Preface takes aim at the foundation of servitude in the fear and superstition of the common people, its ire is directed against the 'real schismatics' and 'troublemakers', or the ambitious clerics who willingly manipulate the fear of the *vulgus* for their own political advantage, as well as allied would-be monarchs in their midst.[50] By contrast, Spinoza sets out a method of naturalistic, historico-political analysis of special revelation and

---

[46] XV, 45; CWS II, 282.
[47] XV, 37; CWS II, 280.
[48] *Ep.* XXX [to Henry Oldenburg]; CWS II, 14.
[49] For a good survey of the *TTP*'s historical context, see Israel 2001: chs 10–11, James 2012: ch. 1 and Malcolm 2002: 44–52.
[50] *TTP* XX, 42; CWS II, 352. A knowing nod to the growing political allegiance between Prince William I of Orange and hardliners within the Dutch Reformed Church opposed to the liberal republicanism of its stadtholder and regents; Spinoza draws on the controversy around the Synod of Dort in the previous paragraph (XX, 41).

scripture 'with an unprejudiced and free spirit', affirming 'nothing about it, and to admit nothing as its teaching, which it did not very clearly teach me'.[51]

In asserting that 'Scripture leaves reason absolutely free' and 'has nothing in common with philosophy', Spinoza was rejecting the 'dogmatists' like his friend Meyer, or Maimonides, an important influence upon the work, which read scripture as a philosophical text that is consistent with reason.[52] Spinoza was also rejecting the 'skeptics' like Alfakhar,[53] a contemporary of Maimonides, and contemporary Calvinists by proxy, who emphasise scriptural infallibility and faith over reason. Instead, the 'revealed word of God' would not be found in certain books or textual passages but in the lessons of the prophets, to obey God with all one's mind by practising justice and loving-kindness. This is the end of both philosophy and theology; their means to it differ vastly, the former demonstrated by reason through the common notions and intelligible to all with sufficient understanding (as per the quote that prefaced the last section), the latter upon the imagination of prophets, which instils willing obedience to these precepts in the common people.

The above gloss reflects the twofold political epistemology of the *TTP*, but the account is still troubled by some of those disquieting issues around the social good of such an epistemically weak, false and unreliable knowledge pondered earlier. For the imagination can also become the basis for prejudice, superstition and mass fear, manipulated by those who seek to bring us back to our 'ancient servitude' explored in Chapter 1. The analysis of prophecy in the *TTP*'s first two chapters brings little relief. The first defines prophecy as 'certain knowledge of some matter which God has revealed to men', and then goes on to argue why natural knowledge presents a more reliable basis for understanding God (and is indeed 'divine') than that possessed by a prophet.[54] The prophet's revelation depends on the imagination alone, which is 'random and inconstant', resulting in a vast number of contrary descriptions of God.[55] Chapter 2 states that prophecy is 'inferior to natural knowledge', and warns that 'those who eagerly search the Prophetic books for wisdom, and knowledge of both natural and spiritual matters, go completely astray'.[56] It would seem by Spinoza's reasoning that prophecy is an

---

[51] Praef., 20; CWS II, 72.
[52] Praef., 24; XV, 1; 4; CWS II, 72; 272; 272.
[53] XV, 5; CWS II, 273.
[54] I, 31; 33; CWS II, 76; 77.
[55] I, 47; cf. 46; II, 19–23; CWS II, 93; 98–100.
[56] II, 6; 2; CWS II, 95; 94.

inferior, obsolete, if not dangerous basis for knowledge. Our highest good is in 'the knowledge and love of God', and consequently God's commands are simply the 'means required' to realise this in human actions, and the 'rule of life' this entails is divine law.[57] Given that these are naturally intelligible, all that the worship of God truly requires is a sound understanding.

Yet this is beyond what most human beings can achieve, without sufficient education, maturity, motivation and social stability. This judgement upon the necessarily diminished capabilities of much of humankind cannot be understated in the *TTP*. The virtue of prophets is their persuasiveness. The prophets 'had a singular virtue, beyond what is ordinary', and 'cultivated piety with exceptional constancy of heart'.[58] What they lacked in philosophical reasoning, they made up for in vividness of imagination. What distinguishes a true prophet from a false one, then, is not the content of their vision, but the social consequences of their doctrine, which must be directed by 'a heart inclined only to the right and the good',[59] or 'piety and constancy'.[60] For while reason 'seems to show that prophecy and revelation are very doubtful', its 'certainty' and 'authority' over scripture lies in its commendation of 'loving-kindness and justice above all'.[61] Against Maimonides and Meyer, the truth of prophecy isn't to explain things through their natural causes (the domain of philosophy), but to 'fill the imagination' and 'impress devotion in the hearts of the common people', to 'make them obedient, not learned' – in other words, in its socially salutary effects.[62]

Through this argument, Spinoza may be drawing on an earlier tradition in Maimonides, further back into the Islamic Neoplatonic philosophy of Al-Farabi and Ibn Sina (Avicenna), wherein the prophet possesses both a perfected intellect and a perfected imagination.[63] For Farabi, the imaginative faculty concerns only sensibles, whereas the Active Intellect concerns forms, or in Spinoza's terms, God's necessary laws.[64] For Maimonides, prophetic vision comes through the intellect but requires strong imaginative powers to bring forth its doctrine. 'Prophecy is, in truth', he says, 'an emana-

[57] IV, 14; CWS II, 128.
[58] I, 40; 25; CWS II, 91; 85.
[59] II, 10; CWS II, 96. It is 'the chief thing' among three considerations on prophecy, the others being a vivid imagination and the use of a miraculous sign.
[60] II, 31; CWS II, 102.
[61] II, 8; 6; XV, 29; 34; CWS II, 95; ibid.; 279; 280.
[62] VI, 44; XIII, 26; CWS II, 162; 262.
[63] Cf. Maimonides 1963b: 2.36–7.
[64] For further, see Kreisel 2001: 241–6, and Pines's introductory essay in Maimonides 1963a: xc–xcii.

tion sent forth by the Divine Being through the medium of the active intellect', and is 'the highest degree and greatest perfection man can attain'.[65] Spinoza's commitment to a philosophical blessedness cannot agree, nor does the *TTP* share its estimation of the philosophical powers of the prophet. Instead, it may well be that this earlier elevation of the prophet served as a useful theoretical resource for Spinoza to position the truth of the prophet in justice and loving-kindness.

Is this ultimately what such truth amounts to, then? A cluster of readings endorsing the salutary role of the imagination in political thought suggest as much. Susan James calls Spinoza a 'social epistemologist' in this regard: the truth that the prophet communicates is in the social behaviours they encourage, namely 'to love and live in a steadily cooperative fashion'.[66] But a Christian dictum like *love thy neighbour* will not move the minds of many unless one can recognise another as a valid peer or equal, and the importance of engendering this underlying sense of commonality (or shared awareness of being of a common nature with another) comes prior to the mutual assistance that James identifies. Albeit unconsciously, the true prophet must also supply what Gatens and Lloyd call 'socially shared fictions' – illusions that administer real effects in producing a set of ideas individuals share in, becoming or remaining some form of community in the process, and are instrumentally true in the shared good they realise.[67] According to this reading, these are not socially convenient fictions with which the masses are duped, but vivid, emotional narratives in which individuals share and participate. There should be some reservations about the adoption of the term 'fiction' – its implied view of the socially constructed nature of truth is at odds with Spinoza's stringent arguments for the intelligibility of nature according to reason. Nonetheless, these ideas lead to the consideration of prophecy as containing some intrinsic rationality in the socially beneficial effects its teachings realise. But take note of the regular emphasis on effects: Spinoza does not imply anywhere that there is any inherent truth in the prophet's dreams and visions, which are necessarily confused and fragmentary, like all ideas of the imagination.

This is reflected in how Spinoza describes piety (*pietas*, sometimes translated as 'morality') in the *TTP*, which is frequently endorsed, and associated with justice and loving-kindness. In the *Ethics*, it's described as 'the desire to do good generated in us by our living according to the guidance of reason'.[68]

[65] Maimonides 1963b: 2.36.
[66] James 2011: 187.
[67] Gatens and Lloyd 1999: 124.
[68] *Ethics* IV, 37 Schol. 1; CWS I, 565.

Chapter 3 introduces Moses to indicate what this *pietas* or morality amounts to: a law-abiding behaviour which enhances the common good and enables a community to 'liv[e] securely and healthily'.[69] This accomplishment is dependent upon many external causes, and best realised by the guidance of 'wise and vigilant' leaders, whose abilities lie in their understanding of the socio-cultural 'character' (*ingenia*) of the people, and in their commitment to the common good of the subjects. While not a philosopher, the knowledge of a prophet like Moses is demonstrated through the design and organisation of the State according to the dictates of reason, and in his use of imagistic devices to address and enlist his varied subjects. For Spinoza, truth is available to all and is enveloped throughout nature, and the prophet recognises that human beings depend on each other to survive, yet oppose and endanger each other by their passionate, self-interested behaviour.[70] Likewise, some people can have their hopes and fears used by ambitious figures to present themselves as defenders of the public good by persecuting unprotected minorities. Spinoza fears, just as the *vulgus* fears. Utilising their social epistemology of the hearts of the people, and understanding indirectly the three laws of politics of Chapter 2, the prophet presents compelling narratives that persuade many to act according to the dictates of reason[71] – which is to say, cooperatively and peacefully, and not wholly out of fear, but devotion.[72] While this does not make these ideas of the imagination inherently rational – for those whose devotion to justice and loving-kindness is compelled by such visions, they remain passive to them and their knowledge is inadequate, partial – its consequences are in accordance with the dictates of reason.

Moses is the exemplary prophet, in Spinoza's account. He demonstrates a sound knowledge of human nature and politics as a legislator and statesman, devising laws that brought together the stateless, recently enslaved Hebrew people with a series of commands and a group identity as a nation and 'God's chosen people', accessible to their weakened condition and 'childish power of understanding'.[73] This emphasis on willingness and devotion for obedience is interesting, and is what Steinberg highlighted earlier. In one way, it seems to be a central plank of Spinoza's political thought, for laws based on fear will be experienced as a burden, and will be disobeyed as soon as the authority

[69] *TTP* III, 12; *CWS* II, 113.
[70] V, 18; 21; *CWS* II, 143; 144.
[71] *TP* V, 23; *CWS* II, 516.
[72] *TTP* VI, 44; *CWS* II, 162; cf. *Ethics* IV, 54 Schol.; *CWS* I, 576.
[73] *TTP* II, 47; III, 6; *CWS* II, 107; 112.

appears weak or absent.[74] By contrast, laws that involve the 'hope of some good they [the subjects] desire very much' are most effective, for each person 'will do his duty eagerly'.[75] Likewise, in his discussion of miracles, Spinoza argues that the value of scripture is not to 'teach things through their natural causes' but to 'increase wonder' and, consequently, 'impress devotion in the hearts of the common people'.[76] This involves using phrases and ideas that 'can most effectively move people (especially, ordinary people) to devotion'.[77]

In this respect, scripture 'speaks quite improperly concerning God and things', he claims, 'because its concern is not to convince people's reason, but to affect and fill their fantasy and imagination'.[78] While Steinberg and others understandably highlight the societal goods that follow from such 'hope-willingness', it is important to contextualise these arguments within the two separate domains of philosophy and theology, and recall that such devotion is founded upon ideas of the imagination, not the intellect.[79] While its effects can be beneficial, where concerned with an obedience to the common good, Spinoza is careful to remind readers that such representations should not be confused with things understood from the 'natural light'.[80] For the wise, knowledge arises when 'they judge things from the perceptions of the pure intellect, and not as the imagination is affected by the external senses'.[81] The latter is often associated with the reasoning of the common people (*vulgus*), who anthropomorphise God and come to experience God's universal and immutable laws (or the dictates of reason) as a great 'burden'.[82] For them, such freedom appears as servitude. Thus, the merit of miracles, prophetic revelation and other 'imaginary things' is their ability to affect as many as possible. 'It is to these and similar opinions', he writes, 'that a great many events in Scripture are adapted, which therefore ought not to be accepted by the philosophers as real.'[83]

Towards the close of the *TTP*, Spinoza warns against allowing prophets any liberty. The prophets, 'as private men' (an important distinction),

---

[74] V, 22; CWS II, 144.
[75] V, 24; CWS II, 144.
[76] VI, 44; CWS II, 162.
[77] VI, 49; CWS II, 163.
[78] Ibid. repeated XIII, 26; CWS II, 262.
[79] Steinberg 2018: 82.
[80] *TTP* XV, 44; CWS II, 281.
[81] VI, 58; CWS II, 165. This clear distinction between imagination and intellect, appearing more subtly elsewhere in the *TTP*, also bears the influence of Maimonides.
[82] *Ethics* V, 41 Schol.; CWS I, 616.
[83] *TTP* VI, 58; CWS II, 166.

'aggravated people more than they corrected them by the freedom with which they warned, reproached and censured them'.[84] He notes that the number of prophets greatly increased during the Kingdom(s) of Israel, and rightly warns how such ambitious, ignorant figures usurp what is universal knowledge, the knowledge of God, and use it to terrorise and dominate others. For if the prophets did serve a use, that use has now passed. The imaginative processes of prophecy can just as easily be used for the purposes of deception and exacerbating anger and fear, which weakens civil society. They are part and parcel of the 'ceremony and pomp' of religions which support and sanctify the rule of bloodthirsty despots,[85] and which can take over and subjugate the minds of many. Presenting oneself as God's messenger has long characterised 'false' prophets, from Zedekiah and the 400 who misled King Ahab,[86] to the Ottoman Turks associated with religious and political despotism.[87] The sheer difficulty of determining true prophecy from false is a recurring area of dispute in Christian and Jewish scholarship, exacerbated by the tendency of many self-declared prophets to attack existing religious institutions. Like Maimonides, Spinoza notes that, 'today, so far as I know, we have no Prophets'.[88] There's more than a hint of irony in the comment, but its meaning is elucidated when we consider the role of Jesus Christ as a prophet and a philosopher. By Spinoza's outline, Christ has also made all prior prophecy obsolete. Let's consider why.

Jesus Christ, Prophet–Philosopher

Christ appears sparingly throughout the *TTP*, but where he does, he occupies a position between prophet and philosopher. Whereas the prophets grasped the common good only indirectly, and through fragmentary bodily images, the Christ of the *TTP* understands that the 'divine law' is but the totality of reason. Thus 'God sent to all nations his Christ, who would free all equally from servitude to the [externally-imposed] law' (translation modified), inscribing universally true principles 'thoroughly in their hearts'.[89] Unlike the true prophets, Christ's virtue is in the ability to make others think and act more adequately. This universality is key. Christ presents the

---

[84] XVIII, 13; CWS II, 325.
[85] Praef., 9; CWS II, 68.
[86] 1 Kings 22:1–40; *TTP* II, 7; CWS II, 95.
[87] E.g. *TTP* Praef., 9; CWS II, 68; *TP* VI, 4; VII, 23; CWS II, 533; 555.
[88] Maimonides 1963b: 2.36; *TTP* I, 7; CWS II, 78.
[89] III, 45; IV, 34; CWS II, 121; 134.

divine law to all nations, not just the Jews. Moreover, in revealing its core message – justice and loving-kindness – the divine law becomes internalised, and, as Balibar describes, '*always immediately available*'.[90] A similar argument was being made at the same time by the Quakers, Collegiants and Socinians – every man can establish a true and personal knowledge of God.

Yet Christ's power as a philosopher shouldn't be overstated. The *TTP* describes him as teaching according to the affective predispositions of the audience, teaching obscurely through parables when faced with 'the people's [*populus*] ignorance and stubbornness', accommodating himself to the 'mentality' (*ingenium*) of his audience.[91] The same applies to Christ's claim to perform miracles like healing a blind man, which otherwise the *TTP* tends to be quiet if not dubious about.[92] 'I must warn here that I'm not speaking in any way about the things some of the churches maintain about Christ', he writes. 'Not that I deny them. For I readily confess I don't grasp them.'[93] Christ recognises that salvation through reason is impossible for the passion-led *vulgus*, and so, like the prophets before him, uses an image of God as a lawgiver. But to those capable of knowing 'the mysteries of the heavens', he teaches in terms of eternal truths 'and did not prescribe them as laws'.[94] To use our distinction of earlier, for some he works through the imagination, and for others through the intellect.

Unlike the prophet, whose imaginings help individuals to join forces or remain together as communities, Christ's message potentially extends our commonality beyond the narrow limits of ethnic, national or other physically or socially defined communities, and towards a universal collectivity of humanity – what early Christians would call *philadelphia*, brotherly love.

---

[90] Balibar 2008: 42.
[91] IV, 33; cf. II, 56, in terms of the Apostles, and VII, 32; CWS II, 133; 110; 177.
[92] VI, 47; CWS II, 162.
[93] I, 24; CWS II, 84. Oldenburg would challenge him to 'reveal clearly' his thinking about Christ's divinity, where Spinoza is blunter (*Ep*. LXXI [from Oldenburg]; *Ep*. LXXIII [Spinoza's reply]; CWS II, 464–5; 467–8. Curley gives a good discussion of Christ's heterodox position in Spinoza 2016: 53–5. Hunter (2005) poses whether Spinoza was in fact a radical Protestant, something for which I don't find enough evidence. Matheron is also responsible for a second major study of Spinoza, this time of Christ's salvation of the ignorant through obedience (1971). He argues for Christ as principally a philosopher with intuitive knowledge, who sought not to manipulate but to elevate the capacities of the people (e.g. 1971: 97). While it usefully highlights the importance of obedience in Spinoza (as does Steinberg's monograph, discussed earlier), this glosses over his prophet-like reliance on parables. Van Cauter (2016: 158) provides a good, nuanced overview of Matheron's position and wider debates.
[94] *TTP* IV, 34; CWS II, 133.

Spinoza uses this universalist distinction to then explain the division of the Old and New Testament, which might otherwise be explained easily enough by his historico-political analysis of religion: 'before the coming of Christ the prophets were accustomed to preach religion as the law of their country [. . .] but after the coming of Christ the Apostles preached the same to everyone as a universal law'.[95] But do Christ's teachings do enough to raise the *vulgus* beyond a passionate and imagistic (i.e. inadequate) understanding of nature? Garver would argue that this still 'bootstraps' the imagination to what is ultimately empowering, but I don't think it goes far enough in itself for human freedom. Spinoza's Christ has no intention of making the *vulgus* more free and self-determined. We could describe him as a collectivist philosopher, but one whose processes establish communities of the imagination, not collectives of rational understanding. But as a prophet who exemplifies the very best of the possibilities of imagination and faith, Spinoza would have no problem with that.

We can observe a similar process with another of Spinoza's devices for making faith think, as it were, by bringing about reasonable effects that result in societal harmony. In Chapter 14 of the *TTP*, Spinoza sets out to reestablish faith as something entirely separate from philosophy. As he writes, 'faith requires not so much true as pious dogmas, that is, such tenets as move the mind to obedience, even though many of these may not have a shadow of truth in them'.[96] Whereas philosophy is defined by 'universal concepts' whose aim is 'nothing but truth', guided by the dictates of reason, faith aims at nothing more than 'obedience and piety', and has its foundations in 'histories and language'.[97] He therefore sets out seven basic tenets of a universal faith (*fidei universalis*) that should be promoted by the State's supreme power in order to establish piety:

1. God exists, i.e., there is a supreme being, supremely just and merciful, or a model of true life. Anyone who doesn't know, or doesn't believe, that God exists cannot obey him or know him as a judge.
2. He is unique. [. . .]
3. He is present everywhere, or everything is open to him. [. . .]
4. He has the supreme right and dominion over all things, and does nothing because he is compelled by a law, but acts only according to his absolute good pleasure and special grace. [. . .]

---

[95] XII, 24; CWS II, 253.
[96] XIV, 8; CWS II, 265.
[97] XIV, 38; CWS II, 271.

5. The worship of God and obedience to him consist only in justice and loving-kindness, or in love toward one's neighbour;
6. Everyone who obeys God by living in this way is saved; the rest, who live under the control of the pleasures, are lost. [. . .]
7. Finally, God pardons the sins of those who repent.[98]

Indeed, throughout the previous chapter, Spinoza reiterates that the Bible 'requires nothing of men other than obedience', an obedience that consists in loving one's neighbour, and acting justly, charitably and cooperatively, as we've explored.[99] Significantly, this is the goal of Spinoza's social epistemology. It's through this that we can evaluate the 'truth' of true prophecy, which lies in its effects. For Spinoza, it is unrealistic to expect eternal truths to motivate when they are beyond the ken of many. Instead the imagination has served, after Maimonides, to motivate willing belief that is good for everyone. However, unlike Maimonides or Meyer, the tenets of the faith are not on themselves reasonable grounds, for instance a belief in an anthropomorphic, just and merciful being that Spinoza plainly refutes elsewhere.[100] The universal faith instead emphasises good works alone – justice, charity and loving-kindness. It allows 'everyone the greatest freedom to philosophize', and interpret scripture as they wish, so long as they do not harm others – a potent antidote to Calvinist orthodoxy, with its emphasis on divine election, grace and faith.[101]

The seven dogmas also supply imaginative, accessible means by which all can willingly obey what Spinoza later calls the 'supreme law' (*lex*) of the common good.[102] It is a 'path to salvation' available to all, beyond the 'very few [. . .] who acquire the habit of virtue by the guidance of reason alone', our lions of earlier, and who would already be socialised into such a belief system in the first place.[103] Where does this take us, then, to our earlier distinction of the imagination and the intellect? It seems to reflect the Spinozist view of two registers of human flourishing: the imagination and the intellect, akin to the distinction between theology and philosophy, which Spinoza seeks to preserve as an aim of the book. Spinoza's view is grounded on a political realism that philosophy for all isn't a viable expectation.

---

[98] XIV, 25–8; CWS II, 268–9.
[99] XIII, 3; cf. XIV, 3; CWS II, 257; 264.
[100] XIV, 28; CWS II, 269; *Ethics* I, App.; CWS I, 441.
[101] *TTP* XIV, 39; CWS II, 271.
[102] XVI, 10; XIX, 24; CWS II, 284; 337.
[103] XV, 45; CWS II, 282.

This is reflected in the explanation of the seventh teaching of the universal faith, which presents an anthropomorphic view of a forgiving God inconsistent with the view of Part I Appendix. 'So if we did not maintain this', he explains, 'everyone would despair of his salvation, and there would be no reason why anyone would believe God to be merciful.'[104] In other words, the motivation for adhering to justice and loving-kindness would be lost if there were no transcendent guarantee for it. He continues:

> Moreover, whoever firmly believes that God, out of mercy and the grace by which he directs everything, pardons men's sins, and who for this reason is more inspired by the love of God, that person really knows Christ according to the spirit, and Christ is in him.[105]

At the same time, like the philosophy of Christ, Spinoza's reasoning binds him to promoting conditions that can only partially liberate the *vulgus*. That's intentional – the theology/philosophy distinction reflects Spinoza's view that it's unrealistic to expect the many to be able or willing to live according to the demanding conditions of philosophy. Hence we turn to the prophets, who in the *Ethics* are hailed for their use of the sad passions of repentance and humility which, though harmful in themselves, benefit society when used to guide others to act in accordance with reason.[106]

It also extends beyond the Christian tradition who might be considered a prophet – something that irked one Cartesian philosopher, Lambert van Velthuysen, who attacked Spinoza by letter for implying that the Prophet Muhammad could be a true philosopher. 'If he should reply that Muhammad also taught the divine law and gave certain signs of his mission, as the other prophets did', Spinoza replies, 'there will surely be no reason why he should deny that Muhammad was a true prophet.'[107] Further, if his followers 'worship God with the practice of justice and loving-kindness toward their neighbour, I believe they have the spirit of Christ and are saved'. Such views would undoubtedly scandalise Christian readers, who viewed the Ottoman Empire and Islam more widely as an existential threat up until their eventual defeat by combined Christian forces in the late seventeenth century. And indeed elsewhere Spinoza seems to make some broader provocative equivalences. 'Long ago things reached the point where you can hardly know

---

[104] XIV, 28; CWS II, 269.
[105] XIV, 27; CWS II, 269.
[106] *Ethics* IV, 54 Schol.; CWS I, 576.
[107] Ep. XLIII [to Jacob Ostens]; CWS II, 389.

what anyone is, whether Christian, Turk, Jew, or Pagan', he writes in the *TTP* Preface, except by the external dress and adornment of his body, or because he frequents this or that place of worship'.[108] For one downside of such prophets (or rather, their followers) who bring together a wide range of people into one community is that this grouping then tends to define itself against all others, be it in dress, place of worship, or language and customs like those the *TTP* analyses of the Jewish people. Such is the dangerous limitation of communities of faith but not of philosophy. So, while Christ (as a philosopher) was a collectivist, the Church could only ever be communitarian. In Spinoza's time, as the Preface of the *TTP* sees it, Christ's philosophy had become buried in theological prattling, while no state looked to come close to installing a universal faith of the kind Spinoza imagines here.

In the last place, it's worth thinking about what the *TTP* proposes as a part of its refoundation of politics within the theology/philosophy distinction. In Chapter 16, Spinoza presents among his political laws that democracy is the most natural and absolute form of government. Here, as men gather in assemblies, ideas and opinions can be voiced and concord established, as a collective agrees and determines the most reasonable course of action to pursue its shared interests. That also requires free speech and religious toleration. Yet if the *vulgus* are to be left to faith and theology, and their intellectual and bodily development left somewhat neglected in favour of parables and prayer, then that can't fully address the fear or anger they feel, particularly at times of war and civil upheaval, like that of the 1660s and the wars against England, or the constitutional fissuring of the United Provinces between the liberal republicanism of Grand Pensionary Johan De Witt and some of the city regents, and the conservative monarchism of William III of Orange and his supporters in the Calvinist Church.[109] Spinoza's programme would not be enough.

A Collectivity to Come

In *The Arcades Project*, Walter Benjamin characterises the nineteenth century as a 'singular fusion of individualistic and collectivist tendencies'. While the

---

[108] *TTP* Praef., 14; CWS II, 70.
[109] Further aggravated by De Witt's abolition of the office of *stadhouder* in the Perpetual Edict of 1667, traditionally held by a member of the House of Orange. This only served to amplify Orangist unrest, particularly among provinces of the States-General that voted against the Edict, like Zeeland, Friesland and Groningen. We'll follow the unfolding constitutional crisis at the start of the next chapter.

former concept is largely phantasmagorical, the latter is fundamental, and Benjamin is a rich interlocutor to think through some of the problems of collectivity sketched in this chapter. First, on individuality. Unlike all previous eras, the nineteenth century 'labels all actions "individualistic" [...] while subterraneanly, in despised everyday domains, it necessarily furnishes, as in a delirium, the elements for a collective formation'.[110] One could call this concept of individualism a 'superstition', in the terms Spinoza used in Chapter 1, in that it provides a false belief about our self-autonomy in a necessarily social and interdependent world. This can be especially devastating when individuals are disempowered by adverse circumstances, sad passions or deserted of human companionship, and in turn perpetuate these by retreating inwards. It obscures how friends, allies and loved ones nurture us and make our worlds.

By contrast, how might we recognise a 'collective formation'? This point becomes clearer in Benjamin's work on Baudelaire. Here he sketches a concept of 'collective desire' as something that seeks to transcend the 'deficiencies of the social order of production' that otherwise attempt to defeat the promise of the 'new' by commodifying it.[111] Against this individualising, commodifying imperative, he identifies a revolutionary concept of a dormant collectivity and its desire, which takes the form of 'images in the collective consciousness', of a memory of the ancient past which releases hope for a utopian future, 'in which the new is permeated with the old', and in which primal history furnishes the possibility of a return to a classless society, and a call for a collectivity to come'.

Beyond descriptions of the 'collective unconscious' or the 'collective dream' in *The Arcades Project*, we do not find a political outline of this collectivity in Benjamin.[112] It provokes a stern response from Theodor Adorno, who by letter dismissed it as a quasi-Jungian 'archaic collective ego'.[113] The historical subject that would transcend capitalism, the proletariat, was here recast as a dream. Adorno's difficulty with Benjamin's conceptual critique of individualism reveals a broader issue in the thinking of collectivity. As has been argued over the last two chapters, the project of collective empowerment is essential for the individual's freedom and for building effective political movements. Therefore, establishing ways for individuals to recognise

---

[110] Benjamin 1999: 390.
[111] Benjamin 2006: 32.
[112] E.g. 1999: 4, 11, 64, 152, 212, 389–91, 399, 405, 546, 828, 842, 854–5. For more on Benjamin and collectivity, see Lunn 1982: 162–3, and Gelley 2015: xii.
[113] In Lunn 1982: 165; the influence of Durkheim goes uncommented on.

their common nature with others and act in solidarity is of primary concern. Yet that recognition isn't likely to occur spontaneously among everyone. It requires a figurehead or a social or political movement to organise around. Or, it may require a state-wide and state-led education in citizenship.

Georg Lukács, a contemporary of Benjamin though more concerned with the practicalities of political organisation, gives an instrumental account of *becoming conscious* as a stage in collective political mobilisation. In a discussion of the Russian Revolution, he observes that the 'the vague and abstract concept of "the people" had to be rejected, but only so that a revolutionary, discriminating, concept of "the people" – *the revolutionary alliance of the oppressed* – could develop'.[114] Not merely semantics, Lukács observed a redefinition of a vague Enlightenment notion into the more affectively concrete form of the oppressed: a category of individuals brutalised by poverty and hunger amid the war and violence of the tsarist state, which could easily recognise themselves *as* and others *of* the oppressed. Hence, '*only the practical class consciousness of the proletariat* possesses this ability to transform things'.[115] The emergence of their class consciousness is akin to an individual becoming self-determining in their desire, in Spinoza. Where once they were only a passive cause of their action or thought, in coming to recognise (via the assistance of others) the nature of the desire and its effects, they leave behind their isolation and acquire a new understanding of this desire, and a new activity and corresponding joy in realising this desire by themselves.

The question remains how individuals become conscious of their common nature and act in solidarity. For Lukács, such a class consciousness (like that of the revolutionary alliance of the oppressed) can only succeed in realising itself and becoming revolutionary when it overcomes the ideological fetters of individualism. It is a matter of desire – one that seeks to transcend 'the immediacy of empirical reality' into a communist collective unity.[116] Towards the end of *History and Class Consciousness* he argues that the '*conscious* desire for the realm of freedom' is one that necessarily entails 'consciously taking the steps that will really lead to it'.[117] Yet this is not a freedom of the isolated individual, for in 'contemporary bourgeois society individual freedom can only be corrupt and corrupting because it is a case of unilateral privilege based on the unfreedom of others', through unequal relations of private property. This conscious desire therefore renounces individual freedom

[114] Lukács 2009: 22–3.
[115] Ibid. 205.
[116] Lukács 1971: 162.
[117] Ibid. 315.

as presently offered, embracing instead an interdependent and communal identity that makes a 'reality' of the freedom of the individual, in empowering all collectively. Such a freedom requires the 'conscious subordination of the self to that collective will', which to many will smack of Rousseau, and all the attendant problems of the general will where 'man must be forced to be free'.[118]

For Lukács and Benjamin, then, cultivating a shared consciousness is inherently empowering, as an alliance of the oppressed organises the isolated and indignant into a mutually strengthening bond. Both also argued that this alliance (or party) would only succeed by attempting to divest people of their individualist self-perceptions, harmful ideas that 'enlisted' desires and left them in a state of anxious and docile servitude. But as Adorno asked of Benjamin, above, to what extent can such a collective alliance act and think as an individual? And to what extent should it? Like desire, while collectivity can be a foundation of empowerment, it is not necessarily empowering.

For Spinoza, a shared sense of commonality is a prerequisite for a collective to freely desire what correlates to its common good. Rarely does this faculty emerge fully developed in an actual set of individuals. As this chapter has determined, beyond an elementary propensity that brings communities together in an association of a narrowly defined common nature, they require a good deal of prior ability to develop their collectivity, from the universal and necessary imaginative elements (e.g. language, customs) to common notions (e.g. citizenship, recognition and assent to the good of cooperation) to associate, like those of the Hebrew Republic. Their collectivity is also weak if it is merely passively imposed by an authority onto a *vulgus*, rather than embodied by a sovereign *populus*, active, joyous and internally directed, unlike the case of the Hebrews, as we might recall from our study of terminology in Chapter 5.

I'm worried, then, that Spinoza's theology/philosophy distinction isn't ambitious enough even to achieve Spinoza's own modest goals with the *TTP*, set out in those three challenges to Oldenburg. On the one hand, there's something interesting about the *TTP*'s two-pronged political epistemology and even its indirect grasp of its readers' imaginations. While complimenting his 'philosophical reader' and subtly reminding them of their difference from the crude and ignorant *vulgus*, Spinoza also uses a range of rhetorical devices to take over their imaginations. His deep analysis of scripture and its emphasis on an understanding of Hebrew, something few readers would have possessed, serve to wrest control of scripture from the Calvinist preachers

[118] Ibid.; Rousseau 1999: I.7, 58.

Spinoza felt threatened by. His use of the Hebrew Republic under Moses was also attuned to Dutch ears. The very young republic (established officially in 1648) was borne from war with Catholic Spain, and with another large and dangerous Catholic state near its southern border, national resistance myths like Leo Belgicus also drew extensively on the Hebrew Republic of Moses.[119] We should also recall the imaginative power of exemplars, models that guide our intellects, like the 'perfect man' and 'free man' in Chapter 4. Perhaps, if we were to be especially charitable, we could interpret the very Hobbesian character of Chapter 16 as a way to accommodate his politics to a readership familiar with natural right theories and Hobbesian views of nature as mediated by the popular and prolific work of the De la Courts.

Spinoza's political epistemology of the prophet demonstrates how one figure can educate many imaginations. The power of the true prophet was not only in producing compelling, socially beneficial ideas that result in obedience to justice and loving-kindness; the power of Christ as a universal prophet was in extending this commonality outwards to incorporate all nations. Commonality reflects a more simple precept, that *we are only capable of what we can already imagine*, and can be as narrow or wide as the power of our thinking permits.

Elsewhere, though, Spinoza berates the 'childish power of understanding' of the Hebrews.[120] In another section of Chapter 16, Spinoza uses the example of children, parents and slaves to explain how a democratic government would govern its citizens compared to a despotic one. Children are 'not slaves', he writes, even though they must obey all the commands of their parents, because these commands are 'primarily concerned with the advantage of children'.[121] It's an interesting but by no means certain distinction – despots have historically claimed to protect their subjects' safety from internal or external enemies. Spinoza then distinguishes between slave, child and subject:

> a slave is someone who is bound to obey the commands of a master, which are concerned only with the advantage of the person issuing the command;

---

[119] Rosenthal 2002: 225 notes that a painting of 'Moses the Lawgiver' hung prominently in Amsterdam Town Hall from 1664, while Vardoulakis (2019) has observed similar affinities in images of Moses by Ferdinand Bol and Rembrandt. Cf. Petrus Cunaeus's *De Republica Hebraeorum* (1617), which also prominently put such comparisons on the Dutch intellectual map.

[120] *TTP* III, 6; *CWS* II, 112.

[121] XVI, 35; *CWS* II, 289.

a son is someone who does what is advantageous for himself, in accordance with a parent's command; and

a subject, finally, is someone who does what is advantageous for the collective body – and hence, also for himself – in accordance with the command of the supreme power.

Kant would later write of Hobbes that under

such a paternal government [. . .] the subjects, as immature children, who cannot distinguish what is truly useful or harmful to themselves, would be obliged to behave purely passively and to rely upon the judgement of the head of state as to how they ought to be happy.[122]

As Kant concludes, '[s]uch a government is the greatest conceivable despotism'. In the *Ethics*, Spinoza presents the memorable image of a world without ageing, in which some are born infants, and others, adults. The latter would pity the former, Spinoza jokes, because of their fundamental weakness and passivity.[123] Spinoza's paternalism in the *TTP* endorses a political rule in which subjects are raised like children by parents, in ways conducive to their ultimate good. But children must become adults. The two-pronged political epistemology of the theology/philosophy distinction doesn't provide enough resources to explain how that might happen. Spinoza will therefore need a supplementary account of political institutions and processes to explain how they might produce citizens who can freely participate and actively realise the common good.

---

[122] Kant 1991: 74.
[123] *Ethics* V, 6 Schol.; CWS I, 600.

7

The State

Caute. Spinoza's motto (*Caution!*) was imprinted on a signet ring that he wore and used to stamp his correspondence. It's sometimes considered the mark of a man whose thought scandalised intellectual society around him. We might recall some of the outraged epithets of the Introduction, or the apocryphal attack on his life outside the synagogue (or the theatre – the ambiguity or equivalence between these two different sites is another insight into the images of Spinoza). Then there are also the remarks on the *vulgus* to consider, or the political epistemology which consigns philosophy to a few, and theology for everyone else, like in the last chapter.

Spinoza's 'persecution' has long interested readers. The fact of his expulsion from the Jewish community fascinated early biographers, while a variety of progressive and revolutionary political traditions have read Spinoza's heretical or anomalous status as something that presages modernity, or makes philosophy worth fighting for, hence Malcolm X's time for the 'black Spanish Jew' in Chapter 2, or the self-appointed 'precursor' of Nietzsche, or the vitalistic Spinozism of Negri and Deleuze and Guattari earlier. More substantially, extensive research has gone into excavating the clandestine influence of Spinoza over subsequent Enlightenment thought. In the English-speaking world, this position will suggest Jonathan Israel's 1995 *Radical Enlightenment* thesis, but Paul Vernière's 1954 two-volume *Spinoza et la pensée française avant la Révolution* also persuasively connects Spinoza to a range of important thinkers in seventeenth- and eighteenth-century France like Diderot, d'Holbach and Rousseau. Vernière, like Israel, tends to infer from the abuse of 'Spinoza' and 'Spinozists' a vaster subterranean influence, wherein 'Spinozism' becomes the mantle for almost all heterodox thought over the period,[1] one

---

[1] E.g. Vernière 1954: 528–611. The vital intermediary in these refracted Spinozisms is Bayle.

that ascribes to nearly any position critical of anthropocentrism, providence, miracles or expounding monism or materialism the direct influence of Spinoza, rather than other associated causes (like, for instance, the reception of Greek atomism). Nonetheless, we might say that Spinoza's 'persecution' has often been the condition for a 'rediscovery' or 'detour' back into his text.

Indeed, it can be mapped pretty well onto the relatively short life of a man who, after the *cherem*, moved several times across the Province of Holland ('the Jew of Voorburg', as Christiaan Huygens called him), settling in The Hague in what has often been described as a life of quiet and frugal seclusion ('where he lived a very retired life, according to his fancy', writes Colerus).[2] Thus the image of the lens-grinder privately pursuing his vision of the infinite, this 'prince' of philosophers for Deleuze, the 'noblest and most loveable of the great philosophers' in Bertrand Russell's view, the 'quiet man [. . .] dreaming up a brilliant labyrinth', as Borges wrote in a beautiful sonnet, even the 'virtuous atheist' of Pierre Bayle that went on to shape his early eighteenth-century reception.[3] But the image of the solitary philosopher–prince has also reinforced a view that Spinoza was a man not of his time but of a time to come, one whose teachings for the future were recorded in one work, the *Ethics*, whose metaphysics or understanding of God must be unearthed and subject to proper translation in the modern context for which they were intended, continuing a line of the ancient theology.

But that obscures the social and political problems and engagements that characterise a philosopher very much concerned with problems in his own society, and whose work is inexplicable outside of its intellectual and historical contexts. There lies part of the fracture between the freedom-loving individual who beheld a 'perfect man' and writes of an intellectual love of God that is open to all, and the community of which he was a part, or was not a part, as it judged fit. The *TTP* was intended as Spinoza's contribution to that politics, a work that had taken him at least four years (and possibly more, if we consider the possibility that early parts drew on an *Apologia* in Spanish written to justify his beliefs to the Jewish community after his expulsion, as Bayle suggested) – far longer than he would spent on the *TP*, which seems to have been drafted over a year or two.[4] But the fact that a second work on political philosophy was necessary suggests that there were some processes or principles either lacking or no longer adequate in his first attempt.

---

[2] Nadler 1999: 183; Colerus 1880: 419.
[3] Deleuze 1990: 11; Russell 1961: 569; Borges 2000: 229; Bayle 1965: 295.
[4] Bayle 1965: 292.

Were these new innovations (for instance, the 'free multitude', the 'highest good' of the State, or the basic political fact of the affects) necessitated by later revisions to the theory of the affects in the *Ethics*, as Matheron suggests?[5] Had Spinoza sensed some deficiencies in his account of political servitude and the domination of the minds of the many, first intimated in the *TTP*'s Preface but never substantially returned to, resulting in a new formulation of the domination of minds in *TP* Chapter 2? Had Spinoza also become increasingly aware of the implications of collectivity under the shared pursuit of what is led by the understanding to increase living power in common, as had been suggested by the physics of *Ethics* II, Proposition 13 and the unanimity of the *populus* in the *TTP*, but not present in the same work's faith in free tongues and the rational chorus of democratic assemblies?

If Spinoza was not yet asking himself these questions, the changing political weather of the Dutch Republic was asking it of him. Spinoza had come of intellectual age in the 1650s, at the peak of what would become known as the Dutch Golden Age. It was the first decade after the formal recognition of the United Provinces by the Treaty of Westphalia (1648), and the republic was becoming very wealthy from its monopoly of trade with Japan and the vast expansion of the Dutch East India Company. The ports of Amsterdam and Rotterdam were bringing in Japanese silks, Maluku spices, Brazilian sugar, Chesapeake tobacco, Hudson Valley beaver pelts and Chinese porcelain and tea. Book publishing thrived and local industries (many imitating the new imports) like Delftware became hugely profitable. But successes were uneven.

We read in Chapter 2 about the overextended West India Company and the failure to hold onto Brazil (and Angola) against the Portuguese. The Dutch were under attack from various sides, with wars with England (e.g. 1652–4, and 1665–7) hampering sea trade and traffic. But by the late 1660s the Provinces and its liberal, trade-orientated governors had emerged powerful. Grand Pensionary Johan de Witt now felt emboldened to remove by law the title of stadtholder (or de facto head of state) from a young William III of Orange in the name of 'freedom'.[6] It would be the first attempt in the history of the new republic to *de jure* re-establish its political constitution around one sovereign power, the Estates-General, rather than two, with the quasi-monarchical stadtholder from the House of Orange. Spinoza would describe the State as a 'body without a head' with its divided constitution or mixed

---

[5] Matheron 2011: 205. I go deeper into the differences of the *TTP* and *TP* and the influences of Aristotle and Machiavelli over the latter in my article (2019b).

[6] Israel 1995: 4.

government, something which traditional political philosophy had considered a virtue.[7] Spinoza, like Hobbes, instead considered its power dangerously divided and its ultimate authority unclear. De Witt was just about able to succeed, though several provinces voted against the Perpetual Edict of 1667. Supporters of William were becoming increasingly critical of the government's direction and were finding allies in the Dutch Reformed Church. It was in this intellectual climate, with the gradual and conspicuous encroachment upon liberties of speech and philosophy, that compelled the *TTP*.

That is where we left our author in the last chapter. But I want to place what happens next in the *Political Treatise*, with its arguments for freedom through the State, in the context of the Dutch political and constitutional crises that consume it after 1670. Following the subterfuges in publishing the *TTP* anonymously and under a fake imprint, Spinoza initially avoided identification as its author, and returned to the *Ethics*. We'll recall that he wrote to friends in 1671 to prevent a Dutch translation, fearing the consequences for his safety. Early that same year, Johannes Melchior was publicly naming and condemning him as the author of the work (if absurdly misspelling his name to 'Xinospa').[8] Later that year, Johann Graevius at the University of Utrecht had written to Leibniz of 'a most pestilential book' whose author was 'said to be a Jew named Spinoza, but who was cast out of the synagogue because of his monstrous opinions'.[9] We can assume that in many circles its authorship was an open secret.

Equally worrying was the imperilled situation of the republic, which was subject to a surprise joint attack in April 1672 by the English navy and the armies of France, Cologne and Munster. Soon, over half the country was under enemy occupation (much ceded with little resistance), with the unpopular and unprepared government desperately trying to sue for peace. One event of this *Rampjaar* ('The year of disaster') is often highlighted – the ambush and murder of Johan and Cornelis De Witt (another prominent figure in the Estates-General) by a crowd in The Hague on 20 August 1672, the *ultimi barbarorum* who beheaded, butchered and cannibalised the brothers. While unprecedented, this was not an isolated spectacle of insurrectionary violence. Many within the Provinces had been unhappy with the city regents' handling of the war.[10] Why hadn't the government realised

---

[7] TP IX, 14; CWS II, 595.
[8] Israel 2010: 77.
[9] In Nadler 1999: 301.
[10] For more on the Dutch context, see Israel 1995: ch. 31; Price 2014: ch. 5; and Prak 2005: 50–2.

that its apparent ally, England, was plotting an attack, or that France would invade the country through the weakly defended east with the connivance of Munster and Cologne? Why had the provinces been so easily overrun? Why were the regents of Utrecht so willing to capitulate without a fight and sue for peace on the most expensive and egregious of terms? Why was the vital military bastion of Schenckenschans left under the charge of a useless associate of the States Party and given up without a fight?

Fears spread that the regents ('traitors') actually wanted to hand over most of the country to the French, a misapprehension further amplified by the States of Holland's offer to permanently surrender some of the provinces and claims on the Spanish Netherlands to Louis XIV in June.[11] Under military occupation and naval blockade, work and trade ground to a halt. Soon serious riots broke out among unemployed fishermen, artisans, militia and refugees from the occupied territories who filled the remaining free cities – first Dordrecht, then Rotterdam, Amsterdam, Schiedam and Delft over June and July 1672. Many of the rioters were reportedly women, and preachers often fomented and rallied the unrest. The homes of some regents were burned down, and others were chased out. Many protestors displayed their support for William of Orange who, amid war, now reassumed the title of stadtholder in July, left unoccupied for two decades. His supporters condemned the supporters of De Witt as enemies of the public Church who had abandoned Brazil and sought to sell out the 'fatherland'.[12] Johan de Witt gave up his title on 4 August after an earlier knife attack in June. After the death of the De Witts, there were further civil disturbances and local insurrections until the Prince of Orange was 'invited' by his followers to restore order and remove the remaining republican regents. The 'true freedom' was over.

Though no prescription of the *TTP* could have aided the Dutch against the attack, the work had little to say about constitutional matters, the division of executive powers or military defence, and so little instruction for the increasingly polarised and unstable situation the Dutch were in. While they were able to conduct an effective defence by sea and land (the English parliament was just as concerned about God as trade, and pushed Charles II into backing down), the invasion produced a political crisis of legitimacy that led to the collapse of the State's regents and the liberal republican culture celebrated by the De la Courts. Its downfall had been accelerated by an uneven division of power between the pro-Orangist and Calvinist

---

[11] Israel 1995: 801.
[12] Ibid. 802.

Dutch Reformed Church, which enjoyed significant public support, and the mercantile, liberal States faction which made up De Witt's government and supporters, to whom the *TTP* had appealed. Spinoza's appeal for democracy and toleration had been ignored by the many, who now welcomed stricter religious controls and the installation of monarchy. But for Spinoza, the momentary triumph of the *ultimi barbarorum* in the deaths of the De Witts could not be put down to the moral failures of any group of people, but the inadequate constitution of the State.

It seems Spinoza also tried to make a diplomatic intervention. In July 1673 both Colerus and Bayle record him being invited to French-occupied Utrecht to meet with the Prince of Condé, military commander and patron of writers like Molière and Racine. Condé may have been motivated by the latter, but Spinoza, who had earlier turned down a generous stipend from Simon de Vries and a job offer at Heidelberg University two months earlier, was probably motivated by a sense of political duty, perhaps seeing himself as having a part to play in negotiating peace.[13] The trip was a dangerous and fruitless one, and Condé had left by the time he arrived. On return, Colerus reports from his landlord, 'the Mob at the Hague were extremely incensed against him', considering him a spy.[14] Der Spyck once again had to protect Spinoza within his own home.

This threat to his personal safety continued. Over 1673–4 William had overseen a Dutch counterattack that reversed nearly all the gains of the invaders. He was rewarded in January 1674 when the position of stadtholder was made hereditary and perpetual to the house of Orange, making the Provinces a de facto monarchy. The Calvinist preachers were also in the ascendancy. By July 1674, the Court of Holland officially banned the *TTP* as blasphemous (alongside Hobbes's *Leviathan*), as well as in multiple provincial synods.[15] In late July 1675, Spinoza visited Amsterdam to oversee the publication of the *Ethics*, begun around thirteen years earlier, but after being warned of danger to his life should the book be published, he postponed it, writing to Oldenburg once more of his fears and uncertainty.[16] His final years were marked by ill health, but seem to have been occupied initially with planned revisions to the *TTP* to 'remove the prejudices con-

---

[13] Colerus 1880: 422; Nadler 1999: 261; *Ep.* XLVIII [to J. Ludwig Fabritius]; CWS II, 397. Rovere points that Spinoza still accepted a stipend of around 300 florins per annum, enough to not rely on lens-grinding for an income (2017: 350).
[14] Colerus 1880: 423; Bayle 1965: 295; Nadler 1999: 318.
[15] Nadler 1999: 322.
[16] *Ep.* LXVIII [to Henry Oldenburg]; CWS II, 459.

ceived about it', as he wrote in the same letter, upon which little progress was seemingly made.[17] It's more likely that from late 1675 Spinoza had begun work on a project given wholly to politics.

The *Political Treatise* as we have it seems to be mostly complete, its structure following that suggested by a letter to an unnamed friend, probably Jelles, which outlined its chapter plan. Democracy remained incomplete, as did a planned section on laws.[18] Unlike the *TTP* and the *Ethics*, the work is written in a freer style, neither deploying rhetorical and hermeneutic devices involving scripture, nor being in geometric order. It openly acknowledges arguments in the previous two works, something unprecedented in Spinoza's writing, given concerns over anonymity, safety and censorship. It suggests that its audience were the circle of trusted friends who had studied copies of the *Ethics* in circulation, and had commented upon the *TTP*. This new political work emerges out of conversations like those leading to the unnamed friend's suggestion to set Spinoza's political ideas onto the page, revised for a more unstable milieu. Spinoza's late politics would be rooted in a foundation of the political in the affects, mirroring their expanding role for human freedom in the later *Ethics*, and in the ability of a state's organisation (and not individual leadership) to instil and enhance the 'justice and loving-kindness' of its subjects, foundational to 'true religion' in the *TTP*, and now essential to a state's security.[19] It's this final politics of the State as a means of realising collective freedom that we shall now explore.

Freedom is the State

Towards the end of the *TTP*, Spinoza treats the 'ultimate end' of the State.[20] It's an oddly teleological turn in a work elsewhere concerned with political naturalism. We've seen this conflict between exemplars and actualities before, like the free man and the slave, but it becomes more apparent in the later *TP* and its concern with understanding the 'highest good' that

---

[17] Cf. *Ep*. LXIV [to Lambert van Velthuysen]; *CWS* II, 460, which also requests in writing his criticisms of the *TTP*.

[18] *Ep*. LXXXIV [to 'one of his friends']; *CWS* II, 488.

[19] Numerous commentators have observed the expansion of the affects in Spinoza's late philosophy, compared to *TdIE* and *KV*. It is possible that through work on the *TTP*, Spinoza became aware of the affective and imaginative nature of the political, compelling an expansion of what had been one chapter-treatment of the affects into Parts III and IV of *Ethics*, separating human servitude to the affects from our freedom or power over them.

[20] *TTP* XX, 11–12; *CWS* II, 346.

different forms of the State can achieve. There are signs that Spinoza had begun applying this interest in exemplars to politics. In the same letter to Jelles that sought to stop a Dutch translation of the *TTP* in 1671, Spinoza speculated about the need for a new political work on 'the highest good' of the State, beyond merely 'money and honour'.[21] In the *TTP*, Spinoza says that the State can provide three kinds of freedom: an affective kind ('to free everyone from fear'), a social kind ('to act without harm to themselves or to others') and a cognitive kind ('to allow their minds and bodies to develop in their own ways in security and enjoy the free use of reason'). Spinoza concludes that 'the true purpose of the State is in fact freedom'.

Following our analysis in Chapter 5, it achieves this in two ways. First, it provides a minimal level of security, as a group of people join to protect one another's right, serving their own interest and others in turn.[22] Second, and more substantially, the institutions of the State can nurture the underlying power of the people, developing their powers of reasoning in a peaceful, public-spirited and cooperative polity, through democratic assemblies, the protection of philosophy and toleration of free speech. We called this the collectivist argument. But we'll also recall that Spinoza didn't really provide much detail on how the State might do this, or what kinds of state can accomplish this. His endorsements of the liberty of his own state in the *TTP* – '[s]ince, then, we happen to have that rare good fortune' to 'live in a republic in which everyone is granted complete freedom of judgment' – have a ring of irony about them.[23] For his freedom of speech, Adriaan Koerbagh had been shackled. Popular uprisings had now usurped the authority of the provincial governments of the Estates-General and had now overthrown the liberal republic in the name of an ambitious monarch.

In an insightful discussion of this passage, Steinberg challenges what he identifies as a prevailing 'liberal' reading of Spinoza's political good, one concerned with protecting individual liberties rather than affirming a normative conception of the social good.[24] Instead, he largely follows Spinoza in load-

---

[21] *Ep.* XLIV [to Jarig Jelles]; *CWS* II, 391. In his final letter which outlines the plan of the unfinished *TP*, Spinoza says that the fifth chapter will cover 'the ultimate thing a state can aim at' (*Ep.* LXXXIV [to 'one of his friends']; *CWS* II, 488). In practice, the remaining chapters dealing with monarchy, aristocracy and democracy largely deal in ideal models of an optimal sort. The distinction also appears in Chapter 5's discussion of the 'right way' (e.g. natural right, driven by desire and power and not reason) as opposed to the 'best way' – *TP* V, 1; *CWS* II, 528–9).

[22] Cf. *TTP* III, 20; *CWS* II, 115.

[23] Praef., 12; *CWS* II, 69.

[24] Steinberg 2009: 35; cf. 2018: 65.

ing the burden of becoming-freer onto the State. 'A state that is able to procure the *securitas* [an affect of certain hope or peace of mind] of its members will in turn have empowered or liberated them, since it will consequently promote their joy or psychic wellbeing in a reliable way.'[25] Alongside producing a minimal security, the State also increases the power of acting of its citizens, through the stability of its institutions that in turn determine 'as-if' reasonable behaviours, and in providing a general environment of hope, where citizens can flourish.[26] Yet following our criticisms of paternalism in the last chapter, for Spinoza's inference of freedom *as* political to stand up, it must supply a model of how its citizens can actively become more reasonable, rather than merely passively live under reasonable rule.

But in some ways Spinoza's political thinking does undergo a shift towards the position Steinberg recommends. For as Spinoza argues there, 'the path reason teaches us to follow is very difficult', and so those 'who persuade themselves that a multitude, which may be engaged in public affairs, can be induced to live only according to the prescription of reason' are 'dreaming of the golden age of the poets'.[27] The self-expressed goal of his account now, as its title-page attests, is to describe various optimum forms of political organisation wherein 'the peace and security of the citizens are preserved'.[28] If a state is to survive, its 'affairs must be so ordered that, whether the people who administer them are led by reason or by passion, they can't be induced to be disloyal or to act badly'.[29] Whether they do or not is a consequence of the good organisation of their governmental form. Spinoza adds that it 'doesn't make a difference [. . .] in what spirit men are led to administer matters properly', so long as this instrumental good is achieved. For 'freedom of mind, or strength of character', the *Ethics*' highest virtues, are no more than a 'private virtue', whereas 'the virtue of the State is security'. Whether individuals are guided by reason or passion is irrelevant to the overall freedom that living in a well-organised, secure state confers.

This could present a serious obstacle to our earlier argument that freedom is of a general kind across Spinoza's works, with no substantial difference between ethical and political freedom, only the means used to realise it. On the face of it, the 'freedom' of the State, and of the individual, seem to be of very different orders. But we'll recall from our discussion of desire in

---

[25] Steinberg 2009: 52; cf. 2018: 75.
[26] Steinberg 2009: 46–8.
[27] TP I, 5; CWS II, 506.
[28] Title page; CWS II, 503.
[29] I, 6; CWS II, 505.

Chapter 3 that the good of a set of ideas lies in their effects. This point is made more forcefully in the *TTP* with the role of the imagination for religion (as *pietas*) – its good lies not in the inherent truth of its ideas, but in the effects it produces in achieving justice and loving-kindness.

The 'utopias' of the philosophers are dismissed in favour of a new empirical methodology, following the lessons of 'statesmen' who, guided by experience (and Spinoza implies Machiavelli and Johan and Pieter De la Court, the few theorists referred to positively in the text),[30] will aid him 'to demonstrate the things which agree best with practice, in a certain and indubitable way, and to deduce them from the condition of human nature'.[31] Politics is no longer concealed beneath biblical analysis but is presented as a 'science'.[32] Just as in the *Ethics* Spinoza considered human nature as if it were 'of lines, planes or bodies', here the affects are a form of science to be understood with the same 'freedom of spirit' as mathematics, so that one can regard 'love, hate, anger, envy, love of esteem, compassion, and other emotions' as properties like 'heat, cold, storms, thunder, etc., pertain to the atmosphere'.[33] Lastly, we may recall from *Ethics* IV, Definition 8 that virtue is equivalent to freedom or power – Spinoza reminds us again at *TP* II, 7 in any case, while summarising the *Ethics*' account of conatus and desire. The State's virtue or power is in its ability to persevere in existence, withstanding forces externally and internally that will otherwise compel the proportionate ratio of its parts into dissolution and war. To accomplish this, it need not rely on the virtues or vices of a few instrumental figures within it – rather, its reason is realised through the collective citizen body. But the education of these citizens involves, like the aims of theology in the *TTP* before it, producing reasonable effects as much as reasonable ideas, whether motivated 'by reason or by passion' (translation modified), so long as it empowers the lives of the many.[34]

---

[30] Translation modified: Curley chooses 'political practitioners' over 'statesmen', but this seems imprecise. Spinoza refers to 'a very wise Dutchman, V.H.' in *TP* VIII, 31 – V.H. being the initials 'Van den Hove', the Dutch equivalent of 'De la Courts' (*CWS* II, 579). Machiavelli is directly referred to in *TP* V, 7 (*CWS* II, 531). The philosophers referred to are probably Plato, Aquinas, Thomas More, as well as Hobbes (as Matheron argues, 1978: 59), and even, in a tenuous but brilliant claim by Morfino, the calculating and self-interested individual of the *TTP*'s social contract (2017: 24). On the deeper influence and conceptual overlaps between Spinoza and Machiavelli, see Del Lucchese (2009).

[31] *TP* I, 2–4; *CWS* II, 504–5.

[32] I, 4; *CWS* II, 505.

[33] *Ethics* III, Praef.; *CWS* I, 492; *TP* I, 4; *CWS* II, 505.

[34] Curley opts for the more sober 'by reason or by an affect', which minimises Spinoza's own emphasis here. *TP* I, 6; *CWS* II, 506.

By reason or passion . . . There is something of Machiavelli's *Prince* in the remark, and it jars with the highest good that preoccupies Chapter 5. Its conflicting strands are illuminated by the account of freedom and nature that follows it, early in Chapter 2, which render the conceptual necessity and consistency of thinking individual freedom through the State. Spinoza begins with a recap of the *TTP*'s theory of natural right, involving a subtle redefinition bearing the influence of the *Ethics*, where 'freedom is virtue, or perfection'.[35] Against Hobbes, there is no 'freedom' in the natural state, but only in living in the civil state, where together we can offer mutual assistance and live lives of greater well-being and peace.[36] But what if the State we live in is poorly constituted and regularly suffers crises of sovereignty, like the collapses of the *Rampjaar*?

One issue facing Spinoza's endorsement of free speech, toleration and the inherent rationality of large, free democratic assemblies in the *TTP* was the extent to which individuals were able to think and speak freely, or under the coercion of another. Whereas the Preface of the *TTP* reflects on how men can be led by their fear to 'fight for slavery as they would for their survival', defending the regimes of tyrants who ultimately oppress them, the 'theoretical' Chapter 16 considers men in nature who will speak and deliberate by their own reasonable judgement.[37] Contextual matters discussed in Part II necessitate a theoretical explanation as to how the judgement of many can fall under the power of one, in ways not just explicable by hope or fear.

In his gloss of the *TTP*'s natural right in Chapter 2, Spinoza subtly redefines the relation of freedom to independence of thought.[38] He begins by outlining the conatus doctrine, before reformulating desire as a form of consciousness of one's appetites, wherein a desired object's 'good' or 'evil' is relative to its empowerment of a person's specific nature as they judge it.[39] Spinoza then adds a new argument that correlates human power with independence of thought. We considered this earlier in Chapter 1 in the context of servitude, but it's worth returning to in assessing the direction of

---

[35] *TP* II, 7; *CWS* II, 510; echoing *Ethics* IV, Def. 8; *CWS* I, 547.
[36] *TP* II, 15; *CWS* II, 513.
[37] Spinoza uses this term to distinguish his preceding theory of natural right and democracy from the historical analysis of the Hebrew Republic under Moses that follows it (*TTP* Praef., 10; XVII, 1; *CWS* II, 68; 296).
[38] Spinoza will do the same in his gloss of the *Ethics*, redefining Adam's original sin as resulting from being subject to affects that prevented him from using his reason (*TP* II, 6; *CWS* II, 509–10), versus *Ethics* IV, 68 Schol. (*CWS* I, 585), which peculiarly explains it through Adam's imitation of the affects of the animals.
[39] *TP* II, 8; *CWS* II, 511.

the late politics. There, Spinoza gave four situations in which an individual falls under the power of another (*sub potestare habere*). This can involve either body or mind (or both), and to the extent that one is deceived by another, one is subject to their right.[40] By implication, we heard, a mind is 'completely its own master just to the extent that it can use reason rightly'. Spinoza now assesses human power 'not so much by the strength of the body as by the strength of mind' – a slight shift from the ambiguous parallelism in parts of the *Ethics* – and so 'people are most their own masters when they can exert the most power with their reason'.

The argument is made briefly in the manner of a recap, but Spinoza expands his theory of power to explicitly involve a greater degree of independence and self-control. In order for one to be *sui juris*, that is, to be in their own right and have the capacity for citizenship, they require a relative power of self-determination or autonomy to withstand the rights of others who might otherwise seek to exploit them.[41] In concise fashion, Spinoza offers a new foundation with which to tackle the problem of political servitude introduced in Chapter 1 with the *TTP*, through independence of mind. The new condition could provide his account with a much-needed basis to outline how many in a given society (the *plebs* of Chapter 5, who are more easily subject to the sad passions) can begin thinking and feeling in more joyous and active ways.

From this, Spinoza restates his previous arguments for the possibility and advantages of collective power ('if two men come together . . .'),[42] and mutual assistance, from which he derives the necessity of acting together – 'the more they agree as one in this way, the more right they will all have together'[43] – and arrives at his first formulation of collective power in the *Treatise*. While a late addition to the *Ethics* also pointed to how, in coming together for a common purpose, men multiply their right,[44] in the *TP* this language of coordination and collective right is much more prominent. In holding their rights in common, 'all are led as if by one mind', a power that is also greater than the sum of its parts, and foundational to sovereignty in

---

[40] II, 10–11; CWS II, 512.
[41] *Sui juris* (with right) is a concept from Roman (and Greek) law and one discussed by Dutch republican sources like the De la Courts. Aristotle restricted citizenship to those deemed 'self-sufficient' (1981: 1275b13), while Justinian's *Digest* defined the slave as one subject to the power of another, in contrast to the free, self-willing agent. See Weststeijn 2012: 162; James 2009: 226; Kisner 2011: 21.
[42] *TP* II, 13; CWS II, 510, echoing *Ethics* IV, 18 Schol.; CWS I, 556.
[43] *TP* II, 15; CWS II, 514.
[44] *Ethics* IV, 37 Schol. 2; CWS I, 566–8.

all three state-forms.⁴⁵ We'll recall some of the earlier conceptualisation around collective individuality in Chapter 5, which there relied on an integration of bodies producing a common effect. We reflected on the implicit consequences of an equal integration of minds, but found in the *TTP* only mixed resources to think about how a *populus* might be empowered by shared images and beliefs to live more capably together. In the *TP*, such coordination is impossible, however, unless the State's laws are 'according to reason's dictate', and it is in this way that Spinoza's civil state is one guided by reason, rather than coercive conformity.⁴⁶

But what does this reason amount to? For Spinoza, it refers to the common good, the freedom that all can collectively share in and benefit from. Thus Spinoza writes that the State must be established 'so that everyone – both those who rule and those who are ruled – does what's for the common well-being'.⁴⁷ Again, it does not matter if this is done willingly, reasonably or not, so long as their common good is realised – 'whether of his own accord, or by force, or by necessity', they will all live 'according to the prescription of reason'. This prescription of reason is what results in the flourishing of the people, echoing Cicero and the *TTP*, with the third law of politics we identified back in Chapter 2.⁴⁸ The 'people's well-being is the supreme law, or the king's highest right' in a monarchy,⁴⁹ and it is the basic measure of the strength of any polity in the *TP*.⁵⁰

These, in themselves, are not uncommon in early modern republicanism: what's interesting is how they become interlinked with organicist metaphors of the multitude as acting, led or guided 'as if by one mind' [*una veluti mente*] – a phrase that appears numerous times, particularly in Chapters 2–3 – and as one body of citizens.⁵¹ While on an elementary level one can agree with Curley that acting by one mind connotes a 'commonality of purpose', if this were merely Spinoza's point then such a vivid and oft-repeated metaphor would not be expected in an otherwise austere and unsentimental writing style. Spinoza's choice of passive inflections of the verb *ducere* (to lead or guide) instead indicate how a multitude are led and compelled to act in

---

⁴⁵ *TP* II, 16; *CWS* II, 516.
⁴⁶ II, 21; *CWS* II, 510. See also V, 4, which makes this clearer (*CWS* II, 530).
⁴⁷ VI, 3; *CWS* II, 532.
⁴⁸ *TTP* XVI, 10; *CWS* II, 284.
⁴⁹ *TP* VII, 5; *CWS* II, 547.
⁵⁰ E.g. III, 17; IV, 6; V, 7; VI, 3; 8; VII, 3–5; VIII, 20; 44; cf. Hobbes L II.30.1.
⁵¹ Variants appear at II, 13; 15–16; 21; III, 2; 5; 7; VI, 1; and VIII, 6. Organicist metaphors of the body politic are common, appearing in Hobbes, Grotius and, ultimately, Aristotle, e.g. 1981: 1281b5, 1287b30.

common, and in coordination with one another, through a shared set of true ideas.

Led *as one* need not imply that such individuals share the same thoughts. Spinoza's physical digression explains how groups of bodies can unite and share a common *ratio* among each other, becoming one individual through sharing a common order and purpose, while also remaining partially independent and not necessarily agreeing in nature. It's important not to lose sight of the possibility of difference (of natures, or even abilities) that this outline of collectivity suggests – something that the examples in Chapter 5 of the musical band, loving relationship or sports team suggest. The emphasis on reason also accords with Spinoza's epistemology in the *Ethics*, wherein knowledge of the second and third kinds is necessarily a basis of agreement.[52] It also helps us make use of the social epistemology of the *TTP*, for whom the truths of 'true religion' and prophecy are those which result in behaviours of justice and loving-kindness, through being relayed at a suitably imaginative level that can stimulate and guide the minds of the many. Within Spinoza's late politics and its blueprints for secure states, the right of a state is the power of a free multitude, led by one mind or a common set of laws,[53] established in accordance with reason, with the end of their common flourishing.

The Free Multitude

This entrance of the 'free multitude' is interesting. The *TTP* rarely refers to the *multitudo*, usually via quotations of scathing Roman authors (e.g. 'the savage multitude').[54] In the *Political Treatise* the multitude are everywhere, and Spinoza now compares a 'free multitude' from a 'slave' one of a state gained by right of war.[55] In a distinction that echoes the conflict of the free man and slave in *Ethics* V, 41–2 discussed in Chapter 2, the free multitude lives by hope and for life, and live for themselves; in contrast, the subjugated multitude live by fear and to avoid death, and for the benefit of the victor. This distinction is important, indicating how Spinoza positively draws on the common people (*multitudo*) as the basis of political sovereignty where previous references in the *TTP* and the *Ethics* were often scathing and dismissive – the common people (as the *vulgus*) often described as irrational, fearful and violent, a danger as much to themselves as to aloof philosophers.

---

[52] E.g. *Ethics* IV, 31–2, 35; CWS I, 560–1, 563.
[53] *TP* III, 2; II, 21; III, 7; CWS II, 517; 515; 520.
[54] *TTP* XVIII, 24; CWS II, 328.
[55] *TP* V, 6; CWS II, 530–531.

A peaceful and secure commonwealth is one where the free multitude are guided to live in accordance with reason; a warlike and disorderly one where they are subjugated externally by the right of another, and internally by a turmoil of fear, prejudice and hatred.

But while we can agree with Matheron that the multitude are the 'immanent' power of a commonwealth, there is no inherent rationality or 'democratic conatus' in a multitude, who can just as easily be led through servility by a tyrant.[56] This becomes clear in a distinction drawn between *citizens* (*cives*) and *subjects* (*subditos*). Whereas citizens 'enjoy, by civil right, all the advantages of a commonwealth', the *multitudo* are merely subjects, 'bound to obey the established practices of the commonwealth, or its laws'.[57] This is an inherently passive state, obeying the laws out of fear, not free and willing consent. It is akin to the discussion of being 'subject' in mind to another's right earlier. The citizen is *sui juris* whereas the subject is passive and unfree. When Spinoza writes that 'the right of a commonwealth is determined by the power of a multitude that is guided as though by a single mind', from the preceding discussion we can understand that such a freedom or collective power arises from a life in common that is peaceful and mutually supportive, but one also led by the citizens and imposed on subjects.[58] But it does not mean all power to the multitudes. The multitude remain 'not in control of their own right', and the text cannot bear out a wholly liberatory politics of the multitude, as per Negri. They remain 'under the control of the commonwealth, insofar as they fear its power or threats, or insofar as they love the civil order'.[59] Instead, the 'union of minds could in no way be conceived unless the chief aim of the commonwealth is identical with that which sound reason teaches us is for the good of all men'.[60]

But where exactly does the consent of the multitude fit into this schema? While the role of religion and faith is vastly diminished in the *TP*, Spinoza seems to retain some of his reasoning about how one might elevate and intensify the well-being of the common people using indirect means. Whereas the *TTP* redefines piety and religion around the effect of producing 'justice and loving-kindness', we can observe a similar effect in the reorganisation of the basis of three ideal political states through the common affect of the multitude. We'll recall earlier that the multitude remained under the control of

---

[56] Matheron 1997: 217.
[57] *TP* III, 1; *CWS* II, 517.
[58] III, 7; *CWS* II, 520.
[59] III, 8; *CWS* II, 520.
[60] Ibid.

the commonwealth insofar as they felt a common fear, or common hope. Spinoza begins his discussion of monarchy with the observation that human beings are affectively disposed to form communities with one another. It is 'out of a common affect that they will naturally unite and be led by one mind, by a common hope, or fear, or common desire [*desiderio*] to avenge some harm'.[61] One possible aim of the 'science' of Spinoza's politics of human affects is the understanding of how individual desires cohere into common feelings that can be utilised for the security of the State. Given that human beings 'by nature strive [*appetere*] for civil order'[62] yet are also, by the same affective nature, predisposed to ambition and greed, resulting in all manner of conflicts, the State must not merely intervene in such disputes but prevent their very emergence. It achieves this by placing popular sovereignty at the heart of its institutional forms.

Popular Government

There has been a lot of debate about whether Spinoza is consistently a proponent of democracy between the *TTP*, where it is presented as the most natural and absolute form of government, and one without theoretical restriction to citizens, and the *TP*, which limits enfranchisement to a small number of male citizens.[63] Sidestepping that debate somewhat, my proposal is that Spinoza places democratic processes at the heart of all three of his optimal political forms. While the surviving text seems to have more esteem for aristocracy – Spinoza was writing for Dutch readers, and considers the United Provinces as a kind of federal aristocracy historically – it is the principle of popular sovereignty and power which he most consistently backs.

It is on this basis that Spinoza outlines the three classic forms of political organisation. But contrary to his earlier promises, Spinoza does not treat monarchy, aristocracy or democracy 'as they are', but instead as ideal models that each frame this equilibrium of power. He subjects each form to separate systematic treatment, where the aim is security, the problem is societal con-

---

[61] VI, 4; CWS II, 532.
[62] Ibid.
[63] While many readers come to a view like Steinberg (2018: ch. 7) that there is a roughly consistent theory of democracy over the works, I am not so sure. At minimum, the nature and understanding of democracy becomes much narrower in the *TP*, which is why I propose popular sovereignty as another way of thinking about the principle of the people's well-being at the heart of each. Feuer (1987: 161) and Prokhovnik (1997: 108) both make compelling arguments against what the latter calls the prevailing view of the 'normative pre-eminence' of democracy across Spinoza.

flict, and the solution is a neat division of legislative, legal, civil and military powers. Whether it be the right of succession of a monarch, the selection and renewal of aristocratic patricians, or the limited conditions of *sui juris* of the democratic citizen, each model is proposed through an orderly division of functions. Each model of political organisation begins in the agreement and expression of support of representatives of the collective – clan representatives elect a monarch, or arrange for the 'best' to be selected as patricians,[64] or decide among themselves who possesses sufficient experience and right to represent the rest of the collectivity.

Spinoza explains that he will consider 'the best condition of each kind of state', in which their power is most absolute.[65] Yet this model of 'absolute' power does not consist in demonstrating the greatest right to rule, or in possessing the greatest military and economic resources to defend one's state. While democracies were considered in the *TTP* as the most natural form of government in expressing the popular will, Spinoza now reaches for a more fundamental explanation of natural political power. 'For if there's any absolute rule [*imperium absolutum*]', he writes, 'it's the rule which occurs when the whole multitude rules.'[66] It is this expression of absolute sovereignty which is the final means of mutating the classic forms of political organisation.

This explains why the model of monarchy presented is barely monarchical at all, at least by contemporary standards: out of a federation of cities, a state is formed; its subjects are divided into clans, who then *elect* a king.[67] This king is supported by a general council selected from a list of candidates nominated by each clan; this council is responsible for most of the political administration and decision-making, and functions in effect like a sovereign house of representatives governing alongside a president. In contrast to the rise of absolutist monarchies across Europe, Spinoza's model is one where the king must listen to and enact the will of large assemblies, which by virtue of the quantity of opinions presented, will automatically favour the most reasonable course,[68] the same hopeful argument we encountered in the *TTP*. Out of this 'large number of men, it follows that no solution conducive to the people's well-being is conceivable, except for the opinions this council

---

[64] VIII, 2; CWS II, 565–6.
[65] VIII, 31; CWS II, 579.
[66] VIII, 3; CWS II, 566.
[67] VI, 13–15; VII, 25; CWS II, 536; 556. They also elect the patricians of the aristocracy (VIII, 1; CWS II, 564–5). To be fair, elective monarchy had been a common historical practice, for instance during the early Roman Empire and throughout the Holy Roman Empire.
[68] VI, 17–26; VII, 5–13; CWS II, 537–40; 547–50.

reports to the king'.[69] Where divergences occur, the king intervenes and makes an overall decision in the common interest.

Power is dispersed equally among clans and through executive bodies, with a deeply restricted aristocracy retained only for employment as foreign ambassadors. This monarchy even includes the common ownership of property, with equality granted to all subjects as citizens of the clans.[70] One finds this principle at work too in the discussion of aristocracy. Rather than being the rule of a small caste of hereditary nobles or wealthy merchants and landowners, Spinoza transforms it into a democratic meritocracy, whereby out of the same division of clans, the ablest individuals are nominated and voted onto a higher council of patricians. Unlike a monarchy, this form of rule has additional absolute power in that the council elected is sufficiently large and regenerated on a regular basis, that its will, rule and power are consistent and most representative of the desires of the rest of the State.[71]

In each case, the opinions and beliefs of the collectivity are no longer represented through mere freedom of speech, but through institutions of political representation that also function to restrict specific groups from becoming too powerful. The monarch and aristocratic council are limited by the laws of the constitution which must remain eternally inviolate; the power of the army is restricted by creating a citizen-militia; a state religion is created to ensure societal peace, with other religions permitted but heavily restricted.[72] Before Montesquieu's *Spirit of the Laws*, there is a systematic use of checks and safeguards to ensure an equilibrium of power where the multitude's well-being is the highest good. Despite a common pessimism about human nature and sociality in near-contemporary political theorists like Machiavelli, Hobbes, Boxhorn and the De la Courts, Spinoza's account remains entirely buoyed by a faith transferred from the free and reasonable individuals of the *TTP* and the *Ethics*, to the free and reasonable collective individuals of the *TP*, this *civitas* acting 'as if one mind' and absolutely. By our earlier discussions of collectivity, unanimity and living according to reason in Chapters 4–5, this 'one mind' is in thinking and living in universal agreement with the order of nature.

---

[69] VII, 5; CWS II, 547.
[70] Cf. VI, 11–12; VII, 19; CWS II, 535–6; 553.
[71] VIII, 3; CWS II, 566.
[72] III, 10; IV, 4; VIII, 46; CWS II, 521–2; 526–7; 587.

Becoming Civil

The 'end of the civil condition', writes Spinoza, is 'peace and security of life', a state of 'freedom', where men 'pass their lives harmoniously'.[73] Yet while the *TTP* argues that the fundamental instruction of true prophetic revelation and scripture is 'justice and loving-kindness' in our dealings with others, the *TP* travels further in its vision of harmony, of passing a *human* life defined by the true virtue and power of the mind. Whereas *Ethics* Part V wrote in similar terms of a freedom that would be enjoyed by the philosopher prepared to undergo its difficult and rare path, here Spinoza emphasises the role of the State in providing the peace, security and harmony of the multitude, ones which 'have established their laws according to reason's dictate'.[74] But if many individuals are guided as if by one mind by the State's laws, what is to separate Spinoza's endorsement of obedience from the monarchies he also attacks, which lead subjects like 'sheep' and turn them into 'slaves'?[75] What are the rights of the individual or community who might find themselves in opposition to the laws or decisions of their state? And what precisely is the role of the State in educating its members to reason for themselves?

Let's tackle this issue with some hermeneutic charity. Spinoza does not emphasise the good of public education in the ways that contemporaries John Comenius, Bathsua Makin or John Locke later would; however, he viewed a sufficiently free, tolerant society in which science and philosophy flourished as achieving comparable effects.[76] For Spinoza, following Hobbes, there is a subtle emphasis on citizenship, which may conjecturally have necessitated a separate chapter treatment, following the proposed chapter on laws. Spinoza writes that 'Men aren't born civil; they become civil', echoing Hobbes's *De Cive*, that men require 'training' for society, albeit based on a social contract founded in escaping fear and violence.[77] Instead, for Spinoza, human beings are the same everywhere, a claim later made in Chapter 7, and differences in civil behaviours reflect the institutions that determine them to act in a

---

[73] V, 1; V, 5; CWS II, 528–30.
[74] II, 21; CWS II, 515–16.
[75] V, 4 (CWS II, 530), echoing *Politics*, 1280a21.
[76] All three emphasise public education for children, with a Baconian interest in pedagogy (Makin for educating girls in England, 1673). While Spinoza doesn't address pedagogy directly, he had worked as a tutor (*Ep.* IX [to Simon de Vries]; CWS I, 193), and his later *Hebrew Grammar* was produced as a teaching guide. Some intriguing work in educational psychology has drawn on Spinoza, from Lev Vygotsky (e.g. 2017: 209–27; cf. Sévérac 2017) to, more recently, Johan Dahlbeck (e.g. 2017).
[77] TP V, 2; CWS II, 529; DC I.2; cf. Machiavelli 2003: II.29.

certain way.[78] This making of the citizen follows consequentially from the reasonable constitution of the State and its laws. Rebellions, violence or disorder are to be attributed 'not so much to the wickedness of the subjects as to the corruption of the State', a view originating in Machiavelli.[79] But the true virtue of the State is in its continual sensitivity and calibration of its laws, institutions and decision-making to the common feeling of the multitude, one that can be responsive, but also prepared to lead, pursuing courses of action of longer-term advantage than short-term gain.

The influence of Machiavelli also bears on Spinoza's shift in political terminology. Recalling the table of Chapter 5, while the *TTP* is marked by the high frequency of *vulgus* and *populus*, the *TP* mostly uses *multitudo* and *cives*. This reflects a theoretical departure from Hobbes in *De Cive*, who divided social forces between 'the people', 'a *single* entity, with *a single will*', bound by a social contract to transfer their natural right to the sovereign; and the 'multitude', the citizens and subjects who are the disorganised basis of a state.[80] In Hobbes's system, the sovereignty of the *populus* could be expressed 'paradoxically' (as he himself put it) through the singular person of a king in a monarchy. In the *TP*, Spinoza overcomes the Hobbesian contradiction: one's natural right is entirely coextensive with one's power, and given that the *multitudo* are numerically superior in any society, their natural right and power constitutes the basis of the State's security.[81]

All the same, Spinoza's unfinished account does not explain how passive subjects might, on an epistemic level, become active citizens. Spinoza is non-committal and unclear on the generic eligibility for citizenship in democracies, a point Curley also considers a 'serious, and perhaps irremediable flaw'.[82] Nor does Spinoza give any account of how a given multitude might be educated or enabled to attain citizenship. While Hobbes's *Leviathan* attributed some virtue to the education of citizens, considering them 'clean paper' to be inscribed with civic values, Spinoza rests faith in the intrinsic rationality of assemblies.[83] Yet these assemblies are seemingly far more exclusive than their naturalistic presentation in the *TTP* would have suggested. For while popular sovereignty is the basis of any given state, its *potentia* – responsibility or *potestas* for administering its affairs for the

---

[78] *TP* VII, 27; echoing *TTP* XVII, 26; CWS II, 558–9; 301.
[79] *TP* V, 2; CWS II, 529; Machiavelli 2003: III.29.
[80] *DC* XII.8.
[81] *Ep.* L [to Jarig Jelles]; CWS II, 406; *TP* II, 15; CWS II, 513.
[82] Spinoza 2016: 501.
[83] *L* II.30.6.

common good – falls into the hands of a much smaller group of citizens who play a decisive role in Spinoza's three political forms, forming the various councils which determine its decisions or monitor their efficacy.

It is through this commitment to natural right and its relation to reason that Spinoza ultimately forbids servants, foreigners, children, criminals and women from participating in his ideal democracy.[84] In excluding so many, the democratic assemblies would likely reproduce a stale social conformity of members that would inhibit the goods of deliberative plurality argued in the *TTP*. That in place of large, dynamic assemblies that express ideas that 'no one had ever thought of before', might instead arise institutionally defensive and aloof cultures whose 'one mind that might be guided by reason', is, in Sharp's words, 'counterfactual'.[85] In other words, despite its pressing contextual concerns for peace and stability, Spinoza's programme of collective liberation remains fettered by a paternalistic reliance on wise statesmen who might lead, but not necessarily empower, the multitude. Such a paternalism was found wanting in a different way at the end of the last chapter.

The Living State

Spinoza's late political thought is preoccupied by questions of what constitutes civil order and stability. His conclusions suggest it rests on a common set of ideas and affects in a community, a union of minds given form and structure by historical traditions and culture, but above all, by the reasonable organisation and direction of the State. As he remarks later in the *TP*, 'the laws are the soul of the State' (*Anima enim imperii jura sunt*).[86] The sentence is unusual for Spinoza, not only in its concision, but in the singular appearance of *anima* ('soul') in the text. There is also a peculiar dualism at play: in its assignation of the State's material survival to the 'soul' of its laws or constitution, it is reminiscent of a multitude being guided 'by one mind' earlier. How does this square, then, with the rule of the affects and desire over human affairs set out forcefully by the *TP* earlier?

In a recent study, Del Lucchese has perceptively observed the influence of the imagination in both phrases.[87] A mind imagines that it guides the body, just as a community imagines itself to be guided by a common set of ideas or values. We can extend that observation to citizens who imagine that the

[84] *TP* XI, 3–4; *CWS* II, 602–3.
[85] IX, 14; *CWS* II, 594; Sharp 2018: 110.
[86] *TP* X, 9; *CWS* II, 600.
[87] Del Lucchese 2017: 38.

survival of their state rests on a reasonable and fair constitution and laws. This should make them more receptive to the lessons of political experience, and their underlying theoretical principles in human nature, affects and sociality, of Spinoza's late political science. For laws are only as powerful as the utility of obeying them. So long as this constitution or set of laws is correctly established and kept 'inviolate', the State can exist in eternal security. Such inviolability is dependent on the collective attachment of a people to the civil order, which in turn is based on a constitution operating according to reason. The laws cannot remain intact unless they are 'defended both by reason and by the common affect of men'. Without this common affect, those laws that rest 'only on the support of reason' are 'weak and easily overcome'.[88] Benign dictatorships will collapse unless they are founded in the collective feeling or desire of the people, one unlikely to tolerate long what does not accomplish the common good. It is the political import of this common feeling, decisive for statecraft, that Spinoza's late politics takes a final, incomplete journey towards. As the *TTP* remarks, 'nature creates individuals, not nations', and in the final case, Spinoza's model of political eternity in reasonable laws that reflect common feeling supplies a framework wherein individuals achieve greater power in common, as they align their natural right into forms that realise their individual interests and desires, collectively.[89]

In evaluating Spinoza's late political constitutionalism with its Aristotelian claim that all conceivable forms of state had already been discovered, Stuart Hampshire, an otherwise sympathetic reader of Spinoza, found his formulations 'so unreal and sterile'.[90] On the face of it, we might agree. The peculiarly Aristotelian influence on the *TP* is also present in its appreciation for a new naturalistic political science of the affects, its interest in constitutional blueprints, as well as its teleological interest in the 'highest good'. Elsewhere, the relative silence of Spinoza commentators on the *TP* suggests a similar verdict.[91] Being neither Hobbesian, Machiavellian nor neo-Aristotelian, but a peculiar Dutch hybrid of all and none, the work

---

[88] *TP* X, 9; *CWS* II, 600.
[89] *TTP* XVII, 93; *CWS* II, 317.
[90] Hampshire 1953: 191.
[91] This isn't new: though included in the *Opera Posthuma*, the *TP* was rarely discussed by contemporaries and doesn't feature in the biographies of Lucas and Colerus, nor the encyclopaedia entries of Bayle or Diderot and D'Alembert. It's often been unfairly lumped with the older *TTP*, but I think conceptual and contextual matters demand a separation. In the English-speaking world, however, a good new guide has at last appeared (Melamed and Sharp 2018).

repels a simplified interpretation. Indeed, despite the current flourishing of Spinoza studies, comments like these are a reminder of how not of our times Spinoza is. That doesn't just extend to his early modern republicanism, with its Romanic disdain for affairs of the private household (or *oikos* in Greece, from which eventually emerges economics). It also relates to the broader issue of the intelligibility of nature, conceived under a form of eternity, of a virtue open to all and that all can equally obtain.[92] There is a fracture then between individual knowledge and rapture and the necessity (and possibility) of involvement in the community, in thinking through and trying to establish the conditions for collective joy and power.

Writing of Descartes and his method of doubt in *The Human Condition*, Arendt claimed that, in his attempt to deliver certain knowledge of questions like God or the laws of nature that were in her view fundamentally unknowable, Descartes had inadvertently brought about a modern condition of 'world alienation'.[93] In this condition, everything would be doubted except what was within the human mind. Yet while Descartes, like Francis Bacon, shared a Promethean desire to master nature for human ends, Spinoza's works tilt towards understanding God or nature on its own terms, without resting the world in the 'I-am'.[94] In Arendt's later work *On Revolution*, the problematic figure of Cartesian doubt ('*je doute donc je suis*') briefly returns in the context of Robespierre ('L'incorruptible'), the one who doubts others on a moral level, in an attack on the broader moralisation of politics she associated with the French Revolution. Her words remain timely in our own era, where political disagreement is often read in terms of oversimplified, polarised camps, whose actors are judged more on their perceived moral virtue and lack of hypocrisy than on their actual beliefs:

> If, in the words of Robespierre, 'patriotism was a thing of the heart', then the reign of virtue was bound to be at worst the rule of hypocrisy, and at best the never-ending fight to ferret out the hypocrites, a fight which could only end in defeat because of the simple fact that it was impossible to distinguish between true and false patriots.[95]

In its place, and by way of Thomas Jefferson and the ancient Athenian agora, Arendt formulates a defence of the political, one rooted in spontaneity,

---

[92] *Ethics* IV, 36; CWS I, 564.
[93] Arendt 1998: 272.
[94] Ibid. 280.
[95] Arendt 1965: 97.

public expression and disagreement. It would involve the creation of new public spaces for debate and democratic decision-making, of the sort that might overcome the loneliness she considered elsewhere as endemic to modern life.

For Arendt shared, without realising it, a view of politics as inherently conflictual (or agonistic) that had been established in historical terms in Machiavelli, and formulated according to contrasting views of human nature in Hobbes and Spinoza. Yet it's only of Spinoza that we might recognise a possibility of what she considered fundamental to the life of politics – plurality, in a reasonable republic that gathered difference around ways of common living that might best ensure peace and cooperation. But this is a politics that doesn't have much time for the empty heat and noise of dissensus. Spinoza also has strong ideas about how human societies can be governed.

For, as the last four chapters have determined, while Spinoza is concerned with the freedom of the human mind, the means for achieving it lie in the quality of one's relations with others. These relations bring us into being and nurture our development long before we can independently develop our own ideas and understand the causes of our affects, and so the political has a foundational role for enabling the becoming freer of as many as possible, or, as Balibar nicely put it, 'as many as possible, thinking as much as possible'.[96] That's why I challenged readings that Spinoza's politics and ethics are egoistic or merely concerned with individual therapeutics. Our turn instead to a common becoming-freer allowed us to read Spinoza's pessimism about the incapacity of the *vulgus* to live reasonably as being not merely misanthropic or elitist, but concerned with the elementary conditions of empowerment, in a life freed from fear and guided towards cooperation. For no one can be free of the passive affects that riddle and rive Spinoza's dramatis personae. Our natural condition as bodies and minds that are finite and greatly limited by their dependence on other external bodies necessarily places us in conditions of passivity, with resulting affects of sadness and joy. A politics of uncontaminated reason is therefore of little use. Instead, our greatest freedom *or* power – for these are always equivalent terms, and that which reason guides us to realising – is in combining with others of a common nature, thereby increasing our power exponentially, to the extent that our collective can remain harmoniously organised, which is no small feat.

This brought us to a politics of prophecy and the imagination, a universal means of knowledge and one capable of immense social good. Imaginaries

---

[96] Balibar 2008: 98.

can produce and extend feelings of commonality in communities, increasing their cooperative behaviours and multiplying the opportunities for mutual assistance, joy, and the acquisition of common notions. But concerned by the alarming rise of theological power and the looming collapse of the liberal republican party of De Witt, Spinoza drops his politicisation of the imagination and argues for the free circulation of speech. His resulting social epistemology is weak – how are ordinary Dutch Calvinists supposed to become more reasonable, if subject to the mere number of others' uninformed free tongues, or the pomp and ceremony of powerful voices? – and politically unsustainable, providing no apt model for preserving the Dutch Republic, or restoring it, should the theologians and monarchists seize power.

For all the remarkable developments of the *TP* – and in this chapter we have focused on collectivity, and the realisation of civil security through reasonable citizens – the political use of the imagination barely returns, and only in the somewhat cynical manner of elevating the patricians of aristocracy with distinguished clothing and a 'special title', with all following the universal faith of the *TTP*.[97] This weakens the account, especially one whose method founded sovereign power (Chapters 3–4) in natural right (Chapter 2). But by Spinoza's own standards, its method is already fatally compromised: in seeking the 'highest good' and optimum societies that realise the State's virtue in security, he himself fabricates three different utopias, and applies a quasi-teleological model of little use to his ontology of immanent, self-determining power.[98] His models do not explain how forms of political servitude emerge in a given society, nor how they might be contained (say, for instance, if an elitist cult were to become influential among the council members). The *TP* (like the Hebrew exemplar of the *TTP*) gives no account of how subjects are to become more reasonable, having an active and participatory role in causing their own ideas and affects.

Where is the desire for collectivity to emerge from? The *TP*'s states might need some kind of nationalism to sustain them, a common good that is not a universal one, for otherwise the subjects will become restless against the decisions of an elite class of citizens. Without a collectivist republican imaginary or a programme for popular education, it's hard to see how meaningful political empowerment can emerge. Spinoza's preference for deliberative assemblies has little defence against Hobbes's critique that such assemblies

---

[97] *TP* VIII, 47; VIII, 46; CWS II, 587–8.
[98] There is one possible defence: the three optimal societies may serve an exemplar-like function, devices for educating our imaginations to what might be possible, or models to compare existing polities with possible ones. If so, this isn't clear in the text.

were a 'nuisance' and 'inept', particularly when run by ambitious, vain and ignorant citizens who might represent a narrow part of the population, and whose principal efforts in public office are to reward themselves, their friends or financial backers.[99]

Yet the *TP* has many strengths. At last, Spinoza offers something approaching a coherent normative political theory, one in which the common good is realised by the active and desiring participation of individuals in the collective functions of the State. The State doesn't just offer security to its citizens, it also increases their power of acting. The role of unanimity also explains some of the problems of agency for group or plural subjects touched on in Chapter 5: their activity or obligations to each other do not emerge naturally or innately, but reflect dispositions that they must be made capable of. Spinoza's suggestion of *making citizens* is exemplary on this count: one could read it in an Althusserian way and recognise an immanent critique of ideology and social constructions; one could also read it in a traditional republican way as outlining the kinds of civic virtues, affects and desires required to establish more reasonable, cooperative societies.

This sense of collective identity produced by a free, harmonious polity could be considered an emergent property – one that explains the emergence of civil rights and obligations without identifying their subdivision in the minds of individuals. Yet for such an emergent property to enhance the powers of the individuals that comprise its civil order, it needs more than just deliberative political forms. The way of life of becoming freer involves an education of the imagination and joy, so that the possibility and pleasure in events or thoughts that correlate to our actual self-preservation comes to be freely accepted and desired. The last three chapters have now correlated this self-preservation with the common good. While Spinoza's concepts have set up all the pieces for a game of collective desire, spread out over a board of nature's immanent, infinite power, and even provided a theoretical rulebook, he leaves us with no ability to play. What can one do if one does not live in an optimum polity? What can the rebel do to resist, or change entrenched but unfair laws? If the freedom-loving philosopher happened to be born in the contemporary Ottoman Empire, Spinoza's exemplar of political servitude, then the *TP* offers little, on the face of it, beyond quietism.

Then there's something perhaps in the common feeling of the multitude earlier. Sovereignty begins and ends here. It's at the root of our societies: that nothing is more useful to human beings than one another.[100] Becoming freer

---

[99] *DC* X.10.
[100] *Ethics* IV, 18 Schol.; *CWS* I, 556.

begins in what is communal, like common notions, or bonds of friendship, and reasonable communities directed by the love of a common good, their shared life and power. But it is not merely a common thing: Spinoza's desire to identify the highest good of a collective association of reasonable beings requires taking the common as a premise towards universality. The collective power under reason that Spinoza envisions, and which his philosophy of freedom leads him towards, is one that is not limited to a cultural or national kind, but which extends out to infinity, embracing all, neutralising harmful ideas with joyous, collectivising ideas and actions. Becoming-common is the precondition to becoming-universal, and everything begins and ends with desire and the affects. Yet an education of desire and a 'science' of the affects each necessitate a return to thinking about the kinds of collective organisations which can empower one and all. A politics of freedom that deals only with distant revolutionary horizons cannot satisfy the pressing urgency of this problem, yet a politics without a normative conception of the common good, and which lacks the capacity to dream, is of little use either. Reason's republic should not remain a utopia.

Cadenza: *Prudentissimo Viro*

In an article of June 1920, a time when factory occupations across Italy suggested the possibility of imminent revolution, Antonio Gramsci reflected on the importance of cultural and intellectual power. For these occupations and worker councils to succeed, 'the proletariat must also face the problem of winning intellectual power'.[1] To avoid merely reproducing what they sought to overthrow, it required the formation of 'a new psychology, new ways of feeling, thinking and living that must be specific to the working class, that must be created by it, that will become "dominant" when the working class becomes the dominant class'. But Gramsci's analysis at this stage still seemed to imply that the mind of the proletariat was a *tabula rasa*, passive and inert. It had unmet 'metaphysical needs' that, were they articulated effectively by an organised party, could be sure of realising power.[2]

Six years later, Gramsci had been imprisoned by the now fascist government. Like his comrades in the Italian Communist Party and others overseas, Gramsci had underestimated and dismissed the fascists and their popularity as a short-lived and insubstantial movement of the 'petit bourgeoisie' until too late.[3] His *Prison Notebooks* offer a more nuanced reflection on this question of consciousness. Gramsci develops the concept of 'hegemony' to explore how capitalism had remained resilient despite the profound economic crises of 1917–21. No longer proposing the creation of a proletarian consciousness in a void, an *ex nihilo* myth like that of Spinoza's optimum state in the last chapter, Gramsci came instead to recognise that power is mediated not just along state-political or economic lines,[4] but also

---

[1] Gramsci 2000: 70–1.
[2] Ibid. 43, 71, 81–2.
[3] Ibid. 138–9.
[4] E.g. Gramsci 2000: 192–4.

culturally, through the everyday ideas and beliefs people hold about the world.

Had Gramsci been aware of his work, he might have quoted his contemporary, Wilhelm Reich, who also challenged his Marxist contemporaries to focus not merely on 'economism' but on the more fundamental role of culture, tradition and desire in public life.[5] For Reich, the rise of fascism had been established not simply through grievances over military defeat or economic collapse, but through a widespread fear of the chaos of workers' uprisings and an identification, at the level of desire, with authoritarian familial and political structures:

> The lower middle-class bedroom suite [. . .] the consequent suppression of the wife [. . .] the 'decent' suit of clothes for Sunday [. . .] have an incomparably greater reactionary influence when repeated day after day than thousands of revolutionary rallies and leaflets can ever hope to counterbalance.[6]

If 'psychic structure and social situation seldom coincide', as Reich suggests, then the task becomes understanding and disarming the reactive tendencies of desire, so as to more effectively enable its politically liberatory realisation.[7]

Gramsci himself had begun to identify 'the importance of facts of culture and thought in the development of history', and the importance of intellectual–cultural forms of coercion and consent in cementing social relations.[8] Popular beliefs therefore possess a solid material force, shaped into form by ruling ideologies.[9] These hegemonic facts are 'instruments of domination', the features that Spinoza saw as fighting for servitude in the *TTP*, and which for Gramsci must be tackled with the same seriousness as political and economic forms of oppression.[10] To succeed, revolutionaries need to make 'the governed intellectually independent of the governing', through popular education and self-education.[11]

---

[5] Reich 1972: 284–5.
[6] Reich 1993: 69.
[7] Ibid. 64.
[8] Gramsci 2000: 195.
[9] Ibid. 200.
[10] Ibid. 196.
[11] Ibid.; cf. 332–3.

Gramsci's shift may have also been inspired by Marx's third thesis on Feuerbach: 'the educator must himself be educated'.[12] But emphasising education alone was also unviable against the overwhelming forces of fascism and populist fear, he thought. Gramsci reconsiders societies as composed of 'relations of force' at any given conjuncture, which must be understood in a longer 'war of position'.[13] In his analysis, Western states like Italy and Germany differed from Bolshevik Russia in having a much larger and more traditionally entrenched 'civil society' which through religion, popular journalism, a more diffuse distribution of private property ownership, an expediently useless state education system and a conservative authoritarian family structure would continue to reproduce hegemonic domination without the direct intrusion of capitalists or the State, even if workers were to seize every factory. His concerns were akin to Spinoza's thoughts on Cromwell and the English, or on the tragicomedy of Masaniello, the fisherman–tyrant. The 'actual take-over of power in factories must be preceded by concrete preparation for this take-over *in the mind*', as Reich would similarly put it.[14] The war of position therefore necessitated a longer-term campaign to produce a working-class hegemonic and democratic movement capable of becoming popular enough – and self-determining enough – to succeed decisively.[15] Yet given the conservative forces within civil society that nourished the popularity of fascism and predisposed people to be indifferent or even hostile to collective forms, the war of position could only succeed by persuading the Italian people, using their existing frames of reference.

Gramsci came to outline the necessity of what was described in Chapter 4 as *reprogramming*, of a Spinozan kind. Whereas my argument was for educating joyous affects, Gramsci turns to how revolutionaries might reprogramme existing hegemonic structures with a new kind of 'common sense', a belief-set that is construed as common and obviously known, yet socially progressive. It contains two elements: the first is a critique of existing common sense as something 'incoherent' and 'ambiguous, contradictory and multiform' in the minds of individuals, while the second seeks to repurpose these myths and inchoate fragments towards a collectively liberatory end.[16] By critically and plainly exposing the contradictions of existing 'common sense', considered as a form of 'faith' and 'folklore', Gramsci hoped that a more progressive

---

[12] Marx and Engels 1998: 570.
[13] Gramsci 2000: 201–9, 224–6.
[14] Reich 1972: 358.
[15] Gramsci 2000: 225–30.
[16] Ibid. 343, 346.

popular culture and education system would raise the general intellectual level of the people.[17] The shift was against the kind of reasoning of the imagination of final causes, free will and superstitions whose prejudices Spinoza counselled against in *Ethics* I Appendix and the Preface of the *TTP*. It would serve to enable them to recognise the 'submission and intellectual subordination' implicit in everyday cultural and political beliefs and processes.[18] Further, it would enable them 'in renovating and making "critical" an already existing activity', that of everyday discussion and analysis, to more freely recognise their shared oppression and the advantages of joining forces to improve their conditions, a kind of consciousness-raising long before its adoption by feminists in the early 1970s.[19]

It was something which Mark Fisher was working on in his final writing. It concerned the possibility of a new vision of politics he called 'acid communism', which would involve 'the convergence of class consciousness, socialist-feminist consciousness-raising and psychedelic consciousness, the fusion of new social movements with a communist project, an unprecedented aestheticisation of everyday life'.[20] He had in mind a new kind of political and social practice, a new kind of living (and 'not merely theorising' about) political thinking together, through which people might share their feelings and experiences and identify the impersonal socio-economic structures that often indirectly led to their disempowerment at work or in their communities. 'No individuals can change anything, not even themselves', he wrote, but 'collective activation is already, immanently, overcoming individualised immiseration.'[21] The exit from what he called 'the face', or the privatisation of stress, was at the same time an entrance into new ways of thinking and acting together, in ways that were compassionate, generous and empowering. It might lead to a new and more robust form of political association among individuals who valued the difficulty of thinking and the necessity of doing it together – *fellowship*.

Gramsci's concept of hegemony underwent a transformation from a transcendent viewpoint – class consciousness onto a proletarian *tabula rasa*, leading to total revolution – to an immanent one – repurposing common sense by counteracting bourgeois hegemonic views which result in what might be called voluntary servitude, leading to greater popular

---

[17] Ibid. 339, 343.
[18] Ibid. 328.
[19] Ibid. 332; 339–40.
[20] Fisher 2018: 758.
[21] Fisher 2015b.

self-determination. The proletarians who become aware of these hegemonic forms and can challenge them with their own critical reasoning are the 'organic intellectuals'; those that defend conventional civil society and its bourgeois forms are the 'traditional intellectuals'.[22] What Gramsci envisioned in this transformation of common sense was nothing less than the undertaking 'on an intellectual plane [...] what the Reformation was in Protestant countries'.[23]

But who would play the role of Martin Luther or the printing press? Spinoza was all too aware of the necessity and difficulty of confronting powerful interests and the superstitions and other harmful ideas on which they thrived. While his self-portrait as Masaniello may have served to amuse friends, it also reflected the radical, if not revolutionary nature of his philosophical and political positions. In an increasingly dangerous and unstable milieu, the author of the now finished *Ethics* turned to the affects in politics, as we discussed in the last chapter. We'll also recall the influence of Machiavelli, that 'very prudent man [*prudentissimo viro*] [...] on the side of freedom' who, above all, identified that a tyrant cannot be meaningfully removed without also uprooting the common feelings, desires and beliefs which nourish them.[24]

Yet while Machiavelli dismisses utopias to advise would-be princes to 'learn how not to be good', Spinoza takes a separate route, arguing that a well-organised and reasonable state requires no such expedient vices.[25] What differentiates Spinoza's *TP* from its peers is its attempt to derive a political naturalism from its own earlier definitions of reason, affects and natural right. Leaving nothing to *fortuna* or the moods of the monarch, Spinoza's rational republic places a commonly recognised principle of popular sovereignty into the very life, and highest good, of political processes. Yet, in its focus on the scientific principles for stable states, Spinoza left behind the perceptive social epistemology of the *TTP* and its account of the prophet who builds commonality at the level of the imagination. Such a prophet has need not only of weapons, but of something even more powerful by its social epistemology: an understanding and persuasive communication with the hearts of others.

For Gramsci, the value of generating 'organic intellectuals' paled in comparison with generating a mass democratic movement for broader society, led

---

[22] Gramsci 2000: 340–1.
[23] Ibid. 362.
[24] *TP* V, 7; *CWS* II, 531.
[25] Machiavelli 2005: XV, 53; *TP* V, 2; *CWS* II, 529.

by a political party. The question remained: how would such a party become popular, given the forces ranged against it? In his studies of Machiavelli, particularly *Il Principe*, it becomes a '"live" work', one that fuses political ideology and political science 'in the dramatic form of a "myth"'.[26] For Gramsci, the figure of 'the Prince' and the work *Il Principe* combine two attributes of power: the 'doctrinal, rational' nature of power as understood by political science, and the symbolic, utopian nature of the figurehead who 'anthropomorphically' represents and embodies the collective's desire.[27] Gramsci conceives of the party being like a 'modern Prince': a 'collective individual' which embodies and becomes the symbol of the 'collective will'. Like Georges Sorel's 'myth' of the general strike, Gramsci sees potential in the dramatic staging or 'creation of concrete fantasy which acts on a dispersed and shattered people to arouse and organize its collective will'. In terms abstruse enough to evade the prison censor, Gramsci's modern Prince would be a platform for a 'national-popular collective will' to come into formation and self-awareness through 'concrete and rational' goals that would be realised by a popular, universally inclusive and democratic party.[28] It would revolutionise the 'whole system of intellectual and moral relations', revalue all values, resulting in a new *common sense*, with the same certainty as belief in 'divinity or the categorical imperative'.[29]

Its very activity would find itself opposed vigorously by the traditionally powerful, propertied classes, but for Gramsci, historical instances like the Reformation indicated that, with sufficient popular support and consciousness, a shared common sense by way of an 'intellectual and moral reformation' could overcome overwhelming hegemonic forces. It was not that individuals would merely support a dramatised modern Prince party: as Gramsci envisioned, they would *become* it, participating in the 'collective consciousness' of a 'collective individual', like that consciousness glimpsed by his contemporaries Benjamin and Lukács in Chapter 6.[30] Apprehensive of its conformist implications, Gramsci would later add that this collective would be like an orchestra in rehearsal, 'each instrument playing for itself', giving the impression of a 'most dreadful cacophony', but ultimately 'necessary for the orchestra to live as a single "instrument"'.[31]

---

[26] Gramsci 2000: 238.
[27] Ibid. 238–40.
[28] Ibid. 240–3.
[29] Ibid. 243.
[30] Ibid. 244.
[31] Ibid. 245.

It remains unclear what form exactly this dramatic modern Prince might have taken. Peter Thomas conceives it as 'a coalition of the rebellious subalterns', a pedagogical laboratory for intellectual self-liberation.[32] Carlos Nelson Coutinho considers it a feature of Gramsci's broader 'cultural front' that aimed to establish 'the conditions for the hegemony of the subaltern classes, for their victory in the "war of position" for socialism'.[33] While both readings are right to prioritise Gramsci's broader vision for subaltern liberation, they overlook Gramsci's own interest in the strategic and instrumental use of myths and 'common sense' for producing and articulating a liberatory position. His attention to what is already 'operative' might instead connote that a collective subjectivity, and with it a collective desire, can only be produced by reassembling the fragments of popular myths and forms of speech. At the same time, Gramsci's formulations rely on an implicit dualism that elevates the power of 'will' and 'mind' over passive, pliable bodies. The Spinozan view of collective power is far more radical, understanding the political in what the people feel, imagine and enact (or fail to act) as much as think. It is a freedom as much for bodies as for minds. These would be premises for collective liberation – equal access to resources like housing, healthcare and education, a reduction in the working week, a minimum living wage, a carbon-neutral economy, freedom from the necessity of full-time drudgerous work, freedom of speech, right to due process, and so on – articulated in a form already common and immediately sensible, without condescension. Its mythic nature is a critical self-reflection on the composition of political demands.

Like Rousseau's *volonté générale*, Spinoza's *una veluti mente* or even the UN's 1948 Universal Declaration of 'Human Rights', such concepts and demands are also declarative, calling themselves into being, and subsequently naturalising themselves as rights. They are no less real for it because, as the discussion of interdependence in Chapter 6 emphasised, our being is in our contingent and interdependent relations, something which can be rooted back to the individual's ontological empowerment through their desire, outlined in Chapter 4. The question then becomes not merely understanding the prevailing collective imaginaries and harmful ideas that result in different kinds of social conflict and servitude, but thinking strategically and pragmatically about how such forms become hegemonic in the first place, and then, perhaps, how they might be dismantled and transformed. It means 'shifting the relations of forces', as Stuart Hall puts it, 'not so that

---

[32] Thomas 2013: 32–3; cf. 2009: 437–8.
[33] Coutinho 2012: 114–15.

Utopia comes the day after the next general election, but so that the *tendencies* begin to run another way'.[34] While it jettisons utopianism, it leaves room for strategic optimism. It corresponds to what Mark Fisher described as 'communist realism' in a late writing, 'soberly and pragmatically assessing the resources that are available to us, and thinking about how we can best use and increase those resources', without surrendering a sense of 'realism' or 'pragmatism' to the forces of reaction.[35]

But in different ways, Gramsci and Reich were reacting to a totalitarian appropriation of power that belatedly realised Hobbes's vision of the secular state adopting the trappings of a 'mortal God'. Powerful forces of repression and reaction were growing in influence and confidence, curtailing the safety of independent and critical thought. To challenge these dangerous prophetic forces, and the sad affects they mobilised and expressed, political struggle would have to take place at the level of the imagination, desire and the affects. As Reich wrote in 1934, contemporary communist parties have failed to make contact with 'what happens in "people's heads" and their psychical structures'.[36] On the one hand, this meant understanding desire, grasping the subjective worldviews of the working class in terms of what Reich called their 'progressive desires' against the 'traditional bonds' that stifled them, and which would fall under Spinoza's view of harmful ideas.

But it also necessitated a *recapture* of the collective imaginary, a 'takeover *in the mind*', in order to cultivate a power to think critically and self-determinedly. 'As many as possible, thinking as much as possible', as Balibar put it well in the last chapter. By 1946, Reich calls this position 'work-democracy', in which the natural functions of 'vital work [i.e. socially useful], natural love and knowledge' would be enabled to flourish through a socialist democratic, international federation of interdependent worker-led cooperatives.[37] To prevent the re-emergence of mass authoritarian movements, it would not be enough to emphasise the revolutionary nature of desire itself, as Deleuze and Guattari would do with their 'subject groups' in *Anti-Oedipus*.[38] In Reich's view, most of the population must be raised to an elementary level of capability, able to think for itself. They must be able to freely bear 'social responsibility', whose occasional guilty burden is something that mass

---

[34] Hall 1987: 21.
[35] Fisher 2015a.
[36] Reich 1972: 284.
[37] Reich 1993: 313–15.
[38] Deleuze and Guattari 2013: 320–1.

authoritarian movements will promise, dangerously, to divest them of.[39] Cultivating the sense and maturity to bear social responsibility therefore requires democratic state forms to intervene at the earliest stage, to ensure children and young people are sufficiently educated to understand the complexities of desire, and our relationships with and dependence on others.

As Spinoza had argued centuries earlier, the true freedom of the individual would only be realised in a peaceful, cooperative and free community. But this in turn required cultivating sufficient power of thinking and acting within a society to dissipate the power of reactionary counterforces, the seditious theologians Spinoza railed against in the *TTP*. For Reich, it is therefore 'the State's duty not only to encourage the passionate yearning for freedom in working masses of people; *it must also make every effort to make them capable of freedom*'.[40] In a similar line of reasoning to Spinoza, the virtue of the democratic state – democratic not merely in terms of occasional elections, but in the very structure of its administrative, social and economic institutions – is the freedom to live well that it affords.

It's this promise of true freedom of a communal and collective sort that Spinoza suggests to me, from his very different context – one beyond the rule of money, or government of fear and individual ambition; one beyond the ravaging of our natural environment, a contempt for the motives or mental capabilities of others, or a retreat into individual withdrawal and the diminishing rewards of the lonely mind's egoistic survival. But it is also a matter of 'how ideas become practical forces', as Annibale Pastore, Gramsci's philosophy professor at Turin, concisely puts it.[41] Desiring freedom is only possible and made worthwhile when a collective around one shares in that same desire, unburdened of the fear that cements a condition of passivity and popular servitude. The question then becomes how a political movement can realise this inherent power.

---

[39] Reich 1993: 62, 201–4, 224–9, 316–21.
[40] Ibid. 284.
[41] Gramsci 2000: 30.

8

Revolution

In Chapter 7 of the *Political Treatise*, Spinoza replies to critics who might dismiss his politics as mere utopianism. Against those who claim fear, ignorance and violence belong not to humanity as a whole, but just to the common people (*plebs*), he replies, 'everyone shares a common nature'.[1] Instead, 'we are deceived by power [*potentia*] and culture [*cultu*]' (translation modified), and confuse social customs with the natural order, so that the misdeeds of aristocrats are 'honourable and becoming', while those of the poor require punishment. In the process, he disavows the contempt for the *vulgus* that characterised parts of the *Ethics* and *TTP*. No longer are the common people themselves to be blamed for being feckless, ignorant and violent. For 'it's no surprise that "there's neither truth nor judgement in the plebs"', he writes, paraphrasing a line from Tacitus that characterised his own earlier thinking, 'when the rulers manage the chief business of the State secretly, and the plebs are only making a guess from the few things the rulers can't conceal.' Such disorders are inevitable when the workings of the State are concealed from the people.

This emphasis on power and culture is interesting. One of the many effects of the work of Marx and Engels is the now commonly held conception of social power in economic terms. In a striking passage from *Capital: Volume I*, a work that sets out to analyse these terms, Marx punctures the assumption that the economic relations in society between capitalist and worker merely reflect the natural order. 'The advance of capitalist production develops a working class', he writes, which 'by education, tradition and habit looks upon the requirements of that mode of production as self-evident, natural laws.'[2] We'll recall Spinoza's own critique of a certain prejudiced naturalism

---

[1] *TP* VII, 27; *CWS* II, 559.
[2] Marx 1982: 899.

in Chapter 2. For Marx, the 'silent compulsion' of these relations is that the workers are effectively dominated and have their power (their labour and the value created by it) expropriated from them without even fully recognising it.

One of the attractions of Spinoza for a Marxist perspective is that he provides an understanding of power rooted in the imagination, desire and the affects. Though Marx himself had an interest in what he called the 'superstructure' or common set of beliefs in a society,[3] the mental life and affects of the working class are rarely explored in either *Capital* or Engels' study of the working class in Manchester. Reich described this as the danger of 'economism' earlier. While Althusser, Deleuze and Negri endorse the 'materialist' reading of Spinoza, the resources that they derive most concern the ideational, of how power is constituted or restricted at the level of minds as much as bodies.[4]

The deceptions of power and culture, of the 'ceremony and pomp' that makes men fight for servitude as if for salvation, can lead understandably enough to a suspicion of all forms of power, except that constituted perhaps by the mass of the excluded. Thus, the potential Negri reads in the multitude in his own work on Spinoza, and, with Michael Hardt, a potential akin to theories of 'the people' as the excluded, or 'the part of no part' in the thought of Jacques Rancière, or Ernesto Laclau and Chantal Mouffe.[5] But while there is always greater power in a collective of individuals who agree in their nature, that in no way automatically translates to the life of the many different communities that might constitute a given city or a state. There can be communities who share little except anger, hatred or fear, or who define themselves in opposition and superiority to the rest, and actively defend their interests.[6] Political change has, in most cases, not been achieved by amorphous masses of the excluded, but by smaller, well-organised communities bound together by a common set of ideas and integration of bodies (like social familiarity and trust, and in occupying spaces of economic or political importance). We can also live in and among communities whose members

---

[3] Ibid. 175n35.

[4] In this sense, one could compare Spinoza with the work of Michel Foucault, particularly in his understanding of power as constituted through the disciplining of bodies (1991) or a 'governmentality' (2007) in which the mentalities (or *ingenia*, we might say) and knowledge of citizens are organised by the government. See, as starters, Montag 1995, Juniper and Jose 2008 and Casarino 2017.

[5] Rancière 1999: 89–90; Laclau and Mouffe 2001: 176–8; Laclau 2007: 108; Mouffe 2018: 62.

[6] I am thinking here of Ralph Miliband's analysis of the British upper class, 1969: 60.

don't understand much about each other, prefer their own company to those around them, and live with mistaken ideas about their fellows.

Jane Addams, an early twentieth-century pioneer of social work and an overlooked philosopher of democracy, wrestled with these problems while working with the poor of Chicago's Near West Side. Over some years and with great industry, she established the Hull House settlement which provided clubs and classes for local people, and then, in recognition of local needs, established the city's first public playground, gym and bathhouse. Addams lobbied for rubbish collection, restrictions on child labour and for children's education, and against racial discrimination and local political corruption. She and her colleagues lived alongside the poor and learned from them, pursuing a concept of democracy that bridged theory and practice. Over the course of her work, she often reflected on the communities she had dedicated herself to serve, on their beliefs and desires, and on where her plans and initiatives had been out of sync with local feeling:

> All about us are men and women who have become unhappy in regard to their attitude toward the social order itself; toward the dreary round of uninteresting work, the pleasures narrowed down to those of appetite, the declining consciousness of brain power, and the lack of mental food which characterizes the lot of the large proportion of their fellow-citizens. These men and women have caught a moral challenge raised by the exigencies of contemporaneous life; some are bewildered, others who are denied the relief which sturdy action brings are even seeking an escape, but all are increasingly anxious concerning their actual relations to the basic organization of society.[7]

To address this problem of anxiety and loneliness, Addams envisioned a form of democracy that began at the level of the locality and the communal, one grounded in recognising what we called our interdependence earlier. With this would come a democratic knowledge, whereby people would come to learn about each other, and political policy would be directly informed by the needs, beliefs and affects of all citizens, particularly those in need of public services and traditionally excluded.[8] 'The charity visitor finds herself still more perplexed', she reflected, 'when she comes to consider such problems as those of early marriage and child labor; for she cannot deal with

---

[7] Addams 1902: 4.
[8] Addams uses the term 'sympathetic knowledge', not democratic knowledge (e.g. 1912: 11), but in my reading such sympathy is at the heart of a democratic outlook.

them according to economic theories, or according to the conventions that have regulated her own life.'[9] There are many such remarks in her work; while the society described has long changed, the underlying process of non-judgemental, open-minded listening remains pertinent. An 'intimate knowledge of the situation', one sensitive to and in cooperation with others, rather than imposed from outside, leads to a more accurate and sympathetic view of others, and in turn improves the knowledge and resources provided, indirectly empowering the community again.

Democratic knowledge also involves facing up to the uncertainty of the political, which can never be morally pure or free from hypocrisy – indeed it involves the rejection of the moralisation of politics, or its reduction to a zero-sum game of 'rational self-interest' (an oxymoron in terms) – in favour of recognising our basic equality and difference. Something more concerned with relations than individual rights. It's similar to what Gillian Rose had in mind with what she called a 'good enough justice' in *Love's Work*, one that could face up to impossibility of bridging the middle of individual behaviour and judgement and hectoring moral absolutes.[10] As Addams says, '[w]e have learned as common knowledge that much of the insensibility and hardness of the world is due to the lack of the imagination which prevents a realization of the experiences of others'.[11] We could call that faculty of imagination *commonality*. It will also remind us of Arendt's remarks earlier about the necessity of cultivating, after Kant, an enlarged mentality, one in which we extend our perspective to incorporate many others and, in the process, enlarge the scope of our ethics. If we recall John Martin Fischer's analogy of how we walk the path in Chapter 4, we could say that democratic knowledge involves an understanding of how and why others walk that path in their own ways too.

Such a process cannot succeed by an appeal to self-interest, that superstitious belief which mistakenly places the fulfilment of one's own needs through competition and not cooperation with others. This is understandably difficult when 'power and culture' are established on a view of society as a place of ignorance and danger. But for Addams, what would improve the individual's 'struggle for life' – 'decency and comfort, for a chance to work and obtain the fulness of life' – can only be accomplished by these individuals recognising that their desires have a lot in common, and that their nature indeed was the same.[12] 'The demand should be universalized', she writes,

---

[9] Ibid. 38.
[10] Rose 1997: 116.
[11] Addams 1902: 9.
[12] Ibid. 269.

'in this process it would also become clarified, and the basis of our political organization become perforce social and ethical.'

Though Arendt does not write about Addams' work, she may have heard about Hull House while lecturing at the University of Chicago from 1963 to 1967, just after the publication of *On Revolution*. In that volume, Arendt is often dismissive of what she calls 'the social question' (associated with Rousseau and Marx), which considered the relief of poverty as an absolute political goal.[13] It was the pursuit of this, motivated by compassion, that had side-tracked revolutionaries from the pursuit of 'political liberty', she thought, a liberty that valued plurality and democratic decision-making (she had in mind the American Revolution) over the enforced liberation of the French Revolution. For Arendt, what also characterised the new era of revolutions of the late eighteenth century was the pursuit of freedom as a new absolute ideal, 'to find a new absolute to replace the absolute of divine power'.[14] As Condorcet announced, the 'word "revolutionary" can be applied only to revolutions whose aim is freedom'.[15] But the danger of this view of revolution was that it sought to achieve the realisation of an absolute ideal that was impossible. In viewing such an ideal as morally and historically necessary, this kind of revolutionary thought lacked the resources to deal with disagreement, with catastrophic results when such movements gained political power and inevitably encountered opposition.

Prior to this modern understanding, continues Arendt, riots, insurrections and the popular overthrow of a government had been understood in terms of *revolvere*, a revolving from one form of government to another, in line with the Platonic theory that all political regimes were cyclical, a view retained in Aristotle and Polybius. Thus, insurrections often claimed to restore order rather than inaugurate a new order, like Cromwell's English republic, which declared 'freedom by God's blessing restored' in the 1651 Instrument of Government.[16] Revolution, then, was not about realising some ideal on the horizon, an end-of-history moment where all conflict and human suffering are abolished, but about the difficult, contingent and non-normative events in which a new popular government was established, lastingly or not.

This problem of power, culture and the difficulty of political change introduces some questions I want to explore in our final chapter with Spinoza. Throughout the book we've explored what inhibits the desire for freedom,

---

[13] Arendt 1965: 60.
[14] Ibid. 39.
[15] Ibid. 29.
[16] Ibid. 43.

such that individuals cannot or do not recognise their common nature, as well as some forays into establishing a politics of commonality through the imagination, and the State. Does Spinoza's account provide the resources for thinking about another way of recognising commonality and acting together? I think so, and I will make the case for the imitative affect of emulation, which we last encountered in Chapter 4. But first, I want to explore the possibility and difficulties facing a coherent theory of rebellion in Spinoza, and whether it can address some of those problems just outlined. In the process, we'll also consider the affect of indignation, before offering some final remarks about the people, populism and new forms of collectivity that might be robust enough to withstand the challenges to human freedom outlined across this book.

Is it Reasonable to Rebel?

No, is the short answer from Spinoza. In the *Ethics*, obedience to the sovereign is effectively a dictate of reason. Things that bring 'discord to the State' are considered evil, and the free individual, guided by reason, desires to adhere to and 'keep the common laws of the State'.[17] Spinoza repeats in a letter that 'each person ought to love his neighbour and obey the commands of the sovereign power', and a similar language is deployed in the *TP*, that 'the more a man is led by reason [...] the more steadfastly he will observe the laws of the commonwealth and carry out the commands of the supreme power to whom he is subject'.[18] Even if considered unfair, the subject is unconditionally 'bound to carry them out'.[19] As Barbone observes, the 'wise person perceives that obedience *always* promotes his/her greater interests [...] and so he/she does nothing to contravene the sovereign's authority'.[20] These interests lie in the preservation of the State's sovereignty, understood in Spinoza's Hobbesian contractualism as a collective investment of right in the authority of the sovereign. Defying the State's laws thereby contravenes the natural right of one's fellow citizens, something the rational and free human being will readily avoid.

The *TTP* often attacks 'rebellion' (*seditio*), a term connoting the passive and unwitting complicity of the common people in the destruction of their own state.[21] It is said to arise with objective social causes under which citi-

---

[17] IV, 40; IV, 73 Dem.; *CWS* I, 570; 587.
[18] *Ep*. XLIII [to Jacob Ostens]; *TP* III, 6; *CWS* II, 386; 519.
[19] *TP* III, 5; *CWS* II, 519.
[20] Barbone 1999: 106.
[21] Cf. *TTP* XVII, *passim*, particularly.

zens passively fall.²² Spinoza warns the 'troublemaker' and the 'rebel' against wanting 'to nullify the law, seditiously, against the will of the magistrate', insisting that it 'very rarely happens' that sovereigns make absurd commands.²³ If faced with injustice, one should merely submit one's grievance to the sovereign authority and genially await a formal response.²⁴ Even in the case of the English Civil War, where a quasi-democratic revolt against an unpopular sovereign led to a short-lived republican commonwealth, Spinoza is quick to condemn the English people for their 'deadly example' in violating 'the right of a legitimate king' just to replace him with a 'new monarch under another name'.²⁵ It is exceedingly 'dangerous' to change the whole form of the state 'without a danger that the whole state will be ruined', and Spinoza cautions against such imprudence.²⁶

When confronted with similar premises, some commentators have cautioned whether one can describe Spinoza as revolutionary at all. Feuer describes a disillusioned drift towards aristocracy in the *TP* as Spinoza became 'repelled by the mob, its cruelty, its irrationality', an observation Verbeek also makes of the *TTP*, while Den Uyl recasts Spinoza as a 'conservative' advocate of rational egoism.²⁷ This conservative reading of Spinoza has been challenged on two counts by readers persuaded of a politically liberatory Spinoza, one that identifies within his metaphysics of collective power the basis of a theory of political resistance and rebellion. While the enterprise is often fraught with interpretive difficulty and accusations of anachronism – particularly in less historical approaches like Althusser, Negri and Lordon – I think that such a theory can be identified from within Spinoza's own ideas and context.

The first thing to consider is its historical context: the Dutch rebels of the late 1660s and early 1670s were not freedom-loving democrats but the reactionary Calvinists of the Dutch Reformed Church who wished to suppress philosophy and free speech, and supported the monarchical House of Orange. 'Revolution in the Netherlands meant the victory of reaction', as McShea puts it perceptively.²⁸ As Erik Stephenson writes, Spinoza feared a populist insurrection precisely '*against* freedom of speech and the

---

²² *TTP* Praef. 11–12; XVII, 103–8; XIX, 50; XX, 29; CWS II, 69; 319–20; 342; 349.
²³ XX, 15; XVI, 9; CWS II, 347; 284.
²⁴ XX, 15; CWS II, 347.
²⁵ XVIII, 33–4; CWS II, 329–30.
²⁶ XVIII, 30; 37; CWS II, 329, 331.
²⁷ Feuer 1987: 161; Verbeek 2003: 141–3; Den Uyl 1983: 105.
²⁸ McShea 1968: 191.

open-minded respect for religious pluralism' necessary for freedom.[29] We read in the last chapter about how those well-placed fears were realised over 1672, as the government collapsed and a de facto monarchy took over after widespread rioting. Hence the *TTP* describes as 'seditious' the very views of the Calvinists that seek to separate civil law from divine law and self-appoint their authority by 'divine right' over the common good.[30] Such seditious views began to permeate law after 1672, with the downfall of De Witt and his supporters, and the appointment of William as stadtholder, resulting in the ascendency of orthodox Calvinists across the Dutch city councils and civil life.[31]

In response to the triumph of the *ultimi barbarorum*, the *TP* reiterates the need for prudence in politics: 'how imprudent many people are to try to remove a tyrant from their midst, when they can't remove the causes of the prince's being a tyrant'.[32] This point expands on an underdeveloped observation in the *TTP* regarding the English: they failed because they did not 'change the form of the state',[33] as was noted with Masaniello in the Introduction, and so exchanged King Charles for King Oliver. Unless the institutional and cultural forms that produce monarchy and monarchical obedience are fundamentally transformed, they will continue to perpetuate themselves even after a successful insurrection. That said, Spinoza is clear about his objections to sedition as such. In terms of the social contract of the *TTP*, Spinoza tends to follow Hobbes in the view that open rebellion undermines the sovereignty of everyone else in allowing an individual to dispute or hijack the judgement of everyone else, in whom sovereignty is constituted. Della Rocca takes a modified view of this ('rational similarity') to argue that rebellion is unjustifiable for Spinoza under any circumstances.[34] But Spinoza's naturalism and moral anti-realism can lead him nowhere else, no matter how inconvenient in the context of the *TTP*.

The second challenge to the conservative Spinoza reading draws on his political naturalism, wherein 'the right of nature extends as far as its power extends'.[35] This rationale enables Spinoza to refute Hobbes in prioritising democracy as the 'most natural' form of government, as it more effectively involves and realises the natural right, or desire, of the greater part of its

---

[29] Stephenson 2011: 194.
[30] XIX, 14; 19; CWS II, 335–6.
[31] Israel 2001: 286–7.
[32] *TP* V, 7; CWS II, 531.
[33] *TTP* XVIII, 33; CWS II, 330.
[34] Della Rocca 2010: 180–1.
[35] *TTP* XVI, 2; *Ep*. L [to Jarig Jelles]; CWS II, 282; 406.

subjects, upon which its power depends.[36] It also knowingly dispenses with juridical debates of political legitimacy in Grotius and Bodin and absolute power in Hobbes (the latter merely a 'juridical fiction', as Montag observes) by asserting a simpler naturalistic basis, that a state is as powerful as the mental and physical activity and investment of its constituent parts.[37] Hence any socio-political force that can muster enough popular power to overcome and transform an existing state is, by its ability to secure itself, valid. It achieves a revolution in the political order, forcing out the old government and attempting to establish something new (which is, by the cyclical theory, also something old).

This argument is raised by Del Lucchese, Sacksteder, Matheron, Balibar, Klever and many others, and it will no doubt continue to be made.[38] As Montag puts it, there exists 'no system of rule, no matter how apparently absolute, that does not rest on an equilibrium of forces and the ruler who ignores this fact will not rule very long'.[39] This 'insurmountable antagonism', as Montag calls it, is both the condition of reason and what threatens its very stability. Yet Spinoza's political naturalism is a double-edged sword. Arendt puts it well: 'revolutions are more than successful insurrections'.[40] Spinoza's political naturalism accommodates *any* kind of insurrectionary movement that can then establish broad popularity and a degree of peace, be it militaristic, fascist, theocratic or laissez-faire capitalist. Spinoza would say, after Seneca, that 'no one has sustained a violent rule for long',[41] but even the *TTP* could see that very authoritarian societies, as the Ottoman Empire was perceived to be, could function and even thrive in the absence of free judgement and speech.

This raises the question of how democratic and egalitarian political movements can succeed. Two possibilities emerge: *indignation*, explored in the next section, a less common and more apposite response to the problem of political change. Or, a position more familiar to liberatory readings of Spinoza – and involving a reconstruction of Spinoza's account of human liberation in the *Ethics* – that hinges on ethical liberation.

Often commencing with an affirmation of the conatus (for instance, Dumoulié describes it as a modal incarnation of divine power and 'pure

---

[36] XVI, 11; CWS II, 284.
[37] Montag 1999: 65.
[38] Del Lucchese 2009: 60; Sacksteder 1975: 125; Matheron 1988: 295–6; Balibar 1994: 15; Klever 1984: 99.
[39] Montag 1999: 61.
[40] Arendt 1965: 24.
[41] *TTP* V, 22; XVI, 29; CWS II, 144; 288.

positivity'), the merely ethically liberatory Spinoza reading follows a line of thought led by Deleuze in politicising the joyous affects as being themselves empowering.[42] This over-reliance on the passive affect of joy – criticised in Chapter 4 for confusing the symptom of empowerment with its cause – then leads to an over-estimation of the benign thoughts and activities of an intrinsically revolutionary 'multitude' (Negri), or a relationally autonomous collective (Armstrong) or transindividual grouping (Balibar, Sharp), who will automatically act and think together in ways conducive to reason and peace.[43] The liberation of the individual mind collectively enhances those around it.[44]

It's a strong reading and borne out in places by the text, but I have some concerns. The first was raised earlier with Spinoza's intentions about his group subjects, and the emphasis he places on the reasonable state to cohere the people around a shared set of beliefs, customs and actions. Spinoza doesn't seem to suggest anywhere that the liberation of the individual mind could occur for whole communities. Both the *TTP* and the *TP* explore how communities might live by the guidance of reason without necessarily being aware of what these dictates are. It also doesn't really explore the role of other affects by which, for Spinoza, we recognise and respond to others – how someone's suffering or persecution might prompt us, for instance, to stand with and organise defensively around them.

What sparks the initial moment of solidarity, necessary to political association and fellowship? How do individuals join forces to effect social and political transformation through causes that are (at that given point in time) unpopular or little understood? And how should they respond if subject to fierce repression by the State or a certain community within it? These questions bear on the wider history of protest and political resistance. Let's turn, therefore, to what role indignation might play in Spinoza.

Indignation

In the *Political Treatise*, Spinoza observes that when 'disagreements and rebellions are stirred up in a commonwealth', the 'result is never that the citizens dissolve the commonwealth', but instead 'they change its form to another'.[45] Discussing this passage, Del Lucchese notes that Spinoza has

---

[42] Dumoulié 2003: 46; Deleuze 1988: 27–9.
[43] Negri 2003: 194–8; Armstrong 2009: 59; Balibar 1997b: 33–4; Sharp 2011: 35–42.
[44] Stephenson 2011: 26–8; Smith 2003: 200–1.
[45] TP VI, 2; CWS II, 532.

revised his political naturalism since the *TTP*.⁴⁶ Now the State is the natural association that all human beings gravitate towards for the purpose of self-preservation, whether driven by reason or passive affects. By implication, then, discord and sedition are the means by which a state's form is changed. Whereas conflict in a state was imprudent and to be avoided at all costs in the *TTP*, it now becomes 'an ineradicable element of its physiology'.⁴⁷ Finding itself subject to forces of authoritarian control that seek to diminish and divide its collective strength, the multitude experiences 'the affect of *indignatio*' as a 'drive and capacity for resistance'.⁴⁸ Political repression thereby becomes constitutive of the 'life in common', the first shared affect of the multitude.⁴⁹ In this way, the subjects come together to overthrow the government, *revolving* the State's form.

Now, the *TTP* does view politics as inherently conflictual, as the hungry fish of Chapter 16 indicates. But its Hobbesian case for social concord over the natural war of all against all means that it tends to lean heavily against sedition and rebellion. There were strong contextual grounds for that earlier. Likewise, the *TP* warns against disobedience, but its underlying view of politics tends to consider conflict as much more endemic, if not natural, to political processes. Context also matters: war against England and France had focused minds on the security of the State since 1672, which had frayed internally. But to readers like Del Lucchese, Montag and Matheron, this opens a window to thinking about how indignation, as an affect of resistance, might serve as the basis of a naturalistic theory of rebellion and revolution.⁵⁰

What is indignation? For Spinoza, it is an affect that begins in the imagination, being 'hatred towards him who has done evil to another'.⁵¹ It's related to pity, as both require a judgement that the subjected party is 'like us', of a common nature. But in Matheron's reading it is also an imitative affect, that is, one whose joy or sadness is increased when we see another we judge of a common nature being affected by joy or sadness.⁵² For Matheron,

---

⁴⁶ Del Lucchese 2009: 78–9.
⁴⁷ Ibid. 78.
⁴⁸ Ibid. 60.
⁴⁹ Ibid. 62.
⁵⁰ Montag 1999: 66.
⁵¹ *Ethics* III, 22 Schol.; *CWS* I, 507.
⁵² Matheron 1988: 156. Unfortunately, Spinoza does not describe indignation as an imitative affect anywhere in the *Ethics*. On Spinoza's discussion of indignation itself, see *Ethics* III, 22 Schol.; III, DA 20; IV, App. 24 (*CWS* I, 507; 535; 591); on the imitative affects otherwise, see III, 27 Schol.; 32 Schol.; 34; 40 (*CWS* I, 509; 513; ibid.; 517).

when we imagine someone affecting a beloved object with sadness, 'we shall be affected with hate towards him'.[53] He then applies this to an individual living under a tyrant. The tyrant will necessarily be hated because they rule by fear, which causes sadness, and as 'hatred is nothing but sadness accompanied by its external cause', the subject's fear leads to hatred, anger and collective rage on the streets.

While there are some problems with the argument we'll come back to, what Matheron develops with it is interesting. Why do subjects not avenge the hated tyrant, given the fear it produces in them? '[I]f the subjects abstain, it is only to the extent that one or several amongst them, because they feel isolated, has no hope of achieving it'.[54] If a tyranny can prevent individuals from recognising their common nature and grievances, disaggregating their collective power into isolated individual units, then it can reduce instances of collective rebellion. However, when the tyrant steals, kills and destroys on a large scale (e.g. Nero's Rome),[55] many become disempowered and filled with hatred, and soon cannot help but recognise each other's suffering.[56] We might imagine this happening with our men in Chapter 1 whose fellows have spilled their blood so that their leader may have 'a ground for boasting'. By affective imitation, their indignation and hatred are collectively multiplied, and 'each perceives their hatred is universally shared'. In a process akin to the 'social contract', they all 'naturally coalesce' and with 'a union made of force', their indignation becomes a collective power, and insurrection now has 'the greatest chance of success'. The tyrant can then either grant concessions that persuade the indignant subjects to reinvest their right in its authority, or continue its violence against the subjects, with the subsequent collapse of the State into war.[57]

In coming together, the indignant multitude gains the characteristics of a community, focused around a common set of ideas and organisation of allied bodies. For Matheron or Bove earlier in Chapter 5, what we are describing is a collective individual with a collective conatus, even a democratic conatus for Matheron. It's hard to see Spinoza sharing that view,

---

[53] Matheron 1988: 156, itself quoting *Ethics* III, 24 and 27 Cor. 1; CWS I, 507; 509.
[54] Matheron 1988: 416.
[55] *TP* IV, 4; *CWS* II, 527.
[56] An insight independently reached more recently in the social sciences through the concept of 'relative deprivation' and 'perceived injustice'. See Van Zomeren et al. 2008: 505–6.
[57] Matheron 1988: 416–17. Sharp 2013 reaches a similar conclusion on different lines, using Spinoza's recurring quote from Seneca, *violentia imperia nemo continuit diu* ('no one has maintained a violent regime for long').

but it reflects a late twentieth-century understanding of political protest. But it's unclear how the indignant multitude might transform the State so that one tyrant is not merely replaced with another, as per Masaniello or Cromwell. In Chapter 1 we talked about servitude, and how, without sufficient power, this multitude could just as easily fight for the authorities which subjugate it.

The liberation Matheron envisions this elusive 'democratic conatus' resulting in takes place only at the rarefied level of the mind(s). At the end of *Individu et communauté* he outlines a remarkable vision of a 'communism of minds'.[58] Alongside pursuing generosity, prudence, gratitude and obedience to the civil laws – the 'mundane' but socially necessary activities that reproduce the bourgeois liberal state – the philosopher actively works to 'enable all of Humanity to exist as a totality conscious of itself, a microcosm of the infinite Understanding, in the heart of which every soul, although remaining itself, would at the same time become all the others'. It corresponds to the universal as we've conceived it, though leapfrogging imagination, desire and the passive affects we've considered as fundamental to communal (rather than collective) life. This communism of minds seeks to raise the entire human race to the level of collective self-awareness, with neither 'juridical laws nor institutional constraints', thereby seeing the total withering away of the State and a full 'communism of goods'.[59] Knowledge of the third kind *is* collective, he indicates, because of its eternity and universality. Our collective awareness multiplies our knowledge of ourselves as individuals, and as interdependent members of a collective. In the process, it surpasses 'all alienations and divergences' on an affective level, as individuals come to recognise each other adequately as being of an 'interhuman' and common nature.[60]

This visionary idealism is wonderful, and I can't think of any other reading that so powerfully takes the ethical into the political of Spinoza. But once more, in order to carry the weight of the earlier indignation reading, Matheron, Bove and Stolze subsequently reach to a more rarefied view of personal liberation which still doesn't explain progressive political change in the first place. It doesn't address the messiness, ambiguity and risk of facing up to the political as pluralistic, uncertain and mired in difference. We could provide other affects that might support it – Stolze makes a good case for 'militant fortitude' for resistance, using courage and generosity to

[58] Matheron 1988: 612.
[59] Ibid. 612n95.
[60] Ibid. 613.

bind people together and overcome the rule of fear.⁶¹ Steinberg, in a different way, also talks of a political *fortitudo* that arises from the secure polity.⁶² But that's still consequential to the orderly constitution of a reasonable republic being set in place, and, like Spinoza's own limited political prescriptions, doesn't explain how such a state would be first established. And while the individual's liberation and ascension into a communism of minds may be possible for individuals or possibly even small groups, what about most of us, feeling passive and unable to do anything about the great social and political problems around us, like poverty, ecological collapse or violence in our communities? What of the prejudices and powerful fears and forces that bind people to charlatans and hustlers? How do individuals come to recognise a commonality in each other, and how can solidarity be sustained so that communities remain focused and effective in defending their common interests and maximising their power?

Emulation

Let's return to some of the critical issues in Matheron's account of indignation earlier. The first concerns fear. It's not strictly consistent with Spinoza to claim that the subject will react to the tyrant's violence, which causes them fear, with anger and hatred. As Spinoza argues, it's fear of isolation that compels a subject to ally with others in a civil state, and a common fear shared that, like hope, enables a multitude to think as if by one mind.⁶³ Fear, like hope, compels the subject to obey, or follow others who obey. It's an interesting point considered only briefly in Chapter 1. Hope, so decisive for political resistance in the civil rights tradition, like for Baldwin or Dr King, has little salutary place in Spinoza's ethics. Not only is it based on what's uncertain (and so epistemically weak), it also enables us to persist in that weakened state by not quite thinking about it. 'Hope is the worst of all evils', Nietzsche writes in *Human, All Too Human*, 'because it prolongs the torments of men.'⁶⁴ Our civil rights activists might reply that not to hope is impossible.

The second critical issue concerns the passive affects. Being not only a passive affect but also a sad affect, indignation can only cause harm to the

---

⁶¹ Stolze 2014: 569–71. For a much fuller survey of the various affects of resistance in Spinoza and his readers, as well as a critique of idealism and transcendentalism in recent leftist thought, see my essay in *Pli* (2019a).
⁶² Steinberg 2009: 48.
⁶³ TP III, 3; 8; VI, 1–2; CWS II, 518; 520; 532.
⁶⁴ Nietzsche 2007a: §71.

subject who experiences it. In the *Ethics*, it is an 'evil' and a cause of further passivity, and it finds no place for it in the life of the individual guided by reason.[65] At the same time, Spinoza remarks that while the passive sad affects of 'repentance' and 'humility' are not virtues but failures to adequately grasp one's power and desire, they serve a socially instrumental use.[66] Given that those who live according to the dictates of reason are said to be few, 'since men must sin, they ought rather to sin in that direction'. Of course, no one willingly elects this affective pair. Instead it is through prophets who, having 'considered the common advantage', commend these affects, alongside hope and fear, because those who are 'subject to these affects can be guided far more easily [. . .] [to] live from the guidance of reason'.

Indignation is not one of these affects (nor is it, technically, one of the imitative affects given). While it may serve a politically instrumental use in establishing solidarity and energising a people to overthrow a tyrant and change the State's form, there is nothing about it that will necessarily foster a sense of collectivity beyond the point of observing the injury to another we judge of like nature. It led to the 'imprudence' of the English republican regicides earlier. Once the injury ends, so does the indignation, and so the insurrectionaries return home, some possibly repentant. Instead, there is another affect of resistance that may animate the politics of collective desire, without the textual or political problems above, and that is *emulation*.

Emulation is defined as 'a desire for a thing which is generated in us because we imagine that others have the same desire'.[67] It is also one of the imitative affects, but specifically imitates what is judged to be 'honourable, useful or pleasant'. Emulation emerges from the primary affect of desire,[68] and so is neither joyous nor sad, but the only affect of desire that is also imitative.[69] Imagining others sharing the same desire results in 'undoing the divide between ego-centrism and altruism', as Read puts it, revealing the necessarily relational or, for him, transindividual, nature of the affects.[70] At the same time, emulation is not intrinsically empowering – the desire we imagine could be a harmful one, or we might seek to repress a given desire to conform with others with reactionary beliefs – but it redirects attention to the fundamental role of the imagination in forging lastingly powerful

---

[65] *Ethics* IV, 51 Schol.; 73 Schol.; CWS I, 575; 587. Stolze (2014: 569) also recognises it as a sad passion.
[66] *Ethics* IV, 54 Schol.; CWS I, 576.
[67] III, DA 33; cf. III, 27 Schol.; CWS I, 539; 509.
[68] III, 11 Schol.; CWS I, 501.
[69] Cf. Macherey 1998: 392–405.
[70] Read 2016: 30–1; cf. Matheron 1988: 164.

collectives. If we emulate what we judge to be of a common nature, then the question for a project of collective empowerment becomes how we extend our imagination of what is common with us, our *commonality*.

Spinoza provides no ready answer, though the proximate affects offer more illumination. If someone affects another judged like us with joy, we are affected with love towards them, that is, joy accompanied by the idea of an external cause.[71] Inversely, if this same person affects another like us in a way that causes them suffering, we are affected with sadness for the victim, and hatred for this person.[72] This sadness compels us to 'free a thing we pity from its suffering', resulting either in the destruction of this person, or another desire to do a good for the thing we pity, which Spinoza calls 'benevolence', which Bove also lists as one of his affects of resistance.[73] For Spinoza, our internal affective structure is most often defined by our relations to those around us. We strive to accomplish whatever we imagine others to look on with joy, which leads to 'ambition'; and if we believe that our actions have caused others joy, we experience 'self-esteem'.[74] If we imagine others loving, desiring or hating the same object in the same way that we do, we experience our own affect with greater intensity and constancy, and by the same token, the greater the affect by which we imagine a thing we love to be affected towards us, the greater joy or self-esteem we ourselves experience.[75]

We can now identify some foundations for a project of collective empowerment through the affects: by emulation we desire a common good, because we imagine others like ourselves desiring it. In extending our concept of a common nature towards as many as we can, we feel love for those who bring joy to our friends, and in expressing this love, thereby increase our circle of friends. We care for and defend our friends who are injured, benevolently seeking to restore their power, perhaps getting revenge on those who have injured them. Our ambitious desire to accomplish things that cause others joy, that is, which empowers them, will also lead to a feeling of self-esteem when we recognise our worth in enabling others. And when we imagine our friends loving and desiring the same ideas and activities that we do, we love them with even greater constancy, renewing our commitment and solidarity.

However, there is nothing yet to prevent emulation becoming envy, ambition leading to mutual strife or possessive greed, and love or desire from

---

[71] *Ethics* III, 27 Cor. 1; 13 Cor.; CWS I, 509; 502.
[72] III, 27 Cors. 2–3, drawing on 22 Schol.; CWS I, 509; 507.
[73] III, 27 Schol. [2]; CWS I, 509; Bove 1996: 291–5.
[74] *Ethics* III, 29 Schol.; 30 Schol.; CWS I, 510; 511.
[75] III, 31; 34 Dem.; CWS I, 512; 513–14.

being disappointed or spurned,[76] returning us back to solipsism, isolation and personal resistance. The affects, taken in themselves, can never offer a totally secure vehicle for collective freedom. Even generosity and courage, while maintaining defiance against difficulty, don't themselves lead to opposition to a tolerable yet harmful government. Nor do these idealistic programmes necessarily explain what can happen when revolutionaries seize government, and how new affective regimes can be organised and led towards greater joys and cooperation (or vice versa). Nonetheless, as discussed of desire in Chapter 4 and the imagination in Chapter 6, there is no route to human freedom for those in servitude except through the imagination, affects and desire, hence the value of approaching the political through a science of the affects, as suggested by the *TP*.

It is interesting, then, that whereas Spinoza earlier praised prophets for deploying the sad affects of repentance and humility to make others live by the guidance of reason, he did not write of the joyous affects they are paired with also being deployed for prophetic purpose. Where repentance is first defined, it is merely the saddened obverse of 'self-esteem', that is, 'joy accompanied by the idea of an internal cause'.[77] Likewise, whereas humility is sadness 'accompanied by the idea of our own weakness', joy accompanied by our power of acting is 'self-love' or, again, 'self-esteem'.[78] Yet Spinoza then claims that our observation of another's power of acting inclines us to hate or envy them unless we judge them either as an equal or superior to us.[79] If we venerate another because of their prudence and strength of character, this is only because we cannot imagine their virtues to be of a nature common with ours, 'any more than we envy trees their height, or lions their strength'.

What if Spinoza had considered his active affects of fortitude, courage and generosity as necessarily encouraging others to emulate them? Had he done so, he might have presented an account of a figure or movement that does not merely mobilise through sad passive affects like fear, repentance and humility. Such a figure or movement might draw on the affective powers of self-esteem, courage, generosity, fortitude, the cultural processes underlying commonality, and the passive affects of ambition, pity, love and emulation, and would thereby empower a community more than the prophet who merely mobilises through fear or hatred. As Spinoza deduces, joy is stronger than

---

[76] Following III, 22; 31–2; 35; CWS I, 506; 512–13; 514.
[77] III, 30 Schol.; CWS I, 511.
[78] III, 55 Schol. [1]; CWS I, 525.
[79] Ibid. Schol. [2]; CWS I, 526.

sadness in that it involves passing to a state of greater power.[80] Knowledge alone is insufficient to overcome the affects – only a stronger affect can overcome an existing one.[81] They might emphasise the openness and universality of the community addressed, not a merely local, personal, national, ethnic or even international community, but a collective, each mode of nature distinct in itself but becoming, in the final part, one with the whole universe. 'And if we proceed in this way to infinity', Spinoza writes, 'we shall easily conceive that the whole of nature is one individual, whose parts, i.e., all bodies, vary in infinite ways, without any change of the whole individual.'[82]

While grasping that is hard and at times forgotten as fear or hatred take over our minds, this philosophical figure or movement could prevent a republicanism shaped by principles of political and economic equality, plurality, alongside public education, democracy and social justice. While undoubtedly and with good reasons Spinoza ejects the prophets and much of recognisable religion from his political ideals, there is little substitute for these powerful shared belief systems and social organisations in his later work. It leaves unanswered the question that has dogged statesmen but not philosophers: how to transform the hearts and minds of the people?

Populism for Spinozists

In this final part, I'm going to sketch out how current work in populism studies might elucidate this question about how a political movement might organise itself in such a way as to draw on indignation, strengthen itself through emulation and the organisation of minds and bodies, and become a credible democratic entity that can incorporate difference and dissent.

In our own era, populism and the antagonism between 'the people' and the elites have become ubiquitous in political discussion. The term itself is suitably broad enough to incorporate an impossibly vast range of local electoral surprises, often those that gesture away from political and economic liberalism and towards the breakthrough electoral success of nationalist parties of the far right (and less often, the left), usually oriented around one outspoken figurehead. Machiavelli had conceived of politics as a continuous conflict between 'the people' and 'the nobles' long before, and advised princes to build on the strong foundation of the people.[83] But it may be that

[80] III, 21; CWS I, 506.
[81] IV, 7; 14; 18; CWS I, 550; 553; 555.
[82] II, 13, Lem. 7, Schol.; CWS I, 462.
[83] Machiavelli 2005: IX.

the term has resonated more through the absence of other forms of collective political subject (e.g. 'proletariat' or 'working class' which, with changes to the nature of work and improving living standards in the West, has become more difficult to define). But who are the people?

For Simon Critchley, the 'problem of political subjectivity is a question of *naming*', that is, 'of naming a political subject and organizing politically around that name'.[84] This act of political nomination enables an indignant social group (or 'determinate particularity') to become identified as a political subject and, through that, begin to organise politically around that name. Naming the political subject becomes the first act of its becoming such a subject. Laclau makes the same argument in more abstract terms: the name is an 'empty signifier' but one with the capacity to unite a heterogeneous ensemble of demands.[85]

What would that look like in practice? Critchley gives the example of indigenous struggles, whereby those excluded and without (property) rights challenge the State order by asserting their visibility and *right* to the land – an example reminiscent of our discussion of Rosa Parks in Chapter 5.[86] Critchley's insight partially stems from Rancière, who in several short works has advanced a concept of the political subject as the disruptive manifestation of the socially excluded *demos* from a given political order.[87] In what is variously translated as 'the part of no part' or the 'count of the uncounted', Rancière applies the ancient Athenian democratic practices of enfranchising only qualified males – a minority democratic rule, leaving out the larger part of the actual population, and something which Spinoza himself proposed in the *TP* – to describe a continual tension in the political sphere.[88] This is between authorities who seek to enforce a 'consensus' of the political sphere around technocratic, anti-democratic competence, and the 'people' as a manifestation of the excluded who noisily challenge this by asserting their own rights.[89] This disruption constitutes politics, for Rancière. The 'political subject is a capacity for staging scenes of dissensus', and such dissensus constitutes both the foundation and form of the political subject, and the core of political activity.[90]

---

[84] Critchley 2008: 91.
[85] Laclau 2007: 108.
[86] Critchley 2008: 110–11.
[87] E.g. Rancière 2007: 32–5.
[88] Rancière 1999: 6–11; 2010: 33–5.
[89] Rancière 2006: 51–5; 1999: 29–35.
[90] Rancière 2010: 69.

For these authors, the collective political subject does not exist *out there* in nature. From our work on Spinoza, we could say that it is an *ens rationis*, a thing of reason, but one whose conception and enunciation helps gather a given group of bodies and minds together – one that comes into being through its activity. This political subject doesn't have illusions about a 'communism of minds' or the neutralisation of all conflict and disagreement. It faces up to the difficulty of democracy, of organising and working together with bodies and minds very different from ours.

Spinoza has a lot to say about 'the people' and considers their well-being one of his three supreme laws of politics in the *TTP*, but, like all early modern republicans, he conceives of an equality of citizens, not of all subjects. Some of that politics does not translate well into the twenty-first century, nor should it. But we know that Spinoza was very concerned about politics, a concern that deepened over his life, becoming not merely a branch but the most important application of his ethics. His work sought to intervene in different ways, and at desperate points he was willing to risk his own life against the forces of hatred, ignorance and fear. We cannot know what he would make of the threat now posed to the habitability and life of our planet because of an unsustainable, short-term pursuit of profit and economic growth. But the philosopher meditated on what to do about the fundamentally imaginative and affective nature of human life. His counsel seems to suggest than an individual acting alone will not be powerful enough in themselves to establish a basic life. Communities of feeling should be established which become laboratories of thought and spaces of hospitality, kindness, generosity and courage. As Rancière puts it, it requires not founding 'a counterpower susceptible of governing a future society, but simply to effect a demonstration of *capacity* which is also a demonstration of *community*'[91] – a power that begins not just at the level of minds, as many as possible, thinking as much as possible, but of bodies acting together for a more sustainable, just and equitable society than this one.

But it also involves taking the State seriously, as a political aim and plane of political practice. For the State in Spinoza has the power of increasing the abilities of all when it takes to heart the three laws of politics, and (from the *TP*) that politics begins in the affects, in the common feeling which brings people together. Whereas in the *TTP* the wise prophet–statesman Moses knew how to recognise the temperament and needs of the people, in the *TP* there is no reliance on private individuals. Instead its science of politics puts processes of popular government at the heart of its decisions.

[91] Rancière 2007: 49.

Much of its procedural detail reflects the early modern context, and there is little that translates. We need no longer concern ourselves with the fortification of cities, the conscription of a citizen-militia for defence or the social influence of courtiers. Political violence is now focused on civilian life, and today's aristocrats often still do inherit power from birth, but under the new illusion of equality that their immense wealth has been earned by merit and hard graft.

But the principle of putting the people at the heart of politics is timely. Moreover, it doesn't leave the people as the angry, disruptive demos or part of no part as the best we can hope for with politics. Spinoza's political science considers how we might raise and empower one and all through the many processes available to the nation-state in organising the lives of many individuals. Though in our own times the power of nation-states has undoubtedly become circumscribed by the power of multinational corporations and an interconnected global economy, nation-states remain the most powerful communities of different individuals we know, ones with vast potential to redistribute resources or use the force of the law or redirections on the spending power of citizens to transform economic growth and energy consumption to much more sustainable levels. Whereas the radical individualist might respond to our coming ecological crisis by perhaps recycling a little more or buying more local produce, the collectivist recognises that effective political change must be more ambitious, in identifying and working with others of a common nature to figure out how we can transform the nature of work and the economy for all to live more sustainably and powerfully together, and then do everything feasible to achieve that. In that sense, something like a 'reasonable republic' – a state in which the common good of one and all was the first premise of politics, and the multifaceted representation of the people in all aspects of political life its living constitution – remains eminently desirable, if not possible.

A Spinozan populism isn't just one for the streets, then, but provides an ethical and philosophical basis for collectivity as individual empowerment, and popular sovereignty as political stability, which provides ample untapped resources for the major social and economic upheavals expected over the coming decades. Those interested in rebuilding civic society or the planet's wrecked natural habitats can find much of theoretical use. It may only be a matter of time before our beliefs about individualism are regarded as another superstition, with hideous effects in creating lonely, disconnected individuals, an unsustainable pursuit of endless growth for a few and crushing inequalities and ecological crisis for everyone else. Faced with an unprecedented task of global political, social and economic reconstruction, philosophies of interdependence, care, fellowship and collective power could be the greatest worth.

'The mistake of liberal rationalism', writes Mouffe, 'is to ignore the affective dimension mobilized by collective identifications and to imagine that those supposedly archaic "passions" are bound to disappear with the advance of individualism and the progress of rationality.'[92] A Spinozan populism might begin from the fact of the affects and imagination, and use this understanding of our relationality to think about how they might be reprogrammed and led towards more powerful, coherent mobilisations. In announcing itself in whatever form it takes, this expansive, universalist model of the people declares its claim to what should belong to it, even if at present it doesn't. The opposing authority might make concessions or not; the struggle continues or falters. At the same time, a Spinozan populist would reject this Schmittian notion of politics as premised on the friend/enemy distinction, as the ideational staging of a conflict between the pure people and the corrupt elite. Such indignation oversimplifies the complex webs of relationships that compose economic and political power, and often results in a crude moralisation of politics that prevents cooperation and can lead to the persecution of minorities. In that sense, why speak of populism and not democracy?

The agonistic view of politics of Laclau and Mouffe draws on Gramsci, but as the Cadenza indicates, this view of politics as inherently conflictual goes back to Machiavelli (and Spinoza). Let's take up one of the findings about rebellion earlier. For Laclau, there is nothing normatively popular about populism, even if polemically it takes up the moniker of 'the People'.[93] It necessarily remains 'a partial component which nevertheless aspires to be conceived as the only legitimate totality'. We might say that the people are a 'univocal multiplicity', as Guattari describes, whose collective desire 'crystallises' in the articulation of its struggle and its activity.[94] To maintain and persevere in its own being and enjoy a shared sense of self-esteem, a people imagines its demands having universal significance, because these demands are guided by a clear and distinct understanding of nature, and of our common needs and desires.

Marx and Engels presented a similar process in the *German Ideology*. Even before it had established contact across a given society, the industrial proletariat would 'present its interest as the common interest of all the members

[92] Mouffe 2005: 6.
[93] Laclau 2007: 81.
[94] Guattari 2009: 159.

of society', giving 'its ideas the form of universality, and present them as the only rational, universally valid ones', not just as a particular class, but representing the whole of humanity.[95] Even indirectly through the affects and a shared imaginary – what was called a 'common sense' in Gramsci or being 'mutually constituted' with Sharma and Camus in Chapter 5 – a collective political subject aspires to think and act *una veluti mente*; not as if by the mind of a single individual, which is a kind of tyranny, wherein the people are 'led like sheep and know only how to be slaves', as Spinoza puts it, but by a shared understanding and commitment to reasonable ways of living, being those that are intrinsically peaceful, cooperative, joyous and egalitarian.[96] To establish that kind of knowledge, which is also a kind of collective practice, we very much need philosophy. We need a lingering view of the cosmopolitan, universal truth of our oneness with nature.

It really is a case of finding spaces of collective joy and friendship, even to preserve our own mental and physical power. Collective desire is all about 'making hope practical, rather than despair convincing', as Raymond Williams memorably puts it, or, as Gramsci says, pursuing a 'pessimism of the intellect, optimism of the will'.[97] But the Spinozist has no need for hope or fear – she pursues what will increase her power and those around her with a clear understanding of its cause and nature. Our joys can indicate what is empowering – if they're accompanied by processes of causal awareness and consciousness-raising – and as Chapter 4 put forward, by educating our joys, extending our imaginations through broadening our range of experiences, and reprogramming our desires, joys and hopes to correlate with what might actually aid our collective well-being, we will become freer. Friendship and love are the glue of common association, the feeling and result of being among those of a common nature. Such a 'commons' is not rooted in crude cultural norms of 'nature', be it race or gender, but in a shared imaginary and sense of what is common to all, which, by the guidance of reason, becomes a universal, tolerant, peaceable and egalitarian sense. In this way, becoming-collective involves developing a perspective that expands from becoming-multiple, to becoming-common, to becoming-universal, at one with the universal reason of substance's infinite, intelligible power. *One and all*: this Spinoza teaches us.

---

[95] Marx and Engels 1998: 68.
[96] *TP* V, 4; *CWS* II, 530.
[97] Williams 1989: 209; Gramsci 1992: 175.

Conclusion: For One and All

In the Introduction we considered Spinoza's Masaniello moment, and the challenge of thinking in dangerous and difficult times. For important contextual reasons, Spinoza emphasised his own conformity and respect for his country's laws, and his thought remained preoccupied with the problems of servitude, harmful ideas and sad passive affects that shape the political. At the same time, there's a remarkable propensity within his politics to consider the fundamentally inter-relational and interdependent nature of individual freedom, thereby making the ethical political, in a lasting way.

There is a wonderful quote from Bernard Malamud's 1966 novel *The Fixer*, which also prefaces Deleuze's *Spinoza: Practical Philosophy*, on the disorienting effect of reading Spinoza. 'I didn't understand every word but when you're dealing with such ideas you feel as though you were taking a witch's ride', says Yakov Bok. 'After that I wasn't the same man.'[1] Many readers have remarked on the transformational nature of the encounter with his thought, what Yakov calls a 'whirlwind at my back'. Its rigorous definitions and deductive form compel us towards intellectual vistas that can feel ethereal, otherworldly, like that individuation said to begin from the most minute of modes up to the face of the whole universe.

Where has our witch's ride taken us? I want to first recap on what we've covered, and then comment on some lingering lines of inquiry.

Part I began with the problem of servitude in Spinoza, wherein individuals are possessed by harmful ideas of which they are not the adequate cause, but which provide an explanatory frame that gives meaning, if not reward, to their disempowerment. We asked why individuals are not free in the first place, and what prevents us from becoming freer – a dialectical approach to then determine the nature of our freedom. Servitude emerges in one's

---

[1] Malamud 1967: 71.

inability to moderate strong sad affects, and is associated with illusory fears, fortune and superstition, by which ambitious figures exploit and dominate others. This domination can become so effective that subjects fight for their slavery as they would for their survival, experiencing the desire of a powerful individual or class that has taken over its desires so that they are inextricable from their own, and actively defend it.

Part II then gave a comprehensive outline of empowerment. Chapter 3 scrutinised the conatus, resolving interpretative issues and identifying this elemental and dynamic striving to persevere in being as defining all things, correlating to its power, and realised through desire. We then defined desire as a specific kind of consciousness, made up of affects, memories, imaginings (fantasies, purposes), symbols and beliefs and common notions. We advanced a concept of relative freedom, by which individuals become more active through their desire, to the extent that this desire is composed as much of adequate, reasonable ideas as possible. For reason correlates to the true good of human nature, as Spinoza often makes clear, and reasonable desires are those that correlate to our actual self-preservation, resulting in more lasting joys.

This led to a question of what we do with desires in Chapter 4. We can educate ourselves and others in the most lasting of joys, and reprogramme our desires and habits to more freely seek what aids our well-being, while attuned to the causes of akrasia. We can become more self-determining of our desires and effects, using every resource available to become more knowledgeable about them. This will involve at times freely accepting what is necessary in order to remain independent, even empowered and self-determining in a difficult situation, and possibly learn something from it. Our conative relations reveal our interdependence, and our freedom is strengthened collectively through friendship and cooperation. Reason and the social become inextricably one.

Chapter 5 accounted for this coincidence of ethical reason and societal flourishing in Spinoza through the unanimity outline. I proposed that human beings are naturally predisposed to form collective groups, a process of collectivity, and these associations are more secure and effective the more they are grounded on a reasonable common good. While this developed Part II's account of a materialist metaphysics of human power through the concept of interdependence, it also introduced the difficulties for fostering commonality in shared imaginings through which, as Sharma said, we are 'mutually constituted'.

Part III turned to the politics of collectivity, with a chapter each focusing on its different features in the *TTP* and *TP*. Chapter 6 reread the *TTP* to sift out its account of collectivity, focusing on the instrumental role of the imagination. While having the potential to raise the capacities of the many through faith, I was unhappy with Spinoza's critique of the *vulgus* and the lack of facility for enabling individuals to think more reasonably. This became the basis of a persistent critique: if a democratic political theory cannot account for how individuals become more self-determining and able to think for themselves, then its prescriptions are ineffective, and will in practice prove futile.

This critical note continued into Chapter 7, which explored how the *TP* marked a distinct development in Spinoza's thought, placing the agency of becoming freer onto the State, and a more closely defined politics of collective power, led as if by one mind. It identified how a 'common feeling' is what constitutes political power (as *potentia*), but that the realisation and activity of that power occurs through the careful management of the State as a living embodiment of popular sovereignty. For states are only as powerful as their constituent parts' abilities to think and act cooperatively and peacefully. Spinoza's reasonable republic is a remarkable attempt to make the State think through its assemblies, live through its laws, and produce reasonable citizens, an account whose features claim to be derived scientifically from human nature. Yet Spinoza provided little explanation for how individuals would realise a reasonable republic. For if, as he remarks in the *Ethics*, citizens and not slaves are governed and led 'that they may do freely the things that are best', then Spinoza needed to account for the very animation by which individuals combine together and realise the common good, particularly with the intractable problem of servitude identified earlier.[2]

This was addressed in the Cadenza. Collectivity was identified through enabling a *common sense*, being a sense of commonality, and a politicised sense of what is common and belonging to the commons. Yet such a commonality never appears *ex nihilo*, but must be transformed at a collective, political scale: reordering a shared consciousness about political realism and facts in a way akin to reordering the affects, images, beliefs and desires of the individual. For Mark Fisher, this is the domain not merely of the political, but of cultural studies, influenced in its early stages by the Spinozism of Althusser. Change 'cannot be achieved by "politics" alone', but 'culture – in the widest sense'[3] – a revolution of the affects, desires and imagination at the collective level. At the same time, few movements will realise the universal good of enabling as many as possible to become freer unless they can develop

---

[2] *Ethics* II, 49 Schol.; CWS I, 491.
[3] Fisher 2015b.

the ability to think and act self-determinedly in citizens, a democratic social responsibility. In such a way, as Spinoza imagined, the reasonable state could provide a meaningful freedom.

This raised a pertinent question for the last chapter for how we come to desire freedom, particularly in the light of the more pessimistic findings of Chapter 1. In seeking to explain the conditions for political change, we challenged Spinoza's own weak account of rebellion, before turning to Matheron and indignation as an affect of resistance. Though finding some textual problems with indignation itself, the discussion nonetheless led to an identification of emulation as an imitative affect of desire by which individuals could establish meaningful and lasting bonds of solidarity through which to organise political movements and change. This then led to a politics of freedom that could organise around a more expansive view of the people, mobilising the affects and the imagination to develop new collective subjects that can challenge the prevailing political order. Resisting a kind of Cartesian dualism of collective minds leading passive and inert bodies, the argument teased out the importance of a shared political imaginary involving both minds (ideas) and bodies – affects, encounters, sociality, care and solidarity.

For Spinoza's philosophy is concerned with realising the becoming freer of one and all. While freely reckoning with the great difficulties facing such a liberation, it nonetheless identifies its possibility within the political, theological and epistemological structures of his era. Such a freedom is a way of life, where the proliferation and pursuit of ideas, friendship, justice, peace and generosity are their own rewards. Such a freedom is a path, the image Spinoza suggests to us at the end of the *Ethics*, in which what matters most is not the path itself but the way we walk it, as John Martin Fischer remarked in Chapter 4.

In navigating the treacherous themes of servitude, power and desire, and not always successfully, Spinoza's attempt to develop a model of freedom between societies 'as they are' and their most optimal state has illuminated our own. Across the book we've explored the foundation for thinking ethically and politically about *one and all*. That is to say, a thinking of the individual and the collective, the individual as *of* the collective, the collective *as* an individual, and the collective as emerging from (though not reducible to) the desires of individuals, striving to live well together.

For individuation ascends up to 'the whole of nature', or as Spinoza later puts it, 'the face of the whole universe', which is collective being, substance, where he begins the *Ethics*. The dynamic modal metaphysics of power outlined early in Chapter 3 became the basis for thinking about this individuation as it extends across human life. All human beings develop from an initially weakened, passive state. Unable to determine the cause of our effects, dependent for our basic needs and understanding on others, virtually all of us fall prey to the servitude of harmful ideas. We become possessed by uncertain hopes or fears, 'boundless' desires with little grounding in reality, and once we are inevitably heartbroken, seek refuge in the most immediate and comforting of beliefs. In understanding the power of the passive affects, we start to disarm their influence over us. In turn, we also begin disarming our internal domination by authoritarian dogmas, and so pass to a state of greater power, which is also a state of greater unity or common-mindedness. For reason isn't about being gobbled up by a supra-individual in which we lose ourselves amid mass conformity. The great beauty of Spinoza's view of God or nature is that we can all enjoy adequate knowledge of the universal order. We attain our own right, and act as much as from our own nature as we can, rather than from multiple directions that impinge on us, leading to that vacillation that swings us around mercilessly, and to which some resign their own agency, calling it fate, fortune or providence. In becoming *one* ourselves, we are then able to recognise the many advantages of combining with others, sharing our ideas, affecting and being affected as much as we can, and in the process thinking, feeling and doing what we could not alone before.

Friendship, conversation and communal participation are part of becoming freer. This is one of Spinoza's great insights. It jars with the reputation of the aloof, otherworldly philosopher–prince, consumed by the cobwebs of systematic metaphysics. There are good grounds for that interpretation too. But I don't think we can avoid the centrality of sociality, friendship and collective power in his thought for much longer. Our becoming freer doesn't even begin unless we happen to be born and raised in a stable community that can provide for our material needs, and surround us with nurturing relations and institutions that enable our development. As reasonable, freedom-loving individuals, it is our intrinsic disposition to give something back – that is to say, to contribute to the freedom and life of the community by enabling others to think or live reasonably, and participating in our community's affairs to ensure that the common good is being realised. Freedom of an ethical kind is one with freedom of the political, indeed, the former is not possible without the latter.

Nothing is more useful to human beings than each other – well, that is to say, than another who is judged of a common nature, a feature of Spinoza's argument that is less often alighted upon. One who is overwhelmed by sad passions will be of little aid to the freedom-loving individual (though their benevolence to assist the person disempowered by sad passions could help alleviate their servitude, and so would become a source of joy to both). While we are naturally drawn towards those of a common nature, this is an imaginative judgement reflecting a given sense of commonality, and so can be extended outwards, inclusively.

Ultimately, our argument is for the collectivist Spinoza. There are some grounds for considering Spinoza as a radical egoist or individualist, but this is only through a reliance on certain selective passages at the expense of Spinoza's more forthright expositions on society, friendship and the importance of politics elsewhere. We can go even further and call this kind of individualism a 'superstition' in the sense Spinoza understood in Chapter 1: a distorted and inadequate way of viewing nature according to our own 'blind desire and insatiable greed', a misperception that arises when we fail to take into account anything except the pursuit of our desires and the inevitable adversity these encounter.[4] It results in a kind of magical thinking that the only way for the individual to remain robust and resilient under such adversity is to close up to the world and find resources within, to cultivate inner strength or find in an ethics concerned with the freedom of many a mere therapy for individual sad passions. I've used Gillian Rose's idea of 'the broken middle' to think about some of the tension and conflict inherent between the freedom-loving individual and the world around them. We traced that tension back as early as the *Treatise on the Emendation of the Intellect*, and found a fear and a love of the common people playing out across the *Ethics*, *TTP* and *TP* in different ways, as contexts changed and concepts developed (particularly around the affects, imagination and desire).

That's why I suggested in Chapter 5 the formulation of the *Individual–Communal–Universal*. It's an outline of human power which begins at the level of the individual living and desiring what they have judged to be good for them, but which compels individuals to find and associate with others judged of a common nature to better achieve those ends. This kind of community is the sort we'll all know – contingent and based on images, affects, habits, customs and non-elective facts that bind us with others, like friends, colleagues, neighbours, extended family, or members of a religious congregation or political group, and so on. It's shaped by historical and political forces, and these communities can be very loose and incohesive, or more anchored on sad passions or harmful ideas than empowering ones. I wanted to distinguish the communal from the collective in order to start thinking about a model of association and friendship that could be universal and

---

[4] *Ethics* I, App.; CWS I, 441.

unlimited, cosmopolitan in nature and scope, and based on an understanding and love of nature. I had in mind much smaller groupings where real cohesion and integration might be achieved – like in musical rhythm sometimes, or love. With that, I wanted to emphasise the importance of care, generosity and kindness as the conditions for a stronger model of human friendship that I believe Spinoza had in mind with his 'free man', and of a virtue that was open and desirable to all. It's a form of friendship captured by what Mark Fisher called 'fellowship' in the Cadenza.

But in speaking of care, I also want to acknowledge a journey each of us knows from the very earliest of our lives, as powerful women bring us into the world and love us long before any 'social contract' or theory of citizenship becomes relevant. Though theoretical concepts of collectivity are nearly always concerned with political protest on the left (e.g. multitude, 'the People', the proletariat), I think that much more can be theoretically done with communities of care in our everyday worlds. Across our lives, most of us will be involved in the care of a child, or elderly or disabled relative or friend. As well as one or two primary care givers, there's usually a surrounding group offering their support, time, financial assistance. In Spinoza's era, the most obvious and commonly discussed community was the religious congregation, those gathered as a church. Interestingly, Spinoza resists this model without then juxtaposing a tradition of natural law that inverts those values into aggressive selfishness. The reason-led collective, or the community of care, each indicate different forms of human power that are inter-relational and interdependent.

But I also explored something I could see as important in the background thought of the later *Ethics* and *TTP*: the possibility of developing beyond the imagined community of the nation (a creation not of nature but of individuals, says the *TTP*), and towards the cosmopolitan and the universal; towards a non-exclusionary sociality that seeks to get beyond the fetishisation of sameness or difference for its own sake, particularly a sameness based on physical or restricted characteristics like nationality, religion or ethnicity, and instead extending commonality to the entirety of nature, to all human (and non-human) life. Such a universality involves a difficult intellectual love. It doesn't just admire its own view of this oneness, but actively goes about trying to improve the well-being and minimise the harm caused to other life by any means reasonably necessary. 'Activeness in the sense of Spinoza', wrote the great Spinozist and ecologist Arne Næss, 'requires integration and concentration, not tranquillity.'[5] At the same

[5] Næss 2008: 258–9.

time, it recognises that these cosmic vistas of serenity are rare to find and even more difficult to retain amid the squalls of our lives. A true knowledge of good and evil is overcome by the power of strong affects, says Spinoza. The journey of the *Individual–Communal–Universal* is not a long linear path to some distant nirvana, but the ebb and flow of an individual's power. Harmony and peace find their basis in loving reason, a universal currency that's multiplied in its expenditure. The good life, in short, but one only possible together.

For some, there's been an understandable discomfort about pursuing Spinoza's politics of freedom beyond the confines of the late seventeenth century. Across this study, we've identified anachronisms and cautioned the lionising of the multitude. We've questioned whether there's really a democratic or pre-Marxist revolutionary conatus in the common affects of the *vulgus* or *multitudo*. But given that Spinoza's politics concerns underlying principles (and later in the *TP*, a 'science') of the affects, imagination and desire, and their centrality to political affairs, their implications and relevance remain pressing. We need not make Spinoza one of us. Rather, we might consider cultivating what Nietzsche called a 'star friendship' with the philosopher, a friendship of affinity and distance. While the 'almighty force of our projects' drives us apart 'into different seas and sunny zones', our contexts incomparable in vital ways, there's a commonality, a shared interest, if not desire for human freedom, like a 'tremendous invisible [. . .] stellar orbit in which our different ways and goals may be *included* as small stretches' of a path.[6] Such a path has been walked on by many others before. What matters most, we'll recall, is how we walk that path, and our understanding of how others walk it too.

In a remark towards the end of her life, the novelist Ursula K. Le Guin turned to the importance of the imagination for political change. 'We live in capitalism, its power seems inescapable – but then, so did the divine right of kings.'[7] For Le Guin, power is inherently immanent, and no matter how fixed or fate-like any conjuncture appears, the balance of forces can be completely upturned with enough desire and collective power. The quote was later circulated by my late friend, Mark Fisher, to whom I have dedicated this work. As he wrote elsewhere:

> Emancipatory politics must always destroy the appearance of a 'natural order', must reveal what is presented as necessary and inevitable to be a

---

[6] Nietzsche 2007b: §279.
[7] Le Guin 2014.

mere contingency, just as it must make what was previously deemed to be impossible seem attainable.[8]

I often saw these words when I locked up my bike to teach at Goldsmiths, graffitied on a wall by the library. Like Le Guin's remark, they point to the contingent and continually shifting nature of the political, and its shared reality not just at the level of the economical – as Gramsci and Reich both realised – but also in terms of power and culture, at the level of common beliefs, common feelings like hope and fear, and common narratives about the past and future. The harmful ideas of Chapter 1 could also become the powerful, self-preserving imaginaries used by the prophet in Chapter 6. For just as thinking critically in dangerous times can be an initially isolating and depressing experience, as our politics of shared imaginings, indignation and emulation identifies, it is only through the quality and power of our relations with others that we can come to understand, endure – indeed, enjoy – the vicissitudes and vistas of human freedom.

That also means being prepared to adopt a challenging position and not back down. On the 1990 track 'Fight the Power', Chuck D. of Public Enemy puts the problem concisely. 'People, people we are the same? No we're not the same, cos we don't know the game'. Any easy-going, apolitical view that all human beings are one, while cosy and true on a more universal level, can also serve as a platitude that veils inequalities. Collective empowerment must involve challenging what Gramsci called the 'folklore' of erroneous shared beliefs and harmful sad affects that stop us from not knowing the game. These result in a disempowering pessimism about political change, if not complicity in the perpetuity of inequalities, a game that seems rigged or hopelessly mysterious, one which leads to a collective 'self-hatred' in Fanon and Baldwin, until we collectively untangle and understand its workings. 'What we need is awareness' says Chuck D., 'mental self-defensive fitness'. But a power of both bodies and minds. Freedom-loving radicals from across cultures and contexts have made similar such calls for a political freedom of one and all that begins in contemplative thought and common awareness.

In his final work, Mark Fisher was also thinking about how we might begin again to imagine and desire a better world in our own times. He was concerned that collectively we had lost the capacity to imagine what social change and progress would be like, because we were trapped in a state of viewing the current order as natural, inevitable and impossible to change. He called that state 'capitalist realism', something akin to what Marx sketched

---

[8] Fisher 2009: 17.

out at the start of the last chapter.[9] In its place, he had begun thinking about what he variously called a 'common wealth' or 'red plenty', that is, a world without toil or poverty, a world where people might luxuriate in free time and new spaces of collective joy.[10] Paraphrasing Herbert Marcuse, he was searching for the traces of 'the spectre of a world which could be free', one enveloped in the history of cultural experimentation and radical democracy.[11] Such spaces of fellowship, collective power and freedom are hard to find and don't often last. Nonetheless, they are always possible. As Fisher quotes Fredric Jameson, they can sometimes intrude and disturb our everyday worlds, 'like a diseased eyeball in which disturbing flashes of light are perceived or like those baroque sunbursts in which rays of from another world suddenly break into this one'.[12] But whereas Jameson settled for a distant utopianism on the horizon, Fisher was a thinker of immanence, and envisioned 'a carnival that is achingly proximate, a spectre haunting even – especially – the most miserably de-socialised spaces'.[13] We might call it the carnival of collective desire.

Such a politics of collective desire locates the political in everyday life, and makes use of all opportunities for becoming freer with others in the most modest of ways, from friendship and teaching to community work and political campaigning, and many other things besides. It accepts the inherent risk of getting it wrong and encountering adversity that such a practice of collectivity entails. It recognises that the fracture between the individual and the communal is also a fracture between a certain disappointed realism and the idealism of pursuing exemplars and models of the highest good that we encounter in Spinoza. It is a productive if irreconcilable fracture. Though Spinoza's model of empowerment is founded on descriptive laws, it is indelibly normative, indicating what human beings might best experience, if we collectively put our minds to it, realising our common if not universal good. From the foregoing argument for the collectivist Spinoza, such a freedom is for one and all.

---

[9] Fisher 2009.
[10] Fisher 2018: 754.
[11] Ibid. 753.
[12] Fisher 2016.
[13] Fisher 2018: 765.

Bibliography

Abensour, Miguel (2015) 'Spinoza et l'épineuse question de la servitude volontaire'. *Astérion*, 13. http://asterion.revues.org/2594 (last accessed 16 April 2020).
Addams, Jane (1902) *Democracy and Social Ethics*. New York: Macmillan.
Addams, Jane (1912) *A New Conscience and an Ancient Evil*. New York: Macmillan.
Ahmed, Sara (2014) *Willful Subjects*. Durham, NC: Duke University Press.
Alencastro, Luiz Felipe de (2018) *The Trade in the Living: The Formation of Brazil in the South Atlantic, Sixteenth to Seventeenth Centuries*, trans. Gavin Adams and Author, rev. Michael Wolfers and Dale Tomich. Albany: SUNY Press.
Allison, Henry (1987) *Benedict de Spinoza: An Introduction*. New Haven: Yale University Press.
Althusser, Louis (1997) 'The Only Materialist Tradition, Part 1: Spinoza', trans. Ted Stolze. In Warren Montag and Ted Stolze (eds), *The New Spinoza*. Minneapolis: University of Minnesota Press.
Althusser, Louis (1999) *Machiavelli and Us*, ed. François Matheron, trans. Gregory Elliot. London: Verso.
Althusser, Louis (2005) *For Marx*, trans. Ben Brewster. London: Verso.
Arendt, Hannah (1965) *On Revolution*. New York: Penguin.
Arendt, Hannah (1970) *On Violence*. New York: Harvest.
Arendt, Hannah (1979) *The Origins of Totalitarianism*. New York: Harcourt Brace.
Arendt, Hannah (1992) *Lectures on Kant's Political Philosophy*, ed. Ronald Beiner. Chicago: University of Chicago Press.
Arendt, Hannah (1998) *The Human Condition*. Chicago: University of Chicago Press.

Ariosto, Ludovico (2008) *Orlando Furioso*, trans. Guido Waldman. New York: Oxford University Press.
Aristotle (1981) *Politics*, trans. T. A. Sinclair. Harmondsworth: Penguin.
Aristotle (1998) *Metaphysics*, trans. Hugh Lawson-Tancred. Harmondsworth: Penguin.
Armstrong, Aurelia (2009) 'Autonomy and the Relational Individual: Spinoza and Feminism'. In Moira Gatens (ed.), *Feminist Interpretations of Spinoza*. Pennsylvania: University of Pennsylvania Press, pp. 43–64.
Armstrong, Aurelia, Keith Green and Andrea Sangiacomo (2019) *Spinoza and Relational Autonomy*. Edinburgh: Edinburgh University Press.
Arnett, James (2016) 'Daniel Deronda, Professor of Spinoza'. *Victorian Literature and Culture*, 44.4, pp. 833–54.
Atkins, Dorothy (1978) *George Eliot and Spinoza*. Salzburg: Universität Salzburg.
Atlan, Henri (2018) *Cours de philosophie biologique et cognitiviste. Spinoza et la biologie actuelle*. Paris: Odile Jacob.
Baldwin, James (1968) *The Fire Next Time*. London: Michael Joseph.
Balibar, Étienne (1994) *Masses, Classes and Ideas: Studies on Politics and Philosophy before and after Marx*, trans. James Swenson. London; New York: Routledge.
Balibar, Étienne (1997a) 'Jus-Pactum-Lex: On the Constitution of the Subject in the *Theologico-Political Treatise*', trans. Ted Stolze. In Warren Montag and Ted Stolze (eds), *The New Spinoza*. Minneapolis: University of Minnesota Press.
Balibar, Étienne (1997b) *Spinoza: From Individuality to Transindividuality. A Lecture Delivered in Rijnsburg on May 15, 1993*. Delft: Eburon.
Balibar, Étienne (2005) '"Potentia multitudinis quae una veluti mente ducitir": Spinoza on the Body Politic'. In Stephen H. Daniel (ed., trans.), *Current Continental Theory and Modern Philosophy*. Evanston, IL: Northwestern University Press, pp. 70–99.
Balibar, Étienne (2008) *Spinoza and Politics*, trans. Peter Snowdon. London; New York: Verso.
Barbone, Steven (1999) 'Power in the *Tractatus Theologico-Politicus*'. In Paul Bagley (ed.), *Piety, Peace, and the Freedom to Philosophize*. Dordrecht: Kluwer.
Barbone, Steven (2002) 'What Counts as an Individual for Spinoza?'. In Olli Koistinen and John Biro (eds), *Spinoza: Metaphysical Themes*. New York: Oxford University Press, pp. 89–112.
Bayle, Pierre (1965) *Historical and Critical Dictionary. Selections*, trans. Richard H. Popkin. Indianapolis: Bobbs-Merrill.

Benjamin, Walter (1999) *The Arcades Project*, trans. Howard Eiland and Kevin McLaughlin, ed. Rolf Tiedemann. Cambridge: Belknap Press of Harvard University Press.

Benjamin, Walter (2006) *The Writer of Modern Life: Essays on Charles Baudelaire*, ed. Michael W. Jennings, trans. Howard Eiland, Edmund Jephcott, Rodney Livingston and Harry Zohn. Cambridge, MA; London: Belknap Press of Harvard University Press.

Bennett, Jonathan (1984) *A Study of Spinoza's 'Ethics'*. Indianapolis: Hackett.

Blake, William (2008) *The Complete Poetry and Prose*. Berkeley: University of California Press.

Boerio, Davide (2016) 'The "Trouble of Naples" in the Political Information Arena of the English Revolution'. In Joad Raymond and Noah Moxham (eds), *News Networks in Early Modern Europe*. Leiden: Brill, pp. 779–804.

Borges, Jorge Luis (2000) 'Spinoza', trans. Willis Barnstone. In Alexander Coleman (ed.), *Selected Poems*. London: Penguin.

Bove, Laurent (1996) *La stratégie du conatus: affirmation et résistance chez Spinoza*. Paris: Vrin.

Bove, Laurent (2002) 'De l'étude de l'État hébreu à la démocratie: La stratégie politique du conatus spinoziste'. *Philosophiques*, 29.1, pp. 107–19.

Brienen, Rebecca Parker (2006) *Visions of Savage Paradise: Albert Eckhout, Court Painter in Colonial Dutch Brazil*. Amsterdam: Amsterdam University Press.

Campbell, Karlyn Kohrs (1973) 'The Rhetoric of Women's Liberation: An Oxymoron'. *Quarterly Journal of Speech*, 59.1, pp. 74–86.

Campos, Andre Santos (2012) *Spinoza's Revolutions in Natural Law*. New York; Basingstoke: Palgrave Macmillan.

Campos, Andre Santos, ed. (2015) *Spinoza and Law*. Abingdon; New York: Routledge.

Camus, Albert (1991) *The Rebel*, trans. Anthony Bower. New York: Vintage.

Camus, Albert (2005) *The Myth of Sisyphus*, trans. Justin O'Brien. London: Penguin.

Carriero, John (1991) 'Spinoza's Views on Necessity in Historical Perspective'. *Philosophical Topics*, 19.1, pp. 47–96.

Carriero, John (2005) 'Spinoza on Final Causality'. In Daniel Garber and Steven Nadler (eds), *Oxford Studies in Early Modern Philosophy, Volume II*. Oxford: Clarendon Press, pp. 105–47.

Casarino, Cesare (2017) 'Grammars of Conatus: Or, on the Primacy of Resistance in Spinoza, Foucault and Deleuze'. In A. Kiarina Kordela and Dimitris Vardoulakis (eds), *Spinoza's Authority: Resistance and Power in Ethics*. London: Bloomsbury, pp. 57–86.

Cicero (1931) *On Ends*, trans. H. Rackham. Cambridge, MA: Loeb Classical Library.
Cicero (1999) *On the Commonwealth and On the Laws*, ed. and trans. J. E. G. Zetzel. New York: Cambridge University Press.
Cioran, E. M. (1970) *The Fall into Time*, trans. Richard Howard. Chicago: Quadrangle.
Cohen, I. Bernard (1964) '"Quantum in se est": Newton's Concept of Inertia in Relation to Descartes and Lucretius'. *Notes and Records of the Royal Society of London*, 19.2, pp. 131–55.
Colerus, Johannes (1880) 'The Life of B. de Spinosa'. In Frederick Pollock, *Spinoza: His Life and Philosophy*. London: Kegan Paul.
Coutinho, Carlos Nelson (2012) *Gramsci's Political Thought*, trans. Pedro Sette-Camara. Leiden: Brill.
Critchley, Simon (2008) *Infinitely Demanding: Ethics of Commitment, Politics of Resistance*. London: Verso.
Curley, Edwin (1988) *Behind the Geometrical Method: A Reading of Spinoza's Ethics*. Princeton: Princeton University Press.
Curley, Edwin (1996) 'Kissinger, Spinoza, and Genghis Khan'. In Don Garrett (ed.), *The Cambridge Companion to Spinoza*. New York: Cambridge University Press.
Curley, Edwin and P.-F. Moreau, eds (1990) *Spinoza: Issues and Directions: The Proceedings of the Chicago Spinoza Conference*. Leiden: Brill.
Dahlbeck, Johan (2017) *Spinoza and Education: Freedom, Understanding and Empowerment*. London; New York: Routledge.
Damasio, Antonio (2003) *Looking for Spinoza: Joy, Sorrow, and the Feeling Brain*. London: Heinemann.
DeBrabander, Firmin (2007) *Spinoza and the Stoics: Power, Politics and the Passions*. London; New York: Continuum.
Deleuze, Gilles (1988) *Spinoza: Practical Philosophy*, trans. Robert Hurley. San Francisco: City Lights.
Deleuze, Gilles (1990) *Expressionism in Philosophy: Spinoza*, trans. Martin Joughin. New York: Zone Books.
Deleuze, Gilles (1995) 'Postscript on Control Societies', in *Negotiations*, trans. Martin Joughin. New York: Columbia University Press.
Deleuze, Gilles and Félix Guattari (2013) *Anti-Oedipus: Capitalism and Schizophrenia*, trans. Robert Hurley, Mark Seem and Helen R. Lane. London; New York: Bloomsbury.
Del Lucchese, Filippo (2009) *Conflict, Power, and Multitude in Machiavelli and Spinoza: Tumult and Indignation*. London; New York: Continuum.

Del Lucchese, Filippo (2016) 'Spinoza and Constituent Power'. *Contemporary Political Theory*, 15, pp. 182–204.

Del Lucchese, Filippo (2017) 'The Symptomatic Relationship between Law and Conflict in Spinoza: *Jura communia* as *anima imperii*'. In A. Kiarina Kordela and Dimitris Vardoulakis (eds), *Spinoza's Authority: Resistance and Power in the Political Treatises*. London: Bloomsbury, pp.27–44.

Della Rocca, Michael (1996) 'Spinoza's Metaphysical Psychology'. In Don Garrett (ed.), *The Cambridge Companion to Spinoza*. New York: Cambridge University Press, pp. 192–266.

Della Rocca, Michael (2008) *Spinoza*. New York; Abingdon: Routledge.

Della Rocca, Michael (2010) 'Getting His Hands Dirty: Spinoza's Criticism of the Rebel'. In Yitzhak Y. Melamed and Michael A. Rosenthal (eds), *Spinoza's Theological-Political Treatise: A Critical Guide*. Cambridge: Cambridge University Press, pp. 168–91.

Den Uyl, Douglas (1983) *Power, State and Freedom: An Interpretation of Spinoza's Political Philosophy*. Assen: Van Gorcum.

Derrida, Jacques (2016),*Of Grammatology*, trans. Gayatri Chakravorty Spivak. Baltimore: Johns Hopkins University Press.

Descartes, René (1985) *The Philosophical Writings of Descartes: Volume I*, trans. J. Cottingham, R. Stoothoff and D. Murdoch. Cambridge: Cambridge University Press.

Descartes, René (1989) *The Passions of the Soul*, trans. Stephen Voss. Indianapolis: Hackett.

Descartes, René (1995) *The Philosophical Writings of Descartes: Volume II*, trans. J. Cottingham, R. Stoothoff and D. Murdoch. Cambridge: Cambridge University Press.

Dumoulié, Camille (2003) 'Spinoza, or, The Power of Desire', trans. Lorenzo Chiesa. In *Pli: The Warwick Journal of Philosophy. Volume 14: Spinoza: Desire and Power*, pp. 44–52.

Eliot, George (1997) *Felix Holt, the Radical*. Ware: Wordsworth.

Eliot, George (2020) *Spinoza's Ethics*, ed. Clare Carlisle. Princeton: Princeton University Press.

Fanon, Frantz (2004) *The Wretched of the Earth*, trans. Richard Philcox. New York: Grove.

Fay, Brian (2017) 'What George Eliot of *Middlemarch* Could Have Taught Spinoza'. *Philosophy and Literature*, 41.1, pp. 119–35.

Feitler, Bruno (2009) 'Jews and New Christians in Dutch Brazil, 1630–1654'. In Richard L. Kagan and David D. Morgan (eds), *Atlantic Diasporas: Jews, Conversos, and Crypto-Jews in the Age of Mercantilism, 1500–1800*. Baltimore: Johns Hopkins University Press.

Feuer, Lewis (1987) *Spinoza and the Rise of Liberalism.* New Brunswick, NJ: Transaction.

Feuer, Lewis (1995) *Varieties of Scientific Experience.* New Brunswick, NJ: Transaction.

Fischer, John Martin (2007) 'Compatibilism'. In Author, Robert Kane, Derk Pereboom and Manuel Vargas, *Four Views on Free Will.* Oxford: Blackwell, pp. 44–83.

Fisher, Mark (2004) *Spinoza, k-Punk, neuropunk. K-Punk.* 13 August 2004. http://k-punk.org/spinoza-k-punk-neuropunk/ (last accessed 16 April 2020).

Fisher, Mark (2009) *Capitalist Realism: Is There No Alternative?* Ropley, UK: Zer0 Books.

Fisher, Mark (2015a) 'Communist Realism'. *K-Punk,* 5 May 2015. http://k-punk.org/communist-realism/ (last accessed 16 April 2020).

Fisher, Mark (2015b) 'Abandon Hope (Summer is Coming)'. *K-Punk,* 11 May 2015. http://k-punk.org/abandon-hope-summer-is-coming/ (last accessed 16 April 2020).

Fisher, Mark (2016) 'Baroque Sunbursts'. In Nav Haq (ed.), *Rave: Rave and Its Influence on Art and Culture.* London: Black Dog.

Fisher, Mark (2018) 'Acid Communism'. In *k-punk: The Collected and Unpublished Writings of Mark Fisher, 2004–2016,* ed. Darren Ambrose. London: Repeater.

Ford, III, James Edward (2018) 'Interrupting the System: Spinoza and Maroon Thought'. In A. Kiarina Kordela and Dimitris Vardoulakis (eds), *Spinoza's Authority, Volume I: Resistance and Power in the Ethics.* London: Bloomsbury.

Foucault, Michel (1991) *Discipline and Punish,* trans. Alan Sheridan. London: Penguin.

Foucault, Michel (2007) *Security, Territory, Population,* ed. Michel Senellart, trans. Graham Burchell. Basingstoke: Palgrave Macmillan.

Frank, Daniel and Jason Waller (2016) *Routledge Philosophy Guidebook to Spinoza on Politics.* Abingdon; New York: Routledge.

Friedman, Saul S. (2017) *Jews and the American Slave Trade.* Abingdon; New York: Routledge.

Gabbey, Alan (1980) 'Force and Inertia in the Seventeenth Century: Descartes and Newton'. In Stephen Gaukroger (ed.), *Descartes: Philosophy, Mathematics and Physics.* Brighton: Harvester, pp. 230–320.

Galileo (2008) *The Essential Galileo,* ed. and trans. Maurice A. Finocchiaro. Indianapolis: Hackett.

Garber, Daniel (1994) 'Descartes and Spinoza on Persistence and Conatus'. *Studia Spinozana,* 10, pp. 43–67.

Garrett, Don (1990) '"A Free Man Always Acts Honestly, Not Deceptively": Freedom and the Good in Spinoza's *Ethics*'. In E. Curley and P.-F. Moreau (eds), *Spinoza: Issues and Directions*. Leiden: Brill, pp. 221–8.

Garrett, Don (1994) 'Spinoza's Theory of Metaphysical Individuation'. In K. F. Barber and J. J. E. Garcia (eds), *Individuation and Identity in Early Modern Philosophy*. Albany: SUNY Press, pp. 71–101.

Garrett, Don (1996) 'Spinoza's Ethical Theory'. In Don Garrett (ed.), *The Cambridge Companion to Spinoza*. New York: Cambridge University Press, pp. 267–314.

Garrett, Don (2002) 'Spinoza's *Conatus* Argument'. In Olli Koistinen and John Biro (eds), *Spinoza: Metaphysical Themes*. New York: Oxford University Press, pp. 127–58.

Garrett, Don (2008) 'Representation and Consciousness in Spinoza's Naturalistic Theory of the Imagination'. In Charlie Huenemann (ed.), *Interpreting Spinoza*. Cambridge: Cambridge University Press, pp. 4–25.

Garrett, Don (2009) 'Spinoza on the Essence of the Human Body and the Part of the Mind that is Eternal'. In Olli Koistinen (ed.), *The Cambridge Companion to Spinoza's Ethics*. New York: Cambridge University Press, pp. 284–301.

Garrett, Don (2010) '"Promising" Ideas: Hobbes and Contract in Spinoza's Political Philosophy'. In Y. Y. Melamed and M. A. Rosenthal (eds), *Spinoza's Theological-Political Treatise: A Critical Guide*. Cambridge: Cambridge University Press, pp. 192–209.

Garver, Eugene (2018) *Spinoza and the Cunning of the Imagination*. Chicago: University of Chicago Press.

Gatens, Moira (2009, ed.) *Feminist Interpretations of Spinoza*. Philadelphia: University of Pennsylvania Press.

Gatens, Moira (2012) 'Compelling Fictions: Spinoza and George Eliot on Imagination and Belief'. *European Journal of Philosophy*, 20.1, pp. 74–90.

Gatens, Moira and Genevieve Lloyd (1999) *Collective Imaginings: Spinoza Past and Present*. London: Routledge & Kegan Paul.

Gazzaniga, Michael S. (2012) *Who's in Charge? Free Will and the Science of the Brain*. London: Constable & Robinson.

Geggus, David, ed., trans. (2014) *The Haitian Revolution: A Documentary History*. Indianapolis: Hackett.

Gelley, Alexander (2015) *Benjamin's Passages*. New York: Fordham University Press.

Giancotti Boscherini, Emilia (1970a) *Lexicon Spinozanum: A–K*. The Hague: Martinus Nijhoff.

Giancotti Boscherini, Emilia (1970b) *Lexicon Spinozanum: L–Z*. The Hague: Martinus Nijhoff.

Gilbert, Jeremy (2014) *Common Ground: Democracy and Collectivity in an Age of Individualism*. London: Pluto.

Gilbert, Margaret (2006) *A Theory of Political Obligation*. Oxford: Oxford University Press.

Goetschel, Willi (2016) 'Spinoza's Dream'. *Cambridge Journal of Postcolonial Literary Inquiry*, 3.1, pp. 39–54.

Gramsci, Antonio (1992) *Selections from the Prison Notebooks*, ed. and trans. Quintin Hoare and Geoffrey Nowell Smith. New York: International Publishers.

Gramsci, Antonio (2000) *The Gramsci Reader: Selected Writings 1916–1935*, ed. and trans. David Forgacs. New York: New York University Press.

Grotius, H. (2005) *The Rights of War and Peace. Book II* (1625), ed. R. Tuck. Indianapolis: Liberty Fund.

Guattari, Félix (2009) *Chaosophy: Texts and Interviews 1972–1977*, ed. Sylvere Lotringer, trans. David L. Sweet, Jarred Becker and Taylor Adkins. Los Angeles: Semiotext(e).

Gueroult, Martial (1969, 1974) *Spinoza*. 2 vols. Paris: Aubier-Montaigne.

Hall, Stuart (1987) 'Gramsci and Us'. *Marxism Today* (June), pp. 16–21.

Halmi, Nick (2012) 'Coleridge's Ecumenical Spinoza'. In Beth Lord (ed.), *Spinoza Beyond Philosophy*. Edinburgh: Edinburgh University Press.

Hampshire, Stuart (1953) *Spinoza*. Harmondsworth: Penguin.

Hampshire, Stuart (2005) *Spinoza and Spinozism*. New York: Oxford University Press.

Hardt, Michael and Antonio Negri (2000) *Empire*. Cambridge, MA: Harvard University Press.

Harvey, Warren Zev (2012) 'Gersonides and Spinoza on Conatus'. *Aleph: Historical Studies in Science and Judaism*, 12.2, pp. 273–97.

Hegel, G. W. F. (1990) *Lectures on the History of Philosophy. Volume III*, ed. R. F. Brown, trans. R. F. Brown, J. M. Stewart and H. S. Harris. Berkeley: University of California Press.

Hegel, G. W. F. (2004) *The Phenomenology of Spirit*, trans. A. V. Miller. New York: Oxford University Press.

Hobbes, Thomas (1840) 'The Whole Art of Rhetoric', *The English Works. Volume VI*, ed. William Molesworth. London: John Bohn.

Hobbes, Thomas (1998a) *Leviathan*, ed. J. C. A. Gaskin. Oxford: Oxford University Press.

Hobbes, Thomas (1998b) *On the Citizen [De Cive]*, ed. and trans. Richard Tuck and Michael Silverthorne. Cambridge: Cambridge University Press.

Hobbes, Thomas (1999) *The Elements of Law, Natural and Politic*, ed. J. C. A. Gaskin. New York: Oxford University Press.

Huenemann, Charles (2014) 'Review of Matthew J. Kisner and Andrew Youpa (eds), *Essays on Spinoza's Ethical Theory*'. *Notre Dame Philosophical Reviews*, 14 September. https://ndpr.nd.edu/news/essays-on-spinoza-s-ethical-theory/ (last accessed 20 May 2020).

Hume, David (2007) *A Treatise of Human Nature. Volume I*, ed. David Fate Norton and Mary J. Norton. New York: Oxford University Press.

Hunter, Graeme (2005) *Radical Protestantism in Spinoza's Thought*. Aldershot: Ashgate.

Israel, Jonathan I. (1995) *The Dutch Republic: Its Rise, Greatness, and Fall, 1477–1806*. Oxford: Oxford University Press.

Israel, Jonathan I. (2001 [1995]) *Radical Enlightenment: Philosophy and the Making of Modernity 1650–1750*. Oxford: Oxford University Press.

Israel, Jonathan I. (2006) *Enlightenment Contested: Philosophy, Modernity, and the Emancipation of Man 1670–1752*. New York: Oxford University Press.

Israel, Jonathan I. (2010) 'The Early Dutch and German Reaction to the *Tractatus Theologico-Politicus*: Foreshadowing the Enlightenment's More General Spinoza Reception?' In Yitzhak Y. Melamed and Michael A. Rosenthal (eds), *Spinoza's Theological-Political Treatise: A Critical Guide*. Cambridge: Cambridge University Press, pp. 72–100.

Israel, Jonathan I. and Stuart B. Schwartz (2007) *The Expansion of Tolerance: Religion in Dutch Brazil (1624–1654)*. Amsterdam: Amsterdam University Press.

James, Susan (2009) 'Freedom, Slavery, and the Passions'. In Olli Koistinen (ed.), *The Cambridge Companion to Spinoza's Ethics*. New York: Cambridge University Press, pp. 223–41.

James, Susan (2011) 'Creating Rational Understanding: Spinoza as a Social Epistemologist'. *Proceedings of the Aristotelian Society, Supplementary Volume LXXXV*, pp. 181–99.

James, Susan (2012) *Spinoza on Philosophy, Religion and Politics: The Theologico-Political Treatise*. New York: Oxford University Press.

Juniper, James and Jim Jose (2008) 'Foucault and Spinoza: Philosophies of Immanence and the Decentred Political Subject'. *History of the Human Sciences*, 21.2, pp. 1–20.

Kant, Immanuel (1991) *Political Writings*, trans. H. B. Nisbet, ed. H. Reiss. Cambridge: Cambridge University Press.

Kant, Immanuel (1998) *Critique of Pure Reason*, trans. and ed. Paul Guyer and Allen W. Wood. Cambridge: Cambridge University Press.

Kelly, Mark G. E. and Dimitris Vardoulakis (2018) 'Balibar and Transindividuality'. *Australasian Philosophical Review*, 2.1, pp. 1–4.

King, Martin Luther, Jr (1992) *I Have a Dream: Writing and Speeches That Changed the World*, ed. James Melvin Washington. New York: HarperCollins.

Kisner, Matthew J. (2008) 'Spinoza's Virtuous Passions'. *Review of Metaphysics*, 61.4, pp. 759–83.

Kisner, Matthew J. (2011) *Spinoza on Human Freedom: Reason, Autonomy and the Good Life*. Cambridge: Cambridge University Press.

Kisner, Matthew J. and Andrew Youpa, eds (2014) *Essays on Spinoza's Ethical Theory*. Oxford: Oxford University Press.

Klever, Wim (1984) 'Power: Conditional and Unconditional'. In C. De Deugd (ed.), *Spinoza's Political and Theological Thought*. Amsterdam: North-Holland Publishing, pp. 95–106.

Koistinen, Olli, ed. (2009) *The Cambridge Companion to Spinoza's Ethics*. New York: Cambridge University Press.

Koistinen, Olli and John Biro, eds (2002) *Spinoza: Metaphysical Themes*. New York: Oxford University Press.

Kordela, A. Kiarina (2007) *$urplus: Spinoza, Lacan*. New York: SUNY Press.

Kordela, A. Kiarina and Dimitris Vardoulakis, eds (2017) *Spinoza's Authority: Resistance and Power in Ethics*. London: Bloomsbury.

Kouvelakis, Stathis (2003) *Philosophy and Revolution: From Kant to Marx*, trans. G. M. Goshgarian. London; New York: Verso.

Kreisel, Howard (2001) *Prophecy: The History of an Idea in Medieval Jewish Philosophy*. Dordrecht: Kluwer.

Kwek, Dorothy H. B. (2015) 'Power and the Multitude: A Spinozist View'. *Political Theory*, 43.2, pp. 155–84.

Lacan, Jacques (1997) *The Seminar of Jacques Lacan Book VII: The Ethics of Psychoanalysis*, ed. Jacques-Alain Miller, trans. Dennis Porter. New York: W. W. Norton.

Laclau, Ernesto (2007) *On Populist Reason*. London; New York: Verso.

Laclau, Ernesto and Chantal Mouffe (2001) *Hegemony and Socialist Strategy: Towards a Radical Democratic Politics*, 2nd edn. London; New York: Verso.

Laclau, Ernesto and Chantal Mouffe (2007) *On Populist Reason*. London; New York: Verso.

Lærke, Mogens (2014) 'Spinoza's Language'. *Journal of the History of Philosophy*, 52.3, pp. 519–47.

Latour, Bruno (2014) 'On Some of the Affects of Capitalism'. Lecture given at the Royal Academy, Copenhagen, 26 February 2014. http://www.bruno-latour.fr/sites/default/files/136-AFFECTS-OF-K-COPENHAGUE.pdf (last accessed 16 April 2020).

Lawford-Smith, Holly (2015) 'What "We"?' *Journal of Social Ontology*, 1.2, pp. 225–49.
LeBuffe, Michael (2009) 'The Anatomy of the Passions'. In Olli Koistinen (ed.), *The Cambridge Companion to Spinoza's Ethics*. New York: Cambridge University Press, pp. 188–222.
LeBuffe, Michael (2010a) *From Bondage to Freedom: Spinoza on Human Excellence*. New York: Oxford University Press.
LeBuffe, Michael (2010b) 'Theories about Consciousness in Spinoza's Ethics'. *The Philosophical Review*, 119.4, pp. 531–63.
LeBuffe, Michael (2015) 'The Doctrine of the Two Kingdoms: Miracles, Monotheism, and Religion in Spinoza'. *British Journal for the History of Philosophy*, 23.2, pp. 318–32.
LeBuffe, Michael (2018) *Spinoza On Reason*. New York: Oxford University Press.
Le Guin, Ursula K. (2014) 'Ursula K. Le Guin's speech at the National Book Awards'. *The Guardian*, 20 November 2014. http://www.theguardian.com/books/2014/nov/20/ursula-k-le-guin-national-book-awards-speech (last accessed 16 April 2020).
Leibniz, G. W. (1989) *Philosophical Essays*, trans. Roger Ariew and Daniel Garber. Indianapolis: Hackett.
Lin, Martin (2004) 'Spinoza's Metaphysics of Desire: The Demonstration of IIIP6'. *Archiv für Geschichte der Philosophie*, 86.1, pp. 21–55.
Lin, Martin (2006) 'Spinoza's Account of Akrasia'. *Journal of the History of Philosophy*, 44.3, pp. 395–414.
Lin, Martin (2009) 'The Power of Reason in Spinoza'. In Olli Koistinen (ed.), *The Cambridge Companion to Spinoza's Ethics*. New York: Cambridge University Press, pp. 258–83.
Lloyd, Genevieve (1994) *Part of Nature: Self-Knowledge in Spinoza's Ethics*. London; Ithaca: Cornell University Press.
Lloyd, Genevieve (2002) *Routledge Philosophy Guidebook to Spinoza and the Ethics*. New York: Routledge.
Locke, John (1997) *An Essay Concerning Human Understanding*. London: Penguin.
Locke, John (2003) *Two Treatises of Government*, ed. Peter Laslett. Cambridge: Cambridge University Press.
Lord, Beth (2011a) 'Review of Michael Mack, *Spinoza and the Specters of Modernity: The Hidden Enlightenment of Diversity from Spinoza to Freud*'. *British Journal for the History of Philosophy*, 19.2, pp. 339–42.
Lord, Beth (2011b) '"Disempowered by Nature": Spinoza on the Political

Capabilities of Women'. *British Journal for the History of Philosophy*, 19.6, pp. 1085–106.

Lord, Beth, ed. (2012) *Spinoza Beyond Philosophy*. Edinburgh: Edinburgh University Press.

Lordon, Frédéric (2014) *Willing Slaves of Capital: Spinoza & Marx on Desire*, trans. G. Ash. London; New York: Verso.

Lukács, Georg (1971) *History and Class Consciousness: Studies in Marxist Dialectics*, trans. R. Livingstone. Cambridge, MA: MIT Press.

Lukács, Georg (2009) *Lenin: A Study on the Unity of this Thought*, trans. N. Jacobs. London; New York: Verso.

Lunn, Eugene (1982) *Marxism and Modernism: An Historical Study of Lukács, Brecht, Benjamin, and Adorno*. Berkeley: University of California Press.

Macherey, Pierre (1998) *Introduction à l'éthique de Spinoza. La troisième partie: la vie affective*. Paris: Presses Universitaires de France.

Machiavelli, Niccolò (2003) *Discourses on Livy*, trans. Julia Conaway Bondanella and Peter Bondanella. New York: Oxford University Press.

Machiavelli, Niccolò (2005) *The Prince*, trans. and ed. Peter Bondanella. New York: Oxford University Press.

Mack, Michael (2010) *Spinoza and the Specters of Modernity: The Hidden Enlightenment of Diversity from Spinoza to Freud*. London: Continuum.

Macpherson, C. B. (1962) *The Political Theory of Possessive Individualism*. Oxford: Oxford University Press.

Maimonides, Moses (1963a) *The Guide of the Perplexed, Volume I*, trans. Shlomo Pines. Chicago: University of Chicago Press.

Maimonides, Moses (1963b) *The Guide of the Perplexed, Volume II*, trans. Shlomo Pines. Chicago: University of Chicago Press.

Malamud, Bernard (1967) *The Fixer*. London: Penguin.

Malcolm, Noel (2002) *Aspects of Hobbes*. New York: Oxford University Press.

Manzini, Frédéric (2009) *Spinoza: une lecture d'Aristote*. Paris: Presses Universitaires de France.

Marshall, Eugene (2008) 'Spinoza on the Problem of Akrasia'. *European Journal of Philosophy*, 18.1, pp. 41–59.

Marx, Karl (1982) *Capital, Volume I*, trans. Ben Fowkes. Harmondsworth: Penguin.

Marx, Karl and Friedrich Engels (1998) *The German Ideology. Including Theses on Feuerbach and the Introduction to the Critique of Political Economy*. New York: Prometheus.

Marx, Karl and Friedrich Engels (2008) *The Communist Manifesto*. London: Pluto.

Massumi, Brian (1992) *A User's Guide to Capitalism and Schizophrenia.* Cambridge, MA: MIT Press.

Matheron, Alexandre (1971) *Le Christ et le salut des ignorants chez Spinoza.* Paris: Aubier-Montaigne.

Matheron, Alexandre (1977) 'Le *Traité Théologico-Politique* vu par le jeune Marx'. In *Cahiers Spinoza* I. Paris: Éditions Réplique, pp. 159–212.

Matheron, Alexandre (1978) 'Spinoza et la decomposition de la politique thomiste: Machiavelisme et Utopie'. *Archivio di filosofia* (*Lo spinozismo ieri e oggi*) 46.

Matheron, Alexandre (1986) *Anthropologie et politique au XVIIe siècle* (*Études sur Spinoza*). Paris: Vrin.

Matheron, Alexandre (1988) *Individu et communauté chez Spinoza.* Paris: Éditions de Minuit.

Matheron, Alexandre (1994a) 'Les fondements d'une éthique de la similitude'. *Revue de métaphysique et de morale*, 99.4, pp. 475–91.

Matheron, Alexandre (1994b) 'L'indignation et le conatus de l'Etat spinoziste'. In M. Revault D'Allones and H. Rizk (eds), *Spinoza: Puissance et ontologie.* Paris: Kime, pp. 153–65.

Matheron, Alexandre (1997) 'The Theoretical Function of Democracy in Spinoza and Hobbes', trans. Ted Stolze. In Warren Montag and Ted Stolze (eds), *The New Spinoza.* Minneapolis: University of Minnesota Press.

Matheron, Alexandre (2011) 'Le probleme de l'evolution de Spinoza du *Traite theologico-politique* au *Traite politique*'. *Études sur Spinoza et les philosophies et l'âge classique.* Lyon: ENS.

McShea, Robert J. (1968) *The Political Philosophy of Spinoza.* New York: Columbia University Press.

McShea, Robert J. (1969) 'Spinoza on Power'. *Inquiry*, 12.1–4, pp. 133–4.

Melamed, Yitzhak Y. (2011) 'Spinoza's Anti-Humanism: An Outline'. In C. Fraenkel, D. Perinetti and J. E. H. Smith (eds), *The Rationalists: Between Tradition and Innovation.* Boston: Kluwer, pp. 147–66.

Melamed, Yitzhak Y. (2013a) 'Review of Michael Mack, *Spinoza and the Specters of Modernity*'. *European Journal of Philosophy*, 21, E1–E2.

Melamed, Yitzhak Y. (2013b) *Spinoza's Metaphysics: Substance and Thought.* New York: Oxford University Press.

Melamed, Yitzhak Y. and Michael A. Rosenthal, eds (2010) *Spinoza's Theological-Political Treatise: A Critical Guide.* Cambridge: Cambridge University Press.

Melamed, Yitzhak Y. and Hasana Sharp, eds (2018) *Spinoza's Political Treatise: A Critical Guide.* Cambridge: Cambridge University Press.

Mertens, Frank (2007) 'Franciscus van den Enden: Works: *Kort Verhael van Nieuw-Nederland* (1662)'. http://users.telenet.be/fvde/index.htm?Works4c (last accessed 16 April 2020).
Miliband, Ralph (1969) *The State in Capitalist Society*. London: Basic Books.
Miller, Jon (2005) 'Spinoza's Axiology'. In Daniel Garber and Steven Nadler (eds), *Oxford Studies in Early Modern Philosophy, Volume II*. Oxford: Clarendon Press, pp. 149–72.
Miller, Jon (2007) 'The Status of Consciousness in Spinoza's Concept of Mind'. In Sara Heinämaa, Vili Lähteenmäki and Pauliina Remes (eds), *Consciousness: From Perception to Reflection in the History of Philosophy*. Dordrecht: Springer, pp. 203–20.
Montag, Warren (1995) '"The Soul is the Prison of the Body": Althusser and Foucault, 1970–1975'. *Yale French Studies*, 88, pp. 53–77.
Montag, Warren (1999) *Bodies, Masses, Power: Spinoza and His Contemporaries*. London: Verso.
Montag, Warren (2005) 'Who's afraid of the Multitude? Between the Individual and the State'. *South Atlantic Quarterly*, 104.4, pp. 655–73.
Montag, Warren and Ted Stolze, eds (1997) *The New Spinoza*. Minnesota: University of Minneapolis Press.
Montaigne, Michel de (2003) *The Complete Essays*, trans. M. A. Screech. London: Penguin.
Moreau, Pierre-François (1994) *Spinoza: L'expérience et l'éternité*. Paris: Presses Universitaires de France.
Moreau, Pierre-François (1997) 'Fortune and the Theory of History', trans. Ted Stolze. In Warren Montag and Ted Stolze (eds), *The New Spinoza*. Minneapolis: University of Minnesota Press.
Morfino, Vittorio (2017) 'Memory, Chance and Conflict: Machiavelli in the *Theological-Political Treatise*'. In A. Kiarina Kordela and Dimitris Vardoulakis (eds), *Spinoza's Authority: Resistance and Power in the Political Treatises*. London: Bloomsbury, pp. 7–26.
Mouffe, Chantal (2005) *On the Political*. Abingdon; New York: Routledge.
Mouffe, Chantal (2018) *For a Left Populism*. London: Verso.
Nadler, Steven (1999) *Spinoza: A Life*. New York: Cambridge University Press.
Nadler, Steven (2001) *Spinoza's Heresy: Immortality and the Jewish Mind*. New York: Oxford University Press.
Nadler, Steven (2008) 'Spinoza and Consciousness'. *Mind*, 117, pp. 575–601.
Næss, Arne (2008) *Ecology of Wisdom*, ed. Alan Drengson and Bill Devall. Berkeley: Counterpoint.

Negri, Antonio (2003) *Savage Anomaly: The Power of Spinoza's Metaphysics and Politics*, trans. Michael Hardt. Minneapolis: University of Minnesota Press.

Negri, Antonio (2004) *Subversive Spinoza: (Un)contemporary Variations*, ed. Timothy S. Murphy, trans. Timothy S. Murphy, Michael Hardt, Ted Stolze and Charles T. Wolfe. Manchester; New York: Manchester University Press.

Nietzsche, Friedrich (1982) 'Postcard to Overbeck'. In Walter Kaufmann (ed. and trans.), *The Portable Nietzsche*. New York: Viking Penguin.

Nietzsche, Friedrich (2007a) *Human, All Too Human*, trans. R. J. Hollingdale. Cambridge: Cambridge University Press.

Nietzsche, Friedrich (2007b) *The Gay Science*, ed. Bernard Williams, trans. Josephine Nauckhoff and Adrian Del Caro. Cambridge: Cambridge University Press.

Noys, Benjamin (2010) *The Persistence of the Negative: A Critique of Contemporary Continental Theory*. Edinburgh: Edinburgh University Press.

Nussbaum, Martha C. (2018) *The Monarchy of Fear*. Oxford: Oxford University Press.

Ovid (2004) *Metamorphoses*, trans. David Raeburn. London: Penguin.

Pascal, Blaise (1966) *Pensées*, trans. A. J. Krailsheimer. Harmondsworth: Penguin.

Peden, Knox (2014) *Spinoza Contra Phenomenology*. Stanford: Stanford University Press.

Peden, Knox (2015) 'Response to My Critics – On Seeming Right'. *Politics, Religion and Ideology*, 17.1, pp. 96–100.

Pereboom, Derk (1994) 'Stoic Psychotherapy in Descartes and Spinoza'. *Faith and Philosophy*, 11, pp. 592–625.

Pettit, Philip (2001) 'Collective Intentions'. In N. Naffine, R. J. Owens and J. Williams (eds), *Intention in Law and Philosophy*. Farnham: Ashgate, pp. 241–54.

Pettit, Philip and David Schweikard (2006) 'Joint Actions and Group Agents'. *Philosophy of the Social Sciences*, 36.1, pp. 18–39.

Plato (1997) 'Theaetetus', trans. M. J. Levett, rev. Myles Burnyeat, in *Complete Works*, ed. John M. Cooper. Indianapolis: Hackett.

Prak, Maarten (2005) *The Dutch Republic in the Seventeenth Century*, trans. Diane Webb. Cambridge: Cambridge University Press.

Price, J. L. (2014) *Dutch Society: 1588–1713*. Abingdon: Routledge.

Prokhovnik, Raia (1997) 'From Democracy to Aristocracy: Spinoza, Reason and Politics'. *History of European Ideas*, 23.2–4, pp. 105–15.

Pufendorf, Samuel (1994) 'On the Law of Nature and of Nations'. In *The Political Writings*, ed. Craig L. Carr, trans. Michael J. Seidler. New York: Oxford University Press.

Rancière, Jacques (1999) *Dis-agreement: Politics and Philosophy*, trans. Julie Rose. Minneapolis: University of Minnesota Press.

Rancière, Jacques (2006) *Hatred of Democracy*, trans. Steve Corcoran. London; New York: Verso.

Rancière, Jacques (2007) *On the Shores of Politics*, trans. Liz Heron. London; New York: Verso.

Rancière, Jacques (2010) *Dissensus: On Politics and Aesthetics*, ed. and trans. Steven Corcoran. London; New York: Continuum.

Ravven, Heidi M. (2002) 'Spinoza's Rupture with Tradition – His Hints of a Jewish Modernity'. In Heidi M. Ravven and Lenn E. Goodman (eds), *Jewish Themes in Spinoza's Philosophy*. Albany: SUNY Press, pp. 187–224.

Read, Jason (2016) *The Politics of Transindividuality*. Leiden: Brill.

Reich, Wilhelm (1972) *Sex-Pol: Essays, 1929–1934*, ed. Lee Baxandall, trans. Anna Bostock, T. DuBoise and Lee Baxandall. New York: Vintage.

Reich, Wilhelm (1993) *The Mass Psychology of Fascism*, trans. Vincent R. Carfagno, ed. Mary Higgins and Chester M. Raphael. New York: Noonday.

Rice, Lee (1985) 'Spinoza, Bennett, and Teleology'. *Southern Journal of Philosophy*, 23.2, pp. 241–53.

Rice, Lee (1990) 'Individual and Community in Spinoza's Social Psychology'. In E. Curley and P.-F. Moreau (eds), *Spinoza: Issues and Directions. The Proceedings of the Chicago Spinoza Conference*. Leiden: Brill.

Rilke, Rainer Maria (2004) *Letters to a Young Poet*, trans. M. D. Herter Norton. New York: W. W. Norton.

Rose, Gillian (1992) *The Broken Middle: Out of Our Ancient Society*. Oxford: Blackwell.

Rose, Gillian (1996) *Mourning Becomes the Law*. Cambridge: Cambridge University Press.

Rose, Gillian (1997) *Love's Work*. London: Vintage.

Rosenthal, Michael A. (2002) 'Why Spinoza Chose the Hebrews: The Exemplary Function of Prophecy in the Theological-Political Treatise'. In Heidi M. Ravven and Lenn E. Goodman (eds), *Jewish Themes in Spinoza's Philosophy*. Albany: SUNY Press, pp. 225–60.

Rosenthal, Michael A. (2003) 'Spinoza's Republican Argument for Toleration'. *The Journal of Political Philosophy*, 11.3, pp. 320–37.

Rosenthal, Michael A. (2005) '"The Black, Scabby Brazilian": Some Thoughts on Race and Early Modern Philosophy'. *Philosophy & Social Criticism*, 31.2, pp. 211–21.

Rosenthal, Michael A. (2017) 'Spinoza's Political Philosophy'. In Michael Della Rocca (ed.), *The Oxford Handbook of Spinoza*. Oxford: Oxford University Press, pp. 408–33.

Rousseau, Jean-Jacques (1999) *The Social Contract*, trans. Christopher Betts. New York: Oxford University Press.

Rovere, Maxime (2017) *Le Clan Spinoza*. Paris: Flammarion.

Russell, Bertrand (1961) *A History of Western Philosophy*. London: Allen & Unwin.

Rutherford, Donald (2008) 'Spinoza and the Dictates of Reason'. *Inquiry*, 51.5, pp. 485–511.

Rutherford, Donald (2010) 'Spinoza's Conception of Law: Metaphysics and Ethics'. In Yitzhak Y. Melamed and Michael A. Rosenthal (eds), *Spinoza's Theological-Political Treatise: A Critical Guide*. Cambridge: Cambridge University Press, pp. 143–67.

Saar, Martin (2013) *Die Immanenz der Macht: Politische Theorie nach Spinoza*. Berlin: Suhrkamp Verlag.

Saar, Martin (2014) *The Immanence of Power: From Spinoza to 'Radical Democracy'*. Uitgeverij: Spinozahuis.

Sacksteder, William (1975) 'Spinoza on Democracy'. In Maurice Mandelbaum and Eugene Freeman (eds), *Spinoza: Essays in Interpretation*. La Salle, IL: Open Court, pp. 117–38.

Sacksteder, William (1984) 'Communal Orders in Spinoza'. In C. De Deugd (ed.), *Spinoza's Political and Theological Thought*. Amsterdam: North-Holland Publishing, pp. 206–13.

Sangiacomo, A. (2015) 'Spinoza and Relational Autonomy: An Outline'. In M. Eckert and G. Cunico (eds), *Orientierungskrise. Herausforderung des Individuums in der heutigen Gesellschaft*. Regensburg: Roderer, pp. 19–27.

Santayana, George (1913) 'Introduction', Spinoza's *Ethics and 'De Intellectus Emendatione'*, trans. Andrew Boyle. London: J. M. Dent.

Sartre, Jean-Paul (1968) *The Communists and Peace*, trans. M. Fletcher. New York: Braziller.

Sartre, Jean-Paul (1989) *No Exit and Three Other Plays*, trans. Stuart Gilbert. New York: Vintage.

Sartre, Jean-Paul (1992) *Notebooks for an Ethics*, trans. D. Pellauer. Chicago; London: University of Chicago Press.

Schmaltz, Tad M. (2015) 'Spinoza on Eternity and Duration: The 1663 Connection'. In Yitzhak Y. Melamed (ed.), *The Young Spinoza: A Metaphysician in the Making*. New York: Oxford University Press.

Schmid, Hans Bernhard (2014) 'Plural Self-Awareness'. *Phenomenology and the Cognitive Sciences*, 13.1, pp. 7–24.

Schopenhauer, Arthur (1974) 'Counsels and Maxims'. *Parerga and Paralipomena, Volume One*, trans. E. F. J. Payne. Oxford: Clarendon Press.

Sen, Amartya (2009) *The Idea of Justice*. Cambridge, MA: Harvard University Press.

Sévérac, Pascal (1998) 'Passivité et désir d'activité chez Spinoza'. In F. Brugère and P.-F. Moreau (eds), *Spinoza et les Affects*. Paris: Presses de l'Université de Paris-Sorbonne, pp. 39–54.

Sévérac, Pascal (2005) *Le devenir actif chez Spinoza*. Paris: Honoré Champion.

Sévérac, Pascal (2017) 'Consciousness and Affectivity: Spinoza and Vygotsky'. *Stasis*, 5.2, pp. 80–109.

Sharma, Kriti (2015) *Interdependence: Biology and Beyond*. New York: Fordham University Press.

Sharp, Hasana (2011) *Spinoza and the Politics of Renaturalization*. Chicago: University of Chicago Press.

Sharp, Hasana (2013) 'Violenta imperia nemo continuit diu: Spinoza and the Revolutionary Laws of Human Nature'. *Graduate Faculty Philosophy Journal. New School for Social Research*, 34.1, pp. 133–48.

Sharp, Hasana (2018) 'Family Quarrels and Mental Harmony: Spinoza's *Oikos-Polis* Analogy'. In Yitzhak Melamed and Hasana Sharp (eds), *Spinoza's Political Treatise: A Critical Guide*. Cambridge: Cambridge University Press, pp. 93–100.

Sharp, Hasana (2019) 'Generosity as Freedom in Spinoza's *Ethics*'. In Jack Stetter and Charles Ramond (eds), *Spinoza in Twenty-First-Century American and French Philosophy*. London: Bloomsbury, pp. 277–88.

Simondon, Gilbert (1989) *L'individuation psychique et collective*. Paris: Aubier.

Smith, Steven B. (1997) *Spinoza, Liberalism, and the Question of Jewish Identity*. New Haven: Yale University Press.

Smith, Steven B. (2003) *Spinoza's Book of Life: Freedom and Redemption in the Ethics*. New Haven: Yale University Press.

Spinoza, B. (1910) *Short Treatise on God, Man and his well-being*, ed. trans. A. Wolf. London: Adam and Charles Black.

Spinoza, B. (1925) *Spinoza Opera*, ed. Carl Gebhardt. 4 vols. Heidelberg: Carl Winter.

Spinoza, B. (1985) *The Collected Works of Spinoza, Volume I*, ed. and trans. Edwin Curley. Princeton: Princeton University Press.

Spinoza, B. (2000) *The Political Treatise*, trans. Samuel Shirley, introduction and notes by Steven Barbone and Lee Rice. Indianapolis: Hackett.

Spinoza, B. (2007) *Theological-Political Treatise*, ed. J. Israel, trans.

M. Silverthorne and J. Israel. Cambridge; New York: Cambridge University Press.
Spinoza, B. (2009) *Opera*, ed. C. Gebhardt. Heidelberg: Carl Winter [1925]. Online text edition: http://spinoza.tk (last accessed 16 April 2020).
Spinoza, B. (2016) *The Collected Works of Spinoza, Volume II*, ed. and trans. E. Curley. Princeton; Oxford: Princeton University Press.
Steinberg, Justin (2009) 'Spinoza on Civil Liberation'. *Journal of the History of Philosophy*, 47.1, pp. 35–58.
Steinberg, Justin (2010) 'Spinoza's Curious Defense of Toleration'. In Yitzhak Y. Melamed and Michael A. Rosenthal (eds), *Spinoza's Theological-Political Treatise: A Critical Guide*. Cambridge: Cambridge University Press.
Steinberg, Justin (2014) 'Following a *Recta Ratio Vivendi*: The Practical Utility of Spinoza's Dictates of Reason'. In Matthew J. Kisner and Andrew Youpa (eds), *Essays on Spinoza's Ethical Theory*. Oxford: Oxford University Press, pp. 178–96.
Steinberg, Justin (2016) 'Affect, Desire and Judgement in Spinoza's Account of Motivation'. *British Journal for the History of Philosophy*, 24.1, pp. 67–87.
Steinberg, Justin (2018) *Spinoza's Political Psychology: The Taming of Fortune and Fear*. Cambridge: Cambridge University Press.
Stephenson, Erik H. (2011) 'Spinoza and the Ethics of Political Resistance'. PhD thesis, McGill University.
Stetter, Jack and Charles Ramond, eds (2019) *Spinoza in Twenty-First-Century American and French Philosophy*. London: Bloomsbury.
Stolze, Ted (2014) 'An Ethics for Marxism: Spinoza on Fortitude'. *Rethinking Marxism*, 26.4, pp. 561–80.
Strauss, Leo (1982) *Spinoza's Critique of Religion*. New York: Schocken.
Strauss, Leo (1988) *Persecution and the Art of Writing*. Chicago: University of Chicago Press.
Tatián, Diego (2018) 'La potencia de los esclavos. Conjetura sobre un silencio de Spinoza'. *Co-herencia*, 15.28, pp. 224–44.
Taylor, Dan (2019a) 'Affects of Resistance: Indignation, Emulation, Fellowship'. *Pli*, 30, pp. 23–46.
Taylor, Dan (2019b) 'The Reasonable Republic: Statecraft, Affects, and the Highest Good in Spinoza's Late *Tractatus Politicus*'. *History of European Ideas*, 45.5, pp. 645–60.
Terence (1874) *The Comedies of Terence*, trans. Henry Thomas Riley. New York: Harper.
Thomas, Peter D. (2009) *The Gramscian Moment: Philosophy, Hegemony and Marxism*. Leiden: Brill.

Thomas, Peter D. (2013) 'Hegemony, Passive Revolution and the Modern Prince'. *Thesis Eleven*, 117.1, pp. 20–39.

Tosel, André (1984) *Spinoza ou le crépuscule de la servitude*. Paris: Aubier-Montaigne.

Van Bunge, Wiep (2012) *Spinoza Past and Present: Essays on Spinoza, Spinozism, and Spinoza Scholarship*. Leiden: Brill.

Van Bunge, Wiep, Henri Krop, Piet Steenbakkers and Jeroen Van de Ven, eds (2011) *The Continuum Companion to Spinoza*. London; New York: Continuum.

Van Cauter, Jo (2016) 'Spinoza on History, Christ, and Lights Untameable'. PhD thesis, Ghent University.

Van Groesen, Michiel, ed. (2014) *The Legacy of Dutch Brazil*. New York: Cambridge University Press.

Van Rompaey, Chris (2015) 'Language and Meaning in the *Ethics*. Or, Why Bother with Spinoza's Latin?' *Parrhesia*, 24, pp. 336–66.

Van Sluis, Jacob and Jonnis Musschenga, eds (2009) *De boeken van Spinoza*. Groningen: Bibliotheek der Rijksuniversiteit Groningen; The Hague: Haags Gemeentearchie.

Van Zomeren, M., T. Postmes and R. Spears (2008) 'Toward an Integrative Social Identity Model of Collective Action: A Quantitative Research Synthesis of Three Socio-Psychological Perspectives'. *Psychological Bulletin*, 134.4, pp. 504–35.

Vardoulakis, Dimitris, ed. (2011) *Spinoza Now*. Minneapolis: University of Minnesota Press.

Vardoulakis, Dimitris (2019) 'The Figure of Moses: The Origins of Authority in Spinoza'. *Textual Practice*, 33.5, pp. 771–85.

Verbeek, Theo (2003) *Spinoza's Theologico-Political Treatise: Exploring 'the Will of God'*. Burlington, VT: Ashgate.

Vernière, Paul (1954) *Spinoza et la pensée française avant la Révolution*. 2 vols. Paris: Presses Universitaires de France.

Viljanen, Valtteri (2011) *Spinoza's Geometry of Power*. Cambridge: Cambridge University Press.

Viljanen, Valtteri (2014) 'Spinoza on Virtue and Eternity'. In Matthew J. Kisner and Andrew Youpa (eds), *Essays on Spinoza's Ethical Theory*. Oxford: Oxford University Press, pp. 258–72.

Villari, Rosario (1985) 'Masaniello: Contemporary and Recent Interpretations'. *Past and Present*, 108, pp. 117–32.

Virno, Paolo (2004) *A Grammar of the Multitude*, trans. Isabella Bertoletti, James Cascaito and Andrea Casson. Los Angeles: Semiotext(e).

Von Duuglas-Ittu, Kevin (2008) 'Spinoza the Merchant: The Canary

Islands, Sugar and Diamonds and Leprosy'. *kvond*. http://kvond.wordpress.com/2008/08/09/spinoza-the-merchant-the-canary-islands-sugar-and-diamonds-and-leprosy/ (last accessed 16 April 2020).

Vygotsky, Lev (2017) *Notebooks: A Selection*, ed. Ekaterina Zavershneva and René van der Veer. Singapore: Springer.

Watson, Richard (2007) *Cogito, Ergo Sum: The Life of René Descartes*. Boston: David R. Godine.

Weststeijn, Arthur (2012) *Commercial Republicanism in the Dutch Golden Age: The Political Thought of Johan & Pieter de la Court*. Leiden: Brill.

Williams, Raymond (1989) *Resources of Hope*, ed. Robin Gable. London; New York: Verso.

Wilson, Margaret D. (1996) 'Spinoza's Theory of Knowledge'. In Don Garrett (ed.), *The Cambridge Companion to Spinoza*. New York: Cambridge University Press, pp. 89–141.

Wiznitzer, Arnold (1954) 'The Number of Jews in Dutch Brazil (1630–1654)'. *Jewish Social Studies*, 16.2, pp. 107–14.

Wiznitzer, Arnold (1956a) 'Jewish Soldiers in Dutch Brazil (1630–1654)'. *Publication of the American Jewish Historical Society*, 46.1, pp. 40–50.

Wiznitzer, Arnold (1956b) 'The Jews in the Sugar Industry of Colonial Brazil'. *Jewish Social Studies*, 18.3, pp. 189–98.

Wolfson, Harry Austryn (1962) *The Philosophy of Spinoza: Unfolding the Latent Processes of His Reasoning*. Cambridge, MA: Harvard University Press.

Wordsworth, William (2000) 'The Prelude', *The Major Works*, ed. Stephen Gill. New York: Oxford University Press.

X, Malcolm, and Alex Haley (1973) *The Autobiography of Malcolm X*. Harmondsworth: Penguin.

Yovel, Yirmayahu (1989, 1992) *Spinoza and Other Heretics*. 2 vols. Oxford: Princeton University Press.

Zac, Sylvain (1963) *L'idée de vie dans la philosophie de Spinoza*. Paris: Presses Universitaires de France.

Index

Abensour, Miguel, 38
Aboab, Isaac, 44, 62*n*
'acid communism', 217
act, to
   activeness, 253
   affects, 100, 239
   capacity for, 77
   misanthropy antidote, 118
   power of, 111
action, causes non-recognition, 68
active
   causes, 90
   Intellect, 172–3
Adam, original sin, 197
Addams, Jane, 225–7
adequate cause, 247
Adorno, Theodor, 182, 184
affects, 9, 90, 95, 98–9, 108, 131, 166
   active, 100, 239
   causes variety, 141
   conflictual nature of, 152
   imitative, 161, 233, 237
   joyous, 112, 134
   new naturalistic political science of, 208
   passive, 96, 103, 105–6, 210
   power of present, 157
   power relative, 109
   sad, 149
   sad passive, 237, 241
   science of, 72, 239
   strong, 254
'affirmationism', 12

afterlife, riches, 24
'Age of Discovery', European, 42
agency, 80–1
   group, 156
Ahmed, Sara, 146
akrasia, problem of, 96, 104, 106, 108, 111–12, 248
Al-Farabi, Islamic Neoplatonic philosophy of, 172
Alencastro, Luiz Felipe de, 41*n*
Alfakhar, 171
Allison, Henry, 82
Alquié, Ferdinand, 8
Althusser, Louis, 8, 25*n*, 34, 59, 120, 143, 212, 224, 229
   Spinozism, of, 249
Alvares brothers, 63*n*
ambition, 100, 149
ambitious figures, 174
   clerics, 142, 151, 170
   fears exploiting, 248
   manipulative, 33, 49
American Constitution, 62
amor mundi, 113
anger, servitude affect, 100
Anglo-Dutch War, First, 41
Angola, 41
Anniello, Tommaso, 2
anonymity, opportunity, 147
anthropocentrism, 188
   delusions of, 24
   tendency to, 169
anxiety, 225

appetite(s) (*appetitus*), 98
  as human conatus, 97
  desire distinction, 102
  restraining of, 28
Aquinas, Thomas, 47, 79, 191n, 196n
Arendt, Hannah, 35, 113, 132, 147, 153, 209–10, 226–7, 231
  lonely subject, 155
Ariosto, Ludovico, *Orlando Furioso*, 85, 91n, 93
aristocracy, 202
  contemporary aristocrats, 243
Aristotle, 10, 48, 51, 53, 198n, 227
Armstrong, Aurelia, 59, 159n, 232
Arnett, James, 125n
ataraxia, Epicurean, 114
'atheism', reputation for, 170
Atkins, Dorothy, 125n
Atlan, Henri, 87n, 119n, 148n, 158n
Augustine, 58, 79, 113
automation, 132
Avicenna (Ibn Sina), 84n, 172
awareness, 156–7, 255
  causal, 245
  collective, 173, 235
  self-, 219

Bacon, Francis, 209
balance of forces, 254
Baldwin, James, 36, 147, 236, 255
  The Fire Next Time, 61
Balibar, Étienne, 8, 10n, 30, 33, 39, 59n, 73n, 145n, 150–2, 177, 210, 221, 231–2
Balling, Pieter, 44, 167
'banality of evil', 35
Barbone, Steven, 73n, 119, 140, 144–5, 228
Battle of Vienna, 32
Baudelaire, Charles, 182
Bayle, Pierre, 5, 129, 187n, 188, 192
beatitudo, 103, 110
becoming-common, 213
behaviour, 99
Belgicus, Leo, 185
benevolence, 238
benign dictatorships, 208

Benjamin, Walter, 184, 219
  The Arcades Project, 181–2
Bennett, Jonathan, 10, 74, 76, 81–3, 98n, 107, 110, 136, 140, 148n
biconditional formula, 99
Biro, John, 10n
Black African slavery, justifications for, 40
Blake, William, 113
  'Auguries of Innocence', 91
blessedness, 4, 58
Blijenbergh, Willem van, 5
Bodin, Jean, 231
Boétie, Étienne de la, 33n
Bol, Ferdinand, 185
Bolshevik Russia, 216
Book of Exodus, 26
Borges, J.-L., 188
Bove, Laurent, 77n, 143, 234–5, 238
Boxel, Hugo, 2, 3n
Boxhorn, Marcus Zuerius, 135n, 204
Brazil, Dutch foothold, 41
Brienen, Rebecca Parker, 41n
'broken middle' concept, 130
bureaucratic processes, 132

Calvinists
  anti-Cartesian, 27
  church, 181
  contemporary, 171
  orthodoxy, 179
  'seditious', 230
Campbell, Karlyn Kohrs, 61
Campos, Andre Santos, 46n, 50n
Camus, Albert, 14, 113, 245
Canary Islands, 41
capitalism
  capitalist realism, 255
  contemporary, 156
Carlisle, Clare, 125n
Carriero, John, 79n, 84n
caution (*caute*), Spinoza's motto, 187
Cavailles, Jean, 8
Cervantes, Miguel de, 94n
  Don Quixote, 95
cheerfulness, 30, 103
chess, 1, 126–7
Chicago, Hull House Settlement, 225–7

choice
  delusions of, 68
  illusory feeling, 70
Christianity
  Christian natural law, 47–8
  mystical aspects, 126
Chuck D. of Public Enemy, 'Fight the Power', 255
Cicero, 48, 50, 55, 79, 80, 129n
  De Re Publica, 49
Cioran, E. M., 113
citizen(s) (*cives*), 151–2, 201
  education of, 196
  elite class of, 211
  equality of, 242
  making of, 206, 212
citizenship
  capacity for, 198
  eligibility for, 206
  'training', 205
civil rights, 46
  movement, 146
  tradition, 236
civil society, 162
  emergence of, 134
civil war, 118
clans, 204
class consciousness, emergence of, 183
clerics, ambitious, 29
Cohen, I. Bernard, 80
Coleridge, Samuel Taylor, 111n, 126
Colerus, Johannes, 1, 62, 129, 146, 188, 192, 208
collective
  belonging, 136
  'consciousness', 219
  desire, 7, 10
  'formation', 182
  freedom politics, 121
  identity as emergent property, 212
  imaginary *recapture* of, 221
  -individual tension, 131, 133
  individuality conceptualised, 199
  life, 136
  reason-led, 253
  relationally autonomous, 232

collective power, 96
  advantages of, 198
  Gramsci's view of, 220
  Spinoza's ideas and politics, 149, 153
collectives, 140
collectivism, argument for, 135, 139, 194
collectivity, 13, 105n, 132–3, 159, 161, 166–7, 200, 249
  concept of, 6
  desire for, 211
  'dormant', 182
  implications of, 189
  importance of, 162
  individual empowering, 243
  political, 157, 248
  Sartre's view of, 155
  spectrum of, 147
  universal, 131
collegial (*collegialiter*), 54–6
Comenius, John Amos, 205
common affect(s), 153, 201–2, 208
common good, 72, 179, 208
  utility of, 56
common notions, 48n, 90, 96, 102, 107–10, 142, 153, 166–7, 171, 184, 211, 213
common people (*vulgus*), 57, 128
  denunciation of, 31
  hostility to, 129
'common sense', 249
  repurposing, 217–18
'common wealth', 256
commonality, 130, 142, 185, 226, 228, 236
  issue of, 162
  passive affects jeopardising, 136
  politics of, 15
  sense of, 153, 252
  shared sense of, 184
'commons', 245
communal participation, self-interest argument, 134
communal-universal distinction, 14, 133
'communication', politics of, 152
'communism of minds', 131n, 235
Communist Manifesto, 89n

Communities
  exclusionary, 147
  of faith limitations, 181
  reason led, 141
  religious congregations, 253
compatibilism, 67
competition, 127
compulsion, 19
conatus, 13, 19, 47, 51, 76, 81–2, 84, 90, 92, 102, 141, 161, 231, 248, 254
  argument, 70, 82
  collective notion, 143
  'democratic', 235
  desire, 196
  drive of, 69
  human, 97
  manifestations of, 98
  mind's, 110
  New Science based, 79
Condé, Prince of, Louis II de Bourbon, 192
Condorcet, Marquis de, 227
consciousness, 38, 96, 98, 101, 111, 214
  -raising, 61, 217, 145
contractualism, Hobbesian, 228
cooperation, benefits of, 45
'counter-power', multitudinal, 161
Coutinho, Carlos Nelson, 220
Critchley, Simon, 241
Cromwell, Oliver, 5, 227, 235
  Spinoza's thoughts on, 216
'cultivation of reason', recognition of, 52
cults, 146
  elitist, 211
Cunaeus, Petrus, 185n
Curley, Edwin, 24n, 48, 50n, 52n, 54n, 73n, 77n, 82, 84n, 129n, 135, 150n, 196n, 199, 177n, 206

D'Alembert, Jean-Baptiste, 208n
D'Espinosa, Michael, 43
D'Holbach, Paul-Henri, 187
Dahlbeck, Johan, 205
Damasio, Antonio, 148n
De la Court, Johan, 10, 55n, 135n, 185, 191, 196 198n, 204

De la Court, Pieter, 10, 55n, 135n, 185, 191, 196 198n, 204
De Vries, Simon, 192
De Witt, Cornelius, 190, 192, 230
  murder of, 190
De Witt, Johan, 146, 181, 189, 192, 211
  murder of, 5, 190
DeBrabander, Firmin, 107n
Declaration of the Rights of Man, 62
Del Lucchese, Filippo, 157, 196n, 207, 231–3
Deleuze, Gilles, 10n, 32, 34, 37–8, 39n, 59, 71, 83–4, 88, 107, 120, 187–8, 221, 224, 232, 247
  Spinoza: Practical Philosophy, 9
  Spinozism of, 8
Delgado, Pinto, 94n
deliberation, capacity for implied, 54
deliberative assemblies, 54–5, 211
Della Rocca, Michael, 10n, 80, 81n, 82, 230
democracy (ies), 49, 139, 150, 202–3, 225
  argument for, 54
  difficulties of faced, 242
  free deliberation of, 6
democratic assemblies, exclusions, 207
Den Uyl, Douglas, 119–20, 144, 229
Der Spyck, Hendrik van, 192
Derrida, Jacques, 158
Desanti, J-T., 8
Descartes, René, 21–2, 24, 67, 79, 159n, 164, 209
  critiqued, 80
  Meditations, 129
  mind-body duality, 20
desire(s) (*cupiditas*) 3, 7, 9, 37, 47, 53, 56, 90, 92, 96–7, 100, 102, 221, 239, 248
  affects, 101
  analysis of, 116
  appetite distinction, 102
  causes of non-recognition, 69
  collective, 77, 245
  common, 202
  consciousness incorporated, 98–9, 108
  debilitating reprogramming, 36

desire(s) (*cont.*)
  delusions, 95
  different experiences of, 69
  'emergent property', 119
  faculty of absence, 112
  for survival, 51
  immoderate, 49
  joy arisen, 109
  mind's consciousness, 101
  'molar', 38
  passive affects, 100
  politicising, 12
  -politics relation, 8
  politics of collective, 256
  reactive tendencies of, 215
  reprogramming, 106, 114, 115, 118, 248
  Spinoza's definition, 68
  'wilful', 146
despair, 61, 245
Dias, Henrique, 44, 62
dictates of reason, 53n, 71, 137, 174–5, 178, 237
Diderot, Denis, 187, 208n
disempowerment:
  collective state of, 29
  effect avoidance of, 116
  ideas about, 56
  universal claims for, 146
disobedience, 233
drawing, 1
Dumoulié, Camille, 231, 232n
Duns Scotus, 79
Durkheim, Émile, 182n
Dutch Brazil
  Jewish experience of, 45
  slavery, 62
Dutch East India Company, 189
Dutch Reformed Church, 27, 170n, 190, 192
  reactionary Calvinists, 229
Dutch Republic, 211
  changing politics, 189
  1672 joint attack, 192
  republican tradition, 135
Dutch West India Company, 40–1
'dynamic essentialism', 84

'Earthly city', 58
'economism', 224
education, emphasis, 216
  public, 205
effects, -final causes confusion, 24
Eichmann, Adolf, 35
Eliot, George, 126, 137
  Spinoza's translation, 125
elitism, 161–2
  cults, 211
Emperor Nero, 81
empowerment, 25, 248
  collective, 152, 238, 255
  elementary conditions of, 210
  model of, 6
  Spinoza's model of, 256
emulation, 100, 237–8, 240, 250
  definition, 127
Engels, Friedrich, 89, 223–4, 244
England
  Civil War Spinoza condemned, 229
  regicides 'imprudence' of, 237
  wars with Holland, 189
Enlightenment ideals, 130
'enlisting', 37
epistemology
  political, 166
  social, 173
  Spinoza, 10
equilibrium of forces, 231
ethical liberation, 231
Ethics, 4, 6–7, 27, 70, 72, 83, 114
  Appendix, 20, 57
  collectivity outline, 133
  denounced, 5
  Part IV, 120
  sociality and individuation, 13
Euripides, *Hippolytus*, 103
exemplars, 38, 111, 136–8, 174, 193–4, 211–12, 256
extension, 71, 84

Fabritius, J. Ludwig, 192n
fascism, rise of, 215
faith, 178
  tenets of, 179

'false consciousness', 25n
  belief, 27
'false' prophets, 176
Fanon, Frantz, 36, 147, 255
Fay, Brian, 125n
fear
  debilitating nature of, 33
  and hope, 21
  of isolation, 236
  'of the masses', 150
feeling, communities of, 242
'fellowship', 217, 253
Feuer, Lewis, 44n, 202n, 229
fictions, 'socially shared', 173
final causes, seeking predisposition, 21
Fischer, John Martin, 119, 226, 250
Fisher, Mark, 34, 155, 217, 221, 249, 253–6
  Acid Communism, 156
flattery, 24
'folk essentialism', 157
Ford, James, 44n
fortune, 30, 116, 251
  concept of, 26
  Spinoza's definition, 25
Frank, Daniel, 10n
free man, the, 6, 29, 59–60, 69, 74–5, 107, 110, 127, 136–40, 160, 200, 253
'free multitude', 151, 200–1
'free republic', idea of, 32
free speech, 35
free will, 68, 74, 104
  argument against, 72
  Cartesian view, 105
  critique of Cartesian, 20
freedom
  as beatitude, 76
  concept of relative, 248
  definition of, 67
  desire inhibitions, 227
  different orders of, 74
  difficulty of, 20
  human illusion, 75
  necessity contrast, 73
  of thought, 47
  political, 6

  practice of, 250
  relational, 39, 159
French Revolution, 209, 227
Freud, Sigmund, 9
Friedman, Saul S., 43n
friendship, 6–7, 50, 60, 96, 103, 105n, 117, 136–8, 152, 251–2

Gabbey, Alan, 7n
Galileo, 79, 90
Garber, Daniel, 81n
Garrett, Don, 53n, 76–7n, 80–4, 99n, 112, 136n
Garver, Eugene, 106, 162, 168–9, 178
Gatens, Moira, 10n, 125n, 145n, 173
'gaze of the other', 154
Gazzaniga, Michael S., 119n
Gebhardt, Carl, *Opera*, 148n
Gelley, Alexander, 182n
German Idealists, 11
Gersonides, 79n
Giancotti Boscherini, Emilia, 54n, 148
Gilbert, Jeremy, 120
Gilbert, Margaret, 156
Giraffi, Alessandro, 2n
God
  anthropomorphic, 21, 175
  as power, 82
  false beliefs of, 27
  'godless', Spinoza accused, 5
  'intellectual love' of, 19, 21, 91, 137–8, 169
  judgements of, 22
  knowledge of, 19, 118
  modes of power, 83
  nature of, 57
  necessary existence of, 74
  neo-Aristotelian views, 20
  obedience 'servitude', 24
  potentia of, 71
  sin pardoning, 179
  Spinoza's, 25
'Godless' Spinoza accused, 5
Gods, anthropomorphic, 115
Goetschel, Willi, 44n
Gongora, Luís de, 94n

good, the, 3
  collective political, 117
  greater, 38
  life, 111
Gracian, Baltasar, 94n
Graevius, Johann, 190
Gramsci, Antonio, 215–16, 218–19, 221–2, 244, 255
  'common sense' notion, 216, 218, 245
  hegemony concept, 220
  Machiavelli reading, 15
  Prison Notebooks, 214
Grotius, Hugo, 45, 46, 51, 53, 63, 231
  laws of nature, 41
  slavery rationalised, 42
grouping, transindividual, 232
Guattari, Félix, 32, 37–8, 39n, 120, 187, 221, 244
Gueroult, Martial, 8, 144

Haiti (Saint Domingue) rebellion, 62
Haley, Alex, 60n
Hall, Stuart, 220
Hampshire, Stuart, 129, 208
Hardt, Michael, 9n, 224
harmful ideas, 25, 49, 220–1, 247
  consequences, 31
  remedies, 112
  servitude of, 251
  susceptibility to, 60
harmful sad affects 'folklore', 255
Harrington, James, 59
Harvey, Warren Zev, 79n
hatred and fear, 7
  disempowering, 30
Hayek, Friedrich, 119
Hebrew Republic, 25n, 26, 133, 184, 197n
  Moses' law, 34, 185
Hebrews, servitude of, 26
  under Moses, 150
Hegel, G. W. F., 11, 126
hegemony, Gramsci's concept of, 214, 217
Heidegger, Martin, 153
Heidelberg University, 192
Heraclitus, 157

Hobbes, Thomas, 21, 46, 48–51, 54–6, 58–9, 80, 106, 126, 135, 152, 186, 190, 196n, 197, 204–5, 210–11, 221, 230
  contractualism, 120
  Elements of Law, 127
  fear emphasis, 52
  influence of, 47, 134
  Leviathan, 169n, 206
  'mortal God', 127
  social contract version, 53
Holland
  1672 riots, 191
  Spanish Hapsburg rule, 26
  war with Catholic Spain, 185
hope
  civil rights traditions, 61
  politics of danger, 33, 237, 245
  -willingness' societal goods, 175
hopes and fears, 22, 26
  common people, 33
  fluctuating, 31
  vacillation between, 23
Horace, 94n
Huenemann, Charlie, 10, 11n
human freedom
  political life centrality, 138
  politics of, 4
human mind, mutability of, 4
human nature
  associative, 140
  pessimism about, 204
  political, 51
  first universal law, 51
  second universal law, 53
  third universal law, 54
human society, despisers of, 58
humanism, Renaissance, 26, 128
Hume, David, 5, 70, 115, 119, 126
'humility', 237
humour, Spinoza's, 2
Hunter, Graeme, 1n
Huygens, Christiaan, 188

ideas, adequate/inadequate, 97, 102–3, 109–12
identity, personal, 88

INDEX

ideology, formation of, 34, 120, 183, 212, 215
idle talk, 153
ignorance, isolation of, 60
images of things, 167
imaginary shared, 245
imagination, 4, 9, 22, 34, 69, 90, 96, 101, 112, 131, 142, 153, 162, 165–6, 177, 207, 239
   centrality of, 113
   delusions of, 168
   education of, 13
   faculty of, 172
   instrumental role of, 249
   knowledge of limits, 169
   politics of, 154
   -reason relation, 12, 162
   value given, 113
   varieties of, 167
imaginative function, 'strategic', 136
imitation, affective, 161, 233–4, 237
immanence, case for, 73
impotence (*impotentia*), 24–5, 27
impulse (*hormé*), 79
independence, of thought, 28
indigenous struggles, land rights, 241
indignation, 15, 231–3, 235–7, 240, 244
   as resistance affect, 250
   becoming collective power, 234
individual
   empowerment political concern, 90
   freedom as collective good, 136
   God's power modal unit, 131
   self-conception, 154
   self-development delusion of, 118
individual-communal-universal
   distinction, 14, 133, 252, 254
individualism
   ideological fetters, 183
   as superstition, 182
individualist, radical, 243
individuality
   atom-like illusion, 59
   'emergent property', 148
   'formal', 143

individuation, 88, 143, 158, 247, 250
   anthropocentric, 145
   collective, 146
   order of, 139
   power through, 89
indoctrination, vulnerability to, 29
ingenium, 21, 22n, 60, 177
'insofar as it is in itself', 80
intellect, rule of, 4
   Spinoza's intellectualism, 165
intentionality, collective, 156
interactions, 'active/passive', 87
interdependence, 13–14, 133, 220, 248
'internal objectivity', collective thought, 155
'interpreters', ambitions of, 22
intuitive science, 74–5, 90, 102, 167, 177
Israel, Jonathan, 10, 43, 47, 52n, 54n, 170n, 187, 189–90n

James, Susan, 10n, 55n, 170n, 173, 198n
Jameson, Fredric, 256
jealousy, 85, 93
Jefferson, Thomas, 209
Jelles, Jarig, 44, 193–4
Jesus Christ, 14, 26, 170
   collectivist, 181
   figure of, 163
   parable use, 177
   philosophy, 180
   universal law, 178
   universality, 176
joy(s) (*laetitia*), 100–1, 114–15, 212, 238–9
   affects of, 105
   collective, 245
   education of, 114, 162, 166
   instrumentality of, 113
   joyous affects empowering, 232
   joyous desire test, 117
   passive, 108
Judaism, 'New Christians' returned to, 43
Judeo-Christian scripture, 170
judgment, role of, 56
justice, 172
   and loving kindness, 201
Justinian Digest, 198n

Kant, Immanuel, 21, 26, 63, 153, 159n, 186, 226
Keter Torah Yeshiva, 44
Kierkegaard, Søren, *angst*, 108
kindness, 253
King Ahab, 176
King, Martin Luther, 61, 236
Kisner, Matthew J., 10n, 31n, 71n, 136, 137n, 159n, 198
Klever, Wim, 231
knowledge, 6, 115, 117, 240
  adequate, 161, 167
  democratic, 226
  good and evil, 105
  inadequate, 96
  passive, 168
  rule of, 4
  self-interest instances, 137
  true, 109.
  see also common notions; intuitive science
Koerbagh, Adriaan, 129n, 194
Koistinen, Olli, 10n
Kordela, A. Kiarina, 8, 10n
Kouvelakis, Stathis, 89n

Lacan, Jacques, 115
Laclau, Ernesto, 224, 241, 244
Lærke, Mogens, 129
Latour, Bruno, 9n
law, divine-human, 50
Lawford-Smith, Holly, 156
laws of nature, three, 50–5
Le Guin, Ursula K., 254–5
LeBuffe, Michael, 98n, 106n, 107n, 138n, 165–6
Leibniz, Gottfried Wilhelm, 80, 83, 146, 190
Levites, the, 35
Liberal Dutch government/republican culture, collapse of, 163, 191
libertarianism, 119
life, fullness affirmation, 113
limits, acceptance of one's, 116
Lin, Martin, 82–4, 106n
listening, non-judgmental, 226
Lloyd, Genevieve, 145n, 173n

Locke, John, 42, 45, 59, 62, 88, 99, 120, 127, 159n, 205
loneliness, 225
  foundational totalitarianism, 35
  mass, 132
  self-discovery potential, 147
Lord, Beth, 10n
Lordon, Frédéric, 37–8, 229
love, 85, 93, 95, 127, 138
Lucas, Jean Maximilien, 208n
Lucian, 94n
Lucretius, 80
Lukács, Georg, 183–4, 219
Lunn, Eugene, 182n
lust, 100
Luther, Martin, 218

Macherey, Pierre, 8, 237n
Machiavelli, 26, 196, 204, 210, 240, 244
  Il Principe, 197, 219
  influence of, 206, 218
  Spinoza's reading of, 15
Macpherson, C. B., 59, 120
  'possessive individualism', 86
magical thinking, individualism as, 252
Maimonides, 14, 149, 171–2, 176, 179
Makin, Bathsua, 205
Malamud, Bernard, *The Fixer*, 247
Malcolm, Noel, 135
Malcolm X, 60, 187
manipulators, fear generating, 142
Marcuse, Herbert, 256
'marrons', European society, 44
Marshall, Eugene, 106n
Martial, 94n
Marx, Karl, 2, 8, 89, 120, 223
  Hegelianised, 143
  Marxists, 143
  'silent compulsion' notion, 224
  The German Ideology, 244
  third thesis on Feuerbach, 216
Masaniello, 1–3, 230, 235, 247
  self-portrait, 218
  Spinoza's drawing of, 5, 60
  tragicomedy of, 216
Massumi, Brian, 9n

mathematics, Spinoza's praise for, 91
Matheron, Alexandre, 8–9, 15, 21n, 59,
    83–4, 131n, 136, 143, 145, 151,
    177n, 189n, 201, 231, 233–6, 250
May 1968, 'air' of, 8
McShea, Robert, J., 144, 229
mechanics, 4, 59
medicine, 4, 59
Melamed, Yitzhak Y., 10n, 11
melancholy, 118
    'melancholics', 58
Melchior, Johannes, 190
meritocracy, democratic, 204
metaphor, construction, 145
Meyer, Lodewijk, 129n, 169, 171–2, 179
Miliband, Ralph, 224n
military service, 32
Miller, Jon, 98n
miracles, 175, 177
misanthropes
    critique of ascetic, 157
    dismissal of, 117
    recluse, 162
modes, 82, 154
    finite, 71, 73, 75, 82–3
Molière, 192
monarchy, 203
    'of fear', 161
Montag, Warren, 8n, 10n, 44n, 151, 231,
    233
Montaigne, Michel de, 60, 105, 164
Montesquieu, Charles de, *Spirit of the
    Laws*, 204
More, Thomas, 196n
Moreau, Pierre-François, 26, 57, 145n
Morfino, Vittorio, 196n
Morteira, Saul Levi, 44–5, 62, 79
Moses, 131, 150, 164
    knowledge of *ingenium*, of the people,
        174
    paternalistic state, 35
    prophet-statesman, 242
    reasonable laws of, 27
Mouffe, Chantal, 224, 244
'multitude' (*multitudo*), 9, 151–2, 200,
    212, 232
    'grammar' of, 153

guided, 207
lionising of, 254
power of, 3
see also 'free multitude'
Musschenga, Jonis, 94n
mutual
    advantage, 7
    'aid' recognition, 52
    Participation, 159
    'responsiveness', 156
    utility, 139

Nadler, Steven, 43n, 76n, 94n, 98–9n,
    146n, 188n, 190n, 192
Næss, Arne, 253
naming, 241
Naples, 1647 uprising, 1–2
Nassau-Siegen, Johan Maurits von,
    41–2
nationhood
    exclusionary, 163
    imagination of, 163
    nationalism, 38
    resistance myths, 185
'natural intellect', 164n
natural law, 50
natural right, 46–7, 56, 58–9, 76, 197
    concept of, 51
    law of, 52
naturalism
    political, 230
    prejudiced, 223
nature, 12
    anthropomorphic purpose view, 21
    'entirety' of, 140
    Hobbesian view, 185
    human reason unconstrained, 48
    intelligibility of, 209
    laws of, 57
    mastering, 209
    non-contingent, 74
    purpose and design, 20
'necessity', 19
Negri, Toni, 8, 10n, 44, 73, 120, 151, 161,
    187, 201, 229
    multitude reading, 224
    Savage Anomaly, 9

New Holland
  Brazil colony, 13
  Jews settled in, 43
  Portuguese retaken, 44
'new humanity', 156
Newton, Isaac, 80
Nietzsche, Friedrich, 11, 187, 236, 254
Novalis, 11
Noys, Benjamin, 11–12
Nussbaum, Martha, 118n, 161
  'practical' hope, 61

obedience, 9, 26, 46, 165, 174, 177n, 179
  consented, 55
  doctrines of, 169
  laws, 208
  political, 34
  powerful binds of, 37
  social, 164
  to the sovereign, 228
Old/New Testament division, 178
Oldenberg, Henry, 72n, 79n, 128, 164, 170, 177n, 192n
'omens', 23
ontology
  relational, 152
  Spinoza's, 83
Opera Posthuma, 5, 129n, 208n
opinion, 29, 167
  slaves, 60
'organic intellectuals', 218
Ostens, Jacob, 24n, 228n
Ottoman Empire/Turks, 33, 176, 231
  as existential threat, 180
  coercive model, 54
  servitude example, 32, 212
  'slavery associated', 28
Ovid, 94
  Metamorphoses, 103

pactum, 151
parallelism, 97
Parks, Rosa, 146–7, 241
Pascal, Blaise, 105, 114
'passions'
  archaic, 244
  freedom from, 74, 119
  sad, 106–8, 138
  Spinoza's appreciation of, 126
  strong, 105
passive affects, 61, 69
  joys, 37
  power of, 251
  shared, 130
passivity, 12, 23, 28–9
  socio-political implications, 30
Pastore, Annibale, 222
paternalism
  criticisms of, 195
  Spinoza's, 186, 207
Peden, Knox, 8, 90, 143
'people', the (populus), 7, 149–52, 242
  empowered, 199
  welfare emphasis, 55
perception, capacity to, 87
Pereboom, Derk, 107n
Perez de Montalvan, Juan, 94n
perfection, 117
Pernambuco, Brazil, 40
  refugees from, 44
Perpetual Edict 1667, 190
'persecution', Spinoza's, 188
perseverance, 115, 141
pessimism, heartbroken, 113
Petronius, 94n
Pettit, Philip, 156
Philips Pelt, 43
philosophy, as liberatory, 4
'physical digression', Ethics, 70, 86–7, 139–40, 144, 200
piety (pietas), 173–4
pipe smoking, Spinoza, 106
Plato, 91, 196n
  Meno, 113n
  Phaedrus, 104
  Theaetetus, 22
plebs, 149, 223
political
  constitutionalism, 208
  domination desire involvement, 70
  epistemology, 170–1
  lasting change, 5
  legitimacy, 231

protest 20th-century understanding, 235
realism, 249
representational institutions, 204
shared imaginary, 250
sovereignty, 200
violence, 243
Political Treatise, 7, 28, 48, 54, 120, 193
   Chapter 7, 223
politics
   moralisation of, 209
   psychological interest in, 166
   refoundation of, 181
   Schmittian notion, 244
   as science, 138
Polybius, 227
popular
   government possibility, 48
   sovereignty principle, 218
populism, Spinozan, 243–4
   studies, 240
'possessive individualism', 59, 86, 120
Potential
   /actuality dissolution, 72
   affects control, 71
   difference, 13, 72–3
potestas, 72
power, 13, 47, 84, 100, 104
   ability to imagine, 168
   checks and safeguards, 204
   collective, 59, 144
   conative, 89
   'constituent', 157
   exclusion from, 130
   -freedom relation, 81
   'intensity' of, 88
   metaphysics of, 12, 90, 127, 135
   modal metaphysics, 250
   ontology of, 76
   potentia form, 70
   theory of, 198
   totalitarian appropriation of, 221
   understanding of, 224
Prak, Maarten, 190n
prejudice, 20, 22, 26, 29, 35, 37–8, 45, 57–8, 68, 128, 169, 171, 217, 236
Price, J. L., 190n

Prokhovnik, Raia, 202n
proletariat, the, 182
   as 'tabula rasa', 214
prophecy, 162, 171
   politics of, 210
   truth calculating, 179
prophet(s), 14, 58, 175, 177, 180, 185, 218, 237, 239
   ambitious potential, 176
   persuasiveness, 172
   role of, 163–4
   -statesmen, 165
protest movements, 146
'psychological egoism', 119
'psychotherapy reading', 74, 107, 109, 120
Public
   democratic decision-making, 210
   education, 4
Pufendorf, Samuel von, 45, 99

Racine, Jean, 192
Ramond, Charles, 10n
Rampjaar, collapses of, 197
Rancière, Jacques, 224, 241–2
Rand, Ayn, 119
rational self-interest, zero sum game, 226
Ravven, Heidi, 69
Read, Jason, 8n, 37, 237
'reality', 87
reason, 34, 59, 75, 112
   acquire sufficient, 49
   attraction on, 199
   dictates of, 71
   laws of political, 58
   republican ideal, 50
'reasonable republic', sketch of, 14, 243
reasoning, flawed process of, 57
rebellion, 3, 15, 53, 157, 228, 250
Recife Brazil, 1636 synagogue, 43
recta ratio vivendi, 52, 107
'red plenty', 256
Reformation, the, 219
Reich, Wilhelm, 38, 215–16, 221–2, 224, 255
'relational autonomy', 159
relations of force, 216
relative freedom, 76

religion, imagination for, 196
Rembrandt, 185
'repentance', 237, 239
reprogramming, 116
republica, 151
republican imaginary, collectivist need, 211
republicanism
  De la Courts Dutch, 53
  early modern, 199
  liberal, 181
  social justice hope, 240
resistance, 'militant fortitude' for, 235
Rice, Lee, 119, 140, 142–5
rights, individual-collective, 52
Rilke, Rainer Maria, *Letters to a Young Poet*, 91
Robespierre, 209
Robinson, Henry Crabb, 111n
Roman republicanism, *salus populi*, 55
Rose, Gillian, 130, 132, 155, 226, 252
Rosenthal, Michael A., 10n, 44n, 137n, 151n, 185n
Rousseau, Jean-Jacques, 184, 187, 220
Rovere, Maxime, 62, 129n, 192n
Russell, Bertrand, 188
Rutherford, Donald, 50n

Saar, Martin, 73n
Sacksteder, William, 143, 231
sad passions, 168
  disempowering, 252
sadness (*tristitia*), 3, 100–1
Sangiacomo, Andrea, 159n
Santayana, George, 90
Sartre, Jean-Paul, 14, 118, 149, 154–6
'savage multitude', 160
Schmaltz, Tad M., 76n
Schmid, Hans Bernhard, 156
Schmitt, Carl, 142n
Schopenhauer, Arthur, 118
Schuller, George, 98n, 104n
Schwartz, Stuart B., 43n
second-wave feminism, 61
sectarianism, 118

security, 56
  State's virtue, 195
sedition, rebellion, 228
self, the, 3, 70
  -awareness, 156
  -containment, 114
  -control, 117
  -determination, 198
  -empowerment individual, 119
  -esteem, 238–9
  -hatred, 147, 255
  -interest, 50, 53, 96, 137
  -organisation, 147
self-preservation, 83, 212
  principle of, 51, 79
  theories of, 77
Sen, Amartya, 118n
Seneca, 35, 81, 129n, 148, 231
sensual pleasures, wariness of, 85, 93, 95
Sephardic Jews, Dutch Portuguese speakers, 43
servitude, state of, 7, 20, 23, 27, 31, 49, 56, 103, 247
  affective, 161
  'ancient', 171
  awareness of, 104
  internal state, 12
  passivity formed, 24–6, 89
  problem of political, 198
  'symbols' of, 28
Sévérac, Pascal, 37
Shakespeare, William, 95
shame, complex racial politics, 36
Sharma, Kriti, 157–8, 245, 248
Sharp, Hasana, 6n, 10n, 58–9n, 136, 152n, 207, 232, 234n
Ship of Theseus paradox, 88
Shirley, Samuel, 145n
Short Treatise, 110
signal cell transduction, 157
Silverthorne, Michael, 52n, 54n
Simondon, Gilbert, 8
  'transindividuality', 152n
'singular things', 86
'slave'
  fear paralysed, 103
  Spinoza's use of term, 29

slavery, 12
  blindness to transatlantic, 62
  fight for, 32
  rationalisations of, 42
  trade, 41, 43
Smith, Steven B., 107n, 232n
smoking, desire to stop, 106, 113
social contract, 46, 52, 144, 150–1, 230
  Moses', 28
social relations, ensemble of, 8
  internalised narratives, 34
sociality, 251
  non-exclusionary, 253
  socialisation(s), 118
'society' 154
solidarity, 250
  motivation, 232
  sustained, 236
Sorel, Georges, general strike 'myth', 219
speech, free circulation of, 211
Spinoza, Benedict de, 43
  anomalising, 11
  book collection of, 94
  collectivist, 59, 121
  conservative reading of, 229
  flourishing studies of, 209
  Hebrew language facility, 184
  knife attack on, 129
  late politics of, 200
  materialist reading of, 120
  multitude theorists, 62
  Neoplatonic reading, 154
  'persecution of', 60, 128–9n, 187–8
  politicised interpretations, 9
  Stoic reading of, 112
  threats to, 192
Spinoza, Gabriel, 43, 45n
Spinoza, Rebecca, 45n
'star friendship', 254
State, the, 7, 9, 14–15, 21, 56, 72, 151, 174, 190, 208, 228, 242–3, 249
  collective functions of, 212
  division of functions, 203
  environment of hope creation, 195
  fear-based, 145
  formation of, 53
  forms of, 194

freedom purpose, 194
  -individual relation, 144
  laws, 199
  new models, 142
  popular sovereignty, 202
  'revolving', 233
  security provision, 205
Steinberg, Justin, 10n, 22n, 33, 46n, 99, 114, 136, 165–6, 174, 177, 194–5, 202, 236
Stephenson, Erik, 229, 230n, 232n
Stetter, Jack, 10
Stoics, 79, 112
  stoicism, 116
Stolze, Ted, 8n, 10n, 235, 236n
strategic optimism, 221
Strauss, Leo, 129n, 161
stress, privatisation of, 217
striving, as efficient cause, 81
subjective/objective distinction dissolved, 154
subjectivity
  collective, 89
  political, 241
subjects, passive state, 201
sugar, 41
suicide, 81–2
superfluous people, prospect of, 132
superstition, 23, 26, 31, 129
  imagination basis, 171
suspicion, Hobbesian, 128
Synod of Dort, 170n

Tacitus, 223
Tatián, Diego, 41n
Terence, 94, 148
the 'masses', 33
The German Ideology, 89
Theological-Political Treatise (*TTP*), 6–7, 188, 203
  anonymously published, 190
  audience for, 27
  banned, 192
theology
  /philosophy distinction, 184–6
  power of, 165
theory-practice distinction, 133

think tanks, 146
Third universal law, 54
Thomas, Peter D., 220
Thomasius, 5
thought, attribute of, 71, 78, 84, 97
titillation, dangers of, 108
Toussaint Louverture, 62
transatlantic slavery, blindness to, 62
'transindividuality', concept of, 8, 152n
Treatise on the Emendation of the Intellect, 3
Treaty of Westphalia, 189
Trump, Donald, 61
'truth', 164
Tschirnhaus, Ehrenfried, 67, 69, 72, 80
Twitter, 155
Tyranny, scale importance, 234

UN (United Nations), Declaration of Human Rights, 220
unanimity, 139, 142, 212, 248
uncertainty, 130
'union of bodies', 139
United Provinces, 26, 181, 189, 202
universal faith, tenets of, 163, 169, 178–81
'universal hospitality', 63
universality, 213
University of Chicago, 227
University of Utrecht, 190
'univocal multiplicity', 244
'utopias', dismissed, 196

vacillation, 104
Van Blijenbergh, Willem, 82n
Van Bunge, Wiep, 10
Van Cauter, Jo, 177
Van den Enden, Franciscus, 62n, 94
Van der Dussen, Adriaen, 41, 43
Van der Spyck, Hendrik, 192
Van Gent, Pieter, 129
Van Oldenbarnevelt, Johan, 6
Van Rompaey, Chris, 129n
Van Sluis, Jacob, 94n

Van Velthuysen, Lambert, 5, 180, 193
Van Zomeron, M., 234n
Vardoulakis, Dimitris, 8n, 10n, 185n
Verbeek, Theo, 229
Vernière, Paul, 187
Viljanen, Valtteri, 10n, 73n, 76–7n, 80–1, 82n, 83–4
Virgil, 94n
Virno, Paolo, 153
virtue, 109, 196
    definition of, 75
VOC, 42
'voluntary servitude', 34n
Von Duuglas-Ittu, Kevin, 44, 45n
Von Nassau-Siegen, Johan Maurits, 40
vulgus, 149–52, 187
    contempt for disavowed, 223
    fear manipulated, 170
Vygotsky, Lev, 205n

Waller, Jason, 10n
'war of position', 216, 220
West India Company, 189
Weststejin, 135n, 198n
will (*voluntas*), 98
William of Orange-Nassau, 5, 27, 170n, 181, 189, 191–2
Williams, Raymond, 245
Wilson, Margaret D., 76, 98n
Wiznitzer, Arnold, 43, 44n
Wolfson, Harry Austryn, 10, 79, 84n
women, 85, 93
wonder, 22, 133
Wordsworth, William, 111n
'work-democracy', 221
world alienation, 209

xenophobia, 36, 37

Youpa, Andrew, 10n
Yovel, Yirmayahu, 44n

Zac, Sylvain, 143
Zedekiah, 176

EU representative:
Easy Access System Europe
Mustamäe tee 50, 10621 Tallinn, Estonia
Gpsr.requests@easproject.com